ON THE EDGE OF THE GLOBAL

A Series Sponsored by the East-West Center

CONTEMPORARY ISSUES IN ASIA AND THE PACIFIC

John T. Sidel and Geoffrey M. White, Series Co-Editors

A collaborative effort by Stanford University Press and the East-West Center, this series focuses on issues of contemporary significance in the Asia Pacific region, most notably political, social, cultural, and economic change. The series seeks books that focus on topics of regional importance, on problems that cross disciplinary boundaries, and that have the capacity to reach academic and other interested audiences.

The East-West Center promotes better relations and understanding among the people and nations of the United States, Asia, and the Pacific through cooperative study, research, and dialogue. Established by the US Congress in 1960, the Center serves as a resource for information and analysis on critical issues of common concern, bringing people together to exchange views, build expertise, and develop policy options. The Center is an independent, public, nonprofit organization with funding from the US government, and additional support provided by private agencies, individuals, foundations, corporations, and governments in the region.

NIKO BESNIER

On the Edge of the Global
Modern Anxieties in a Pacific Island Nation

Stanford University Press · *Stanford, California*

Stanford University Press
Stanford, California

Printed in the United States of America on acid-free, archival-quality paper

Library of Congress Cataloging-in-Publication Data

Besnier, Niko, author.
   On the edge of the global : modern anxieties in a Pacific island nation /
Niko Besnier.
      pages cm. — (East-West Center Series on Contemporary Issues in Asia
and the Pacific)
   Includes bibliographical references and index.
   ISBN 978-0-8047-7405-5 (cloth : alk. paper)
   ISBN 978-0-8047-7406-2 (pbk. : alk. paper)
      1. Culture and globalization—Tonga. 2. Tonga—Social life and customs.
3. Tonga—Civilization. I. Title. II. Series: Contemporary issues in Asia and
the Pacific.
   DU880.B47 2011
   996.12—dc22
                                        2010043060

Typeset by Thompson Type in 9.75/13.5 Janson

Contents

Figures, Tables, Charts, and Maps

Figures

Tables

Chart

Maps

Note on Tongan Orthography and Transcription Conventions

The Tongan language has twelve consonants (*f h k l m n ng p s t v '*) and five vowels (*i e a o u*), roughly identical to the sounds of the International Phonetic Alphabet (IPA) that are written with the same symbols, except for *ng*, which is a velar nasal (IPA ŋ), and the inverted apostrophe, which represents a glottal stop. Vowels can be phonemically long, in which case the letter is superposed with a macron (e.g., *ā*). This orthography is standardized. Standard reference works on the language continue to be C. Maxwell Churchward's grammar (1953) and bilingual dictionary (1959), although the latter is soon to be superseded by a monolingual dictionary compiled by Melenaite Taumoefolau.

In several chapters, I analyze brief excerpts of talk. The conventions I follow in the transcripts are those established in the sociological tradition of Conversation Analysis, through the work of Gail Jefferson in particular, designed to provide analytic information on the prosodic quality, rhythm, and nonlinguistic vocalizations audible in the recording. While these conventions have been subjected to criticism, they are nevertheless useful because of their readability and the fact that their widespread scholarly usage makes them easily recognizable. Following is a key to relevant transcription conventions.

(1.2)	length of significant pause in seconds, between or within utterances
(.)	untimed pauses (for pauses of less than 0.3 seconds)
word-	abrupt cut-off
WORD	forte volume

hhhh	exhalation (number of character indicates approximate length)
.hhhh	inhalation
wo::rd	nonphonemic segment gemination
?	rising pitch (not necessarily in a question)
,	slightly rising pitch
.	falling pitch (not always at the end of a sentence)
!	animated tempo
word = = word	turn latching (no pause between turns)
((whisper))	information for which a symbol is not available
( )	inaudible material
(word)	conjectured material
[1985:4:B:360–700]	transcript and page number or recording counter

Preface

In much of the postcolonial Global South, people's lives today are suffused with anxiety. Anxiety emerges in association with many different dynamics, the most obvious of which is economic uncertainty: In many societies, while a small minority of people appears to be getting richer, the bulk of the population increasingly sinks into poverty while having to listen to local elites and powerful outsiders urging them to be more frugal. The global economic collapse at the end of the new millennium's first decade has only aggravated these dynamics. Anxiety is what motivates people to seek greener pastures in wealthier countries, in the hope that geographical mobility will translate into economic mobility. At the destination, however, many find themselves as impoverished as where they started if not more so, with the added burden of living in fear of immigration checks and facing the prospect of a shameful empty-handed return home. Anxiety, however, is not a matter only of economics but is often cultural. It is, for example, a matter of who belongs where, as many societies are experiencing "the return of the local," a revalorization of notions of belonging, continuity, and tradition, cultural essentializations in the service of a politics of inclusion and exclusion (Geschiere 2009: 1). Citizens of Western nations are not the only ones to experience anxiety about the influx of immigrants. In the developing world as well, migrants from other places, the descendants of local people who migrated, and the images and practices that they bring are often deemed threatening to the economic, political, and social order. These tensions all contribute to an ongoing "malaise of modernity" (Jolly 2001: 198, echoing Taylor 1991) created by conflicts between groups, positions, symbols, and projects.

This book explores the workings of this malaise in one society on the edge of the global, the island kingdom of Tonga. It analyzes the way in which segments of this small-scale society develop different understandings of what modernity is, how it should be made relevant locally, and how it should mesh with tradition. A pivotal feature of my argument is that the anxieties that Tongans experience in the twenty-first century are the product of both continuity and rupture with the past and that they are also generative of this continuity and rupture. In this respect, my analysis departs from analyses of comparable cases that associate change with anxiety and continuity with comfort. I am also suspicious of facile explanations associating reproduction with localness and change with outside "influences." Instead I demonstrate that, in a society that is deeply connected to the outside world through its diasporic migrants, change not only comes from elsewhere but is also generated locally. It is here that I am likely to part company with many Tongans, both intellectuals and ordinary citizens, who make sense of the world in which they live through a scenario that can be paraphrased as, "Everything was fine until new ideas were brought in from the outside." Similar arguments dominate naïve Western representations, such as those that inform coverage of Tonga in the international media, as Western journalists frequently arrive in Tonga convinced that they have stepped into a slightly ludicrous tropical time warp, with its seemingly feudal political system and its large-bodied people. I argue that, instead of pointing accusatory fingers at the allegedly disruptive intrusion of modernity in an otherwise tranquil tradition-steeped society, we should seek to understand Tongan anxiety as being the product of a convergence of the forces of history, tradition, and locality on the one hand and, on the other, the forces of the present, modernity, and the global. The relevance of this analysis reaches well beyond the shores of Tonga, to many other societies of the Pacific Islands and, further afield, the Global South.

Many ethnographies of global flows have focused on migrants and the strategies that they develop in coping with multiple allegiances and identities. Less commonly, anthropologists have followed the movements of commodities, ideas, and images across geographical locations, producing some of the more innovative works in contemporary anthropology (e.g., Foster 2008, Gewertz and Errington 2010, Hansen 2000, Lakoff 2006). This book takes a different approach, while maintaining at the same time a congruent focus with these other works: The frame of cultural reference is what moves and is located elsewhere, while the agents stay in place.

I first went to Tonga as a nineteen-year-old, fearless in my naïveté, having just obtained an undergraduate degree in mathematics after a rather odd upbringing in various countries. I was searching at the time for a variety of interrelated experiences: ethnographic fieldwork (although my idea of what that involved was more than a little vague); adding another language to my repertoire; and the romance of the exotic. I arrived in early 1978 in Vavaʻu, the larger northern island group of Tonga, with the little money I had earned doing construction work in San Francisco, and was almost immediately employed teaching English and mathematics in one of the secondary schools, run by the Wesleyan Church. I lived in a small village, which satisfied my quest for exoticism, in a Tongan style coconut-frond house (*fale Tonga*) that a kind family had built for me in hope that it would bring in a salaried household member but into which the villagers' roaming pigs would periodically conduct infuriating raids. I managed, perhaps, not to offend too many people. But I did acquire a reasonable competence in the language and got a glimpse of the fact that the exotic is not as simple as it appears at first glance, particularly when other people control it. I left Tonga again at the end of that year to pursue graduate work in linguistics at Stanford, but in less than a year I found myself drawn back to the Pacific Islands. A variety of improbable circumstances soon took me to other locations in the region, particularly Tuvalu. I returned to rural Tonga for several extended visits through 1982, for a total stay of about half a year—then did not visit again for a dozen years, being fully involved with fieldwork in Tuvalu and starting a career in anthropology.

In 1994, 1995, 1997, and 1999–2001, I again conducted fieldwork in Tonga, this time in Nukuʻalofa, the country's capital. By then my Tongan had become a little rusty and was competing with my knowledge of Tuvaluan, but I did manage to reacclimatize, this time, to the capital city's distinctively Tongan urbanity. I focused on constructions of gender, in particular on *fakaleitī* or *leitī*, transgender (or "effeminate") men whose lives and experience were more often the subject of romanticized constructions than serious analysis in anthropology and in the popular imagination in New Zealand, where I was living and teaching anthropology during that period. It is through *leitī*'s eyes that I began to appreciate how Tonga at the end of the millennium both differed from and was fundamentally continuous with Tonga in the 1970s, how urban Tonga both disengaged from and was deeply connected to rural Tonga, and how Tongans' lives are deeply enmeshed with a world well beyond the shores of their island nation. I began to understand how capitalism, consumption, and development in contemporary Tonga articulate with traditionalism, exchange, and a resilient sense of humor. It is this paradoxical co-existence of different modes of experience that formed the focus of the fieldwork I conducted for half a year in 2008, shortly after the country experienced some of the most significant changes in its modern history.

This book focuses on seven different sites of social life, the choice of which does not result from a theoretically articulated agenda. I became intrigued with them because they seemed to encapsulate, to me as an analyst and for the agents who frequent them, particularly evocative aspects of modernity in Tonga. Agents' negotiations over the meaning of modernity in these sites spotlight objects and bodies, whose materiality constitutes a point of convergence of ideologies, emotions, political positions, personal projects, state policies, and global discourses. Agents' focus on objects and bodies can be understood both particularistically and comparatively. For Tongans, objects represent a pivot for the articulation of what they see as the traditional order and the modern condition, as is illustrated most vividly by the dramatic increase in the importance of the prestation of traditional textile valuables, alongside rampant capitalism. Similarly, bodies are at the foreground of modernity-conscious Tongans' preoccupations and outsiders' commentaries about their society.

The particular role that objects and bodies play in the articulation of past, present, and future is not confined to the specifics of the Tongan context. Bodies and objects are intensely cultural at the same time as agents strive to naturalize them, as many anthropologists of modernity have highlighted. Perhaps not surprisingly, the sites on which my fieldwork focused all occupy public spaces where Tongans come together and negotiate what it means to be modern. Another anthropologist may well not have paid much attention to them, as they are all quite banal and resemble, on the surface at least, cognate contexts of social life in industrial countries. My attention was drawn to these sites in large part because of my prior lengthy experience conducting fieldwork on remote or at least rural regions of the Pacific. It is because they contrast with village life in Tuvalu and Tonga, and yet articulate social dynamics recognizable from this other life, that I found them particularly fascinating.

My methodology has varied considerably in the various stages of fieldwork and in different sites. In the 1990s and 2000s, I spent time doing "deep hanging out" (Geertz 1998), particularly in the sewing shop of the person who had become a close friend, Malakai Fonua (a.k.a. Lady Mara). I saw the shop move twice, to finally operate from one of Tonga's first shopping centers, a row of now rather dilapidated shops and offices surrounding a parking lot. I interviewed people in different locations, sometimes in depth, other times superficially, and conducted a few surveys. Whenever possible, I recorded people interacting with one another in naturalistic settings, using the techniques and analytic methods with which I am familiar from linguistic anthropology and utilizing successive generations of technologies (from old-style cassette recorders to digital ones, minidisk recorders, and digital recorders, from Hi-8 video to mini-DV, from PAL to NTSC), dishearteningly complicated to convert, harmonize, and preserve.

By 2008, Malakai had taken over the management of the hair salon next to his sewing shop, and when I returned he set me up along with my research assistant in the largely unused "reception area" of the salon. From there my research assistant, a gifted young woman who juggled five or six jobs at any given time, conducted interviews with patrons. I could also take part in or eavesdrop on conversations between patrons of the various businesses in the shopping center. Elsewhere, I talked, casually or formally, to a wide array of people, including government officials, intellectuals, business people, and ordinary folk, young and old, women, men, and everyone else. These conversations took place in restaurants, offices, shops, marketplaces, church premises, street corners, the gym, private homes, inside taxis, and occasionally around urban kava circles (informal gatherings around a bowl of the national drink, a mild narcotic)—although the kava I had already imbibed in villages in the late 1970s and early 1980s was enough for a lifetime. I spoke Tongan whenever possible, true to many Tongans' and my own conviction of the importance of language maintenance, or English when it clearly was my interlocutor's preferred language for conversation with me. Later, in 2009, when I was conducting fieldwork among rugby players and other Tongan immigrants based in Japan (which informs this book, although the ethnography is being written up elsewhere), some of my interviews were in Japanese.

While this ethnography makes frequent reference to the contrast between urban and village life and focuses primarily on the former, I shy away from defining this work as an instance of "urban anthropology," that is, an anthropology that focuses on the issues (frequently "problems") commonly associated with urban living: anonymity, conflict, crowding, and so on. The first caveat is that, frankly, Nuku'alofa's urban patina remains rather unconvincing from a comparative perspective. The town is small and its hustle and bustle confined to a small area surrounding the produce market, the police station, the prime minister's office, and the main street, Tāufa'āhau Road. On Saturday afternoons, it empties out. The poorly maintained roadways, the vacant lots (which have multiplied in the aftermaths of arson fires and rioting in November 2006, which I will describe shortly), and the freely roaming pigs, fowls, and packs of dogs do little to foster an atmosphere of cosmopolitan urbanity. Villagers from around the island of Tongatapu come to town with ease, formerly by truck, now by bus and private car. Some commute on a daily basis, others make the trip on Saturday mornings to buy vegetables at the produce market or sell used clothing at the secondhand marketplace. While the quality of life in Nuku'alofa (or lack thereof) sets it apart from life in villages and outer islands, the two are at the same time so deeply interconnected that any attempt to keep them segregated would miss out on important aspects of life in urban Tonga.

Since the turn of the millennium, Tongans have become intimately familiar with social research, as squadrons of experts of all stripes have been descending on the country in increasing numbers to conduct surveys on every imaginable social and other "problem" (such as teenage pregnancy, obesity, youth "disaffection"). Most of these (generally) well-meaning but overpaid, fly-in-fly-out experts in the employ of New Zealand or Australian development agencies, or associated with the United Nations or other international bodies, work under time pressure. While they index Tonga's global ties and regional modernity, their understanding of the local context is often minimal. In their reports, they often invoke a highly reified notion of "culture," portraying it as a hurdle to be surmounted before development can take place, as is typical of the "modernization" discourse operative around the world. In other reports, "culture" is something to be "respected" but ultimately ignored, echoing the well-rehearsed way in which Māori and Pākehā (white) biculturalism is implemented in New Zealand (Goldsmith 2005). The choice of overseas contractors to conduct this work is frequently a condition for donor funding, a fact that does not fail to irritate Tongan intellectuals, who justifiably feel that they are much better qualified to do the work. The avalanche of social research has introduced into the Tongan vocabulary a neologism borrowed from English, *sāvea*, "survey." In 2008, the easiest way to explain what I was up to was to use this term, for better or for worse, although it was not always a complete misrepresentation. Occasionally, confusion arose in the minds of government officials: Because all experts on flying visits need to be chaperoned by a particular ministry, which ministry was in charge of me?

For many Tongans, the fieldwork I conducted made little sense. I was not addressing "social problems" in any straightforward way. I was investigating "culture," but Tongans have very clear ideas of what culture is, and what I was researching was not it. For them, an anthropologist worth his or her salt should concentrate on aspects of Tongan culture that matter: rituals of rank, land tenure, brother–sister relations, *koloa faka-Tonga* "Tongan valuables," poetic genres, and the intricacies of traditional dancing. And, indeed, most anthropologists who have written about Tonga have focused on these topics, often grounding them in a distant Tongan past and underexamined assumptions of historical continuity. To quote George Marcus's apt words, "Even the very best contemporary ethnographic work in Tonga has constantly been contextualized and measured in terms of Tongan society at the time of Captain Cook [that is, the late eighteenth century] or Tongan society in the time of Tupou I [that is, the nineteenth century]" (2000: 526). (In the foregoing discussion, I will refer occasionally to information about early Tonga, but with a full awareness of their diachronic locus.) Anthropologists' compression of history reflects Tongans' own erasure of history. The nation-making mythology, for example, portrays the trajectory from the mid-nineteenth century to contemporary times as a period of unbroken stability, despite ample evidence of serious conflicts in the formation of the country's modernity.

Because they "skip" a century or more, few anthropologists working in Tonga have paid much attention to such modern-day agents as small-scale entrepreneurs eking out a living selling secondhand goods, needy people pawning their valuables, and young men lifting weights at the gym. For Tongans themselves, an analytic interest in these topics amounts to a slightly ridiculous celebration of the trivial and the contemporary. For example, when I presented an early version of the chapter on the secondhand marketplace at an educational institution in Nuku'alofa, one prominent Tongan intellectual politely voiced the opinion that I was creating "a tempest in a teacup." "You must be joking!" was the reaction of a close friend, a member of Nuku'alofa's business elite, when I told him that I had analyzed the secondhand market-place as a site of modernity. "Maybe you would have been better off doing fieldwork in a village," he added tactfully some time later, as this book was nearing completion. More often than not, Tongans naturalize their and each other's everyday actions, explaining them by appealing to universal principles, such as the need to feed one's children and make improvements to the house where one's parents live. For mainstream Tongans, the dynamics of moder-nity that I analyze in this book are just sensible strategies for living, pragmatic action that need no explanation and are grounded in anything but culture. It is this naturalization, in fact, that makes them such good capitalist subjects.

Of course, the reactions that my research triggered reveals more about Tonga's traditional and transforming senses of rank and emerging class sys-tem than about the irrelevance of an anthropologist's research. Rank and class are deeply implicated in an ethnography that focuses on people in precarious social positions seeking to forge ahead with their lives, making ends meet as well as they can, and searching for self-respect in a competitive society where people are so quick to dismiss each other. Ironically, the denial of coevalness that Johannes Fabian (1983) attributes to anthropology also characterizes elite Tongans' position vis-à-vis their own less fortunate compatriots. It is signifi-cant that this ethnography focuses on sites that are often frequented by peo-ple who are themselves a bit of an embarrassment: the low-ranking, the poor, the young, the unemployed, the transgender, the charismatic Christians, and the criminals deported from countries of the diaspora. And here I am faced with a dilemma. Because our task as anthropologists is not to prove that our informants are wrong, I do not seek to demonstrate that the impatience with which elite and middle-class Tongans have greeted my research is ill founded. Backgrounding this work is the view that what one finds important or trivial, as anthropologists or subjects, is deeply embedded in a politics of positional-ity deserving of analytic attention. In the conclusion, I will return to the idea that the impatient and dismissive local reactions to my fieldwork are in fact constitutive of modernity, in Tonga and elsewhere.

This book seeks to demonstrate that what appears trivial or undignified at first glance may not necessarily be so under further scrutiny, this strategy be-ing, after all, one of the best tricks of anthropology. Consequential insights can be gained about 'Tonga, and about the modern condition in locations comparable to Tonga, by searching for meaning in the day-to-day practices of ordinary or marginal people, their struggles to find material comfort and to define what this comfort is, and their search for a modicum of dignity, perched as they are on the edge of the global, deeply enmeshed in capitalism and yet not quite of it. We cannot simply seek an understanding of this society's problems in purely economic terms, or by invoking a "breakdown of society" thesis, as many attempt to do in Tonga and elsewhere. Rather, this understanding is to be found in the space where the material intersects with the imagination.

Nor can we invoke "the outside world" or "the spoilt generation" to explain the sociopolitical changes that are rocking contemporary Tonga, as well as many other similar corners of the world. These invocations nevertheless constitute a hegemonic discourse of blame in Tonga, where many people feel that the problems that the country is experiencing are caused by "influence" from elsewhere. This discourse overlooks a number of important issues. One is that depicting the relationship between Tonga and the rest of the world as one of "influence" seriously oversimplifies the issues. Others are the facts that Tonga is deeply connected to the rest of the world and that Tongans are not simply the passive recipients of images from elsewhere. Tongans have always been their own interpreters of what has percolated from elsewhere, and the current generations are no exception.

This book is based on my engagement with Tonga and its people that is now entering its fourth decade. This length of time has provided plenty of opportunity to accumulate indebtedness, and I will necessarily overlook many people in these acknowledgments. From their extraordinary support of the odd twenty-year-old that I was in my early years in Tonga, I must belatedly thank Patricia Ledyard Matheson and Father Georges Callet. Since those days, I have cherished my ongoing friendship with Tupou Tonutonu and with Mary and Pesi Fonua, who stalwartly continue to run the Matangi Tonga news website and allowed me to reproduce several photos.

For the last decade and a half years, I have cherished the friendship and trust of Malakai Fonua, a.k.a. Lady Mara. Malakai has consistently provided me with insights (despite her frequent exasperation with the inanity of my questions), enormous quantities of food, and invaluable help with practicalities, all from behind her sewing machine, as she rules the world of Tongan fashion with an iron fist. Hair salon employees and numerous regular visitors to the two shops enlivened my life with jokes, gossip, and serious discussions: Vaisima Langi, Lōmiō Mafi (Romanda), Lasa Taufaʻao, ʻĀmini Fonua (Little Princess Amyland), and the incomparable Sōsefo Foliaki (Susitina), who regaled us with her daily Bollywood performances at 5 PM sharp. I also thank the many friends in Tonga who have made my stays so enjoyable, including the late Naoko Afeaki, Lingi Angilau, the late Futa Helu and Kaloni Helu, Make Helu, Sisiʻuno Helu, Mia Karalus, Joey Mataele, Pila Poʻoi, Geoff Smith, H. K. Yeoh and Julie Wong, and many others. Paul Johansson-Aitu deserves a very special word of thanks for his generosity and hospitality.

My fieldwork was greatly enhanced by the help I received from two assistants, Tyron Langi (in 2000–2001, as well as occasionally in 2008) and Nenase Afu (in 2008). Nenase was a particularly insightful and competent co-fieldworker. Juggling multiple jobs, deeply involved in the affairs of kinship and church, at ease with everyone (even though she left the island of Tongatapu for the first time only recently), Nenase represents all the complexities of contemporary life in Tongan. Working with her has been a privilege.

I have discussed the issues with which I deal in this book with people in Tonga from whose intellectual insights I have greatly benefited, even though they do not necessarily agree with my interpretations. These include the Baron of Kolomotuʻa the Honorable Fielakepa, the late Naoko Afeaki, Shirley Beaman, Semisi and Grace Fakahau, Caroline Fusimālohi, Mataele Fusituʻa, the late Futa Helu, Paul Johansson-Aitu, Viliami Liavaʻa, Monalisa Palu, ʻAna Taufeʻulungaki, Viliami Tautuaʻā, Berry Taukolo, Dennis Tuʻinukuafe, and Raelyn Lolohea ʻEsau. Over the years, the following anthropologists and other scholars of Tonga and the Tongan diaspora have enriched my thinking and refined my understanding: Marie-Claire Bataille-Benguigui, Georges Benguigui, Gaia Cottino, Wendy Cowling, Joseph Esser, Steve Francis, Tamar Gordon, Paul van de Grijp, Adrienne Kaeppler, Tēvita Kaʻili, Takuya Kitahara, Helen Lee, Françoise Marsaudon, Makiko Nishitani, Michael Poltorak, Cécile Quesada-Moaeteau, Kenʻichi Sudo, the late Jehanne Teilhet-Fisk, Besi Wood-Ellem, and Heather Young-Leslie. For their collegiality and enduring friendship I single out Sue Philips, Mary Good, and Ping-Ann Addo (with whom I coauthored an earlier version of Chapter Four). I am grateful to Geoff White for his efforts and enduring friendship and collegiality, to the editorial board of the series for their important advice on earlier versions of the manuscript, and to Deborah Gewertz and Don Brenneis, colleagues of extraordinary quality, who generously reviewed the manuscript on an anonymous basis for the press. At very short notice, three people whose friendship I treasure and scholarship I admire, Anne Allison, Susan Brownell, and Maria Lepowsky, intervened with hands-on help and encouragement, at times when they were seriously needed.

Gaia Cottino, Yannick Fer, Mike Goldsmith, Mary Good, Marvin Harrison, Helen Lee, Ian Lincoln, Fernando Orejuela, Cécile Quesada-Moaeteau, Sue Philips, Mattijs van de Port, Graeme Reid, Matt Tomlinson, and Elisabeth Wood-Ellem all read parts of this book and offered important critical comments. The late Naoko Afeaki, Jenny Alexander, Barak Kalir, Birgit Meyer, Laura Miller, Linda Seligmann, Melenaite Taumoefolau, Elisabeth Wood-Ellem, and H. K. Yeoh provided useful references and information. Librarians Lynette Furuhashi, Stuart Dawrs, Jan Grainger, Tamara Monster, and Phil Parkinson sent me extracts of Tongan phone directories. Jochen Jacoby drew the maps with care and enthusiasm. Editor Stacy Wagner and the staff at the Press were a pleasure to work with. During the writing process, I benefited from the intellectual collegiality of Gerd Baumann, Anneke Beerkens, Stuart Blume, Yolanda van Ede, Alex Edmonds, Marieke van Eijk, Marianne Franklin, Thomas Blom Hansen, Anita Hardon, Barak Kalir, Shifra Kisch, Birgit Meyer, Annelies Moors, Oskar Verkaaik, Mattijs van de Port, Vincent de Rooij, Alex Strating, Sharika Thiranagama, Jojada Verrips, and Jarrett Zigon. In Amsterdam, Peter Geschiere and Frances Gouda are my intellectual muses.

Prior versions of portions of the text have been previously published, in some cases in quite different form: Chapter Three as "Consumption and Cosmopolitanism: Practicing Modernity at the Second-Hand Marketplace in Nuku'alofa," *Anthropological Quarterly* 77: 7–45 (2004); Chapter Four as "When Gifts Become Commodities: Pawn Shops, Valuables, and Shame in Tonga and the Tongan Diaspora," coauthored with Ping-Ann Addo, *Journal of the Royal Anthropological Institute* [n.s.] 14: 39–59 (2008); Chapter Five as "Transgenderism, Locality, and the Miss Galaxy Beauty Pageant in Tonga," *American Ethnologist* 29: 534–566 (2002); and Chapter Six as "Modernité, corps et transformation de soi: Les salons de coiffure aux îles Tonga (Polynésie occidentale)," *L'Homme* 197 (2011). I thank the George Washington University Institute for Ethnographic Research, the Royal Anthropological Institute,

Blackwell Publishing, the American Anthropological Association, and the editorial office of *L'Homme* for granting permission to further develop the ideas that appeared in those publications. The Prime Minister's Office of the Government of Tonga granted permissions to conduct the fieldwork on which this book is based. For funding I am indebted to Yale University's Social Science Faculty Research Fund (1994), Victoria University of Wellington's Faculty of Humanities and Social Sciences Research Fund (1998), the Marsden Fund of the Royal Society of New Zealand (1999–2001), the Wenner-Gren Foundation (1999–2001), the Amsterdam School for Social Science Research (2008), and the Netherlands Organization for Scientific Research NWO (2008).

Finally, I thank Mahmoud abd el Wahed for his unconditional support, in this project as well as many other aspects of life. I dedicate this book to his family and mine.

ON THE EDGE OF THE GLOBAL

Chapter One

Straddling the Edge of the Global

On November 16, 2006, the center of Nuku'alofa, the capital of Tonga, became the scene of mayhem that until then no one had thought possible in
the otherwise peaceful kingdom. It began with Tongans from all walks of
life crashing through shop windows and helping themselves to anything in
sight: food, liquor, appliances, furniture, electronic equipment, and so on.
Then benzene drums were trucked in, and the town went up in flames. A
sizeable number of shops, offices, and government buildings burned to the
ground. Originally designed to target specific buildings, the fire quickly
went out of control, goaded by a dry and fickle summer breeze. Cars were
overturned and set on fire. An anonymous European tourist videotaped the
events. The extensive footage, bootlegged copies of which would sell briskly
in Nuku'alofa shops in subsequent months, captured looters in a celebratory
mood mugging for the camera, oblivious to the fact that the police would
later use the film as incriminating evidence in court. Eight looters entered
the burning offices of a phone company, not realizing that the door was self-
locking. Their remains were later found, charred beyond recognition, one
with packs of stolen plastic phone cards melted onto his body. The trucks
that had brought in the benzene were quickly organized to carry the loot
back to suburbs and outlying villages. While on a global scale of violence,
defined by genocides and natural disasters, the event did not even register as
a blip, it was locally experienced as a day of infamy, to which Tongans would

Photo 1.1.   Nuku'alofa, November 16, 2006: Looting and buildings on fire.

come to refer as "16/11" (in Tongan, *taha ono taha taha*), tacitly evoking the New York event that had preceded it by five years despite the profound differences in intention, magnitude, and consequence (Figure 1.1).

The looting and arson took place in a climate of anxiety of an unprecedented nature since the beginning of the country's modern history. This beginning can arguably be located in the mid-nineteenth century, when the nation emerged as what Tongans often proudly call "the last remaining Polynesian kingdom," managing with some difficulty to keep at bay the colonial takeovers that the neighboring polities endured. As the twentieth century was drawing to a close, the delicate political and social edifice on which the Tongan state had rested was beginning to unravel through a series of interrelated circumstances. The most visible of these was the increasing insistence emanating from some quarters of Tongan society for democratic participation in a government hitherto structured by a rigid rank-based order. This insistence was primarily associated with a "Pro-Democracy Movement," founded in the early 1980s by a group of vocal educated commoners and later renamed "Human Rights and Democracy Movement of Tonga" (HRDMT). Pressure to democratize also emanated from overseas (and, some cynics point out, more crucially so): from the International Monetary Fund, the World Bank, the World Trade Organization, and the two major powers in the Pacific region, New Zealand and Australia. For these latter, demonstrating a faith in "good governance" had become a precondition for economic assistance to their poorer island neighbors.

In 2005, to appease growing dissent, the reigning king, Tāufaʻāhau Tupou IV, appointed to the prime ministership Feleti (Fred) Sevele. Holder of a PhD in human geography from the University of Canterbury in New Zealand, Sevele was at the time a Pro-Democracy parliamentarian and prominent businessman. The appointment of a progressive well-educated commoner to the post was a radical departure from tradition, as prime ministers until then had all been members of the royal family or close associates. It surprised the people and raised hopes, particularly as it took place in the wake of a series of embarrassing scandals, such as the government's illegal sale of Tongan passports and the mismanagement of the proceeds (which evaporated completely, apparently into the pockets of an American con artist who had befriended the king). But the mood did not last. Beginning on July 25, 2005, the underpaid civil service staged an unprecedented six-week general strike, marching to Parliament with a petition endorsed by 2,000 signatories and camping out for weeks at Pangai Siʻi, ceremonial grounds located across from the Royal Palace. Civil servants were demanding that the government raise salaries to keep up with the price hikes of the last few years, the effect of double-digit inflation and a falling currency on an economy crucially dependent on imports. In the preceding years, members of parliament (including HRDMT members) and cabinet ministers had regularly voted substantial salary raises for themselves.

After some haggling, the government granted the civil service a 60 to 80 percent raise, bringing the biweekly starting salary of junior employees up to T$140.[1] For a while, order was restored, and optimism returned. The aging king then constituted, with financial assistance from Australia and New Zealand, a National Committee for Political Reform (NCPR), at the head of which he appointed his late brother's son, ʻUluvalu Prince Tuʻipelehake. The committee visited all the islands of the group, as well as expatriate communities in New Zealand, Australia, and the United States, holding "conversations" (*talanoa*) with townspeople, villagers, and migrants. On July 5, 2006, however, before the NCPR had completed its mission, a drag-racing American teenage girl sideswiped the car in which 'Uluvalu was travelling on the freeway in Menlo Park, Northern California, an area with a high concentration of Tongan migrants. The prince, his well-respected spouse Princess Kaimana, and their driver were all killed. Sitiveni Halapua, a Tongan development studies scholar who directs one of the programs at the East-West Center in Honolulu, stepped in to finish the work of the committee and in August presented its recommendations to the king, who was lying in an Auckland hospital. The king, aged 88, died on September 10, 2006, and Crown Prince Tupouto'a, then aged fifty-eight and unmarried, became King George Tupou V.

Without warning, the government disbanded the NCPR and appointed a new committee, whose recommendations it chose to accept instead of the NCPR's. In early November, parliamentarians (including HRDMT members) voted themselves another 60 percent pay raise. HRDMT politicians then fissioned, as some jumped the fence to the government's side. 'Akilisi Pōhiva, the self-appointed voice of the movement since the 1980s, and several other opposition politicians abruptly withdrew their support for the NCPR's recommendations and, on November 16, staged a march in the center of town. Crowds assembled at Pangai Si'i. While breakaway prodemocracy politicians were in negotiations with the prime minister in his office, a stone's throw from Pangai Si'i (and, indeed, a few stones were thrown at the building), the crowd moved to the business district, and the looting began. The premeditated nature of the arson that followed is unquestionable: Only selected buildings were originally targeted, several of which belonged to the prime minister, while the businesses owned by prodemocracy politicians and their wealthy and ambitious supporters were spared. In 2009, some still stood alone on street corners, surrounded by empty lots where other buildings once stood, shameful reminders of a crisis that many previously thought impossible, still haunting imaginations months and years after the government lifted the state of emergency that followed.[2]

Many Tongans find the events too upsetting to even talk about, in a society that traditionally considers the public expression of conflict and anger outside the prerogatives of rank deeply disruptive. However, different narrative versions of the events "from above" continue to pepper conversations, preoccupy intellectuals, and fill newspaper columns. They also emerge in the international press when news is slow, bearing titles such as "Trouble in Paradise" or some predictably unimaginative alternative (for example, Teague 2007), in tune with the tone of condescending mockery that often characterizes international press coverage of Tonga. But, like all events of its kind, the looting and burning of Nuku'alofa were not simply the product of political intrigue by a few, a failed coup d'état inspired by the successive coups that neighboring Fiji has endured, or the action of a youthful mob looking for trouble and excitement. Rather, an understanding of 16/11 must be embedded in a larger historical, social, and cultural context, in addition to a political one.

Aspects of this context that are commonly invoked include the increasing anxiety that many people in Tonga are experiencing about their welfare, the sudden and unexplainable influx of immigrants from the People's Republic of China, and the breakdown of tradition that many believe is taking place, as "respect" (for hierarchy, tradition, government, and so on) is being sapped, ostensibly by overseas influences. This book seeks to cast a much wider analytic net than commonsensical analyses do when attempting to explain 16/11, as well as more generally the profound transformations that Tongan society underwent in the last decades of the twentieth century. I am particularly intrigued by some of the details of the 16/11 events that are easy to overlook and that today fuel the mocking contempt that better-off Tongans sometimes express for their less worldly compatriots: the looters mugging for the tourist's video camera, naïvely oblivious to the workings of modern police surveillance; the eight young men's tragic lack of familiarity with self-locking doors; the phone cards melted onto the charred body of one of the victims; and the fridges, washing machines, and beer cartons being cheerily carted away through smashed store windows.

These details betray complexities grounded in a considerably broader context than the tragedy itself. This context is constituted by the hopes, anxieties, and frustrations that ordinary Tongans are experiencing as their society retains a robust self-image of continuity while at the same time undergoing profound change. In the last half century, the society has transformed itself from a relatively stable organic entity into a diasporic, pluralistic, and deeply modern society. Islanders have moved in large numbers to New Zealand, Australia, and the United States, while Chinese immigrants and other agents from elsewhere (including transnational corporations, overseas governments, nongovernmental organizations [NGOs]) have played an increasingly determinative role in the affairs of the country. This book focuses on the ways in which Tongans negotiate the resulting tensions between traditionalism and modernity in everyday contexts. An understanding of what happened on 16/11 must be grounded in the uneasy structures of difference that have emerged in Tongan society since the 1960s and in the fractures that transverse it today. In turn, these must be embedded in a theoretical understanding of the modern condition, to which I now turn.

Tongan Modernity in a Theoretical Context

Unlike sociology, which has been preoccupied with modernity since its nineteenth-century origin, anthropology has long been saddled with its image as the social science of the "primitive other." It was only in the last decades of the twentieth century that anthropologists turned their attention to the nexus of material and ideational dynamics commonly referred to as "modernity," compelled by the realization that the societies in which we work are "exotic no more." Whether they live in the crowded neighborhoods of Cairo or Mumbai, poverty-stricken areas of the United States, African forests, or faraway islands of the Pacific, people are deeply cognizant of the world-scale structures of interconnection in which they are embedded. Even when hegemonic representations orientalize them as "people without history" or when they orientalize themselves as being on the edge of the global, as Tongans do, in the global but not quite of it, people everywhere are deeply implicated in the modern condition. Modernity is with us, wherever we are.[3]

Attempting to define modernity is a notoriously hazardous enterprise because of the diffuse, shifting, and ungrounded nature of the category (Yack 1997). Language often provides little guidance. This is the case of the Tongan language, in which the rather vague term *onopooni* "these modern times," which contrasts with *onoʻaho* "days of yore," is the closest in meaning to *modernity* in English, although sometimes the English word is borrowed into Tongan as *mōteni*.[4] *Tradition*, in contrast, is captured precisely and recognizably by the ubiquitous phrase *anga faka-Tonga*, which people gloss as "the Tongan way" when speaking English and generally equate with "culture" tout court (another term, *fakatukufakaholo*, foregrounds continuity with the past). The discrepant ways in which the Tongan language treats tradition and modernity comprise a revealing index of the unstable nature of modernity in contrast to the solidity that people ascribe to tradition, in the Tongan context as well as more generally.

Drawing inspiration from Marx and Weber, Anthony Giddens, one of the foremost contemporary theorists of modernity, locates it at the convergence of four large-scale forces: capitalism, or the production and circulation of commodities in a market context; industrialism, or the transformation of nature through technology; surveillance, or the institutional control over citizens; and military power, or the state monopoly over violence (1990: 55–78). These forces are interdependent, but none is reducible to the others. Together they produce what Giddens calls "time–space distanciation," the process of separating time and space from a local grounding and from one another, which he contrasts with a "social integration" that premodern persons generate through straightforward copresence (D. Gregory 1989: 187–190). Distanciation is generated, for example, by the disjunction between production and consumption under capitalism, as distance and time separate those who produce from those who consume, who as a result become mutually irrelevant. Another illustration is surveillance: video cameras roaming over different spaces at once, storing images of anonymous people's actions that can be viewed at a later date for the purpose of unmasking anonymity, of which the tourist's camera in Nuku'alofa on 16/11 offers a particularly relevant illustration. Time–space distanciation enables what Giddens posits would have been impossible before the rise of modernity, namely the "lifting out of social relations from local contexts of interaction and their restructuring across indefinite spans of time–space," a process that he terms "disembedding" (1990: 21).

At the same time, people still interact with one another on a daily basis and do not experience the Nietzschean nihilism that one would expect to emerge in disembedded lives. In particular, while people everywhere increasingly consume commodities generated by absent producers or produce commodities that absent others will consume, they still come face-to-face with familiar people, inhabit familiar spaces, and fill their daily lives with routines governed by a familiar sense of time. For Giddens, disembedded social relations are also subject to "reembedding," namely a recontextualization into a familiar space and time. For example, the shopping mall in the modern urban landscape is specifically designed to inspire security and familiarity, despite the fact that it is almost exclusively occupied by chain store franchises, virtually identical all over the urban world and controlled by forces invisible to most (1990: 141). It is this very possibility of the disembedded to undergo domestication that generates in people trust in modernity and faith in its possibilities, despite the specter of dehumanization that hovers over it.

Anthropologists have been particularly seduced by the creativity involved in reembedding, the sense that people are not passive flotsam and jetsam in an ocean of time–space distanciation, but active subjects. They have taken great pains to demonstrate that modernity does not just happen but that it is shaped by agents who engage with it while pursuing their localized life projects. Agents do so with the help of one powerful tool, the imagination, which provides grounding to disembedded dynamics even when other resources are lacking. Focusing on this creativity undermines the totalizing image of modernity that Giddens proposes and allows for its transformation when it operates outside the late capitalist Western nation-state. The imagination that people everywhere (not just shoppers in the malls of Western Europe and North America) bring to the modern condition can shape it in ways that Western common sense may find surprising. Anthropologists take particular delight in relativizing this common sense with ethnographic material from elsewhere and demonstrating that it is neither sensical nor common (Foster 2008: 14–17).

Arjun Appadurai argues that globalization has given this vague concept, the imagination, a centrality than it never had before: Crossing paths with flows of objects, ideas, and images of an unprecedented density, people partake in the enchantment of imagined possibilities of personal and social transformation. Imagining has become a routinized activity, whereas in earlier times it may have been a bracketed event: "Fantasy is now a social practice" (1996: 54). Of course we do not know for certain that fantasy in premodern times was not also a social practice. Furthermore, works inspired by Appadurai tend to overemphasize the production of the imagination in modernity, presenting the expanded horizons of the imagination as the product of globalization. In fact, the imagination was there before anyone was talking about the modern, albeit perhaps in a different configuration. Before James Cook reached their shores, heralding an unprecedented expansion of their horizons, there is little doubt that some Tongans at least were perfectly capable of imagining life on other islands, the prospect of new exchanges, and the possibility of moving to other locations. Rather than seeing the imagination as being in a one-way relationship with modernity, one should see the latter as constitutive of a particular kind of imagination, rendered necessary by particular aspects of the modern, such as the material precarity engendered by neoliberal conditions.

In addition, modern global flows often only afford fleeting and tantalizing, but ultimately unrealizable, glimpses of possibilities, as global modernity is just as often a matter of closure as it is a matter of movement (Hannerz 1996; Heyman and Campbell 2009; Meyer and Geschiere 1999). For many around the world, global flows of people, ideas, and images are just as likely to generate frustration as they are to open up new horizons, through what Trouillot (2001: 129) calls "the global production of desire," glimpses of "the good life" that are beyond the reach of most. Closure takes very concrete forms for Tongans, for whom obtaining visas just to visit other places is extraordinarily difficult. More abstractly, the inhabitants of the developing world are deeply aware of the forces that anchor them in positions of "underdevelopment," "tradition-steeped" societies, or the "savage slot," positions that the industrial world needs to define itself as the legitimate proprietor of modernity (Ferguson 1999, 2002; Trouillot 1991) in the same fashion that the self requires an abject other to produce the ever-ongoing work of self-definition (Kristeva 1980). This "contradiction," as Liechty (2003: xi) characterizes it, is the context in which many people have to generate a sense of self, come up with the resources that they need to survive, and negotiate social relations with others around them, regrounding into the local context disembedded fragments of social life from both their own immediate life-worlds and life-worlds from faraway locations.

Plurals

In the 1990s, the recognition that modernity is always shaped by the local led many social scientists to talk of "multiple modernities," "other modernities," "vernacular modernities," "local modernities," "parallel modernities," "alternative modernities," and "indigenous modernities." These assertions of plurality and difference, at times a little too celebratory for their own credibility, nevertheless expanded in healthy ways totalizing characterizations of modernity à la Giddens.[5] Localized modernities resemble forms of modernity familiar from postcapitalist contexts but exhibit specific engagement with local particularities, generating their own possibilities and constraints. Driving calls for modernity's pluralization were powerful critiques of modernity emanating from postcolonial and subaltern studies (for example, Chakrabarty 2000; Prakash 1999), from a colonial periphery on whose shoulders Europe had long rested while appropriating modernity for itself. We were now very far from earlier unilinear models of "modernization" that characterized the "Third World" as potentially achieving a modern condition once it accepts development and sheds its bothersome obsession with tradition. No longer viewed as a stage in history, modernity was now conceptualized as the staging of history (T. Mitchell 2000: 23), hence its susceptibility to multiply, shift, and be disrupted.

The pluralistic approach to modernity was motivated by efforts to come to grips with not only the relationship among different kinds of modernities (particularly postindustrial versus other) but also the tension between modernity and what it is commonsensically supposed to follow or displace, "tradition." Already Bruno Latour (1991 [1993]) had claimed that "we have never been modern" because everything in the modern condition is a hybridization of the traditional and the modern. According to him, the project of modernity consists of two efforts: separation (or purification) between persons and things, culture and nature; and translation (or mediation or hybridization), whereby categories separated by the first project become entangled with one another again. For most anthropologists, however, concepts such as "purification" and "hybridization" come with their own problems (Crehan 2002: 58–67; Palmié 2006; Piot 2001). The very concept of "hybridization" presupposes preexisting pure ingredients, while in fact the elements that mix to produce a hybrid form are themselves pure only because they are ideologically produced as such. Hybridity also implies improvisation and chance, implications that fail to do justice to the structural ways in which modernity and tradition converge in many contexts. Latour's approach thus runs the danger of obscuring the politics operative in both separation and translation. Finally, separated and hybridized forms may be each other's products rather than autonomous entities. For example, as many anthropologists have demonstrated (for example, Geschiere 1997), tradition can be the product of modernity rather than its antecedent. While the dynamics that produce the pure forms are worthy of attention, my preoccupation in this book is of a different kind. I am concerned with the work of keeping tradition and modernity apart, as I document Tongans strenuously distancing themselves from hybridity while their lives are in fact suffused with it. For them, despite their own embracement of modernity, it opposes and threatens tradition, even though both emerge from the same social and cultural forms.

Not unexpectedly, the enthusiasm with which anthropologists have relativized modernity has been subjected to criticism. One of the sharpest is Englund and Leach's (2000) contention that scholars have promoted modernity to the status of metanarrative. Through their efforts to identify it in their ethnographic materials wherever they think it exists, anthropologists have lost track, they claim, of one of the key features of ethnography: reflexivity. Echoing a similar debate over the concept of culture that raged in the 1990s (Brightman 1995; see also Sahlins 1999), other commentators ask what one actually gains by replacing the singular form of the word *modernity* with its plural form (Gaonkar 1999). "The vocabulary of alternatives can still imply an underlying and singular modernity, modified by local circumstances into a multiplicity of 'cultural' forms" (T. Mitchell 2000: xii; see also Knauft 2002: 18–20).

Approaching the problem from the vantage point of an expertise in linguistic anthropology, Spitulnik (2002) argues that anthropologists would have much to gain from paying greater attention to the language of modernity. She distinguishes between terms that refer, in particular languages, to modernity on the one hand from, on the other, ways of speaking that signify "being modern." The term itself may have no straightforward or single equivalent in many languages, as is the case of Tongan. Modernity in Tonga and elsewhere is not so much talked *about* as it is *enacted* and *performed*. In Tonga, this enactment is embedded in the frequent use of borrowings from English (the language of modernity par excellence), code switching between English and Tongan, and the use of cutting-edge expressions of various kinds. However, any of these communicative strategies can "mean" different things in different contexts because they operate as indexes rather than symbols, and thus their meaning is deeply contextual and a matter of evocation rather than reference.[6]

Particular acts, linguistic and other, index modernity when they co-occur with other forms that also potentially allude to modernity. For example, at the secondhand marketplace in Tonga, code switching between English and Tongan in a conversation about fashion in New Zealand is driven by the desire to be seen as modern in a setting where consumption, "shopping," and imported goods all figure center stage and work as modernity-alluding signs themselves. Furthermore, particular performances arouse responses, both immediate, in the form of conversational turns, and delayed, in the form of gossip, for example. As I will illustrate later, Tongans are very quick to criticize each other's performances, ascribing descriptors such as *fie Pālangi* "pretending to be a Westerner" or *fie me'a* "pretending to be more than one is" to people who claim more of a modern identity than they are capable of substantiating or who seem too eager to turn their back on tradition. By "reading" these clues, intentions can be unpacked, and subjectivities can be analyzed.

Arguments from linguistic anthropology do not militate for or against a pluralistic position on modernity, but they do suggest that when modernity is the object of so much attention, desire, and anxiety, it had better be the sustained focus of ethnographic inquiry (see Osella and Osella 2006: 570). However, one has to be particularly attentive not just to the commentaries that people offer on the topic itself but also, and more importantly, to the conduct of their own interactions, to their responses to each other's positionings, and to the location of semiotic forms, both verbal and nonverbal. And it is through this ethnographic attention to the particulars of everyday lives that we realize that the desire for modernity is more than just the ethnographer's unreflexive projection. Attention to this desire, in places on the edge of modernity such as Tonga, situates ethnography squarely in its reflexive mold, but a reflexivity mold that is perhaps more complex than meets the uniformed ear, as it is one that requires that we listen attentively to what people say to one another, how they say it, and when. At strategic moments in this book, I will highlight the methodological power of linguistic anthropological methods, which presuppose not only a finely honed understanding of particular languages but also an understanding of the relationship of language to social action and cultural form.

Bifocality

A focus on modernity and its twin, globalization, raises questions about the scale and location of the ethnographic focus, questions that are not specific to modernity but that are nevertheless foregrounded by it. Being modern in a local context represents a cultural and material engagement with two coterminous realms of reality: at one extreme, large-scale dynamics of state-level, regional, and global forces; and, at the other extreme, the forces of grounded locality. These realms of reality are of course not neatly separated but blend and overlap with one another, necessitating a constant engagement with them in the course of daily life. This engagement is what Edward Said called, in reference to exiles, "a plurality of vision": "Because the exile sees things both in terms of what has been left behind and what is actual here and now, there is a double perspective that never sees things in isolation"

(1984: 44). Here I expand Said's insight beyond the experience of the exile: It is not just them whose vision is plural but also those whose movements are not straightforwardly characterizable as exile, as well as those who remain in place, who are equally cognizant of other perspectives on who they are and what they do, of other possibilities for action, and other contexts for understanding the present. All engage in what can be termed "bifocality" (Peters 1997; Rouse 1991).

Agents engage in this bifocality, living and interacting in the "nearsightedness" of the here-and-now while constantly focusing into the distance for the possible presence of faraway spectators, as well as everything else that comes in between. It is what gives to the modern condition a shifting, contingent, and unpredictable quality, or, to use Bernard Yack's bold wording, the "large degree of incoherence [operating] in the life of modern individuals" (1997: 36). Attempting to come to terms with this quality, anthropologists have taken two contradictory analytic directions, as Webb Keane (2003) demonstrates. One approach consists in focusing on global interconnections, be they structures of political economy, colonialism, history, or rootlessness. This approach makes its object of analysis the "disjunctures and differences" constitutive of global dynamics, viewing modernity as a matter of mobility of people, ideas, resources, and signs, questioning the naturalization of place as the locus of culture, and using estrangement from the particular as an analytic strategy to uproot the subject (Appadurai 1996; Gupta and Ferguson 1992). Another approach advocates a particularistic focus on intimate lived experience and the immediacy of the local, accessible to the ethnographer through personal identification with the ethnographized subject (L. Abu-Lughod 1991). This latter approach underlies endeavors to understand modernity in the micropolitics of performativity, through which people alternatively embody, evaluate, or mock modernity (Schein 1999).

Calls for both particularism and analytic estrangement come with limitations (Keane 2003). Privileging mobility and displacement runs the danger of isolating subjects as autonomous entities in control of their world and liberating them from the strictures of place and culture, leaving unattended local political economic regimes that keep them in place. A focus on the particularities of lived experience rests on the conviction that the intimacy of private worlds is somehow more genuine than other forms of being, an assumption that has long been demonstrated to be problematic, at least since Erving Goffman (Gal 1995). It also obliterates the politics of representation, enabling the ethnographer to conflate his or her own metalanguage with local forms. Finally, it runs the risk of calling attention to local continuities between a premodern order and the particularities of the localized modernity and of turning a blind eye to radical change, which anthropologists have been notoriously ill equipped to account for in the first place (Robbins 2007).

One way to avoid the pitfalls of both particularistic and deterritorialized approaches is to focus on the fact that modernity does not operate uniformly across all contexts of social life. Rather, agents give it different shapes in different contexts, tying it to different large-scale processes and to the different foci of their farsightedness. It is surprising that anthropologists of the modern have rarely engaged with the fact that modernity does not "mean" the same thing to different people within the same society, an insight that differs from more common calls for the recognition of "multiple modernities." In any given society, not everyone is equally invested in modernity because it does not offer an identical range of possibilities and does not represent the same kinds of constraints for everyone. Modernity fascinates some but repels others. Minimally, modernity is gendered, just as it provides differing avenues to members of different age groups and generations, ranks, and other forms of social difference (for example, S. Cohen 2004; Rofel 2002). In turn it becomes a vehicle for social difference, as agents incorporate their own and each other's positioning in their projects of self-making. How can we engage with these complicated processes of differentiation and identification?

In this book I seek to denaturalize place but also recognize the continued importance of locality as a nexus of political action and ideological elaboration. This stance recognizes that modernity is configured differently, not only for different social groups but also in the different locations of the social geography within which people organize their daily existence. This approach goes a long way in solving the problem of scale to which Keane draws attention: While people engage with modernity on a microscopic scale, they also index differing large-scale configurations. For example, at the secondhand marketplace in Nuku'alofa, objects offered for sale originate overseas, some having been shuttled back and forth between different corners of the Pacific Basin before finally landing there, just as secondhand clothes do in other parts of the world on other edges of modernity (Hansen 2000). But they are also evaluated in terms of local standards of quality, appropriateness, and desirability, evaluations that sometimes involve complicated face-to-face negotiations among local agents. At Pentecostal and charismatic churches, people sing and dance in celebration of God and of their liberation from the strictures of local tradition-alism, at the same time as they partake in a world-scale discourse of conversion, prosperity, and "happiness." Young women competing in Tonga's annual Miss Heilala beauty pageants strive to perform a rigidly defined tradition while also competing for a chance to take part in pageant circuits in the Pacific Island re-gion and beyond. The articulation of specific forms of modernity in particular local sites with large-scale forms of modernity is always fraught. For example, the poor results that Tongan beauty pageant winners have generally obtained in regional pageants are related to the fact that the "modern traditionalism" lo-cally expected of them is irrelevant to the international circuit: There, in con-trast to the national pageant, no one particularly cares whether a particular Miss South Pacific contestant is competent in her local language and able to perform the national dance with exacting grace. At the same time, shifts be-tween coexisting body aesthetics, from health- and wealth-indexing plumpness to cosmopolitan sveltness, subject contestants to different kinds of evaluative scrutiny, the location of which is not always predictable. The stories I tell in this book are open ended, subject to unexpected revisions in the same way that the past that I also chronicle has been the context of unexpected turns.

As these examples illustrate, apprehending the local meaning of moder-nity requires a subtler engagement with the ethnographic context than one that would attempt to identify what modernity means "for Tongans," a fall-back on Durkheimian presuppositions of social cohesion whose specter still haunts many works on local forms of modernity. Different groups and dif-ferent agents orient themselves differently to modernity, but they also do so in reference to the immediate context in which they are located, consisting minimally of the people who surround them, while at the same time engag-ing with different aspects of globality. Various sites present different ranges of possibilities and constraints for the intersubjective negotiation of mo-dernity. Focusing on how the local and the global are configured in specific settings provides an ethnographic handle on two forms of rupture: One is spatial, as agents engage with modernity in its multiple forms in the spatial geography contexts of their daily existence; the other is temporal, enacted in modernity's distanciation, embedded in the belief that change is necessary, unavoidable, and exciting (which often operates, paradoxically, hand-in-hand with a faith in continuity and tradition).

The ethnography I present here has particularly implications for an un-derstanding of a certain kind of local–global engagement, namely that of diasporic societies, which are increasingly numerous in the contemporary world. As I will elaborate in the next chapter, Tongan society is now dispersed throughout the Pacific Basin and the rest of the world. Despite being preoccupied in their daily existence by the vicissitudes of urban living in New Zealand, Australia, and the United States, many overseas Tongans retain a strong orientation to their island homeland. The constitution of Tongan migratory culture (dispersal, homeland orientation, persistence) does motivate treating it as a classic diaspora, at least at this moment in history, even in light of Brubaker's (2005) caution against the liberal use of the category. It also explains why Tongans (both overseas and island based) experience in particularly vivid ways tensions between the local and the global and between tradition and modernity. As James Clifford argues, "The term *diaspora* is a signifier, not simply of transnationality and movement, but of political struggles to define the local, as distinctive community, in historical contexts of displacement" (1994: 308). These struggles operate intersubjectively, but they also operate between particular contexts of everyday life.

An agentive force of significance in these struggles is the state. As many have now argued, the news of the demise of the state under pressure from global forces has been greatly exaggerated (for example, Hirst and Thompson 1999; Trouillot 2001). The state continues to mediate between the local and the global, through both its presence and invisibility. A Tongan example of the state's control of global–local relationships is the recent change in citizenship legislation. In 2008, dual citizenship became legal, enabling expatriate Tongans to become citizens of their host country and people of Tongan descent but lacking Tongan citizenship to apply for it. But the state's presence is also recognizable in other aspects of Tonga's engagement with modernity: in the secondhand marketplace entrepreneurs' creative engagement with customs officials, charged with collecting an increasingly substantial proportion of the country's revenues while also coping with their own dwindling buying power as employees of a neoliberal state; in the proliferation of pawnshops, as civil servants who took early retirement packages offered by the government anxious to downsize the civil service invested their money in the commodification of traditional valuables; and even in the Pentecostal Church's prosperity faith, as one overseas-based congregant uses a sudden windfall from God to buy one of the beachfront homes that the government has put up for sale.

State entities that mediate the articulation of the local and the global are not confined to Tonga. Other states intervene, such as the United States and its punitive response to law breaking by noncitizens, creating a new identity in Tonga, "deportee," that has become the focus of much anxiety and blame shouldering.[7] Immigration policies of all countries of the diaspora are the bureaucratic (and often capricious) regulators of possibilities for and constraints on movements, kinship ties, and futures. The state is a mediator of people's engagement with the local and the global and one that cannot be ignored in an ethnographic engagement with the bifocality of action.

Sites

Underlying my analysis is the recognition that the global and local intersect in particular spaces of social life. To refer to these spaces, I borrow the category "site" from cultural studies. Although the term has also long entered the social scientific vocabulary, its meaning is more often assumed than attended to. A site may be a concrete fragment of space or an abstraction. In either case, it animates structures of power and the ideological scaffolding propping these structures. Sites are always potentially laden with semiotics and suffused with ideologies that agents produce within them (de Certeau 1980 [1984]; Lefebvre 1974 [1991]). A site is thus not just the location where social action takes place but also the context whose ideological and structural configuration authorizes specific forms of social action, and the latter in turn reinforces the ideological scaffolding of the site. For example, as I will demonstrate in Chapter Six, the hair salon enables its middle-aged female customers to fuss over their graying hair, and in turn the specific configuration of the self associated with anxieties over aging becomes part of the meaning of the salon as a site. Most of the sites I will discuss in this book are concrete spatial locations or at least have a strong association to specific locations. Yet their spatial associations are not just local but also global. Acts that take place in each of them (for example, interaction, consumption, evaluation, or projection into the future) keep one eye on the local and the other on the global, instantiations of the bifocality that characterizes the modern condition.

The social action that takes place at sites of modernity is a quintessential example of what is commonly referred to in social theory as "practice." By "practice" I refer, in step with classic definitions (such as Bourdieu 1972 [1977]), to "anything people do," particularly acts that have "intentional and unintentional political implications" (Ortner 1984: 149). But I also foreground connotations of the term *practice*, associated with earlier theorizations, that highlight the tentative, developmental, performative, and coconstructed nature of activity, in which bifocality plays a determinative role. In this sense, practice (and the habitus that emerges out of it) involves the coordination of behavior with inner dispositions through repeated performance (Mahmood 2005: 136). This perspective on practice, which aligns it with what Ferguson (1999) terms "cultural style," takes inspiration from theories of performativity (for example, Butler 1990), although the materials I will discuss emphasize the uncertainty-generating role of "citationality" rather than its confirmatory power. For example, I explore how the people I observed engage in a complex set of activities about which they are not always entirely sure, such as displaying their familiarity with a desirable modern lifestyle, morally appraising various tokens of modernity, and comparing modern lifestyles with practices that are branded as traditional. "Practicing" in its literal sense also subsumes repeating, which is entirely appropriate because the modernity that agents practice often foregrounds consumption, a sphere of social action in which reiteration plays a crucial role (Appadurai 1996: 66–70).

A salient characteristic of the sites where the global and local met is their banality, which explains why Tongans' reaction to my research alternated between bemusement and impatience, as I explained in the preface. The pawnshop, the secondhand marketplace, the gym, and the hair salon are banal because they are frequented or run by people who generally matter little in the eyes of the establishment and because the activities that take place there (trading, bodybuilding, beautifying) are considered trivial compared to the things that "really matter." Even beauty pageants, despite the considerable interest that they mobilize, are ultimately banal. What goes on in these sites is ostensibly about something other than power, politics, and the local significance of the global. Yet, as both Gramsci and Althusser have argued in their respective versions of Marxism, it is precisely in sites that are "about something else" that one can observe politics at its most effective. It is in the triviality of the everyday, the ordinary, and the "unrecognized" (Lefebvre 1988: 78) that one should expect to uncover the tensions that underlie people's lives, be they tensions of power and hegemony or of politics in its broadest sense (Besnier 2009a).

Viewing modernity as embedded in specific sites calls for a nuanced approach to modern subjectivities. It recognizes that modernity's plurality not only results from different societies implementing different ideas of what it is but also derives from different members of the same society experiencing it differently and associating these differences with specific sites. Modernity arises out of intersubjective negotiations among people, and it is in the crevices of different subjectivities that we should seek an understanding of what changes and what stays the same and allow for the possibility that modernity's enthusiasm for change may in fact be remarkably similar to tradition's fervent allegiance to continuity.

Selves

Universalizing approaches to modernity claim that it endows its subjects with new possibilities for self-creation and self-understanding. Anthony Giddens sees this "opening up," as it were, of new forms of self-making as constitutive of reembedding, which activates a self-awareness that is part-and-parcel of the modern condition (Giddens 1991; see also Taylor 1989). In this view, for example, modern intimate partnership is a "pure relationship" between two individuals based on the will to be together, which comes with its own problems but supposedly liberates the subjects from the designs of other agents (Giddens 1992). The pure relationship allegedly contrasts with premodern forms of intimacy, where it is subsumed by family alliances, in comparison to which it pales in importance, and where intimacy outside of marriage is simply irrelevant. "Kinship ties of various kinds were the prime external anchoring of the individual's life experience in most pre-modern contexts," states Giddens (1991: 147), significantly in the past tense.

While suggestive, grand comparative schemes such as these are deeply problematic. While admitting that it is not devoid of difficulties, Giddens celebrates the sovereign self in self-congratulatory undertones. Who would choose to be slave to kinship over free choice and self-determination? Of course, Foucault (1975 [1979]) made us aware long ago that the celebration of the autonomous modern self masks more subtle and insidious forms of structural domination than those at play in premodernity. Other classic critiques of the autonomous self have argued that it is a feature of the *male* modern self, predicated as it is on the denial of dependence, relationality, and identification with others (particularly the mother) during psychosocial development (Chodorow 1978). Historians, anthropologists, and other social scientists have argued that the autonomy of the modern self is contingent on a particular context of materiality, enabled by economic and moral conditions marked for class, ethnicity, race, and many other structural dimensions of difference (for example, Abercrombie, Hill, and Turner 1986; di Leonardo 1991; Ehrenreich 1989). It is easy to feel autonomous when one has the money to pay for everything (except perhaps loyalty and love). For those whose existence continues to hinge on the support of kin and other humans, as well as those who depend on the last remaining safety nets of crumbling welfare states, assertions of autonomy present a more risky game than for those who lead a comfortable middle- or upper-middle-class existence.

Giddens's and others' understanding of modernity as bringing about a radical transformation in self-making echo long-standing discourses of a similar kind in anthropology, although anthropologists have been more preoccupied with the premodern self than the modern self. The most frequently cited passage on the topic must be Geertz's decades-old pronouncement:

> The Western conception of the person as a bounded, more or less integrated motivational and cognitive universe, a dynamic center of awareness, emotion, judgment, and action organized into a distinctive whole and set contrastively both against other such wholes and against its social and natural background is, however incorrigible it may seem to us, a rather peculiar idea within the context of the world's cultures. (1976: 225)

Other anthropologists since then have offered more subtle and more useful analyses of culturally grounded difference in how the person is constituted. Among them figures Marilyn Strathern's (1988) influential characterization of the Melanesian self as "partible" or "dividual" (in contrast to "individual"), that is, the pivot of relationships already formed before birth, through gift giving, marriage alliances, and the transmission of body fluids. At birth, the dividual person is already enmeshed in a world of exchange and becomes, through marriage and reproduction, the conduit of additional exchanges that echo prior instances. This characterization of the Melanesian self rings loud bells of recognition for anthropologists who have worked in comparable ethnographic contexts. This is an identity that is deeply dependent on others and burdened with obligations, too ashamed to focus on the needs of the self, its body permanently stooped in a posture of apology and self-abasement.

Nevertheless, both Giddens's autonomous modern self and Strathern's dividual person in exchange-steeped Melanesia are essentialized constructs.

They potentially serve as useful anchoring mechanisms for an analysis of social action, but one must also come to grips with the fact that no single formulation of the self is ever completely hegemonic, in Melanesia or anywhere else. Many Melanesianists have found their rural fieldwork sites to be inhabited by radical individualists who strongly emphasize ideals of personal autonomy and the valorizing of individual agency, even if these ideals are in constant conflict with concurrent values of sharing, selflessness, and action on behalf of kin group (for example, Kulick 1992; Lepowsky 1993; Sykes 2007; Wardlow 2006). More often than not, different formulations, associated with different positions in the socioeconomic structure or cultural order, are in competition with one another. In Melanesia as well as Polynesia, the dividual self competes with ideological orientations that actively seek to disembed the self from structures of exchange, remove it from the tyranny of obligation, and distance it from expectant others. This self comes to resemble the autonomous entity that Giddens ascribes to Western capitalist modernity even though these processes are not always the product of a growing or aspirational modernity (Gewertz and Errington 1999). In addition, at different moments and in different sites, agents can enact different forms of the self, different orientations to exchange and obligation, and different life projects (Brison 2007; Wardlow 2006: 111–112). But the ghost of the dividual self always haunts people's lives, even if they actively seek individuality.

It is precisely this efflorescence of discourses of the self that I find relevant to my ethnographic materials. Better-off Tongans are quick at disparaging "Tongans," by which they generally mean their less fortunate compatriots, for being "lazy" and for having a "handout mentality." The oft-cited tongue-in-cheek "proverb," *Ko e koloa pē ʻa Tonga ko e fakamālō* "Tonga's wealth is 'thank you,'" implies that the only thing that Tongans offer in exchange for others' generosity is gratitude. Elites' unfortunate statements to this effect have been recorded and circulated widely by Western journalists eager to find evidence that high-ranking Tongans have "lost touch" with ordinary people, a point with which quite a few Tongans nevertheless concur.[8] A discourse of "empowerment" and "self-reliance" permeates development projects and the multiple "youth-focused" projects that have sprouted since 16/11, urging youth to develop both new economic strategies and a new sense of self. These projects generate disappointment more often than self-reliance, as their recipients find out the hard way, no matter how much self-reliance they embed in their sense of self, that it serves them very little unless they have money to back it up. In this book, I analyze many instances of people sitting on the edge of, on the one hand, kinship- and tradition-suffused ways of thinking and acting and, on the other hand, a life project asserting autonomy and self-fashioning. Entrepreneurs at the secondhand marketplace, who sell goods despite the stigma of selling in a gift-exchanging tradition, pawnshop owners who flirt with the immorality of profit making, and beauty pageant contestants exhibiting themselves to the evaluative gaze of large audiences while performing tradition are all testing the waters between dividual and individual forms of selfhood, some cautiously, others boldly. Even the few landmarks that tell them where the boundaries of acceptability lie are constantly shifting, providing little guidance.

An important aspect of competing discourses of the self is the fact that they are all relational. Autonomy and dividuality (and everything else in between) are always defined and enacted in reference to one another. Dividuality is relational by definition, but it is also relational in a more subtle way. To whom is one indebted, with whom does one exchange, from whom does one expect remittances from overseas? To whom can one sell objects rather than just giving them, to whom can one charge interest and collateral rather than just loaning money outright, knowing full well that it will never be repaid? In the Pacific Islands as elsewhere in the developing world, development studies scholars have long debated whether remittances dwindle over time but have asked these questions only in economic terms. Remittance sustainability is in fact intimately tied to the antagonism between different types of discourses of the self and different ways of defining one's life project. Autonomy is also paradoxically relational: The discourse of self-reliance and empowerment always operates in terms of what it distances itself from, namely obligation to others and the communalism of tradition. The relationality of both autonomy and dividuality can be understood as a matter of relative distanciation (to conjure one of the useful tools that Giddens offers). The autonomous self of the modern person distances itself from a dividual self, on which it can reflect, which it can criticize, or with which it can negotiate its own position. By coming to the hair salon to have their hair cut stylishly short in preparation for the funeral of a kin or affine, middle-aged women honor tradition and kinship obligation but do so in a way that still allows them to inscribe modernity on their bodies (Chapter Six). Distance is thus a matter of reflexivity, be it personal, national, or social. It can also be geographical, particularly in the context of a diaspora that serves as the conduit for the constant movement of people (Chapter Two). Geographical, reflective, and relational distances are all interrelated.

As should be evident from these brief examples, ideas of the self are never divorced from materiality. In this book, I approach modernity as being a matter of both cultural and material forms: It can offer new ways of thinking and new material resources to some and provide others only fleeting glimpses of these resources. Restaurants in Nuku'alofa, sporting menus in which each entrée costs half the weekly salary of those who are fortunate to be employed, tap novel ways of eating and relating to food: menus in English, theoretically deferential service, dishes brought in succession, and a rank-leveling micropolitics of space whereby *kakai ma'olunga*, "important people," can be seated next to and at the same level as those ordinary folk who can afford to be there (see Liechty 2005; Yan 1997). In contrast to the abundance of food, large serving sizes, and hearty and silent communal eating at traditional feasts, restaurant patrons sit in small groups and are served plate-size servings designed to be pleasing to both taste buds and the eyes, with bite-sized eating alternating with conversation. The distinction in eating style, which echoes the tension between working- and middle-class manners in Western Europe (Bourdieu 1979), is now a clear marker of difference of which Tongans have a heightened awareness. At more upscale restaurants, people pull money out of their wallet in an open way, rather than handing crumpled bills in a closed fist as non-middle-class people do at the produce market or village shop, in a gesture that iconicizes the embarrassment of the monetary transaction. Restaurant patrons are also visible to those who cannot afford the fare, a point that is not lost on the former: The owner of an upscale eating establishment, the interior of which is visible from the town's busiest street, tells me that customers often ask him to be seated by the bay windows that open onto the street so that they can be seen from the outside.

Objects and Bodies

The convergence of culture and materiality that I analyze across different sites showcases two important "tools" with which people negotiate the meaning of modernity, objects and bodies. As Mauss (1925 [1983]) demonstrated long ago, humans' relations to objects and the relations that they create between themselves through objects determine a host of other dynamics in society and culture. What we can add to Mauss's static functionalism is the fact that agents relate to objects over time, and that this relationship encapsulates wide-ranging sociocultural transformations: "Just as people use objects to invent tradition, they also use them to invent the future" (Wilk 1995: 98). In what follows, I analyze how people negotiate the relationship between past and future, continuity and change, and locality and extralocality through contemporary exchange practices, which encompass both consumer goods and traditional objects of no immediate practical use, such as textile valuables that display all the characteristics of archetypal gifts but are nevertheless commodified. Indeed, no gift, gift exchange, or gift economy conforms exactly to its Maussian idealizations, and Tongan textile valuables are no exception.[9] A focus on objects and the transformations that they undergo—be they sold, bought, given, recycled, pawned, or commodified—provides a particularly useful window onto the workings of modernity: How is it enmeshed with structural dynamics of gender, transnationalism, and capitalism, but also with morality, emotion, and self-making?

The body is the other medium with which people position themselves with respect to modernity. This insight also has a long genealogy. "The first and most natural technical object of man," declares Mauss, "and at the same time his technical tool, is his body" (1934 [1983]: 372, my translation). Politicizing both Mauss and Merleau-Ponty, Bourdieu (1972 [1977], 2004) takes the body as one of the prime vehicles of social and cultural capital. It is through "body hexis" (movements, facial expressions, posture, decorations, inscriptions, clothing) that we orient ourselves vis-à-vis the world around us. Because everyday existence is lived through the body, it serves to constantly reinforce this orientation, acting as a mnemonic device that constantly reminds the agent how structure is organized. From Foucault I retain that technologies of the self, one of four technologies of governmentality (alongside technologies of production, sign systems, and power), "permit individuals to effect by their own means or with the help of others a certain number of operations on their own bodies and souls, thoughts, conduct, and way of being, so as to transform themselves in order to attain a certain state of happiness, purity, wisdom, perfection, or immortality" (1997: 225). Technologies of the self are also more effective than other technologies in regulating behavior because they do so through covert and individualized means by conflating power (that is, the structural definition of how operations are constructed) and agency (that is, the actions through which the subject performs the operations), turning structural power into the subject's personal project. These insights have already given rise to a vast corpus of analyses of the way in which politics, inequality, and the cultural order become naturalized through the body in various societies and at different historical moments.[10]

Not surprisingly, the politics and cultural attributes of modernity can be inscribed on the body, and this can take place through a variety of means, from the trivial to the dramatic. But the body can just as easily operate as a vehicle of tradition, particularly in contexts where tradition is an answer to threatening or oppressive forms of modernity: Such is the case of the political uses of body paints and other adornments by indigenous peoples fighting for their land in Brazil, and of tattooing, which is experiencing a remarkable renaissance in areas of Polynesia where identity politics is particularly tense (that is, New Zealand, Hawai'i, and Tahiti).[11] But the inscription of modernity or tradition on the body is also potentially open to contradictions both within the single body and across societies: The "traditional" outfit worn by Herero women in Botswana can encode both disapproval of Western ways and a sense of national and ethnic identity (thus extricating modernity from the grip of the West), but its unwieldy bulkiness also anchors its wearer in an ultimately confining domestic sphere (Durham 1999). Tattoo designs that denote kinship and belonging for Māori and Pacific Islanders acquire an entirely different meaning when inscribed, in tattoo parlors of Amsterdam and Los Angeles, on the bodies of "urban primitives" on a Rousseauesque quest for a spirituality that they believe modernity has eroded (Rosenblatt 1997). This multiplicity of possible linkages associated with a single garment worn by a single person, or the same form worn by different people, in fact derives quite logically from the indexical nature of the body and its parts.

What this indexicality also entails is that the body operates as a transformative tool, one that serves to convey different positions and on which one can read claims about the subject's position in the world at large. Transgender men parading in elegant evening gowns or outrageous contraptions on the pageant catwalk claim a cosmopolitanism that their marginal status does not allow them to claim in their ordinary existence. Pentecostal congregants dancing in ways that otherwise would subject them to ridicule demonstrate their liberation from the fear of shame through faith in God. Seemingly insignificant forms of body hexis acquire great importance where social and cultural transformation is at stake, precisely because of the mnemonic power of the body (Bourdieu 1972 [1977]: 94; Brownell 2001: 124). Engaging with this power encourages us to turn our attention to the transformative potentials of body hexis, rather than emphasizing, as Bourdieu does, its reproductive character.

A focus on the body is particularly relevant to the ethnographic context on which this book is based, as bodies, and in particular body size, are at the foreground of modernity-conscious Tongans' preoccupations and Western commentaries on Tonga. Tongan bodies are on average some of the largest in the world, as well as some of the most vulnerable to "lifestyle diseases" associated with lipid retention, particularly in the context of changes in the economic organization of domestic life that are erasing physical work and increasing the fatty content of day-to-day food intake. Modernity has introduced new ways of conceptualizing the body, alongside a new problematization of the body, making a focus on the body a particularly appropriate handle on the meaning of modernity for the contemporary Tongan context. But these new ways, I will demonstrate, can take on diverse and unpredictable meanings in the hands of different agents.

Where objects and bodies intersect, one finds gender. Objects are gendered through their production, consumption, and circulation, and bodies are gendered by default. Gender will thus occupy a prominent place in my discussion, not surprisingly either because sites, as forms of "space" and "spheres," are also strongly gendered, as many classic works have demonstrated (for example, Bourdieu 1970; Rosaldo 1974). The way in which Tongan sites are gendered, however, cannot be straightforwardly captured by assigning different sites to different genders. This gendering is subtle, perhaps a reflection of the complexities of gender hierarchy in this society, where women are of higher rank than their brothers but of lower rank than their husbands. The complex relationship between gender and modernity illustrates that social and cultural signs are assigned value in contested ways. The operation of this field of contestation is what this book seeks to understand.

What Comes Next

I have argued in this chapter for an approach that views fracture and reembedding as processes that are constantly in dialogue with one another at the local level. More specifically, it is not just the global (or the modern state or modern institutions) that fragments relations but also the local, hence my focus on "sites" of modernity that are embedded in a local context but also associated with different modernist projects. I argue that Tongan modernity is not a monolithic entity but one that emerges variously in different sites, with different relationships to a larger global context. In Chapter Two, I provide the ethnographic background of these sites, focusing in particular on how Tongan modernity is informed by diasporic dispersal but is also profoundly colored by enduring structures of rank and thus interwoven with a strong sense of traditionalism.

The ethnographic analysis of specific sites of Tongan modernity begins with Chapter Three, which focuses on the secondhand marketplace, where people (predominantly women) sell clothing and other commodities that they receive from relatives overseas in place of monetary remittances. The marketplace foregrounds deeply modern ideas about fashion, propriety, and entrepreneurialism that are also the subjects of unstable moral evaluation. Objects, this time of a kind defined as deeply traditional, remain in the foreground in Chapter Four, which analyzes the ubiquitous pawnshops that accept as collateral for loans ritually important textile valuables (mats and barkcloth) that women manufacture. The commodification of these objects that takes place at the pawnshop is enmeshed with the complexities of gender, emotion, and morality.

In Chapter Five, the body as a vehicle for the performance of modernity comes to the foreground. I compare two types of beauty pageants: one for young women, in which contestants are expected to display competence in traditionalism; and another for transgender men, in which contestants strive to present themselves as modern cosmopolitan subjects. All contestants find these respective expectations difficult to satisfy. In Chapter Six, I catch middle-aged women having their hair done at the salon, cultivating images of busy professional women with little time to do their own hair but with money and interest to have it done by stylists. In Chapter Seven, my attention switches to young men who inscribe a certain form of modernity onto the body by working out at the one gym in the country. They nurture a hyperdeveloped physique that conforms to a particular representation of the powerful warrior of a hypothetical past but that also indexes the bodybuilder's physique of international competitions. Chapter Eight turns to the way in which the body inscribes a religious modernity at Pentecostal and charismatic churches, which frees the subject from dynamics associated with traditional Christianity and traditional life in general, such as kinship obligation and the fear of shame. In the conclusion, I evaluate how the Tongan ethnographic material sheds light on processes of modernity on the edge of the global, their relationship to tradition, and the dilemmas that they present for agents' day-to-day existence. I also return to the events of 16/11, interpreting them in terms of ethnographic understandings of modernity and tradition developed in the intervening chapters.

Chapter Two

Tonga's Modernity

If we take, with Anthony Giddens and many others, the emergence of the state and accompanying institutions as one of the fundamental features of the modern condition, we can arguably locate the beginning of Tonga's engagement with modernity in the mid-nineteenth century. Until then, the islands were organized as a loose association of autonomous chiefdoms, and the population, which had settled the archipelago around 3,000 BP, lived in small scattered settlements. In 1845, an ambitious minor chieftain, Tāufaʻāhau (c. 1797–1893), who originally ruled over the Haʻapai group in the center of the archipelago (Map 2.1), conquered the rest of the group and unified it under his rule. This achievement took place at a time when the presence of Westerners was intensifying, and Tāufaʻāhau's conquest was made possible by the backing of British Wesleyan missionaries. In 1875 he became King George Tupou I, the founder of the dynasty that continues to rule the country. In the same year he also promulgated a constitution, which remains in place today, modified by a number of amendments. It codifies a governing structure headed by the sovereign and supported by a land-holding nobility consisting of thirty hereditary titles and six land-holding noble's assistants, legitimated by a faith in Christian principles. This constitution was inspired by the Kingdom of Hawaiʻi's constitution, which itself was based on the constitution of the United States. It is modern in its theoretical guarantee of

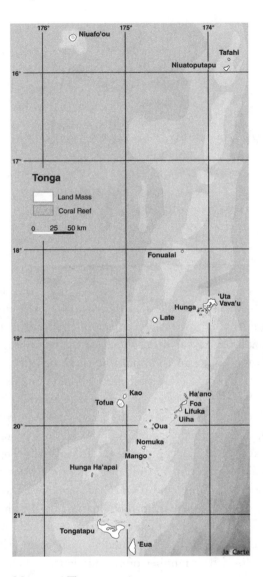

Map 2.1.   Tonga.

equal treatment for all citizens (thus abolishing slavery), although it also enshrined a rigid social stratification and defined numerous legal exceptions.

Contrary to present-day historical representations, which emphasize
stability and continuity, the nineteenth and early twentieth centuries were

periods of serious conflicts, including civil wars, dynastic struggles, conflicts between churches, and the bothersome intrusions of colonial powers and resident foreigners. These conflicts were primarily the concern of the high-ranking, the powerful, and meddling outsiders. Commoners had little choice but to take the side of the chiefs to whom they were subordinate, and they were often the victims of these conflicts. George I's successor, his great-grandson George Tupou II (1874–1918), is generally considered a ne'er-do-well womanizer who started taking an interest in the affairs of the state only when it was too late. The British representative essentially forced him in 1900 to sign a "Treaty of Protection" that absorbed Tonga into the colonial empire as "protected state," a status that was abrogated only in 1970 (Campbell 2001: 128–45; Fusitu'a and Rutherford 1977). Modern-day Tongans often stress with pride that their country never succumbed to colonial rule, in contrast to other Pacific Island polities (Samoa, Fiji, Tahiti, and Hawai'i), although in fact the British interference in Tongan affairs was common and Tonga's power of self-determination limited.[1]

George II had married a chiefly woman named Lavinia Veiongo against the will of the country's high-ranking leaders, which had created serious conflicts. He had with Lavinia only one legitimate daughter, who succeeded him as Sālote Tupou III (1900–1965). Sālote spent the first decades of her reign struggling against nobles' opposition to her but eventually emerged as a deeply revered sovereign (Wood-Ellem 1999). During her reign, the U.S. armed forces occupied Tonga in 1942–1945, a transformative moment in the history of the country that gave the citizenry a glimpse of a much larger world of wealth and foreshadowed the country's subsequent historical course. At the coronation of Britain's Queen Elizabeth II in London in 1953, Sālote rode, despite the pouring rain, in an open carriage as a sign of respect for the sovereign to whom she was a vassal. This memorable act, and her smiling and towering presence, gained her enduring international recognition, solidly embedding Tonga in the deeply reified images of Polynesia operative in the Western psyche since the Enlightenment. Under the reign of her son, Tāufa'āhau Tupou IV (1918–2006), the country underwent fundamental transformations, to which I turn presently. Tupou IV struggled to engage with change while maintaining the status quo with mitigated results, particularly toward the end of his life. Events like 16/11 that marked the first years of the reign of the present king, George Tupou V, can be partly understood as resulting from the late king's inability to seriously deal with change.

While enshrined in a modern constitution, the current government is based on a structure defined by the relationship between chiefs and commoners, which goes back to very ancient times. In pre-Christian days, chiefs ensured the welfare of the people through their divinity, or at least divine origins, but also claimed absolute control over their subjects' actions and lives. While Christianization and state formation in the nineteenth century modified the terms of this covenant, it continues to color the relationship between ruler and ruled (Lātūkefu 1974; Marcus 1978). The royal family and the hereditary aristocracy continue to be the recipients (and, theoretically, redistributors) of large amounts of material tribute, which circulate in the opposite direction from the propitiousness that derives from the sacredness of rank. The churches of various Christian denominations are enmeshed in a comparable relationship with their congregations, through which church representatives are the recipients of gift giving while they exhort God to protect the congregation. Astute aristocrats and church leaders adeptly reinforce the sacred entitlement underlying rank with occasional "man of the people" gestures (Marcus 1980, 1989). It is only in the first few years of the new millennium that a reconsideration of the rank-based structure has hesitantly taken place. This reconsideration is not an easy process, given the extent to which the social structure, the state, the churches, and culture are enmeshed with one another (Moala 2009).[2]

LIVING AND MOVING

At the 2006 census, the country's population totaled 101,134 inhabitants. Nuku'alofa, with 34,058 inhabitants, is home to over a third of the country's population. Tongans, however, are constantly on the move, between islands or island groups, from village to town and vice versa, and across international boundaries, and a radical transformation of their relationship to place figures prominently among the changes that the society experienced in the late twentieth century. Internal migration from the country's outer islands to Tongatapu, the country's largest island (generally referred to as "Tonga"), is said to have started in the aftermath of a severe hurricane that devastated Ha'apai and Vava'u in March of 1961 (Lewis 1982). Population movement has steadily increased ever since, gradually deepening the population imbalance between rural outer islands and urbanized Tonga (Table 2.1). As a result, the sleepy little town that Nuku'alofa was in the 1950s (Map 2.2) has been

TABLE 2.1
Changes in the population over two decades
by island group and rounded percentages of total population.

Island group	1986		1996		2006	
Tongatapu	63,794	66.0%	66,979	67.1%	71,260	69.1%
Vava'u	15,175	15.7	15,715	15.7	15,485	15.0
Ha'apai	8,919	9.2	8,138	8.2	7,572	7.3
'Eua	4,393	4.5	4,934	4.9	5,165	5.0
Niua	2,368	2.5	2,018	2.0	1,652	1.6
Tonga	94,649	100.0	97,784	100.0	101,134	100.0

Source: Tonga Department of Statistics 2008b: 1.

transformed into the much larger and densely populated town that it is today (Map 2.3).[3]

People migrate to Tongatapu for a wide variety of reasons. An oft-cited motivation is children's schooling, not a trivial factor in a society in which education has long occupied a prominent place in people's life designs. While all island groups today have government- and church-run high schools, schools on Tonga are better equipped and hold greater prestige than schools elsewhere in the country. In addition, Form 7 (preuniversity year) is available only at the government high schools on Vava'u and Tonga. For children on the smaller islands of the Ha'apai and Vava'u groups, transportation by motor launch to the local urban centers, where secondary schools are located, is often complicated, costly, and sometimes dangerous. One solution is boarding; another is for families to simply move to Nuku'alofa.

People migrate to the city because the country's medical services are concentrated there, to take advantage of its (relatively) bright lights, the fact that it serves as the departure point for overseas migration, and its elaboration as the core of the hierarchical and centralized social order. Particularly destructive hurricanes, such as Isaac in 1983, have resulted in rural–urban migration surges. Kinship-related events like funerals bring people to the main island for extended stays. The most important attraction of the city, however, is the lack of economic opportunities elsewhere. On the small islands of Ha'apai and in the northernmost "two Niuas" (*ongo Niua*, Niuatoputapu and Niuafo'ou), where the population is steadily decreasing, the economy is confined to subsistence agriculture and fishing, which have become low-prestige activities. In Ha'apai in particular, cultivable land is scarce and agriculture difficult. Arable land on Vava'u, the second largest island group, is plentiful,

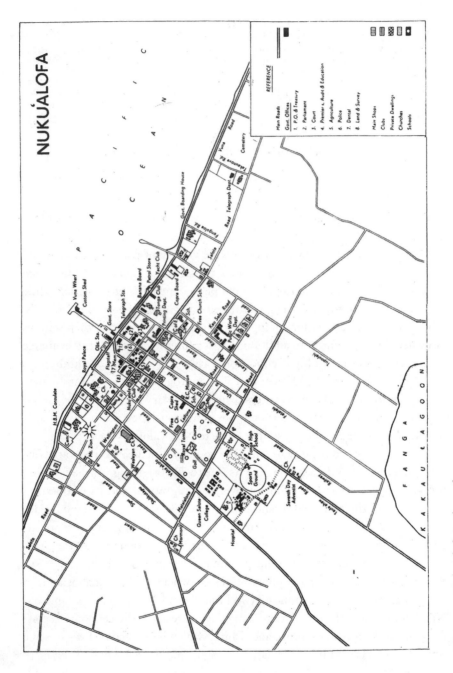

Map 2.2. Nuku'alofa in the early 1950s.

(Source: Bain 1954: 80)

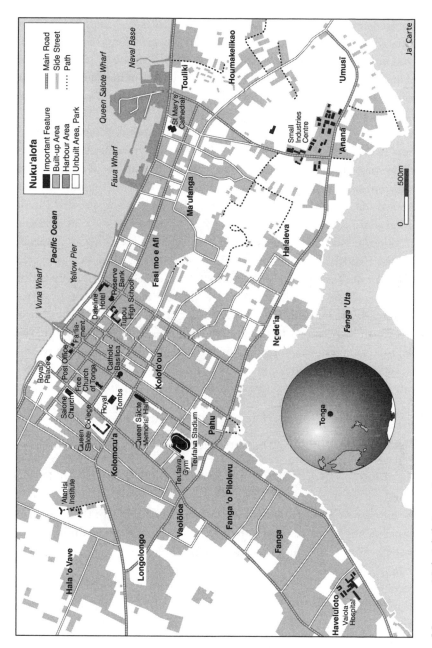

Map 2.3. Nuku'alofa in 2008.

and the transformation of the group into a tourism destination in the last two decades of the twentieth century has slowed down out-migration. Vava'u's population has been more stable than that of other outlying island groups. Common wisdom maintains that when Vava'u Islanders migrate, they move as individuals, but when Ha'apai Islanders migrate, the entire family moves, locking homes and abandoning property.[4]

In addition to moving from rural to urban locations, Tongans migrate overseas in large numbers (Figure 2.1). Overseas migrations result in a net migration rate of −19.8 per 1,000, one of the highest in the world, and explain the apparent demographic contradiction between the youthfulness of the population (median age 19.6) and the slow population growth (Table 2.1). Migrants' most common destinations are urban centers of New Zealand (principally Auckland and Wellington), Australia (Sydney and Melbourne), and, in the United States, Hawai'i, California, and other West Coast states, as well as Utah. Tongans have also settled more or less permanently in Fiji (where many attend the University of the South Pacific) and American Samoa, although the importance of Tonga's contemporary links to these locations pales in comparison to those with New Zealand, Australia, and the United States. Individual Tongans are also found everywhere in the world, including some very unlikely places. The multiple destinations of Tongan migrations, the border-crossing existence of many Tongans, and an enduring focus on the homeland and a common identity (at least in theory) make Tongan society a quintessential diaspora.

Tongans often express ambivalence about moving to locations that already have high concentrations of their compatriots, such as South Auckland in New Zealand, San Mateo in California, and Lā'ie in Hawai'i. On the one hand, these locations offer kinship networks, churches, organizations, and familiar surroundings, while on the other hand they are the context of heightened obligations (*kavenga*), the risk of adolescents becoming involved in gang activities, and potential exposure to damaging gossip and rivalries that can result in deportation if one is undocumented.

Throughout prehistory, Tongans were great travelers. Beginning 3,000 years ago, canoe voyagers from points east were the islands' first settlers. Over the centuries, Tongans evidently maintained regular contacts with other peoples over vast distances. Contacts with neighboring islands, particularly Samoa, Fiji, Wallis ('Uvea) and Futuna, and Rotuma, are chronicled in the oral history of the last millennium and probably go back even further in

Figure 2.1. Waiting for newly issued passports at the Immigration Division in Nuku'alofa, one of the busiest government departments (March 2008).

time (Helu 1999: 233–250). Prehistoric Tongans traveled for many different reasons, including establishing new settlements; running away from defeat or punishment; acquiring objects such as Fijian weapons, canoes, and pots, and Samoan fine mats or *kie Ha'amoa* (Kaeppler 1999); borrowing dances from 'Uvea and Futuna; getting tattooed by Samoan specialists; seeking spouses and other kinds of alliances; and waging war. Since early postcontact times, Tongans have worked as seamen on whalers or trade ships and as laborers on copra and sugarcane plantations throughout the Pacific, in Queensland, and beyond. In the nineteenth and early twentieth centuries, Tongans worked as missionaries, first in Samoa and Fiji, then in what is today Papua New Guinea, 2,500 miles east of Tonga, where they were particularly numerous in the Wesleyan missions ('Atiola 2007; Crocombe and Crocombe 1994; Lātūkefu 1978). Some left the islands involuntarily, as is the case of the victims of the raid, in 1863, on the small isolated island of 'Atā, 100 miles southwest of Tongatapu, by an Australian freelance slave trader (then referred to as "Blackbirder"), which kidnapped 144 islanders or 41 percent of the island's population and sold them to Peruvian slavers. They were probably taken to work on guano fields or in domestic servitude in Peru, from where none ever returned (Maude 1981: 83–87).

The early modern period represents a major break in that it was a period of unusual sedentariness, during which people were grounded more than ever before, their movements constrained by colonial and early state restrictions on ocean travel. A radical change took place in the late 1960s as people began to move again, this time in very large numbers and over vast distances. The triggering factor was "work schemes" through which the New Zealand government invited temporary guest workers from the Pacific Islands to alleviate manual labor shortages during economic boom years, which coincided with increasing Māori indigenous activism (inspired by civil right movements of the 1960s) and Māori's increasing refusal to be confined to menial employment. As is classically the case of such schemes, the guest workers stayed on. Subsequently, many took advantage of the open-border arrangement between New Zealand and Australia and settled in the latter, attracted by Australia's larger-scale economy, in a pattern that would eventually come to be called "backdoor migration" Down Under. Around the same time, the Church of Jesus Christ of Latter-day Saints began facilitating Tongan migration to the United States, a point not lost on the numerous Tongans who have converted to this faith and continue to do so.

While it is tempting to view contemporary migrations as simply the latest symptom of a timeless compulsion to move going back to prehistory, as some have done, this approach obliterates the fact that Pacific Islanders' migratory enthusiasm has fluctuated in the course of history and obscures the important role that colonialism, the state, poverty, and structures of economic dependence play in encouraging or discouraging migrations (Goss and Lindquist 2000: 398). Ancient and modern movements both resemble and differ from one another. Precontact travel bound islands together, creating and reinforcing what Tongan intellectual 'Epeli Hau'ofa (1994) memorably called a "sea of islands," an island world connected through kinship despite the obstacle of the sea. In contrast, contemporary Tongan movements appear at first glance to bypass this Oceanic world and reach out to a world of industrialism, capitalism, and modernity. When observed more closely, however, Tongan diasporic dispersal does not so much bypass the Oceanic world as it expands it. When Tongans go overseas, they predominantly move to either an intensely and self-consciously Polynesian world, in the case of urban New Zealand and Hawai'i, or one that they have Polynesianized, as in the case of Campbelltown (New South Wales), Oakland (California), and Salt Lake City (Utah). These are worlds, often invisible to the dominant groups, where the churches are Tongan, businesses cater to Tongans and employ Tongans, and Tongans inhabit entire neighborhoods. "There [is], in Northern California, a Tongan world within a world," Small (1997: 70) aptly notes, a remark that applied equally to other urban centers of the diaspora.

Tongans often explain their desire to migrate by foregrounding education, which is of course more dignified than alleviating poverty. Overseas education became available to the more fortunate citizens beginning in the 1930s. Newington College, a Methodist Church school in Sydney founded in 1863, established a special relationship with the island nation by accepting its students, including Prince Tupouto'a (later Tāufa'āhau Tupou IV) and his younger brother Prince Fatafehi Tu'ipelehake, later prime minister and the father of 'Uluvalu Prince Tu'ipelehake, killed in the July 5, 2006, road accident in Menlo Park that I mentioned in the opening section of Chapter One. Being the first school in Australia to play rugby, Newington College was also instrumental in introducing the game to Tonga, where it would eventually become the national sport. Other people of rank, including Queen Sālote in the early years of the twentieth century, attended secondary institutions in New Zealand. Appropriately for a society where ranked precedence matters, Prince Tupouto'a was the first Tongan to receive, in 1942, a BA, from the University of Sydney.

Gradually, the availability of educational opportunities democratized, and increasingly large numbers of young Tongans sought government scholarships funded by foreign donors or else used their own funds to educate children overseas, sometimes bankrupting entire families. Tonga eventually became the most educated Pacific Island nation, or at least the most "degreed." The enthusiasm with which commoners embraced education as a means to upward mobility illustrates the mimetic quality that suffuses relationships of rank, whereby the high ranking provide a model that ordinary folk emulate. This mimesis, reminiscent of Thorstein Veblen's concept of "pecuniary emulation" (1899 [1994]), operates for example in campaigns led by royals and nobles for the improvement of living conditions (for example, becoming fit, healthy living, picking up trash). The terms of this mimesis are different from the mimesis that anthropologists have commonly focused on, whereby the colonized (or the developing world) appropriates, reverses, and sometimes ridicules the colonizer's attributes.[5] Here, the mimesis is rooted in a deeply local logic of rank, and it refers only indirectly to colonial and postcolonial relationships. It enabled Tupou IV to establish himself, even before his accession to the throne, as the "education monarch," encouraging ordinary people to seek academic training by following his own example.

Education is not only a tool of upward mobility but also the conduit of migration, particularly because employment opportunities for the highly qualified are scarce in the island context. Government scholarships oblige recipients to work for the bureaucracy for five years, and, while some of the educated come back to fulfill this obligation, others simply stay overseas or migrate to the countries where they were educated after fulfilling their obligations. Since the 1980s, young Tongan men trained at the Tonga Maritime Polytechnic Institute have been working on ships owned by transnational corporations, earning more than their compatriots working in the fields and factories in New Zealand.

By the mid-1970s, moving overseas was deeply embedded in all life projects, and Tongans had developed a "migratory disposition," that is, a logic of life strategies and organized action in which migrating is desirable, possible, and inevitable (cf. Piot 2010 on Togo).[6] Equally prominent in people's minds today, however, are the increasingly challenging state regulatory practices that constrain border crossing, in the form of increased difficulties in obtaining visas and the official repression and populist vilification of "overstayers" in New Zealand and Australia and "illegal aliens" in the United States. For example, in 2008, obtaining a tourist visa to the United States involved filling out online an application form and security form (which presupposes access to the Internet or being indebted to someone who does), making an appointment with a immigration officer based at the U.S. embassy in Fiji, paying a US$120 fee (nonrefundable if the visa is denied, as is frequently the case), and travelling to Fiji for the appointment. The exercise demands considerable knowledge, skills, and expenses. In 1999, Australian and New Zealand immigrations departments imposed stringent restrictions on visa issuance, even for visitors and patients seeking medical attention, in the form of bonds (for example, A$5,000) that immigration authorities forfeit for the most insignificant reasons, such as a change in travel plans. At the time of this writing, New Zealand no longer requires these bonds, but Australia still does. In Australia, deeply conservative former immigration minister Philip Ruddock in the 1990s repeatedly targeted Tongan citizens as some of the most serious culprits who "unlawfully . . . outstayed their welcome," a situation for which he felt draconian measures were called for (Minister for Immigration and Citizenship 1996). These measures and the scapegoating discourse supporting them come and go, but, even when they are dormant, they always threaten to reemerge.

In the early years of diasporic dispersal, the dominant discourse about displacement centralized, in addition to education, the desire "to build a house back in the village." This discourse presupposed that migrants relocated overseas only temporarily and that they would go back home when they had reached their goals. It has since quietly fallen silent, as diasporic dispersal gradually came to be seen as a permanent condition that requires no explanation. Second- and third-generation Tongans grow up in the diaspora, acquiring in the process various levels of competence in "doing being Tongan" (to borrow a phrase from ethnomethodology) and various degrees of allegiance to the island nation. Some become "born-again Tongans" driven by the assiduous pursuit of often reified and romanticized forms of island identity after having initially turned their back on it, as witnessed in the sometimes agonizing online postings on discussion boards such as Kava Bowl and Planet Tonga (Franklin 2005; Lee 2003: 172; Lee 2007; Morton 1998: 19). The resulting picture is of a "Tongan identity" being claimed around the world by a highly diverse constituency, with different priorities and levels of engagement with the traditional island-based order.

Generally speaking, Tongans move for predictable reasons. The dominant attraction of urban centers of the Pacific Rim is the belief that they provide better life opportunities than are available in Tonga, be it in terms of employment, education, health care, or welfare. In those locations, Tongans are employed in many sectors, particularly if one takes into account members of the second and third generations. A few have done very well, some because they started out privileged, others through a combination of hard work and sheer luck. But many continue to occupy low-level positions as cleaners, construction workers, food-service employees, and baggage handlers at airports (which nevertheless afforded until recently airline discounts for trips home), or "live-in" (*līvini*) taking care of elderly or incapacitated middle-class Westerners. Yard work (*'iaati*) in Hawai'i has become a Tongan niche because it involves climbing up coconut trees and felling nuts to prevent property owners from being sued in case one accidentally hits a passerby. The yard workers' relatives then sell the nuts to tourists.

When they move to more unusual destinations, Tongans are usually following a specific purpose. Tongan residents of Japan, for instance, are likely to be married to a Japanese national, be studying on a Japanese government scholarship, or be part of the worldwide circulation of professional rugby players, contracted by professional teams for the unmatched brawn and skill that many Tongan rugby players display, which brings them substantial revenues as well as admiration in Tonga ('Esau 2007, Besnier and Kitahara 2009). Tongans in Iraq were part of a contingent of several dozens supporting the U.S. invasion between 2004 and 2008, serving as camp security with funding from a U.S. government anxious to present itself as supported by an international coalition. When Tongans move to Beijing for a few years, they are most likely to do so through the tertiary education scholarship program that the People's Republic of China instituted after 16/11 to try to smooth frayed relations between Tongan nationals and Chinese immigrants.

The most recent census figure (2001) for Tongans in New Zealand is 40,700, Australia 15,000, and the United States 36,800.[7] By all accounts, these numbers are much too low, and more realistic estimates of the total overseas Tongan population hover between 100,000 and a quarter million. Arriving at an accurate count of Tongan-identified persons living overseas is difficult, one reason being the unstable nature of many Tongans' overseas residency. Many move between Tonga and the diasporic nexuses or among the different diasporic nexuses, working for short stints on tourist visas to bring money home to last until the next overseas visit. Migrants are often undocumented, living in industrial countries as long as they manage to dodge immigration authorities, and they are thus likely to shy away from representatives of state authority such as census enumerators (Lee 2003: 19–21). Citizenship laws complicate the picture: Until 2007, the Tongan government forbade dual citizenship, although it was a widely known secret that many held two passports, particularly among the elites who maintain homes in both Tonga and an industrial country. In 2007, the law changed; from 2008, applicants who can demonstrate Tongan descent can claim Tongan citizenship, and citizens who naturalized in another country can legally retain their original nationality. Citizenship and identification were thus not coterminous until recently, and the effect of these discrepancies on census figures in industrial countries is unknown.[8]

Although it began only in the 1960s, diasporic dispersal now affects every family in the islands and colors every aspect of the economy, society, and culture. At any given moment, most nuclear families have at least one member overseas. Virtually everyone is dependent, in one way or another, on economic links to overseas relatives. The most concrete form of this dependence is the remittances with which Tongans working overseas sustain their island-based relatives. In 2000–2001, remittances constituted close to 20 percent of the average total household income for the entire country (T$2,542 out of T$12,871), while wages and salaries constituted 35 percent. In the June Quarter of 2007 (a period I chose at random), remittances accounted for 54 percent of national foreign receipts. These figures have steadily increased over the years: Remittances accounted for 26.3 percent of the 1990–1991 GDP and 37.2 percent of the 2000–2001 GDP, figures that are among the highest in the world. Of course, these figures concern purely monetary data, and an approach that is more sensitive to people's lived experiences would undoubtedly reveal an even more dramatic picture.[9]

Remittances from diasporic Tongans represent an essential economic lifeline not only at the national level but also for individual households (Figure 2.2). A significant proportion of households, particularly among rural migrants living in Nuku'alofa, have no income and sometimes no regular access to any resource other than remittances. In fact, regular remittances from a dependable relative with a reasonable job overseas are often better than relying on a locally employed family member, whose salary is considerably lower and whose responsibilities to many are greater and more immediate. Remittances allow some families to live well and present themselves as prosperous in social and even sometimes material capital. The resulting picture is that waged employment is a poor predictor of economic well-being. It is only one aspect of the creative, opportunity-driven, and enormously resourceful way in which people "make do." Of course, dependence on faraway relatives who are themselves dependent on the fickleness of labor markets is theoretically more fragile than financial autonomy, although two important factors mitigate this fragility: the fact that financial autonomy is available to very few people in Tonga and the fact that kinship relations involve asymmetrical obligations between specific kindred, such as brothers being obligated to support sisters throughout their lives.[10]

Family income varies seasonally and does not always coincide with cycle of needs, such as having to purchase school uniforms in February, meet church obligations in May and September (for some denominations), and contribute to funerals and weddings on an unpredictable basis. To meet these fluctuating demands, people supplement remittances with loans and communal

Figure 2.2.   Bumper stickers advertising money-transfer corporations, which for many years were the only businesses engaged in advertising (2000).

saving schemes. For the majority, capital accumulation through savings on an individual or family basis is difficult, as money evaporates very quickly to meet the day-to-day needs of the immediate family and larger circle of reciprocity. Communal saving is made possible through the microcredit enterprises of clubs and other groups, particularly kava-drinking cooperative clubs (*kalapu*). On a daily basis, these clubs serve kava, a mildly narcotic drink extracted from the powdered root of a relative of the pepper plant mixed with water, drunk by men as part of both highly significant rituals and everyday routines, which represents one of the key symbols of Tongan tradition. Kava-drinking clubs, which are increasing in importance (along with kava consumption), also regularly hold fund-raising drinking parties, inviting nonmembers over the radio and raising money for different purposes, particularly overseas university scholarships. In addition, loans from banks and pawnshops are an almost universal fact of life, enabling families to meet prestation obligations, such as regular gift giving to the church, but also to purchase household items. Sometimes loans are taken out to pay off prior loans, an increasingly common practice despite the fact that most people find it deeply problematic.

Migrations leave their mark on people's lives in subtler ways than just matters of money. Ties between diaspora and homeland and among different nexuses of the diaspora are kept alive by constant back-and-forth movements of goods, ideas, news, symbols, as well as people, including children and the elderly travelling on their own and the sick seeking overseas medical treatment not available in the islands. Fashions, images, desires, and feelings circulate between the islands and the diaspora. Transnational travel has become part and parcel of everyday life. *Te ke folau?* "Are you flying [overseas]?," a gentleman asks of an elderly female relative whom he encounters at Fuaʻamotu Airport, on a casual tone that encapsulates the mundanity of travelling. *Naʻá ke haʻu ʻanefē?* "When did you arrive [in Tonga]?," a woman shouts across the parking lot next to Talamahu Market to an acquaintance living overseas. Tongans today routinely assume that people have been in New Zealand, Australia, or the United States when they have not seen them for a while (*Fuoloa hoʻo pulí!* "You have not been around for a long time!"). As is the case elsewhere, these dynamics demand a much more subtle understanding of migrations than that provided by the simplistic "push-and-pull" models that have long held sway in migration studies (cf. Rouse 1991).

At first blush, the ease with which people travel contrasts paradoxically with the difficulties that many have in making ends meet, until one understands that travelling can be an investment strategy. A visit to relatives in New Zealand, Australia, and the United States provides the opportunity to work, more or less legally, for a few weeks. The construction or yard-maintenance crew that a successful relative controls enables men to make some money without drawing the attention of immigration authorities. Other people combine visits to relatives with entrepreneurial schemes, selling *koloa faka-Tonga* "Tongan valuables" (mats and barkcloth) or handicrafts produced in Tonga and repackaged as "Polynesian" souvenirs in the tourist markets of Hawaiʻi and Fiji.

Travelling does require an initial investment, including the airfare and the expenses involved in obtaining visas. Airfares, however, became cheaper in 2006, when a new airline opened routes to Australia and New Zealand, breaking the monopoly that Air New Zealand had maintained in the wake of the successive bankruptcies of carriers owned by the Tongan government, members of the royal family, and their associates. Lower airfares and greater flight frequency enable the relatively well-off to think of "a weekend in Auckland" (a three hours flight away) as within their reach. Despite daily struggles to meet life's basic needs, the less fortunate use their network of kinship reciprocity or pawn their Tongan valuables to travel, but, unlike repaying a pawnshop loan or an overdue power bill, travelling offers the hope of material, as well as emotional, returns.

The resulting picture for most Tongans is one in which *muli* "overseas" is simply an extension of the Tongan world, albeit surrounded by more challenging shoals than island locations (for example, visa requirements, transportation costs, constraints on food in luggage, unfamiliar conditions), which most are amazingly adept at navigating. It also highlights the blurred distinction between moving overseas, spending extended but temporary periods of time overseas, and simply visiting overseas-based relatives, an insight that Francis (2003) captures by demonstrating the centrality of "movement as everyday action" in the Tongan habitus.

Some overseas Tongans move back to Tonga. Tired of New Zealand dampness and urban life, some retirees settle back in their village of origin. International agreements regarding the transportability of pensions and accessibility of medical services make such moves increasingly easier. Some successful overseas Tongans combine their overseas ventures with a wealth base in the kingdom. Others try their luck at business and other ventures in Tonga, some with little experience in "doing being Tongan." They achieve various degrees of success, depending on the capital they brought with them, their cultural competence, and their commitment to kin and other obligations (Liava'a 2007). "I can bring the comforts of New Zealand here," one man in his mid-30s with dual citizenship asserted to me in 2008 over cappuccinos at a fancy café in Nuku'alofa, wearing a baseball cap and (inappropriately short) rugby shorts, "and I can always take a holiday in New Zealand if Tonga gets to me."

At the other end of the spectrum, some Tongans come "back" to the islands under conditions not of their own choosing. Such is the case of second- or third-generation diasporic children who are "sent back" to live with relatives in Tonga, particularly when they are perceived to be in need of some good old-fashioned Tongan discipline. This "tradition" places a strain on everyone. Most prominent among involuntary returnees are deported "overstayers" and "illegal aliens," as well as noncitizen permanent residents of industrial countries who have been caught up in criminal activities (particularly drug dealing and gang violence), imprisoned, and deported at the end of their sentence. These youths may have spent their entire life in New Zealand, Australian, or American cities, and "return" to Tonga totally unprepared to deal with life in the islands, its collectivism, and its relative lack of amenities. These "deportees" (*tīpota*), who hang out along with their local admirers on Nukuʻalofa street corners and around Teufaiva gym, some sporting hip-hop fashions (for example, turned-around baseball caps, 50 Cent T-shirts, droopy drawers), emerged as a distinct and prominent category in the early years of the millennium. They are blamed for bringing unwanted forms of modernity (such as drug consumption, break-ins, rapes, lack of respect) and for allegedly instructing local youths in the fine art of law breaking. These dominant representations do not entertain the possibility that the criminal activities that landed them in prison in the diaspora in the first place are sometimes related to the enormous pressure that some young overseas Tongans are under to provide for parents and relatives, a strong encouragement to take money-generating shortcuts such as drug dealing. Thus the undesirable modernity associated with deportees is possibly much more closely allied to tradition-maintaining structures of obligations than anyone admits.

FOREIGNERS

While Tongans circulate across a diasporic world with surprising ease, non-Tongans are also moving to Tonga. People from neighboring islands have always resided in Tonga—marrying in, being brought back as prisoners during war raids, or simply arriving for any one of many circumstantial reasons. The genealogies of the high ranking include ancient connections to Fiji, Samoa, and Wallis and Futuna, all within 600 miles of Tongatapu. Some Tongans today trace their ancestry to Fijian and Solomon Islander indentured laborers who were brought to Tonga to work on plantations owned by European and part-European families in the 1920s and 1930s. More recently, people from all over the Pacific have come to study, seek their fortune, or find church leaders.

Westerners began to arrive almost as soon as contact with the Euro-American world intensified at the beginning of the nineteenth century, but life in Tonga was generally very rough for them, at least until George I managed to dominate his opponents and convert everyone to Christianity within a few years of his own conversion in 1834. A usual array of missionaries, sailors, runaway convicts, beachcombers, traders, adventurers, and politicians (sometimes self-appointed) peppers the course of Tonga's history. Many were trouble, interfering in internal affairs and fomenting conflict (Gunson 1977; Rutherford 1971; Wood-Ellem 1999: 74–83). Some outsiders were incorporated into the Tongan polity, originally by being eaten and, after Christianization rendered cannibalism unfashionable, through marriage, adoption, and business partnerships. Large and important families descend from late-nineteenth-century European and North American traders, sometimes still bearing their names, and in some cases sporting a telltale *haafekasi* "mixed-blood" (from the English colonial term "half-caste") appearance, which Tongans find appealing, and social demeanor, about which Tongans have mixed feelings. From the mid-nineteenth to the mid-twentieth century, European traders, primarily of German extraction, as well as British, Scandinavian, and North American, controlled commerce. At least until World War I, the dominance of Germans was related to the German Empire's colonial presence in neighboring Samoa. Germans were particularly numerous in Vava'u, Tonga's major island group geographically closest to Samoa, 350 miles to the northeast.

Some traders worked for pan-Pacific business conglomerates, such as J. C. Godeffroy & Sohn, which settled in Tonga in 1867. After flirting with insolvency in 1878, it was reconstituted into the Deutsche Handels- und Plantagen-Gesellschaft der Südsee Inseln, which some have called the world's first transnational megacorporation, until it folded at the end of World War I (Firth 1973). The Tonga branch of Levuka-based Morris Hedstrom was established in the early 1900s, absorbed into the Sydney-based Carpenter Group in 1956, and sold to local interests in 1980. It dominated local trade along with Sydney-based Burns Philp, which came to Tonga in 1899 and remained until the 1990s. On at least one occasion, in 1910, foreign traders jettisoned competing Tongan-run cooperatives with the complicity of the British Consul (Rutherford 1981).

Trading combined the import of consumer goods, sold in larger stores in urban centers, with the export of copra and other resources from the land, forest, and sea (vanilla, bananas, cotton, sandalwood, and dried sea cucumbers or bêche-de-mer). In the early twentieth century, a few Japanese, Indians, and Chinese also operated in Tonga, despite the legal restrictions that the Tongan government imposed in 1919 on immigration from Asia (as well as other Pacific Islands). The part-European, part-Indian, or part-Japanese (or, in very few cases, part-Chinese) descendants of these early traders continue to figure prominently among the country's business elite. Although

Figure 2.3.   Boarded-up *fale koloa* owned by a small-scale entrepreneurial Tongan family, bankrupted after two years in the mid-1990s by family obligations and now used as storage room (Nuku'alofa, April 2008).

Tongan-owned business ventures did pick up somewhat after the establishment of the Tonga Development Bank in 1977, few Tongans with no foreign ascendants have traditionally succeeded in commerce. The ubiquitous *fale koloa* "roadside trade stores" dotting the landscape bear witness to this problem: under Tongan ownership, the businesses invariably succumb to the draining power of kinship obligations (Figure 2.3).

Since the 1960s, more or less temporary residents have included various investors (including a wave of Sicilians in the 1980s) and an unending parade of consultants, experts, and aid bureaucrats. Despite legal restrictions, a few Fiji Indians and Chinese set up businesses. Young Mormon missionaries on their two-year mission have stood out in the latter part of the twentieth century for being well trained in language, young, clean-cut, often ripe for marriage (a frequent occurrence), and, more importantly, backed up by a formidably wealthy infrastructure that promises emigration to the United States. Starting in the early 1970s, volunteers from various national organizations (the U.S. Peace Corps, Australian ASA, New Zealand VSA, British VSO, Japanese JICA, and French Coopération) followed, occasionally leading to cross-cultural marriages, most often to reasonably cordial temporary relations.

Historically, Tongans have treated Westerners, or *Pālangi*, in mitigated fashion.[11] Early visitors were there to be killed and their possessions taken, as illustrated by the classic story of the unsuspecting James Cook bestowing the name "Friendly Islanders," which has since been milked for all its worth, onto a people who were too busy arguing over how best to murder him to actually perform the deed. Christianization and the growing awareness that old-fashioned measures did not always yield satisfactory results softened Tongans' response to *Pālangi*, but the never-quite-completed colonial presence meant that foreigners never gained the ascendance that they did in other colonies (for example, Bashkow 2006). In particular, Tongans generally view their relationship with the modern condition as being under their own control rather than being mediated by Westerners. While foreigners came to be quite numerous at various historical moments, Tongans had relatively little contact with them. In classic Polynesian fashion, Queen Sālote III tried to elevate *Pālangi* to nominal chiefly status to prevent them from meddling in Tongan affairs (Wood-Ellem 1999: 78). Not everyone respected this elevation: Basil Thompson, a then prime minister with few allies, reported that "the manner of the average Tongans to a white man whom he dislikes and does not fear leaves much to be desired. I found myself jostled off the road by men on horseback, and subjected to many other petty annoyances" (1894: 78). These impressions find echoes in relations between Tongans and *Pālangi* today.

Of course, Tongans in the diaspora interact on a daily basis with mainstream New Zealanders, Australians, and Americans, as well as members of ethnic minorities (including Māori, other Pacific Island immigrants, ethnic Australians, African Americans, Hispanics), as co-workers, classmates, employees, neighbors, friends, and occasionally employers. However, overseas Tongans, particularly of the first generation, tend to keep to themselves, forming their own worlds around churches, choir groups, kava-drinking circles, nightclubs, and civic organizations, invisible to many mainstream citizens of the towns in which they are embedded, except perhaps in New Zealand and Hawai'i, where the presence of "Pacific Islanders" is much better recognized than in Australia and on the American mainland. White New Zealanders, Australians, and Americans are largely irrelevant to diasporic

Tongans of the first generation, except for the narrow functions that they have in their lives.

This irrelevance is even greater in Tonga, where, unencumbered by kinship privileges and obligations, *Pālangi* are extraneous to a system structured by relations of respect based on kinship and rank. At worst, they are the objects of derision and contempt. Adolescents crack jokes at foreigners' expense in the streets in Tongan, assuming that they will not understand. Children feel perfectly entitled to address them: "Goodbye! Goodbye!" they shout obsessively (a translation of the greeting that Tongans exchange when interacting minimally, *'alu ē!*, literally, "go then!"). Addressed to a Tongan adult, such impudence would earn them a good smack from a grown-up.

Historically, the foreigners whom kingdom-based Tongans have come across have formed a motley crew, and it has changed little since. People react with little fuss to *Pālangi* who conform to their expectations to be decently dressed, honorably transported, and properly bathed and perfumed. They accord them honorary high rank, shuffling them to the top table at feasts, for example, or making them sit on a chair while everyone else sits on the floor. But when a *Pālangi* fails expectations, indifference quickly gives way to contempt, as when foreigners, out of ignorance or willful egalitarianism, disregard rank and decorum. Cruise ships that disgorge for a short day scantily dressed tourists confirm the unappealing aesthetics of *Pālangi*-hood, in the indecorous unsightliness of pale, flabby, or skinny flesh; sweaty bodies ill-adapted to the heat; and legs unable to sit tailor fashion.[12] During my 2008 fieldwork, a Dutchman, who had been employed as a teacher until recently, was selling hamburgers from a large plastic container precariously balanced on his bicycle handlebars. "Are you so hungry," commented an elderly Tongan lady to me, reenacting a fictitious conversation she would have had with this man, "that you have to sell hamburgers by the roadside?"[13]

The early 1990s saw the sudden arrival of immigrants from the People's Republic of China (PRC). What brought them is shrouded in ambiguity, but in popular perceptions at least it is anchored in two events. One is the Tongan government's abrupt switch in diplomatic allegiances from Taiwan to the PRC in 1993. The Taiwanese mission left overnight, but not without taking computers it had donated to an education institution, leaving the cables dangling. The PRC had become crucial to the activities of a corporation called Tongasat, founded in 1988 and owned by the Princess Royal, that leases satellite orbital slots over Tongan airspace. The second event was a scheme in the 1980s and early 1990s by King Tāufaʻāhau IV to sell Tongan passports to noncitizens (Crocombe 2007: 163–165; Van Fossen 1999, 2007). This venture ended when the public outcry in Tonga could no longer be ignored, but it did manage to provide a Tongan passport to the likes of Ferdinand and Imelda Marcos as well as a number of wealthy Chinese, most of whom have nevertheless probably never set foot in the islands.[14]

Even though the relationship between these various events and the spectacular emergence of Chinese immigration is unclear to most Tongans, Chinese people continue to arrive, sometimes penniless. For them, Tonga is the "last migration frontier," alongside Fiji, the Solomon Islands, and Papua New Guinea, countries that have experienced similar recent waves of migrants from the PRC. Most are in Tonga for the sole purpose of making money and have little commitment to the local context. They form a heterogeneous and deeply fragmented group, some relatively wealthy while others are simple country folk. The fragmentation is most prominently inscribed in ethnic diversity. Many are from Fujian, a society, like Tonga, with a deeply engrained migratory disposition; a few are from Guangzhou; and yet another few are reputed to be Beijing urbanites who escaped after the 1989 Tiananmen events. In contrast, long-term Chinese residents, some of whom have been in Tonga since 1974, hail from Taiwan and Hong Kong. There are business people, former villagers, and even a few tradespeople who ply their trade very quietly. The majority came with Chinese passports, on temporary business visas of unclear provenance, and it is doubtful, contrary to popular belief, that the Tongan passport sales scam had much to do with Chinese immigration. Many poorer Chinese are villagers who were conned with promises of jobs, high incomes, and migration to New Zealand, and ended up being stranded in Tonga, indebted to "snakeheads" and relatives back home, unable to return or move elsewhere.

Chinese migrants have taken over most of the small-scale roadside *fale koloa* (Figure 2.4). Many Chinese shopkeepers stumbled on retail as a way to eke out a living, observing appallingly long working hours as they keep the shops open around the clock and close them only when required by the Sabbath law, living in miserable conditions in cramped quarters in the back, in conditions that they apparently consider better than what they left behind in Fujian. In Chinese hands, the shops have become profitable businesses. Seemingly devoid of kinship or other obligations (at least to Tongan observ-

Figure 2.4.   Successful *fale koloa* operated by Chinese immigrants, taken over from Tongan former owners (Nuku'alofa, April 2008).

ers), stereotypically hard working, they advertise success precisely where Tongan have hoped and failed. By 2008 they were said to control 70 percent of retail and a significant portion of wholesale business, generating serious competition by importing cheaper consumer goods from China. Little of the resulting profit stays in Tonga, as evidenced by the under-the-table currency exchange that some of the more successful Chinese shops offer, paying high rates for U.S. cash, which is easy to transport out of the country to circumvent Tongan government restrictions on exporting funds.[15]

The Chinese dominance of retail may have displaced poorer Tongans, but it has had little effect on wealthy Tongans' business ventures. As a result, feelings about the Chinese presence divide the poor from the middle classes and elites. The former harbor deep resentment of the Chinese, while the latter generally approve of them, citing the lower prices and the wider range of consumer goods and often contrasting Chinese shopkeepers' round-the-clock work with their poorer compatriots' alleged *fakapikopiko* "laziness, indolence." For less privileged Tongans, resentment takes a number of forms, ranging from straightforward anger to the argument that Chinese businesses may be bringing in cheaper products, but the ingredients are listed in Chinese and therefore Tongan consumers have no idea what they are using. Those harboring resentment never pause to juxtapose the Chinese presence with Tongans' own enthusiastic migrations overseas. Cross-cultural differences at Chinese-owned shops in how service encounters should be conducted do not alleviate the tension: Participants in a typical encounter are ill mannered, aggressive, and suspicious (on both sides), in contrast to the sociability that Tongans nurture among themselves, at least when owner and patron are related or acquainted. The resulting tension has exposed Chinese people to ongoing violence. On 16/11, their businesses were among the prime targets of the looting and arson. After 16/11, Chinese shop owners with more control over their destiny cut down on their working hours because of security, and some made up for it by expanding their shops into minimarkets, which allow for a broader choice of products. This transformation had the paradoxical effect of increasing the prosperity of Chinese retailers in the wake of the riots.

Chinese immigrants have formed two business associations, the Tonga Chinese Federation and the Tonga Chinese Business Association, the memberships of which overlap substantially. Beyond this, however, their own social relations are characterized by deep mistrust. "You do not trust your own brother," is the way in which one of my knowledgeable informants characterizes the spirit that reins among them. Some have entered into contractual arrangements with other Chinese by necessity, those with capital and business licenses employing poorer migrants who have to find a way to survive. Tongans are by and large oblivious to Chinese immigrants' diversity and mutual mistrust. The admiration that some express for their work ethics may indeed be seriously misplaced, while the resentment that others feel may be targeting people who are themselves victims in the first place. Nevertheless, probably unbeknownst to them, Chinese immigrants are deeply enmeshed with the formation and transformation of Tongan modernity, implicated as they are with the increasing diversity of the society, the conditions that force Tongans to migrate, the increasing commodification of exchange, and the relations between elite and nonelite Tongans.

PRODUCTION

The anxiety around the Chinese takeover of commerce must be understood in the context of the broader economic landscape, an understanding of which necessitates a longish excursus into economies of production, historical and contemporary. After Tonga had entered the world economic scene in the late nineteenth century, the country enjoyed a period of relative prosperity thanks to the processing and export of copra, or desiccated coconut flesh (*mataka*). In the industrial world, copra was (and still is) used in the manufacture of numerous products (soap, shampoo, detergent, cosmetics, industrial lubricant, cooking oil, food additives), and became the pillar of the Tongan economy from 1869, when J. C. Godeffroy & Sohn began to buy it in lieu of the more cumbersome coconut oil. By the early 1960s, copra production had effectively ended because of sinking world prices, competition from larger markets such as the Philippines, and Britain putting an end to preferential import policies. While it lasted, however, it enriched those in power in Tonga, primarily Western residents and the high-ranking, as well as, at particular historical moments, a broad slice of the population (Campbell 2001: 192–194). Generally speaking, however, most Tongans' livelihood was grounded until mid-century in subsistence agriculture and remained relatively unaffected by world economic fluctuations.

In the traditional order, the main source of wealth was land, the cornerstone of the relationship between the high ranking and commoners. Tonga's land tenure system, enshrined in the 1875 constitution, parcels out the entire land area of the kingdom to the sovereign, the government, the thirty hereditary nobles, and six nonnoble land-holding chief's representatives (*matāpule ma'u tofi'a*). Government, nobles, and chiefs are in turn responsible for assigning parcels of land to every adult man, who is constitutionally entitled to a 3.34 hectare agricultural allotment (*'api tukuhau*) and a village allotment (*'api kolo*) of 758 to 1,618 square meters, depending on the location. Based on a now completely outdated assumption of sedentariness, this system is in practice complex. It also allows nobles and their representatives to sometimes make burdensome tributary demands on commoners on the occasion of land allocations and transfers.

The traditional cornerstone of the country's productive economy, agriculture, contributed 23 percent of the GDP in 2003–2004 (including fisheries and forestry, which make negligible contributions). In 2001, 64.2 percent of households in the entire country were deemed "agriculturally active," although the percentage for households on Tonga, 54.2 percent, was significantly less than the national average.[16] Animal husbandry, which supplements land cultivation, concerns principally the lean dark-skinned Oceanic pigs, which three-quarters of the country's households keep, leaving them to forage on their own even on city streets, a practice that gives a peculiar kind of urbanity to Tongan towns. Keeping chickens is also common (half of all households), although Tongan taste buds much prefer the fatty chicken parts imported frozen from New Zealand and the United States, if they can be afforded, to the tough and lean local fowl. Fishing as a productive activity has undergone serious decline, involving today only 22.6 percent of Tongatapu's households, although this percentage is higher elsewhere where reef and offshore fishing is more accessible. For those with land, the main activity is the cultivation of root crops, including cassava, sweet potato, taro, and giant taro for everyday subsistence or domestic sale, as well as yams for feasting and ceremonial prestation, alongside pork. Other frequently consumed cultigens include breadfruit, watermelon, bananas, corn, plantains, and varieties of leafy vegetables, in addition to products from the ubiquitous coconut tree, which grows without human intervention. Also prominent in gardens is kava root (*Piper methysticum*) for social and ceremonial consumption and for export, the cultivation of which can yield excellent revenues.

Historically, agriculture has occupied a central place in the national economy, representing between 67 and 92 percent of total exports in the 1990s, for example. These include various crops (yams, taro, kava, bananas) exported in small quantities to various markets, particularly New Zealand, as well as relatively new crops of little local relevance such as vanilla and coffee. Fish exports are negligible because of the lack of infrastructure, which renders the industry uncompetitive in cutthroat world markets. The government does raise revenues from fishing licenses that it issues to foreign vessels harvesting albacore tuna on an industrial scale in Tonga's waters, but the ships take their catches to canning factories in Fiji and American Samoa, generating little income for anyone in Tonga and raising long-term ecological issues. Small Japanese-owned industries process seaweed and bottle the juice of the *nonu* (*Morinda citrifolia*), a bitter-tasting fruit purported to have medicinal properties (although exoticism is its main selling point), exporting it to Japan. Tahiti, however, has cornered the marketing of this product to the rest of the world.

In the 1960s and 1970s, New Zealand offered preferential treatment to banana imports from Tonga, and the cultivation of the fruit dominated agriculture in the islands (Fleming 1996: 73–75; Needs 1988: 68–78). It was killed by a combination of black leaf disease, the turn to neoliberal economics in New Zealand, and competition from much larger markets dominated by transnational corporations owning plantations in such countries as Ecuador. Since the early 1990s, by far the most consequential cash crop for export has been winter squash or pumpkin (*Cucurbita maxima*). Tongans considered it a low-status and only marginally palatable vegetable, and its cultivation for the domestic market had been insignificant until 1987. That year, a group of New Zealand entrepreneurs collaborated with farmers on the main island to grow it for export, having identified a narrow window of opportunity in the Japanese market between the end of production in Kagoshima and Hokkaidō prefectures in early November and the beginning of imports from Mexico in mid-December. Unlike Tongans, Japanese consumers relish squash as a cheap hearty winter vegetable. Within a few years, squash cultivation boomed and, in the early 1990s, half of all farmers on Tonga and many on 'Eua were growing the vegetable, funded by loans from the National Development Bank (Storey and Murray 2001: 297).

As can be expected of a single crop destined to fill a small time slot in a single market, which also happens to have some of the world's most exacting quality standards, the squash industry turned out to be very profitable for a few and unpredictable and problematic for everyone else. Besides requiring sustained land clearing and a lot of attention, squash cultivation necessitates the yearly purchase of seeds, pesticides, fungicides, and fertilizers. The long-term environmental impact of inorganic additives remains to be assessed, but their use is very difficult to control anyway because growers do what they wish on their land. While the vegetable is relatively sturdy, it is also prone to growing deformed (40 percent of any crop), which, along with the often rough handling it receives at the less-than-delicate hands of harbor workers, makes a large proportion of every crop unacceptable to Japanese wholesalers and consumers, whose attention to the visual form of food is notorious. After a few years, Tongan squash began receiving serious competition in Japan from longer local seasons, earlier Mexican production, and imports from other countries such as Vanuatu. Lastly, the brokers who control the route from grower in Tonga to consumer in Japan are widely reputed to work against the best interests of the former.

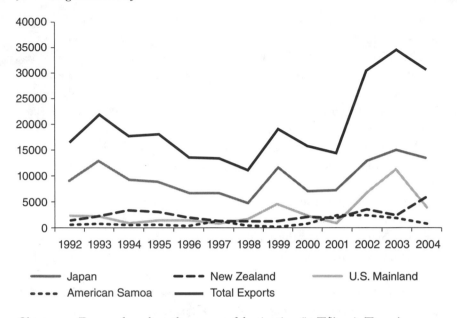

Chart 2.1.   Exports by selected country of destination (in T$'ooo), Tonga's exports to Japan consisting mainly of squash.
(Source: Tonga Department of Statistics 2008c: 50.)

A crisis point was reached in 1994, when veritable mountains of unexportable vegetables were left to rot around Tonga. Chart 2.1 clearly demonstrates the fickleness of the export market. But the figures also show the enduring and determinative role played by squash exports in Tonga's total export market, although they do not factor in the increasingly prohibitive cost of inorganic additives, the losses due to dishonest practices, and the unknown environmental damage associated with the crop. At the time of writing, only growers with access to substantial land, a large capital base, financial cushions, and direct control over the lines of export venture into squash cultivation. The situation does little to alleviate the concentration of income and wealth into the hands of the few.[17]

High-prestige agricultural products, such as yams, pigs, and kava, continue to figure centrally in ceremonial occasions (*kātoanga*) such as funerals, weddings, milestone birthdays, high school reunions, church conferences, inaugurations, and rank- and state-affirming rituals. These products constitute *tokonaki*, the product of men's labor in prestation, presented side-by-side and in symbolic opposition to women's *koloa faka-Tonga* "Tongan valuables," which consist of high-quality plaited mats and barkcloth, described in greater detail in Chapter Four. The continued (and, according to many, increasing) importance of these products in highly visible contexts reflects the persistence of tradition and sustains the illusion of agriculture's enduring significance. In actuality, agriculture has steadily been losing its importance, for a number of reasons. While the Constitution of 1875 in theory guarantees Tongan men access to arable land, the implementation of this right has been seriously constrained by land shortage, population increase and movement, and some nobles' lack of enthusiasm in distributing land.[18] When people migrate from rural areas, they relinquish their land rights. They may enter into informal arrangements with relatives who stay behind, who may keep them supplied in agricultural products, or may rely in their new home on access to a *toutu'u*, borrowed or leased plot of land cooperatively exploited by an agricultural club, kava-drinking club, or church congregation. However, these solutions are fragile, and they generally allow migrants to meet only basic or partial subsistence needs.

Access to land is not the only factor that contributes to the attrition of agriculture. The sector lost its luster in the unreasonable promises and rapid downfall of the squash industry. In the extraordinary enthusiasm with which they embraced squash production, Tongan farmers abandoned more cautious agricultural strategies, to which many have not returned. But it is not only squash that has experienced problematic moments, as domestic markets are commonly flooded with root crops. In March 2008, for example, Vava'u farmers were watching their produce turn bad at the Neiafu produce marketplace, and the hopes that some harbored to take their crops to Nuku'alofa were quickly thwarted by rumors of low prices there, which shoppers still could not afford. Subsistence agriculture is no longer sufficient for survival, and attempting to earn money from agriculture, whether for export or the domestic market, is a high-risk and generally unrewarding proposition. Agriculture has even lost some of its ceremonial significance, as illustrated in the decline of a formerly very important yearly agricultural show attended by the king who every year traveled to all the island group centers. The show echoed the *'inasi* of precontact days, the ritual presentation of the first fruits to the sacred ruler, the Tu'i Tonga (Bataille 1976). This historical resonance was of particular importance in light of the dynasty's long-standing preoccupation with appropriating the symbolic legacy of the Tuʻi Tonga, the last of whom, Laufilitonga, chose to convert to the "wrong" brand of Christianity (Catholicism) and was defeated by Tāufaʻāhau Tupou I in 1826. On Tongatapu, the show was moved in 1988 to make room for the construction of Teufaiva stadium (Chapter Seven), but it never recovered from this ostensibly temporary displacement and eventually disappeared. Beauty pageants and the Heilala Festival are its functional replacement (Chapter Six).

Some observers blame agriculture's unprofitability on growers' increasing reliance on mechanized transportation, fertilizers, and machinery. In the (generic) olden days, these commentators point out, people cleared the land with a bush knife, while today no one wants to do without a tractor or weed eater. Modern-day cultivators are *fakapikopiko*, a term whose referent straddles emotional states such as "languid, lethargic" and personality descriptors such as "lazy, indolent," which also emerges when privileged Tongans compare their poorer compatriots to Chinese immigrants. Women, particularly members of the highly visible cadre of high-achieving women, can be vociferous proponents of this discourse. For example, a prominent intellectual with deep roots in rural Tonga reported to me that village women had repeatedly complained during her recent tour of the islands on an official mission that all their men folk did all day was to sit around and drink kava, leaving to the women the tasks of finding money, providing and cooking food, and taking care of the children. Such comments must of course be taken with a grain of salt, particularly when reported by people who are not themselves engaged in agriculture. But they do point a metaphorical finger to deep-seated gender divisions.

The situation is thus one in which agriculture is the mainstay of the productive economy, but it is no longer profitable, dependable, and prestigious. The nexus of the economy is no longer located in production in any simple sense, but in other sectors: in consumption and the activities that support it and in productive activities located elsewhere, that is, in the diaspora. These activities are "productive" only by a stretch of the imagination, being so thoroughly embedded in the service sector. The effect of the increased reliance on overseas-based activities, which the island-based economy cannot easily counterbalance, can be read in the skewed balance of trade: In 2004 (when squash exports were still substantial), the value of exports was only 15 percent of exports.

In the 1980s, a group of geographers proposed to account for the fragile yet surprisingly resilient economies of Pacific Island microstates such as

Tonga with a model they referred to by the acronym "MIRAB": *Mi*grations, *R*emittances, overseas *A*id, and state *B*ureaucracy (Bertram 1999, 2006; Bertram and Watters 1985; Poirine 1998; and many others). While this proposal has generated vigorous debate among development scholars Down Under, it has generally not captured anthropologists' imagination, at least in the metropolitan traditions of the discipline.[19] This lack of interest is rooted in more than the provincialism of North Hemisphere anthropology. Indeed, a notable characteristic of the MIRAB hypothesis is its elision of agency (Connell 2007: 130; Evans 1999), as it depicts people as simply reacting to the lack of opportunity in their homeland by migrating, or killing time around money transfer offices waiting for funds that their underpaid and overworked relatives send to them from overseas. Anyone who has spent much time among ordinary people in Tonga and elsewhere in the Pacific Islands will immediately see the problems with this image of reactive utilitarianism.

Furthermore, details of the MIRAB hypothesis have not withstood the passing of time. Foreign aid, driven by donors' fickle expansionist interests, is notoriously fragile. So are remittances: Not only predicated on overseas relatives' commitment to their relatives back home (Lee 2007), they also depend on the vagaries of job markets in industrial countries on which overseas Tongans rely. In particular, the effect of the 2008 U.S. subprime mortgage crisis on Pacific Island workers who are overrepresented in the construction and maintenance industry in some of the most vulnerable regions of the United States (such as California) remains to be understood. Also overestimated is the durability of bureaucracy, which has undergone severe erosion as a source of income and general security for ordinary Tongans since the 1990s. Tonga's turn to neoliberal economic policies, following the lead of successive conservative governments in New Zealand and Australia, has led to the privatization of governmental assets, sometimes through amazingly swift action, assiduously backed by a then-Crown Prince Tupouto'a convinced of the value of hard work and the desirability of a hands-off government.[20]

Examples include government's offer in 2006 of retirement packages to streamline the civil service, which large numbers of employees accepted, leaving a government short of labor and suddenly giving a ubiquitous quality to the category "retired." (I analyze one consequence of this action in Chapter Four.) Banks, housing, airport services, wharves, and the National Cultural Centre have been or are being privatized. A more dramatic example was the outright acquisition of electricity supply in 1998 by the then-crown prince and his business associates, which swiftly led to consumers' power bills increasing in some cases by 400 percent (Campbell 2006: 53). The power company was sold back to government in June 2008 for T$26M. As part of the new valorization of the private sector, a telecommunication company has been established by a large transnational telecommunication corporation based in Jamaica, incorporated in Bermuda, owned by an Irishman who declares legal residence in Malta (after a series of misunderstandings about taxes he owed to the government of his previous official residence, Portugal), contracting a Malaysian company to install Chinese equipment by highly remunerated technicians of multiple nationalities, whose interest in and commitment to Tonga are nonexistent. For its launch, the company staged what was perhaps the country's largest ever privately organized event, a free concert featuring Jamaican reggae star Shaggy, who knew nothing about Tonga before arriving, and who, after the obligatory several hours' wait and predictable power cuts, entertained on the waterfront crowds in unheard-of numbers, including uncertain teenagers and village grandmothers putting their grandchildren off to sleep on the sidewalk. The events announced an aggressive marketing campaign to market mobile phone sets and services and compete with the locally owned telephone service provider (Beadle 2008).

The MIRAB hypothesis does suggest (although not very well) some important points relevant to the Tongan national economy and the everyday economics of families alike. One is the extent to which income strategies are grounded on both diversified activities and kinship-based systems of reciprocity (Evans 1999; Munro 1990). Success and survival often rest on the collective work of many family members (not just overseas relatives) and on an opportunity-driven panoply of activities. Families may include one or two young members who are low-ranking civil servants or service-industry employees, but their meager wages manage to cover only a fraction of weekly bills. Thus wages generally constitute a supplement to family income, rather than its core. Other family members may trade at the secondhand marketplace, produce *koloa faka-Tonga*, sell cooked lunch packages door-to-door to office and shop workers, or drive the family car that doubles as a taxi. Neither mutuality nor diversity is limited to the poor, as I will discuss in the next section.

A particularly interesting type of economic activities based on social relations is framed in terms of traditional assistance to the less fortunate, a process referred to as *tokoni*, "help," a ubiquitous term whose literal meaning describes any gift that flows down the ranking system (or that defines recipient as subordinate to giver), from overseas aid to gift giving at feasts. Pawnshop owners, for example, refer to their activities as *tokoni*, "helping" people meet their obligations and goals, obscuring the fact that they also make a healthy profit in the process. A salient example is form filling: visa applications, bank loan applications, and other bureaucratic forms require an increasing level of competence and resources, and people with these assets provide, for a fee, services to others who lack them while still framing their activities as *tokoni*. Some do it casually, while others, more entrepreneurially, have set up businesses that, for example, fill out customers' visa applications, arrange their flight bookings, and loan out fares and "pocket money." Framing business activities in terms of *tokoni* provides a Tongan twist to modern practices, enabling entrepreneurs to appear to stay grounded in tradition while enriching themselves at others' expense, thus deepening the gap between those who have bureaucratic know-how, capital, computers, and easy access to the Internet, and those who don't.

The other point on which the MIRAB hypothesis places its finger is that production is not central to Pacific Island microstates, although we should perhaps try to understand conditions of life not in terms of underproblematized categories such as migration, remittances, and aid from overseas but in more complex dynamics at the convergence of the material and the ideological.

CONSUMPTION

Such an understanding must recognize that Tonga's economy is not so much one of production but one of consumption. The few attempts at manufacturing for export, such as the small-scale production of rugby balls and sweater knitting in the 1990s, have long succumbed to competition from Asia (Connell and Lea 2001: 79). Nonagricultural production for local consumption is limited to food processing such as baking, beer brewing, and sausage making, all from imported raw materials. The majority of successful, as well as more modest, businesses in Tonga gravitate around the import, distribution, and retail of consumer goods. Their business bases in Tonga make up a diversified "portfolio" of ventures, comprised of such unlikely bedfellows as construction, money lending, selling baked goods, DVD lending, and money transfers between Tongan and the diaspora.[21] Supplementing these activities are services such as hotel management, retail, shipping, travel and visa agency services, and overseas "shopping services" for better-off Tongan customers, which process shopping lists through agents in Auckland or Sydney and take care of transport and customs clearance. These practices resemble those of European traders of yesteryears as well as the "multiple livelihood strategies" through which the middle classes maximize wealth and status in other countries of the developing world (for example, Owusu 2008). They also illustrate the centrality in the economy of relations between Tonga and its diasporic nodes.

As many have argued (including Bourdieu 1979; Douglas and Isherwood 1979; Miller 1995), consumption is both material and ideological, in that it is not simply a matter of purchasing products but is encompassed in a cycle of performances, feelings, and desires. In particular, consumption, and more specifically conspicuous consumption, is closely tied to prestige in Tonga through a variety of semiotic means, one of which is size. Size is deeply embedded in the Tongan symbolic order as both an index and an icon of rank, as I will elaborate later. However, because of its semiotic status as an index, size is alienable from rank and can shift to other meaning-making mechanisms without completely leaving its connection to rank. Evidence of the shifting indexicality of size are the enormous houses that some Tongan migrants build, whether or not they return to live in Tonga, dwarfing the homes of their more modest neighbors (cf. Riccio 2001: 585 on Senegal). The conspicuous consumption embedded in megahomes, built in a style that often redefines the meaning of kitsch, enables those who can afford them to lay a highly visible claim to social importance, in parallel to the traditional conflation of importance with rank.

For most Tongans, the conspicuous consumption that emerged in the late twentieth and early twenty-first centuries was not a new phenomenon because they had encountered it in the course of history on several occasions. By the end of the nineteenth century, Tongan elites (high-ranking and part-European families) were enthusiastic consumers of imported goods, just like their Hawaiian counterparts although more modestly, as Tonga did not have the income-generating natural resources that Hawai'i did, such as an abundant supply of sandalwood (Sahlins 1988: 32–36). Photographs of the high ranking portray them dressed in Victorian and Edwardian fineries, and the royal palace, built in 1865–67, signals an ambition of material opulence, even if other buildings dwarf it today. Later, during the U.S. occupation of 1942–1945, ordinary Tongans witnessing the extravagance of wartime America attempted to claim a share of it, which sometimes gave rise to serious conflicts (Campbell 2001: 175–187; Helu 1999: 146–157; Weeks 1987).

Today, few aspects of daily life lay claim to social importance in a more "in your face" manner than the cars that people drive on the country's few roads. Cars, which are more effectively ostentatious than homes because they can be paraded in multiple locations, have become the focus of anxiety in the postmillennium years (cf. Chalfin 2008 on Ghana). Their number rose exponentially during the squash boom, as they were one of the first possessions that farmers sought to purchase with their sudden influx of cash (Storey and Murray 2001: 299). Even as fuel prices are skyrocketing and traffic slows down to a crawl, everyone aspires to own one. "People may live in home with broken louvers and no front door," quips a taxi-driving philosopher in my circle of friends, "but they still want to drive a car." Village buses are virtually gone, and with them a major entrepreneurial activity in the 1970s and 1980s. Formerly a common form of transportation in both town and village and the sign of a certain status, bicycles are now seen as a marker of foreignness, associated with Peace Corps and other volunteers, as well as the object of mild derision (other than as an instrument of middle-class fitness training).

In the last decade of the twentieth century, cars were transformed from unaffordable luxury to barely affordable necessity. When I discussed the matter with Tongan respondents, they invariably argued that they needed a car, and one as large as possible, "to take the children to school." Indeed, the morning traffic around schools now rivals that around California suburban schools. A decade ago, however, children would walk or take the bus to school, methods of transportation that Tongans generally now find lacking in dignity, causing shame (*mā*) and exposing one's children and family to denigrating gossip.[22]

The trajectory of most imported vehicles begins in left-hand-driving Japan: Autos that do not pass the Draconian road-worthiness requirements there are put up for auction, where licensed buyers (including several Tongans) buy and export them to Tonga, as well as to other markets like Pakistan and the Russian Far East. Many cars bear banners advertising companies in the urban centers of Japan, and most still display registration stickers from various Japanese prefectures. There is a general feeling that these vehicles are "dumped" into the Pacific Islands, in a pattern that follows that of many kinds of imported consumer goods: the unacceptable, the out-of-date, or the

Figure 2.5.   Vehicle carcasses dotting the landscape, an increasingly common sight around Tongatapu (April 2008).

barely edible (Gewertz and Errington 2010). Other vehicles are shipped by their owners or their overseas family members from the diasporic nodes.

Because of the largely opportunity-driven way in which automobiles reach Tonga, few can be matched to the right spare parts, demanding creative mechanical ingenuity that some small-scale entrepreneurs have developed into a fine art. The spatial, environmental, and social impact is already showing its magnitude (Figure 2.5): traffic-clogged roads; choking fumes exhaled by poorly tuned engines; frightful car accidents related to drunk driving and other forms of creative driving; and a landscape increasingly cluttered with disintegrating car carcasses (Kawamura 2003). Driving and riding motor vehicles preclude the physical exercise that walking or riding a bicycle formerly provided and are contributing to the alarming rate of obesity and "lifestyle diseases" (particularly diabetes and high-blood pressure) that plague Tonga's modern-day population (Chapter Seven).

Cars, however, are also highly visible symbols of ostentation, partly inspired on the places to which Tongans have migrated (particularly California) and partly grounded in traditional structures of rank. It is not just basic
cars that appear to be the object of Tongans' desires, but SUVs (4×4s), pickup
trucks, and vans, some of colossal proportions, the practical unwieldiness
of which places them squarely within the original definition of "conspicuous consumption." Tongans explain their tastes by invoking the large size
of families and the number of people who regularly expect to be given rides,
as well as the potholes on roads, yet neither family size nor road disrepair
is a logical justification for the bloated vehicles. Rather, large vehicles are
embedded in both a politics of competitive consumption and a semiotics of
rank. The enormous air-conditioned SUVs, tinted windows rolled up, raising clouds of dust or swells of rainwater in their wake; the souped-up trucks
cruising at slow speed blaring hip-hop music; and the jeeps with personalized
license plates or personal names and slogans emblazoned across rear windows all evoke a specific social standing, a particular quality of achievement
and connection. Tongans linked by kinship or dual residence to the United
States receive plenty of reinforcement from mainstream America's fetishization of size (oversized vehicles, overweight bodies, megahomes, enormous
hamburgers, and so on). At the same time, true to the bifocality that characterizes all cultural dynamics in the islands, the size of vehicles operates in
reference to the logic of traditional rank, which is iconicized in the relative
height of people's heads and the social space that they occupy: the heads of
the low ranking must remain below the level of the heads of the high ranking, and the low ranking make themselves small and active in the presence of
the high ranking. Like restaurant eating (Chapter One), cars quietly subvert
this semiotics, as commoners who can afford it can sit just as high in their
SUVs as those of high rank.

Rank informs other aspects of how cars are used. Cars are of course used
for transportation, but they are also for waiting. In the olden days, most
people except the highest ranking would spend considerable time waiting
for buses, village trucks, and interisland launches. Today they continue to
do a lot of waiting (for passports and visas, overdue remittances, customers
in shops, and death), but they do so in cars and vans, fanning themselves as
well as they can in the oppressive heat, occasionally slapping an unruly child,
because waiting in vehicles affords a claim to dignity that sitting on benches
or on the side of the road does not.

Among the indexical allusions that vehicles make to a wealthy and individualistic outside world, links to the urban United States figure prominently in the custom paint jobs (for example, flames, names, slogans, some in telltale Gothic lettering), which index a recognizably American working-class and specifically Latino sensibility (of the "pimp my ride" variety) diffusing outward ethnically and spatially. Some custom paint jobs and other decorations are associated with prior owners in the United States and Japan. When the decorations are customized by the vehicle's Tongan owner or a relative overseas, the form of names etched onto car bodies and rear windows complement this indexical orientation: As if to underline the embracement of a diasporic modernity, many names are the Anglicized version of Tongan names (such as "Steve" for "Sitiveni," or "John" for "Sione"), and the unmistakably American nickname "Junior" appears frequently in custom paint jobs.[23]

At the lower end of the spectrum are old and off-brand cars spewing noxious fumes, rusting bodies plastered with the ubiquitous bright yellow bumper stickers advertising money-transfer transnational corporations. Yet both categories of vehicles are involved in the same general politics of display, competition, and desire that keeps privileging the same people (the high ranking, the wealthy, the lucky) and leaving the rest in the dust. The latter often wonder aloud how some in Tonga can put their hands on so much material wealth, while they themselves have so much trouble making ends meet.

The shift to consumption has given rise to an entire service industry catering to needs that Tongans did not know they had until recently. One example, again associated with cars, is the car-wash business, advertised conspicuously on the license plates of the ostentatiously enormous (and invariably clean) SUVs driven by the owners. Equipped with imported materials, these businesses are designed to rid cars of the dust and mud with which poorly maintained roadways constantly cover vehicles. Real estate agencies, public relations agencies, management consulting firms, and "leadership training workshops" oriented to the disaffected youth of Tonga, none of which were present in 2000, have now sprouted. The insecurity that followed 16/11 and the dramatic increase in break-ins and violence have multiplied security services (including guards, call-and-response services, and patrol vehicles) and have inspired one entrepreneur to import the first armored money truck to the kingdom, a move of which other middle-class Tongans speak approvingly. The upper echelons of these ventures respond to the demands created by the government's economic rationalization and outsourcing, but other ventures of a more modest kind are tied to the desires of ordinary people. For example, the now-essential mobile telephones require repair shops, which make brisk business "unlocking" the mobile phones that Tongans bring in from overseas.

ANGA FAKA-TONGA, "THE TONGAN WAY"

Not surprisingly, the rapid changes in Tonga's economic and social landscape have opened a space for the overelaboration of a traditional order anchored in the past, whose construction is suffused with nostalgia for a calmer and more benign social order. This is the oft-cited *anga faka-Tonga*, to which Tongans refer as "the Tongan Way" when they speak English, which symbolizes all that they deem specific to the island way of doing things and in particular what differs from genericized "Western" ways (as well as, increasingly, Chinese ways).[24]

Like its equivalents operative in other Pacific Island societies, *anga faka-Tonga* is a shifting category characterized by much ideological diversity (Philips 2000, 2004) in that, for example, many see certain forms of historical change as compatible with it. It contrasts ambiguously with the abstract construction of two ways of life, modernity and *muli* "overseas," which usually refers to the West. Tongans associate a number of affects with the Tongan side of the dichotomy. One is *'ofa*, "empathy, compassion, generosity," as well as nonromantic love, the most overelaborated and hypercognized emotion in the local repertoire, which regulates everything from kinship relations to exchange, the relationships between commoners and the high ranking, and the relationship between church members and members of religious hierarchies. Often referred to as "the treasure of Tonga" (Kavaliku 1977), *'ofa* is what drives, for example, people (particularly elderly women) to offer prestation in quantities that are way beyond their means, in the excitement of gift-giving rituals to the high ranking or churches. These actions may be fueled by other emotions and concerns, such as the potential shame (*mā*) of not being able to compete with others, and the drive to gain prestige from giving, but these other concerns do not figure in public representations. (They do in gossip.) For Tongans, *'ofa* is one of the key elements that distinguish life in Tonga from life among *Pālangi*.

Another pillar of *anga faka-Tonga* is encapsulated in the English term *respect*, which in English spoken in Tonga translates the expression *'ulungaanga faka'apa'apa*. (A reciprocal term borrowed from Fijian, *feveitokai'aki*, "to pay attention to one another's needs," is rarely used in everyday talk.) In the first instance, *respect* refers to sister–brother avoidance relations, the respect of children for parents, and the respect of commoners for the high ranking, but it generally bypasses the kind of status-blind respect elaborated in post-Enlightenment Western moral theory. *Anga faka-Tonga* is tied to the maintenance of rank hierarchy (and thus the events of 16/11 were seriously lacking in it), although some who believe in its virtues are also quick to point out that many among today's high ranking "have lost touch" with the people. But all agree that Westerners and the Chinese do not practice or care about respect.

"The Tongan way" also refers to an economic order structured by both obligation and contentment. Tongans talk of a person or family that takes social obligation seriously as *fai fatongia*, "performing duty [required by society]" (for example, giving to church and noble), and *fua kavenga*, "bearing burden [of traditional prestation]." In the old order, *fatongia* referred to the right of chiefs to appropriate commoners' property and labor. Today, it refers to the allegiance to rank and continuity through the prestation of textile valuables, agricultural products, imported food, labor, money, and other resources.

Another manifestation of *anga faka-Tonga* operates through an emotion called *fiemālie*, "contented, comfortable" (cf. Tomlinson 2009: 82–83 on Fiji). References to this emotion are particularly dominant in the nostalgic construction of the homeland in which diasporic Tongans often engage, as do members of other diasporas (for example, Olwig 1996). They also emerge in the frequent harangues to which Tongans subject outsiders comparing life in Tonga and *muli* "overseas." In Tonga, one can eat, sleep, and relax when one wishes; if one is hungry, one just goes to the bush and helps oneself from papaya trees. The frequent focus on papayas is particularly amusing because until recently Tongans did not eat them, feeding them instead to pigs and tourists. In my early naïve days in Tonga in the late 1970s, I would impatiently retort by asking why, then, Tongans were so anxious to move overseas, until I finally understood that what was important about this discourse was not its literal meaning but its self-reassuring effect, in a context dominated by anxieties about material conditions, social change, and identity. In support of this analysis is the fact that Tongans frequently switch, in the same conversation, between the discourse of *fiemālie* and statements that depict quite a different story, such as *'Oku fakaʻofa ʻa Tonga*, "Tonga is pitiable, in a sorry state" (*fakaʻofa* literally means "deserving of *ʻofa*"). Anxiety generates the need for constant reassurance of the basic comfort one can still find in the Tongan way, in contrast to the money-driven, impersonal, individualistic, and godless West. The fact that these two opposites are so deeply enmeshed with one another demands that agents make persistent efforts to keep them apart.

Anxieties surrounding *anga faka-Tonga* are embedded in another affect, "Tongan pride" or "pride in being Tongan," particularly conspicuous among diasporic Tongans. The phrase is ubiquitous in contexts that bring out self-consciousness about identity and desire, such as T-shirts, Internet discussion groups, and personal web pages, particularly those of teenagers on Facebook and Bebo (an Internet social network popular in the Southern Hemisphere). In the course of my fieldwork, "proud to be Tongan" frequently emerged in the negative when people spoke of their reaction to 16/11. Paradoxically, "Tongan pride" is untranslatable into Tongan, the very language of this pride, an untranslatability that provides a glimpse of its genealogy. Its roots are in the diaspora, particularly in Hawai'i and New Zealand, where it has become since the 1960s a ubiquitous marker of everyday politics of indigeneity among Native Hawaiians and Maori respectively, a reaction to the lengthy and devastating colonialism that had discouraged "pride" of whatever kind. I will further comment on these links in Chapter Seven.

Perhaps one of the most visible markers of the mutual constitution of modernity and *anga faka-Tonga* is clothing (Addo 2003). Tongans wear a wide range of outfits, and their fashion choices index different social positionings, from gender to age, from work to cosmopolitanism, and from wealth to rank. While Tongans widely believe that the current status quo is the product of historical immanence, fashion in fact has undergone profound changes from one historical moment to the other. In precontact days, clothing, or rather the relative bulkiness of clothing, indexed rank. Chiefly women and men wore layers of decorated barkcloth wrapped around the middle of their bodies and covered by a plaited pandanus mats, which Captain Cook described as a "curious apron" (Beaglehole 1961: 272), leaving only the upper chest and lower legs exposed. Commoners covered their loins with a single layer of barkcloth, over which they wrapped a girdle of leaves or, if they were in the presence of the high ranking, a mat, as Will Mariner described in the early nineteenth century:

It is proper to mention that, in presence of a superior chief, it is considered
very disrespectful to be undrest. Under such circumstances as the present,
therefore, every one retires a little, and, as soon as he has divested himself of
his usual dress, slips on an apron made of the leaves of the chi [*sī*] tree, or of
matting called gie [*kie*]. The same respect is shown, if it be necessary to undress near a chief's grave; because some hotooa ['*otua*] or god may be present.
(J. Martin 1817: I: 257)

In contrast to some other Pacific Islanders (for example, see Tcherkézoff
2003), Tongans were then and still are extremely reluctant to shed their
clothes before others and, contrary to the belief of naïve Western commentators, this prudery is not the result of missionization. Will Mariner made several references to the indecent nature of nudity in early-nineteenth century
Tonga. For example, writing of a woman who had become insane (or perhaps
perfectly sane but thoroughly enraged) after her child had been sacrificed
to the gods, he states that she "used to . . . dance about to the annoyance
of every body, sometimes with scarcely any clothes on, which is considered
very indecent and disrespectful" (Martin 1817: I: 85). (The hapless creature
became the target of a demonstration of the effectiveness of muskets as she
was walking on the beach one day.)

The growing influence of traders, missionaries, and other external agents
changed the attires that people wore, influence that was motivated in some
cases by a particular sense of morality (for example, missionaries demanding
that women cover their chest), and in other cases by greed. In 1876, European
and American traders persuaded King George I to promulgate a "Law on
Tapa" that prohibited the manufacture of barkcloth and the wearing of clothing made from it so as to force Tongans to buy imported clothing from stores
(Rutherford 1971: 60–1). Even though the law was repealed two years later,
barkcloth never made a comeback as a source of clothing, although its manufacture for ceremonial gift giving survived and continues to this day.

Like many other tokens of modernity, the modern-day image of the sar-
torial respectability of *anga faka-Tonga* was formed in the course of Queen
Sālote's reign (Helu 1999: 291). In contrast to her father, who had chiefs wear
Western-style clothing, the queen encouraged Tongans to don garments
that she was hoping would become a distinctly Tongan style and one that
ordinary people could afford. The style today is typified for women by a tailored matching ensemble of a short-sleeved top and ankle-length skirt called

puletaha, over which they wear a tasseled fiber belt called *kiekie*, and for men by an ordinary shirt and *tupenu* "tailored man's skirt" (sometimes qualified as *faka-Fisi*, "in Fijian style") with a plaited mat, or *ta'ovala*, wrapped around it and fastened with a belt (*kafa*) plaited with coconut-husk fiber, human hair, or horsetail hair. The *ta'ovala* renders the wearing of a necktie superfluous, although members of the more conservative denominations wear one to church services in addition to the *ta'ovala*.[25]

Today, these garments are de rigueur on formal occasions, sometimes as an alternative to formal Western clothing, and their manufacture is largely the responsibility of tailor shops (in 2008, a made-to-measure *puletaha* at Mara's House of Styles cost T$30–45 and a *tupenu faka-Fisi* T$15–20). The *kiekie* and *ta'ovala* come in many variations and are plaited, crocheted, or sewn by women. Some *ta'ovala*, as well as the hair belts used to fasten them (some braided with royalties' hair), are centuries-old chiefly and royal heirlooms brought out only on extremely special occasions (Kaeppler 1999), while cheap contemporary versions are assembled out of plastic-fiber rice bags in answer to the rising cost of plaited mats. Tongan clothing represents several ideals at once, embodying neatness, cleanliness, dignity, and respect for rank, all constitutive of *anga faka-Tonga*. This is particularly true of the *kiekie* and the *ta'ovala*, which in former times had a much more restricted use, being worn either by the high ranking or by the low ranking in their presence. Their use has become commonplace in recent decades, an illustration of the ubiquitous mimetic emulation by commoners of markers of rank and the concomitant association of these garments with a commitment to tradition. For example, to illustrate her shame about the 16/11 events, a mid-level civil servant explained to me in English, "I am no longer proud to be a Tongan, I no longer wear a *kiekie* to church when I am overseas to convey my pride in being a Tongan, today I leave it at home."

The mutual constitution of *anga faka-Tonga* and modernity is iconicized in the multiple combinations of symbols and objects that people wear. Some men wear a *ta'ovala* over trousers, for example. Many T-shirts and "aloha shirts" are decorated with local symbols, which are predominantly printed elsewhere: traditional barkcloth motifs, the national coat-of-arms (*sila*), or references to the national rugby team. The result is a continuum between fashion that indexes *anga faka-Tonga* on the one hand and at the other extreme hip-hop fashion directly borrowed from California inner cities.

Tonga's Modernity

Both historically and synchronically, Tonga's modernity since the 1960s has been intertwined with diasporic dispersal. Little takes place in Tonga without reference to Tongan communities around the Pacific Basin, who constitute both a secondary audience for all social action and points of contact between Tonga and the rest of the world, a point that I invoked in my discussion of bifocality in the introduction. The constant movement of people, objects, ideas, images, and money between Tonga and the diaspora, as well as among the different nodes of the latter, reinforces the continued mutual relevance of island-based and overseas-based Tonga. This sustained interaction has also enabled the emergence of an economic structure that has left behind, for all intents and purposes, the subsistence agricultural production that was operative until the intensification of overseas migration and that is now essentially a consumption-based economy. This seemingly vulnerable economic base has been sustained, at least until the world economic crisis of the latter years of the first decade of the millennium, by income-generating activities located elsewhere, as well as by the resourcefulness that Tongans bring to the task of generating income. But it has also exacerbated the widening of the gap between the rich and the poor and the general feeling that the privileged have little in common with the rest of the society.

The material life of the country and its diaspora is shaped, not surprisingly, by both world economic conditions and local dynamics. Economic projects are also informed by ideological dynamics, many of which are resiliently continuous with the past. I have alluded to the mimesis that is operative in the ranking system, whereby ordinary Tongans take their behavioral cues from the high ranking and, more and more, the wealthy. Another important set of ideological dynamics that underlie the materiality of life is the production of tradition or *anga faka-Tonga*, which goes hand-in-hand with the pursuit of modernity. The following chapters develop these various themes in greater detail.

Chapter Three

Consumption and Cosmopolitanism

The Tongan constitution prescribes that on Sunday no activities take place other than attending church, resting, and eating. Saturday, in contrast, is a day of preparation, principally of food for midday consumption on the Sabbath. In rural contexts, villagers spend the day going to the gardens to harvest root crops, preparing the underground oven (*'umu*), and tidying up house compounds so that they look their best on the day of the Lord.[1] Town dwellers also devote Saturday to preparation, but in the form of shopping: buying food from the markets, roadside vendors, or the supermarkets (for those who can afford it), as well as shopping for a vast array of nonfood items on offer at one of the two secondhand marketplaces, or *fea* (from English "fair"). Since their gradual appearance in Nuku'alofa, secondhand marketplaces have been increasing in size, prominence, and popularity, and have become the focus of weekly outings for a comprehensive cross-section of society. Young and old, women and men, modern subjects and upholders of tradition all seem to heed the exhortation of a tourist-oriented brochure: "Saturday Morning Fair: Join the crowds on the waterfront, and find everything you need" (Vava'u Press 1999, punctuation as in the original). This popularity generates some of the worst traffic congestions in the country.

This popularity has long got under the skin of Nuku'alofa shop owners and was for a long time the focus of many meetings of the Tonga Chamber of Commerce and Industry, a body founded in 1996. Owners of retail businesses that sell clothing, the most prominent item on offer at the *fea*, argue in particular that the *fea* puts them at a distinct disadvantage. While most merchandise sold in Tonga is imported, goods sold at the *fea* are brought in as personal effects and are therefore subject to minimal or no custom duties, in contrast to the substantial sums that shop owners have to fork out to clear merchandise (cf. Scheld 2007: 239 on the Dakar secondhand clothing trade). In 2000, for example, 52 percent on sports clothing, plus 20 percent port handling and T$8 quarantine clearance fees (often applied to each item), to which an across-the-board 15 percent consumption tax (*tukuhau ngāue'aki*, or "CT") was added in April 2005 by the state desperate to generate revenues.[2] Other circumstances contribute to the creation of what shop owners deem to be unfair competition: Small-scale *fea* traders receive their goods from relatives overseas as gifts that supplement or replace cash remittances. As a result, they can afford to sell their wares at dramatically deflated prices, in contrast to shop owners, who have to at least recoup the wholesale prices of the goods they sell. In addition, the events of 16/11 made the inherent vulnerability of shops operating in permanent buildings abundantly clear to their owners, a vulnerability to which makeshift entrepreneurs are immune.

What makes the *fea* so interesting to many people goes beyond a concern for maximizing profits and finding a bargain. First, as I discussed in the previous chapter, elites are the default owners of modernity, yet the marketplace is dominated by the nonprivileged and the socially marginal, busy claiming a stake in how modernity is to be defined and incorporated in the local context. Second, the (relatively) shabby appearance, indecorous character, disorderly social composition, and geographical marginality of the *fea* contradict the dominant association of modernity with cleanliness, order, hierarchy, and centrality. Third, the varied ways in which participants orient themselves to modernity display its multiply layered nature, which is at once moral, psychological, material, interactional, and political, despite dominant local understandings of modernity as a reasonably unified phenomenon. In short, the second-hand marketplace embodies all the complexities and contradictions that arise in the construction of modernity and of the traditional order with which it is contrasted. No wonder it is attractive.

Consumption is at the forefront of what goes on at the *fea*, and like all other instances of consumption, it is part of the social and symbolic context, rather than the simple operationalization of a rationality of cost minimization and profit maximization. "Economism" (de la Pradelle 1995) may be the ideology that agents articulate explicitly, but it is only one of the forces that shape their actions. In particular, consumption makes it possible for agents to fashion ways of thinking and acting that may diverge from and undermine the received patterns endorsed by elites, political and economic institutions, and other powerful agents. In a society that is at once on the edge of the capitalism from which consumption emanates and deeply connected to it, agents filter consumption through local tastes and moralities, but do so in ways that do not necessarily reject outright what they deem locally distasteful. In addition, different local groups and agents perform morality- and taste-imbued acts of consumption for different purposes. In this respect, consumption practices are similar to all other aspects of modernity. The "local," after all, is never as straightforward as it appears at first glance.

Nuku'alofa's Fea

Nuku'alofa's two main *fea* are located in temporary-looking sites on the fringe of town, one at Tu'imatamoana, adjacent to the harbor, the other at Tofoa, a formerly separate village huddled against the western shore of the Vai Mate lagoon, which Nuku'alofa's ever-expanding urbanization has long absorbed (Map 3.1). Speakers of English would describe the *fea* as flea markets (or "swap meets" or "car-boot sales"), as they are reminiscent of these venues in industrialized countries.[3] They offer secondhand goods alongside some new ones to customers who make participating in the *fea* an outing in which sociability figures as prominently as purchasing. Trading is active from dawn till early afternoon every Saturday of the year, and proposals to expand these hours have been vigorously opposed by the Tonga Chamber of Commerce and Industry, echoing comparable struggles between fringe trading and institutional authority in other ethnographic contexts (for example, Richard 2008; Stoller 2002). When stalls are unoccupied, they provide a convenient venue for bingo games.

Historical details about the *fea* are difficult to uncover. Like other activities of the "informal economy," no trail of official paperwork focused on secondhand trading until its popularity could no longer go unnoticed. Prior to the 1980s, the only sources of clothing were tailor shops, where clothes were made to measure, and general stores, which have always offered a limited quantity of low-quality imports. Talamahu Market, the main marketplace

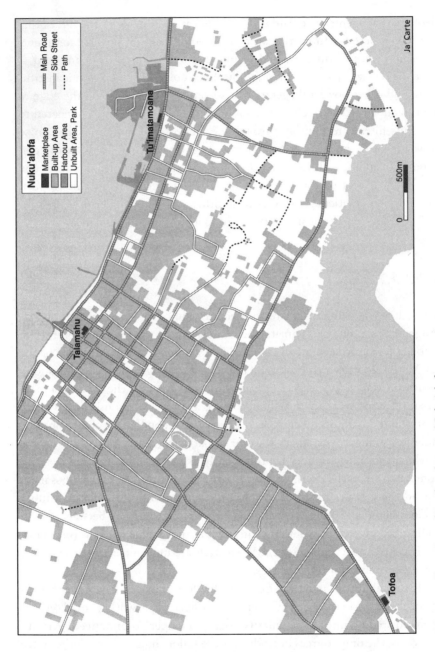

Map 3.1. Location of marketplaces in Nukuʻalofa.

Figure 3.1.   General view of the Tuʻimatamoana secondhand marketplace
(Nukuʻalofa, April 2008).

opened in 1970 in the center of Nukuʻalofa, was dedicated exclusively to the
sale of produce, principally root crops and greens. Stalls selling secondhand
clothing began cropping up in the 1980s among the produce stalls, and by
1990 their number had reached a critical mass. Market Authorities corralled
them together in a temporary location adjacent to Talamahu Market.

In 1995, the government rebuilt Talamahu Market, and during the construction period everyone was moved to a location called Tuʻimatamoana,
owned by the Port Authorities. The new two-story building in the town center was designed to house produce stalls downstairs and stalls for "handicrafts" (a category that includes ambiguously both *koloa faka-Tonga* and
tourist trinkets) upstairs. The latter, however, never became numerous,
in part because the stall rental fee was too high and in part because tourists never arrived in the hoped-for large numbers, and the goods sold upstairs soon diversified to include secondhand goods. Most *fea* stalls stayed at

Tuʻimatamoana, again because of the fees and long-term commitments that running a Talamahu Market stall demanded, although Tuʻimatamoana continues to be viewed as temporary despite its longevity. Its popularity encouraged the Market Authorities to open an additional marketplace at Tofoa in 2000, next to the tourist-oriented National Cultural Centre, already rather decrepit by then. During Emergency Rule following 16/11, Talamahu was out of bounds to citizens, and produce sellers all sought refuge in the stalls of the Tofoa market and alongside the major roadways. In 2008, many had not moved from these strategic positions, which among other things allow them to evade having to pay a daily occupancy fee to the Market Authorities.

Tongans refer to several other sites of consumption-oriented entrepreneurialism as *fea*. One is the upstairs level of the Talamahu Market, which differs from Tuʻimatamoana and Tofoa in that it operates on the same schedule as the produce marketplace, that is, from early morning till late afternoon every weekday. Also called *fea* are makeshift and temporary roadside stalls set up on the side of the road in front of homes and businesses, operated independently by traders with merchandise to sell, which appear and disappear in rapid succession around Nukuʻalofa and the island of Tonga. Neiafu, the main town of the Vavaʻu group, also has a secondhand marketplace, a much smaller version of the Nukuʻalofa *fea*.

Stalls at the two *fea*, which people refer to as *fute* (from the English unit of measure *foot*), form three to four rows, stretching lengthwise between the water and the main road, each approximately 2.5 m wide and 2 m deep. The flimsy makeshift corrugated-iron roofing held by recycled timber or metal posts that in 2001 protected the stalls from sudden weather changes had been replaced by 2008 with thick blue plastic sheeting covering almost the entire area. Traders can be anyone able to pay the daily fee that an employee of the Market Authorities comes to collect during the day: T$6.90 at Tofoa and, at Tuʻimatamoana, T$6 for a covered stall and T$4 for an uncovered one (2008 figures). Traders usually place tarpaulin sheets or rough mats over the alternatively muddy and dusty ground, on which they spread their wares. Resourceful traders also set up folding tables, folding chairs, and coolers, giving their stall a more sophisticated look than those with fewer means and less entrepreneurial flair. Customers approach the stalls from either side, unless the vendor has specifically blocked one side to give his or her stall a front and back, to conform to normative Tongan spatial organization. Vendors volunteer with little prompting the price of particular objects to customers who appear interested, and no bargaining and hawking take place, in contrast to other marketplaces around the world (for example, see Bauman 2001; Kapchan 1996; Lindenfeld 1990). Bargaining is shameful (*fakamā*) for all involved, and customers who try to bargain are not appreciated; such is the case of Chinese customers, whose propensity to do so provides Tongans yet another reason to dislike them.

I engaged in sustained observation of *fea* activities on many Saturdays during my various fieldwork periods, listened to traders and shoppers interact, conversed with them and with market officials, businesspersons, and shopkeepers in Nuku'alofa. My focus was not just on the exchange activities (that is, the exchange of goods for money) but on the context of these activities: the interactions among objects, traders, and customers; the behind-the-scenes interactions between traders and suppliers; and the continuities and differences between social action at the *fea* and social, economic, and symbolic dynamics at play in the rest of the society. In September 2000 and May–June 2008, my assistants and I administered a questionnaire-based survey to thirty and thirty-nine stall-keepers respectively, the latter leading to further interviews. My fieldwork methods were more constrained at the *fea* than in other settings in Tonga, in that participants were not always pleased about being "investigated." For example, several people turned down my requests to photograph or interview them, and I did not feel comfortable videotaping interactions at the *fea*. I will elaborate presently on the analytic significance of these responses.

Objects

Fea traders offer a very wide variety of goods for sale. Most prevalent are used clothes and shoes; household items, including tableware and cleaning products; cosmetics and other personal care items, principally shampoo, cologne, and hairclips; and food, such as root crops, cakes, and bundles of taro leaves (*la'i lū*). Also on offer are pens, sealing tape, ribbons, colored wool, jewels, rubbish bags, water bottles, wigs, gloves, stereos, tires, typewriters, fishing gear, plumbing tools and parts, electrical appliances, plastic flowers, barkcloth, mats, coconut-fiber sennit (rope), and quilts. Table 3.1 inventories six typical stalls at the start of a trading day, providing a glimpse of the variety and typical volume of the merchandise on offer, the variety of the merchandise across

TABLE 3.1.

Inventories of representative stalls, Tuʻimatamoana Fair,
October 14, 2000, (Stalls 1–4) and October 21, 2000 (Stalls 5–6).

Stall 1	Stall 2	Stall 3	Stall 4	Stall 5	Stall 6
5 pairs men's long pants	7 shirts	20 packets noodles	6 hammers	12 pairs long pants	15 pairs shorts
5 dresses	12 T-shirts	2 hair clippers	4 hammer sets	10 pairs shorts	35 dresses
15 tops	1 leather jacket	3 Gameboys	12 screwdriver sets	4 T-shirts	6 T-shirts
2 T-shirts	19 hair-bands	3 boxes washing powder	1 14-piece wrench set	2 dish racks	5 shirts
18 skirts	2 towels	2 pillows	3 hair clippers	3 outdoor baskets	4 pairs ladies' shoes
4 pairs shorts	4 children's dresses	52 pairs gloves	1 adjustable wrench set	4 hot-water bottles	5 cooking spoons
	7 skirts	11 shirts	2 4-piece chisel sets	4 medium washing tins	2 bottles perfume
	1 set fake fingernails	16 dresses	1 grinder	5 large washing tins	30 glass cups
	4 key rings	14 skirts	3 tire pumps	4 pairs tongs	4 plastic jugs
	12 pairs ladies' shoes	6 ladies' tops	6 tape measures	5 pairs sandals	5 pillows
	4 packets sweets	10 pairs ladies' underpants	1 roll sealing tape	14 packets 50-piece clothes pegs	15 ceramic saucers
	1 doll	10 bras	1 manual drill	4 large cooking spoons	15 plastic saucers
		15 baby winter suits	1 electric drill	4 small cooking spoons	1 plastic tin
		7 baby dresses	2 pairs goggles	8 cooking knives	5 toys
		15 cans soft drinks	4 pairs boxing gloves	10 mugs	8 packets drinking straws
			2 10-piece lock sets	6 small coffee cups	8 children's T-shirts
			2 carpenter tool bags	8 saucers	40 meters cloth
			5 levels	10 plastic cups	4 cooking knives
			3 5-piece plier sets	12 drinking glasses	2 glass bowls
			2 handsaws	4 ceramic bowls	4 rolls sticky tape
			2 hacksaws	6 plastic bowls	15 green coconuts
			3 crowbars	6 wine glasses	10 cobs cooked corn
			4 trowels	5 plastic jugs	10 watermelons
			3 pairs scissors	4 glass jugs	
			2 wire cutters	8 trays	
			1 25-piece hex set	4 bath brushes	
			1 8-piece hex set	4 sets clothes hangers	
				5 plastic buckets	
				6 hand towels	

and among stalls, and the range of inventories represented, from clearly specialized inventories to eclectic ones. Interspersed among the stalls offering durable objects are tables selling cooked food such as barbecued chicken and sausages, emulating small barbecue business ventures that dot the urban landscape, and coolers offering drinking coconuts and sodas.

Presentation styles vary considerably, from piles of unsorted and unfolded clothes to carefully arranged displays, with objects organized in categories as in a shop. The care with which goods are displayed reflects the trader's experience: "Regulars" who see the *fea* as a major source of income and selling as an important part of their week have had practice fine-tuning their window-dressing skills and strategize their displays self-consciously, visually foregrounding trinkets (such as toys and bubble-bath kits) that will attract customers but are not necessarily profitable or fashion styles favored by the markets they try to target (for example, young women, parents, elderly ladies). Seasoned stall-keepers tell me that they can never keep up with the demand for certain items, no matter the cost, such as fashionable black trackpants and sports shirts, hip-hop–inspired jeans and jerseys, baby clothes, warm clothing in winter, and large-size black dresses.[4]

Overwhelmingly, stall-keepers at the *fea* obtain merchandise they have obtained from overseas relatives. Ninety percent of respondents in the 2000 survey and 87 percent in the 2008 survey identified relatives as the origin of at least some of their merchandise.[5] Shoppers come to the *fea* with the explicitly articulated expectation that they will be able to buy merchandise otherwise difficult to find or expensive in Tonga. Most goods are brought in from the Continental United States and Hawai'i (60 percent of the stall-keepers in the 2000 survey and 69 percent in the 2008 survey identified their merchandise as primarily of American provenance), reflecting both the residence of traders' relatives and the fact that many shoppers view goods from the United States as particularly desirable. Other goods come from New Zealand (40 percent in 2000, 64 percent in 2008) and Australia (13 percent in 2000, 15 percent in 2008). Traders extract merchandise from multiple networks located in several countries, which explains why the percentages exceed 100 percent.

In Chapter Two, I stressed the importance of remittances for the survival of island-based households. Since the 1980s, however, overseas Tongans have gradually supplemented or sometimes replaced cash gifts with shipments of merchandise, and this merchandise forms the bulk of what is on offer at the *fea*. The marketplace and its merchandise are deeply embedded in structures of kinship relations, sustaining social relations over increasingly wider geographical areas.[6]

Kinship categories that survey respondents mentioned most frequently as the source of merchandise were women's sisters (nine out of thirty in 2000, nine out of thirty-nine in 2008) and women's brothers (seven out of thirty in 2000, eight out of thirty-nine in 2008). The prominence of the former reflects expectations of mutual care (*feʻofoʻofaʻaki*) between sisters, while the prominence of the latter is a reflection of the obligations that men have to their sisters for the duration of their lifetime because of their lower rank. Gifts of marketable goods are part of long-term and large-scale systems of delayed reciprocity. Sixty-three percent of survey respondents in 2000 (41 percent in 2008) indicated that, in return for merchandise, they sent to their relatives *koloa faka-Tonga* "Tongan valuables" (plaited mats and processed barkcloth), which are in particularly great demand in overseas Tongan communities, where the raw material is unavailable and few people would have the time anyway to devote to the time-consuming task of manufacturing them. Some respondents also send their overseas-based relatives coolers of fish and lobsters or cartons of cooked taro and yams. The goods offered for sale can thus have a circuitous career, from commodity to gift to commodity, and they illustrate the complex interplay between both kinds of exchange.

Tongans in the diaspora obtain the merchandise from a variety of sources, including flea markets, garage sales, Salvation Army shops, and discount stores. Those with time on their hands strategize their purchases, looking out for sales in newspapers or combing opportunity racks for end-of-season bargains. They project what will sell well in Tonga, exercising abstract consumer-imagination skills. One trader in 2000 explained to me that her brother worked for an insurance company in New Zealand, which gave him the opportunity to purchase at low cost the contents of fire-damaged homes, the salvageable portion of which he sent to her. In a minority of cases, the merchandise on display is the result of calculated entrepreneurial activity, as I will illustrate presently. A small but conspicuous number of stalls sell merchandise that clearly "fell off the back of a truck" into the hands of Tongan employees of manufacturing companies in industrial countries. For example, for several weeks in the middle of 2000, a stall was offering cosmetics of a well-known high-end brand for a fraction of their normal cost. The otherwise very forthcoming traders became notably evasive when I asked her about the origin of the goods. Tongans and other Pacific Islanders in New Zealand are sometimes apprehended for hoarding illegally obtained goods. One Samoan cleaner, for example, was arrested in 1998 for regularly emptying the lost-and-found box and supply shelves of the public swimming pool where she worked in Wellington, New Zealand; her home was filled with mobile phones and stacks of toilet paper she was planning to send to her island-based relatives.

Overseas Tongans send the merchandise through a variety of means, including sea or air cargo. Some bring the goods as excess luggage when they travel back to Tonga. Recipients generally manage to evade import duties by clearing their goods, for example, during the work shift of a relative employed by the Department of Customs, who will come away from the transaction with a fashionable pair of jeans or two.[7] A few entrepreneurs obtain their goods on their own, benefiting from various factors such as the ability to travel overseas at relatively low cost thanks to a close relative who is employed by an airline company or as part of larger import–export ventures.

The characterization of *fea* merchandise as imports must be mitigated in several ways. First, some *fea* merchandise is quintessentially local, such as the produce (such as bundles of taro leaves or *la'i lu*) that some traders sell. Such is also the case of textile valuables for ritual prestation (*koloa faka-Tonga*), which are now also deeply embedded in the monetized sphere of the economy, both locally and transnationally (Figure 3.2). Other items, such as cakes, are locally manufactured with imported ingredients (for example, flour and sugar). Handicrafts and souvenirs, offered as Tongan products to tourists and Western expats, may or may not be manufactured locally; one prominent dealer occasionally sells large wooden bowls used to mix kava (*kumete*), which he imports from Fiji, as there are very few kava-bowl carvers left in Tonga.

More dramatically, objects with local attachments of one type or other are often the product of multisited manufacture, adding further complexity to the simple characterization of the offerings of the *fea* as either local or not. One stall, for example, offers cotton T-shirts with a large screen-print of Tonga's national seal, a ubiquitous symbol. The traders identified the T-shirts, of interest to both Tongan and overseas customers, as "American" (although the manufacturer's label specified a familiar range of offshore origins, from Indonesia to Mexico) and explained that relatives in Hawai'i screen-printed them from a stencil manufactured in Tonga. Another trader

Figure 3.2.   Yardage of quality barkcloth for sale at Tuʻimatamoana, alongside imported secondhand clothing (April 2008).

has an aunt in California who is a skillful maker of sennit (*kafa*). The stallkeeper extracts raw fiber from the husk of aged coconuts (*pulu*), boils it to satisfy U.S. agricultural regulations, and sends it to her aunt in California, who returns the plaited sennit for sale in Tonga. Yet another stall attracted much attention in early September 2000: Displayed for sale were several women's formal tasseled fiber belts (*kiekie*), intricately crafted in this case with lace, sequins, and imitation pearls, designed to be worn during the *Sepitema*, or annual festival held by the various Christian denominations in September during which women of the congregation offer money and other valuables to the pastor. These particular belts had been manufactured in Lāʻie, Hawaiʻi, by Mormon relatives of the trader (ironically, the LDS Church is one Christian denomination that does not hold a *Sepitema*).

These examples illustrate two points. First, objects commodified or recommodified at the *fea* have had a complex history before they appear under the makeshift awnings of the marketplaces, and this history is embedded in what constitutes them as objects offered for sale. In this respect, of course, they do not differ from many other types of objects in other societies (cf. Hansen 2000). Second, the history of objects embodies narratives of Tongan transnationalism and diasporic dispersal. No longer can local objects, such as coconut fiber sennit, T-shirts emblazoned with symbols of the nation-state, and women's church festival girdles ever be assumed to be "local" in any straightforward sense, that is, assumed to be made in Tonga from Tongan raw materials by Tongan hands. No longer can the flow of goods be assumed to be unidirectional, with "foreign" goods travelling from the diaspora to the islands and "local" goods following a reverse trail. Of course, the complex interplay of the local and nonlocal in the production of "local" objects and symbols is not a new phenomenon. As discussed in Chapter Two, Tongans since precontact days have incorporated objects, practices, and people from surrounding Polynesian groups into local structures. What is novel is the extent to which localness is today produced through the interplay of the local and the transnational.

Traders

Owners of the merchandise usually operate their own *fea* stalls, although relatives and friends often keep them company and help out with transportation and sales.[8] Traders uniformly report that they come to the *fea* to make money. However, they also state that their trading successes are uneven. Sales volume is seasonal, Christmastime being high season, and it differs greatly from stall to stall. The gross sales income among the twenty-five traders in the 2000 survey who reported being at the *fea* in the prior week averages T$119, with a T$8–300 range (s.d. = 82), and among the twenty-nine traders in the same situation in 2008, T$407, with a T$54–1400 range (s.d. = 318). These figures compare favorably with the weekly salaries of public or private sector employees in the same years (for example, around $100 for a service-industry worker in 2008), but it is also highly variable. What is notable is the extent to which the income of *fea* traders has increased over the eight years (assuming the representative nature of the two surveys and the reliability of self-reports), an increase that the significant drop in the value of Tongan currency in the intervening years cannot solely account for.[9]

Traders come from diverse backgrounds but also present some commonalities, best illustrated through a few portraits. Sēini, who prefers to be called

"Jane" (of which "Sēini" is the Tongan-language equivalent), is a forty-five-year-old resident of the San Francisco Bay Area, where she holds a good professional job, and an LDS Church adherent. Around 2000, she came to Tonga twice a year to visit her elderly parents and seventeen-year-old first-born daughter, whom she had left in Tonga to take care of the latter. She also timed the visit during which we met to enable her to attend her high-school reunion. Born in Tonga and speaking both English and Tongan with ease, her presentation of self is unmistakably that of an overseas-based Tonga: Clad in a fashionable rugby shirt and a visor with "Fiji" emblazoned across it, she is forthcoming and gregarious in an inimitable California style. All of her siblings except one have married foreigners. She speaks of the difficulties of flying from San Francisco to Tonga on the limited annual leave available to her, which she manages to extend by swapping duties with colleagues, and self-assuredly compares various airlines and routes (at the time, via Honolulu versus Nadi versus Auckland) for convenience, frequency, fares, and cost of excess baggage. The latter is important: In order to finance her trips to Tonga, she brings the goods she has accumulated in California throughout the year as part of her luggage, paying excess-baggage charges. Jane is a good example of temporary overseas-based *fea* stall-keepers: She radiates an air of cosmopolitanism and is at ease with a multisited lifestyle, embodying the "flexible citizenship" (Ong 1999) of the typical diasporic subject. Like comparable agents in many other parts of the world (for example, Freeman 2001; Konstantinov 1996; Ribeiro 2009), her activities as tourist, family woman, church member, and worker articulate with one another in mutually supportive ways.

'Ofa, in her 50s, also a Mormon, operates a permanent stall on the upper floor of Talamahu in addition to trading on Saturdays at Tu'imatamoana. She "commutes" between Tonga and Inglewood in Southern California (a city with a large Tongan population), spending several months at a time in each location, leaving her stall in the care of a relative when she is in the United States. Her husband and children are all overseas, and she returns to Tonga to take care of her own family, particularly her elderly parents, but also for the explicit purpose of reselling goods.[10] She also transports her merchandise in her luggage, but her trading activities are ongoing, large-scale, and informed by explicit business plans. One of the pioneers in the traffic in consumer goods, she is an astute entrepreneur, but in 2000 she spoke longingly of the days when fewer people engaged in the trade and when sales were consequently brisker and resale prices higher (*kuo holo e fea*, "the fair is not what it used to be"), a complaint that I would frequently hear in 2008. Less cosmopolitan in demeanor than Jane, 'Ofa nevertheless represents another type of transnational Tongan, whose life is materially grounded in both Tonga and California and for whom the *fea* has become a goal in itself, rather than a means to finance airfares.

Traders who engage in complex operations like 'Ofa constitute a small but noticeable minority. Their strategies vary widely, as does the relative importance of selling at the *fea* in the range of trading activities in which they engage. For example, Pita, a member of the mainstream Church of Tonga, bought new shoes in 2000 from a wholesaler in Mainland China, with whom he corresponds with the help of his *Pālangi* son-in-law, and sold them for an appreciable profit to supplement his earnings as a taxi driver. With the benefit of a historical perspective that was lacking back in 2000, Pita emerges as one of the pioneering brokers of the growing importance of the PRC in the local retail scene. In some cases, the *fea* stall is only one of many activities for a particular entrepreneur. The case of Viliami, a "fallen" Mormon and highly visible small-scale entrepreneur, is particularly informative. His stall at the *fea*, to which he attends personally on a sporadic basis, offers different types of goods at different times, depending on his international travel itinerary. He frequently travels to Fiji and Hawai'i with handicrafts for the substantial tourist markets (barkcloth and mat products, wood carvings, bone jewelry), touting them at destination as Fijian, Hawaiian, or "Polynesian" objects, and returns home with T-shirts and other items of clothing that appeal to Tongans and the fledgling tourist market. His home is crammed with raw handicraft materials, *koloa faka-Tonga*, and consumer goods, and doubles as a sweatshop in which half a dozen young female employees make and decorate barkcloth, which they then cut up into small pieces to be packaged as tablemats and coasters. In 2001, I would encounter these objects for sale in the gift shop of the National Museum of Ethnology in Osaka, Japan, signed in the back by Viliami, "Polynesian artist," regardless of the fact that barkcloth manufacture is the exclusive domain of women.

'Ēseta illustrates the case of stall-keepers who utilize both kinship and friendship ties to obtain goods. A member of a small charismatic Christian group with strong overseas ties, which in 2000 included several American missionaries, 'Ēseta, in her thirties, has resided in a Western country in the past but does not travel much now. Like many other traders, she specializes in secondhand clothing. She receives most of the clothes as remittances from overseas-based relatives and gifts from fellow church members, her family in Christ. She and her children wear some for a while before selling them at the *fea*. She enjoys trading, which she does with a pleasant and unassuming demeanor, and finds her trading activities a convenient way of making a living, as it does not tie her to a specific schedule and allows her to attend to family or church activities when needed, echoing a theme that many other traders articulate. (We will encounter 'Ēseta again in Chapter Eight.)

Several sociological generalizations emerge among traders and customers. The most important is the predominance of women among them. This predominance superficially resembles similar patterns found in societies characterized by intensive labor emigration in which women are left behind while men move, and consequently seek out economic, social, and symbolic resources in marketplaces (for example, Kintz 1998). However, in Tonga, both women and men migrate, and while women come to the *fea* to convert nonmonetary gifts from relatives into cash, these gifts originate equally from sisters and brothers (and only marginally from husbands). Thus the Nuku'alofa *fea* is not the product of gendered demographics or exchange patterns in any simple way.

More compelling explanations for the gendering of the *fea* are two factors that have been reported of very diverse societies around the world. The first is the flexibility of marketplace trading. Cross-culturally, the marketplace is often one of the few sites of the economic sphere open to and dominated by women because it provides time flexibility of a kind not offered by other activities, thus allowing traders to attend to kinship and other demands as they arise without jeopardizing trade.[11] Many informants at the *fea* made reference to this advantage: Children, relatives, church activities, funerals, weddings, and other obligations often take precedence over other activities, including income-generating work, particularly on Saturdays. In contrast to waged employment in the labor market, which is easily jeopardized by repeated absences for "personal" reasons, successful trading at the *fea* is not contingent on holding a stall every Saturday. Indeed, among traders who took part in the surveys, a significant number reported not being at the *fea* in the two weeks preceding the survey (17 percent in 2000, 26 percent in 2008). Unlike other income-generating activities, trading at the *fea* allows women to juggle obligations steeped in a traditional order with income-generating activities steeped in a modern order.

The second factor is the cross-cultural association of women with consumption practices and ideologies. Witness for example the way in which women in the postindustrial world have appropriated, with the active encouragement of consumer society, the image of the consuming self more readily than men, having been excluded from cultivating self-worth through wage employment. In Tonga, many women are employed in government, church, and private enterprise, although their numbers thin out as one goes up the employment hierarchy. In addition, women being disqualified from land ownership has meant that they have not benefited directly from export agriculture booms. For many women, trading at the *fea* may be more advantageous economically than salaried employment in the public or private sector, or in certain cases it figures as a parallel activity that some women engage in alongside employment. Perhaps of equal importance is the fact that *fea* trading is pleasurable: As I will discuss presently, many women at the *fea* define themselves as modern persons, in reference to a modernity that embraces consumption as one of its defining cornerstones, an embracement that may be operationalized through either the role of trader (that is, as agent of others' consumption) or customer (that is, as consuming self). The symbolic association of women with consumption, mediated by modernity, is a useful way of contextualizing the predominance of women at the *fea*.

Another important characteristic of the composition of *fea* traders is the over-representation of fringe sociological categories. Church affiliation is a significant index of many aspects of identity. As I discuss in Chapter Eight, the most mainstream religiously defined category of "local Other" is the LDS Church, whose adherents comprised 14 percent of the country's population at the 2000 national census and 17 percent at the 2006 national census. My 2000 random marketplace survey identified over twice the then-current total percentage, and the same exercise in 2008 identified 23 percent LDS church members. This overrepresentation is explained in part by the greater likelihood that an LDS adherent will have relatives in the diaspora, given the active role that the Church plays in facilitating emigration. The reasons, however, are not just social but also cultural: Mormonism is the religion of capitalist modernity par excellence, and its overrepresentation among marketplace traders (as well as pawnshop operators, as explained in Chapter Four) reflects the marketplace's centralization of both capitalist accumulation and projects of modernity.

Evangelical Catholics, Pentecostal and charismatic Christians, and members of other fringe denominations are also overrepresented compared to other contexts, and greatly increased between the 2000 and 2008 surveys. Miscellaneous forms of social liminality that are prominent at the *fea* but are not symbolized by a particular religious affiliation include small-scale entrepreneurs, who often express impatience with forms of prestation and exchange branded as "traditional." Viliami, for example, is an unusual individual in Tonga for being in his forties and unmarried; over lunch, he explains that marrying is too onerous for his taste because a wife's relatives are a financial burden on a successful husband. This kind of stance constructs an image of a traditional order that showcases its burdensome and constraining qualities and sidelines positive features like reciprocity and sociality.[12]

Similarly, traders often distance themselves, in one way or another, from the negative connotations that many Tongans still attach to selling goods, particularly used items. In the traditional order, selling used items is stigmatized as a sign that one is so poor or poorly connected that one had to sell one's belongings to survive and is seen as a problematic cause of *mā* "shame," dynamics that also color the pawning of *koloa faka-Tonga* (Chapter Four). Many traders have decided that they are immune to this emotion and thus place themselves on the margin of the "structure of feelings" associated with tradition but at the same time risking criticism and marginalization for lacking decorum and dignity (compare Rasmussen 2003: 13 on Tuareg transnational artisans).

At the far end of the spectrum of Otherness among *fea* traders are Chinese immigrants, some of whom also own shops in town. Their stalls are invariably larger, better organized, and more specialized than the average Tongan stall, indexing the explicitly and exclusively entrepreneurial motivation of their presence in Tonga. The overall sociological composition of traders therefore imbues the *fea* with an otherness and marginality that I will elaborate when I describe the social practices that take place there.

Fea traders contrast in a number of ways with shopkeepers trading in the center of town. With the exception of the Chinese, there is little overlap between the two groups; in 2000 one shopkeeper asserted that, if he were to set up a stall at the *fea*, fellow retail business owners would have ostracized him. (By 2008, his downtown business had closed down.) Shopkeepers operate a number of permanent commercial establishments in Nuku'alofa, from the roadside *fale koloa* that I described in Chapter Two to supermarkets selling a wide variety of food and nonconsumables, some specializing in hardware, baked goods, or clothing. A few run shops that offer consumer goods (such as hand-painted T-shirts, golf and tennis equipment, hip-hop fashion) to tourists, visiting overseas Tongans, and members of the elite, but at prices well beyond the reach of the average citizen. The more prominent shopkeepers share one characteristic with *fea* traders, namely the fact that they are also predominantly local others: returned migrants, established entrepreneurs with important commercial interests, LDS adherents, part-European descendants of nineteenth-century traders, long-term Fiji Indian residents, and recent Chinese immigrants. However, except for Chinese immigrants, their otherness is more mainstream and privileged than that of *fea* traders: Many shopkeepers are part of elite circles, of which membership in the Chamber of Commerce and Industry is a clear index. Non-Chinese shopkeepers see *fea* traders as threatening not just their commercial interests but also their status as privileged if marginal members of the Tongan establishment.

Customers

Almost everyone in Tonga shops at the *fea*, from the occasional member of the royal family to the low ranking, from wealthy persons to the indigent, from urban sophisticates to villagers, from locally grounded people to returned migrants, tourists, and expats. Because it offers something of interest to everyone, from hip-hop fashion for male teenagers to large-size mourning clothes for elderly women, the *fea* is a great social leveler. Unlike most other contexts of social life in Tonga, it appeals to both Tongans and foreigners: "There is nothing like this in New Zealand," affirmed a Kiwi contract-worker couple in 2000, shopping for clothing to send to their children at boarding school in their home country.

Many customers do not come to the *fea* to buy anything specific. They characterize their trips to the *fea* as an outing (*'eve'eva*) with their spouse or family, during which they are likely to run into friends and relatives. Time spent at the *fea* is "free time," and because this free time is occupied by consumption practices, it embeds customers into a modern lifestyle in which consumption is easily transformed into pleasure and vice versa (Appadurai 1996: 79–83). Customers do not seek to cultivate the kinds of long-term trading partnerships that are so consequential in markets in other parts of the world (Plattner 1989: 210–214), although both groups view socialization over a transaction as an important component of what the *fea* is for. What they see in the *fea* is a place to practice consumption: browse (*siosio pē*), hunt for bargains, compare, and rummage through knick-knacks.

This approach differs from the way customers approach shopping in most Nuku'alofa shops. Many smaller shops are physically designed to discourage browsing, displaying merchandise on shelves separated from the reach of customers by a counter and a narrow corridor where the shopkeeper stands or sits. After 16/11, some shopkeepers (mostly Chinese) turned this design into veritable fortified structures with heavy metal bars keeping customers at bay (look back at Figure 2.5). Even in larger shops with open stacks, browsing customers are often not made to feel welcome (unless they know the shopkeepers), as employees and security guards keep a close watch on their movements. Patrons are expected to know what they need, buy it, and leave. Trying on clothes is difficult. In other words, the acquisition of merchandise at the *fea* and in shops are radically divergent activities, and many shoppers talk about the *fea* as being the only place in Tonga where they can "shop," that is, practice what the self-as-consumer expects to perform: making consumption the central focus of its activities; sensually apprehending objects through touch, smell, and sight; and finding pleasure in desiring, imagining, and acquiring. Furthermore, many shoppers indicated that one of the main motivations for coming to the *fea* was to see and buy goods otherwise not available or affordable. For these shoppers, the *fea* offers goods that enable them, through browsing and acquiring, to maintain a link with a desirable world that transcends the boundaries of the local context. The *fea* thus emerges as a key meeting point between the local and the nonlocal, a prime locus of the practice of bifocality that characterizes modern lives on the edge of the global.

Practicing Modernity

These remarks indicate that the *fea* represents for its participants a great deal more than the simple exchange of merchandise for money but has a host of other meanings for everyone involved, meanings that its enormous popularity suggests as particularly attractive to a broad cross-section of the society. I approach the problem by analyzing interactional vignettes representative of the kind of social practices that participants engage in at the *fea*. Certain semiotic forms operate at the *fea* in particularly dense form that showcases the marketplaces as one of several distinctly modern sites in the society. It is through the repeated co-occurrence of these semiotic forms that the *fea* acquires its particular social and cultural meaning.

In addition to interacting with objects, *fea* participants interact with one another, and informants emphasize the importance of pleasantness and sociability in what attracts them to the *fea*. Customers and traders perform this sociability, for example, by focusing on the objects on display and engaging in detailed talk about fashion, as in the following brief conversation, recorded in August 2000, between two acquaintances:

Trader:	*Sai ia kia koe, Sōnia.*
	"Looks good on you, Sōnia."
Customer:	Yeah- if it fits =
Trader:	((ignoring customer's contingency)) = Ni::ce. (10.0) What size is it?
	(2.0)
Customer:	Eight.
	(3.0)
Trader:	Ohh. (4.0) Too small. (2.0) *'E hao ia 'ia Mālia.* (2.0) *'Ia me'a.*
	"It'll fit Mālia. I mean, what's-her-name."
	(2.0)
	It's might fit you, cuz it looks big!
Customer:	*'Io?*
	"Yes?"
Trader:	Yeah! (2.0) The waist, look!
Customer:	I know-
Trader:	I think it's one of those one that it has to show the belly button.
Customer:	No way!
Trader:	Aaaha-ha-haa!
Customer:	.Haa-ha-hah!
Trader:	That's the in-thing in New Zealand now. Even my kids say, "Mummy, see, it has to show the b-!" Huh! I say, "No::::, no::!" Ahahahuh-hh! Cuz that's the look now!

[Tu'imatamoana, disk 1, 1:47:55-48:47]

This transcript offers a wealth of fascinating details about the modern ambience of the marketplace. The trader begins by presenting a "sales pitch" of a kind rarely heard in other locations and then seizes the opportunity to display her awareness of what's fashionable in New Zealand and hence her worldliness. The shopper comments on the problematic implementation of the foreign style she describes because leaving body parts like belly buttons exposed would be considered highly indecorous in Tonga, despite the gradual trend to wear less among the cosmopolitan youth (Addo 2003; Helu 1999: 288–292). The trader agrees, albeit in what appears to be a face-saving afterthought, and together they construct a body of worldly knowledge about fashion and perform their familiarity with the symbols constituting this knowledge, while also asserting their prerogative to evaluate the local appropriateness of these symbols, carefully monitoring each other's stances. At the end of the excerpt, the trader ascribes to herself and her children an interaction that sounds distinctly modern, one in which children negotiate parents' benign authority over how they should dress in a good-natured tone that emphasizes egalitarianism, in contrast to the slap-happy authoritarianism of parental authority in village contexts. Both trader and customer emerge as cosmopolitan agents, who nevertheless remain grounded in local norms of appropriateness. Tongan women engage in similar talk in other venues, such as the beauty parlor and the seamstress' studio, but one certainly does not talk this way in shops in town.

A notable feature of the conversational excerpt is language choice. Despite two switches to Tongan, most of the interaction is in English, including the directly reported exchange between the trader as mother and her children. While urban Tongans would characterize language choice in this instance (and others like it) as being a personal matter of no consequence, the timing of the code manipulation, its intersubjective negotiation, and its occurrence in the context of the marketplace all suggest a different analysis. Precisely because agents see them as ideologically inconsequential, while they index at the same time a larger historical, political, and cultural context, these microscopic aspects of communication are intensely meaningful (cf. Irvine and Gal 2000; Woolard and Schieffelin 1994).

Grounded in the equivocally colonial past but today more specifically linked to the diaspora, English is the prestige language in Tonga, where it dominates contexts of employment, education, modernity, transnationalism, and new forms of socioeconomic hegemony such as entrepreneurship. However, English "belongs" primarily to the elites, who are intimate with the privilege and cosmopolitanism that the language indexes. In contrast, many nonprivileged Tongans were until recently reluctant to speak English, ostensibly, according to explanations offered, because they fear making linguistic mistakes. In practice, their reluctance is not so much a matter of defective grammatical competence or of being (to use a Tongan friend's priceless characterization) "hurry mouth no grammar" but of not having the social self-assurance to assert oneself credibly as a privileged, modern, and cosmopolitan person without fearing shame (*mā*) and exposing oneself to ridicule. Being an enthusiastic user of English risks being taken as evidence of harboring cosmopolitan pretensions that appear to others to seek to obliterate one's Tonganness, often referred to as *fie Pālangi* "pretending or wanting to be a Westerner," the reverse of what identity-anxious diasporic Tongans refer to as "Tongan pride" (Chapter Two). The dividing line between being "appropriately" modern and *fie Pālangi* is very thin and subject to shifting interpretations.

In this interactional fragment, neither trader nor customer seems particularly concerned with these fears, even though the trader's English displays some of the features typical of broadly accented Pacific Island English, as in "*It's* might fit you" and "one of those one that *it* has to show." The two women are far from unique in their choice of language; while conducting my survey of stall-keepers, I encountered occasional difficulties filling out the questionnaire that I had written out in Tongan when certain respondents insisted on speaking to me only in English. Unlike most other contexts of Tongan social life, the *fea* is a context in which people who are primarily speakers of Tongan interact in English, thereby contributing to its saliently modern and cosmopolitan flavor.

Of additional interest in the conversation fragment is the fact that the trader not only speaks English but also pronounces certain words with an exaggerated New Zealand accent (which I have not transcribed in the above). For example, she renders the first vowel sound of "Zealand" as the central vowel [ə] (schwa, that is, the phonetic value of short unstressed vowels in standard English, such as the last vowel of the word "Zealand"). The phonetic centralization of certain vowels is a characteristic specific to New Zealand English (Bauer 1994), but it is principally the short lax vowel [ɪ] (as in "kid") that can be rendered as such; the first long high tense vowel [iː] is only sometimes centralized in a word like "Zealand" in the speech of very "local" New Zealanders. The trader's linguistic behavior is an example of what sociolinguists call "hypercorrection," which has long been documented in industrial societies as an index of a variety of interrelated sociocultural attributes, including weak solidarity with members of one's own social group and the yearning to be perceived as aligned with a social group that the speaker considers to be socially desirable. Through her exaggerated pronunciation, the trader communicates to others that she is familiar with the subtleties of New Zealand English and, by the same token, with all that the dialect stands for in Tonga, including a certain transnational sophistication and a familiarity with urban modernity. She also distances herself from Tongan-accented English (with some difficulty at the level of syntax) and all that it represents in the New Zealand context, including the stigma of being an underclass "F.O.B." ("Fresh Off the Boat") Pacific Islander, who never centralize their vowels. More subtly, she presents herself not just as part of the context that stigmatizes accented English but also as part of those who do the stigmatizing.[13]

Other *fea* participants express comparable desires to distance themselves from structures of emotions and social arrangements that are branded as "traditional" in other contexts. Such is the case of Viliami, whom I introduced earlier, who expresses an unusual lack of interest in marriage on account of the obligations that marriage imposes on a successful man. In all cases, traders accomplish a number of social acts, which become related to one another in structures of congruence and opposition: They define themselves, albeit in different ways, as modern entities who are aware of a cosmopolitan world of possibilities beyond the strictures of locality and tradition; and they distance themselves, symbolically and materially, from social stances that mainstream Tongan society values, such as *fai fatongia*, "performing duty," and *fua kavenga*, "bearing burden." In a similar vein, an interviewee at the *fea* expresses her impatience with Tongans' poverty by attributing it to their laziness, a theme that commonly surfaces in conversations among privileged Tongans or in privileged sites:

> *Trader:* The Tongan are lazy. I always say that, the Tongan are poor because
> they are lazy, no one should be poor here in Tonga. They should be
> all wealthy, but because they are lazy, they can't even plant a taro. You
> know my home, I plant taro, I plant a- banana, I plant a *lesi* [papaya],
> everything I like, I plant. And now we eat it now. See, the people can't
> seems to- I don't know, it's very hard to dig up something to plant
> something? Naah!
>
> [Tu'imatamoana, disk 1, 1:25:30-26:01]

This kind of rationalization echoes colonial discourses of yesteryear as well as contemporary anti-immigrant discourses in countries such as New Zealand. In Tonga, it echoes the discourse of *fiemālie* that I discussed in Chapter Two, which valorizes "laziness" and can be expressed by the very same people who express impatience with "Tongan laziness" (in addition to the reliance, in both discourses, on the long-suffering papaya). But at the *fea* the discourse of laziness acquires particular salience in conjunction with the modernity that participants construct, a modernity that they contrast with a tradition defined by burdensome obligation and thwarted agency.

Finally, *fea* participants self-consciously position themselves in a modern world that is particularly characteristic of this site. I mentioned earlier some of the hurdles I encountered conducting fieldwork at the *fea*. Traders and customers were reticent about being interviewed, photographed, and researched with a frequency that I have rarely encountered elsewhere in Tonga. I felt that videotaping, for example, fell outside the bounds of propriety. While many participants granted me permission to take photographs, a significant number turned down my requests, a rather unusual response in Tonga. In 2000, one woman barbecuing chicken parts for sale became quite irate (in English) when I asked her (in Tongan) whether I could take her picture, possibly being well aware of the Western journalistic appetite for images of Tongans that perpetrate puerilizing stereotypes of a food-obsessed, obese (as she was), but quaint people. Tongans are anxious about decorum and face, but this concern in most contexts takes other Tongans as a primary frame of reference. In specifically modern sites, however, this concerns becomes bifocal, as it supplements the broader modern world to the locally judgmental context, in this case represented by an inquisitive fieldworker or the possibility of having one's likeness portrayed and circulated in an unfavorable light. The bifocal self-consciousness that many exhibit at the *fea* is congruent with the explicitly modern design of the setting.

The meaning of the *fea* resides at the convergence of a series of dynamics that operate simultaneously through the social practices and symbolic structures that permeate the setting. The *fea* is designed as a site of modernity, in which the consumption-oriented self is defined through the outside world and its material and symbolic resources, or at least the awareness of these resources and of their local relevance, and a bifocal self-consciousness of Tongans' role in the context of a larger world. Participants in the *fea* talk of tradition as more constraining than enabling, and some position themselves in opposition to this traditional order yet reserve the right to select the resources of modernity that they wish to call their own. I am not claiming that the discourses of the self and social practices at the *fea* are consistent because different participants define modernity in potentially divergent ways. Nor am I claiming that what takes place at the *fea* is unique within Tongan society or that it constitutes a complete rupture in time and space. Indeed, one also hears in other contexts that traditional forms of prestation are burdensome, that poor Tongans are poor because they are lazy, and that displaying one's belly button may be in fashion in New Zealand but not Tonga; adherents of the LDS Church are overrepresented in other contexts I analyze in other chapters; and, with increasing frequency, Tongans outside the *fea* are heard speaking English to one another, ignoring the risk of ridicule. Nevertheless, it is the convergence of these symbols and practices, as well as their prominence at the *fea* (that is, the ease with which they can be witnessed or elicited) that provides a particular flavor to the *fea* and places it in a specific relationship to the rest of Tongan society, characterized by both continuity and rupture, and the analytic meaning I give to "practicing" seeks to capture the resulting tentativeness that permeates the setting. Yet social practices witnessed at the *fea* all focus on similar dilemmas: reconciling the potential contradictions between the local and the global, and positioning the self vis-à-vis traditional and modern orders through the active construction of tradition and modernity. Agents opt for different "solutions" to these dilemmas, which range from finding a bargain to finding Jesus, making a profit, and embedding oneself into a larger world.

The *fea* emerges as a context in which segments of the society negotiate their encounter with the rest of the world through the mediation of absent diasporic relations. The encounter is material because objects constitute the focus of participants' attention, but it is also ideational, in that it foregrounds matters of morality, selfhood, and desirability. In addition, participants use this encounter to actively engage in selecting, transforming, and localizing objects and symbols. Shoppers and traders want certain things from the West, from modernity, and from their diasporic relatives, but not others. The encounter is thus one of negotiation and is illustrative of the agency with which many on the world periphery approach their engagement with modernity.

A theme I have stressed but not explained is the *fea*'s marginality to the Tongan social order. The sites are marginal in a literal sense: They are as far from the center of town as one can be without leaving the urban area. They are also on the fringe because of their shabbiness, indecorous character, and temporary appearance, on muddy or dusty sites (depending on the season) and under makeshift awnings that barely shelter traders, customers, and objects in the event of a downpour. The liminality goes further. As I have demonstrated, the *fea* attract the socially marginal, the disaffected, and those who have turned their back on the system. The marketplaces are great social levelers, and participants leave the potentially stifling hierarchy and the social gulf between local and foreigner at the entrance. The *fea* are also the result of a creative approach to the law because most objects are imported through the back door and the origin of some is even a little suspect. These characteristics contrast with hegemonic versions of modernity in Tongan society, which associate modernity with cleanliness, discipline, centrality, and respect for the law, and conflate it with modernization, free-market rationalization, and development, a process with which development-studies approaches to the marketplaces have been complicit (in ways of which the scholars involved are probably completely oblivious).

Despite their popularity, the marketplaces are subtly subversive of the social order, and I venture that it is precisely this covertly subversive role that makes them popular. Modernity in Tonga is, at first glance, the prerogative of the elites, both traditional (that is, the high-ranking) and modern (the wealthy), many of whom belong to mainstream religious denominations, have everything to gain from the maintenance of hierarchy, and believe in carefully managed development and modernization. The elites are those who control the flow of material and symbolic resources brought in from the outside, travel extensively, flaunt their consumption and cosmopolitanism, manage the country's commercial activities through the Chamber of Commerce and Industry, and switch to English whenever they feel like it. By partaking actively in a marketplace on the fringe that nevertheless links them directly to the modern world, the social marginals who are overrepresented at the *fea*, as well as everyone else who is attracted to it, quietly challenge the elite's control of modernity and its relevance to the local context and of the tradition that they construct in contrast to modernity. Under the guise of being a benign source of consumer pleasure seeking and small-scale capitalist entrepreneurial venture, the *fea* provides a context through which Tongans of more or less disadvantaged or marginal status can claim a say in what constitutes modernity and what constitutes tradition and negotiate their place in the interstices. At the same time that they seek an active engagement with the outside world through the *fea*, traders and customers are quietly commenting on local structures of inequality that allow the low-ranking and poor precious few opportunities to voice their discontent. It is precisely the marginality of the *fea* that gives it centrality in people's lives, for it affords them a voice they cannot claim in more mainstream venues. Except perhaps in the events of 16/11, which were quickly repressed, as Scott (1990) would have predicted.

Consumption and Cosmopolitanism

Nuku'alofa's secondhand marketplaces are liminal sites on the geographical and social map, yet they also loom prominently in the society's economic, social, and cultural life. As a buffer zone between modernity and tradition, between the diaspora and the homeland, and between the outside world and Tonga, the *fea* are where the boundaries between these contrasting categories are placed under scrutiny and argued over, both benignly and stridently. Not surprisingly, its dramatis personae are dominated by locally marginals, who seek out this buffer zone for various reasons: Because it helps them deal with their own marginality it provides them with a raison d'être of one form or another, or it recentralizes them in Tongan society. Furthermore, the *fea* are the stage of a subtle but unmistakable struggle between elite and nonelite Tongans over who owns modernity and who has the right to define its relevance to the local context. Modernity at the secondhand marketplace emerges as a contingent, tentative, and complicated category. In particular, it is located at the outcome of social practice, rather than being its antecedent: Traders and customers have only a vague notion of what they are performing when chatting about fashion, code-switching between Tongan and English, and rummaging through knick-knacks, because the self that they are performing is the coconstructed product of the performance.

My discussion began by embracing the widely held anthropological premise that we must seek an understanding of how consumption "works" with reference to local dynamics, a point that can also be applied more generally to the modernity of which consumption is a cornerstone. Indeed, traders and customers partake in the *fea* not just to sell and buy things but also to practice particular social activities and presentations of self that may not be appropriate or relevant to other contexts. People come to the *fea* to localize a larger world of consumption, religious beliefs, social arrangements, and cultural dynamics. However, what this localization entails is complex, and this complexity is highlighted most strikingly by the apparent contradiction between the liminality of the *fea* and its centrality. This apparent contradiction is the consequence of the fact that the local and its relationship to the global are defined on several levels at once (morally, psychologically, materially, interactionally, politically) and that at any given time the boundary between the local and the nonlocal can be drawn differently on different levels.

In addition, consumption and more generally modernity can have many different meanings for different members of society, who may or may not form a sociologically well-defined entity, and this also applies by implication to the tradition that emerges out of modernity. What we witness at the *fea* is not just a celebration of the multiplicity of modernities but also, and more importantly, a critical commentary on local structures of inequality that take for granted that both tradition and modernity are the prerogatives of the high ranking and wealthy. "The concept of the modern itself comes to be understood and utilized by a range of social actors in the context of particular power-laden social relationships both within and between countries" (Walley 2003: 34). The *fea* provides a context for the efflorescence of positions vis-à-vis the social order, as disenfranchised agents use their access to the outside world (through objects, fashion styles, or simply the knowledge that these fashion styles exist) to define their relationship to the traditional order and the social and material inequalities and systems of obligation that sustain them. This is why, at first approach, the *fea* appear to be the local sites, and the Chamber of Commerce and Industry and its membership appear to be agents of modernity, while in fact, upon closer scrutiny, the reverse turns out to be the case.

Chapter Four

When Gifts Become Commodities

In 2006, in an effort to downsize a civil service that, in line with its neoliberal convictions, it considered "bloated," the government of Tonga offered redundancy packages to qualified employees. About 800 civil servants accepted, retiring on June 30 of that year. This event suddenly gave to the category "retired" (*lītaea*) a visibility that it never had before in Tonga. Retirees then faced the question of what to do with the lump sum they had received as part of the redundancy package. The decision that many took may astonish anyone not familiar with modern Tonga: They opened pawnshops.

Tongans refer to the very peculiarly local pawnshops that today dot the urban landscape as *kautaha nō paʻanga*, literally "money-borrowing companies," and when speaking English they use the term "finance company." *Kautaha nō paʻanga* were originally inspired on pawnshops that have long been conspicuous features of industrial and postindustrial city centers of the West (Williams 2004), although informants disagree as to exactly where and when the inspiration originated. They differ in a fundamental way from the Western businesses on which they are modeled in that they accept as collateral for cash loans only traditional textile valuables, or *koloa faka-Tonga*. In 2001, when Ping-Ann Addo and I visited Nukuʻalofa pawnshops, we enumerated eight active businesses, to which my collaborator added one other in Auckland during her fieldwork among Tongan New Zealanders. Street signs in various states of disrepair directed customers to several additional pawning businesses, but they led us to locked-up homes, abandoned years before by people who had left for good. Suddenly, in mid-2006, signs announcing new pawnshops sprouted everywhere, to the dismay of the veterans of the business. The Tonga Telephone Directory had no listings for "financiers" in its yellow pages until its 2008 edition, which lists nine businesses, three with color ads. But this is only the tip of the iceberg: After some phoning around and snowballing, my assistant enumerated no fewer than 126 businesses on Tonga, although a few seemed to have closed in recent months and not all telephone numbers were active. A similar explosion seems to have taken place in Auckland as well, judging from the quantity of advertising in the Tongan-language press.[1]

Pawnshops first appeared in Nuku'alofa in the 1980s, at the historical convergence of two sets of dynamics. One is the gradual emergence of a non-aristocratic elite with ambition and capital derived from entrepreneurial ventures and transnational connections. The other is the decrease in the number of women capable of and willing to manufacture textile valuables, coupled with the ever-increasing demand for the textiles, the increasing unpredictability of ritual events (such as shotgun marriages) where they must be presented, and the increasingly large quantities expected in rituals. Indeed, far from being pushed aside by a capitalism that everyone in Tonga is embracing enthusiastically (even those who have most to lose from it), valuables and their exchange are gaining in significance, a classic case of the proliferation of conservative objects and practices at the same time that agents' lives are increasingly steeped in capitalism, consumption, and modernity. In fact, the production and circulation of valuables figure prominently in a quintessentially Tongan understanding of "development" (*fakalakalaka*), sometimes to the dismay of aid agencies (Horan 2002).

The contemporary prominence of pawning has several consequences. Most straightforwardly, it commodifies textile valuables by systematically ascribing a monetary value to them in an unprecedented fashion. It also restructures social relations: The gift recipient is replaced by the pawnbroker, the giver becomes customer, expertise in assessing the quality of valuables shifts from women to men, and the assessment shifts from people's sociocultural capital to the monetary value of objects.

While pawning appears to radically alter the makeup of traditional valuables and people's relation to them, many aspects of the practice are also consistent with them. In particular, pawning operates within the same cultural logic as gift exchange, in that it is predicated on "shame" (*mā*), an emotion that operates as the covert yet pivotal regulators of exchange, as I discussed in the two previous chapters. People who pawn valuables are exposed to shame, but so are pawnshop owners and the customers who buy unclaimed valuables. However, the distribution of the emotion among the different parties is uneven in scope and quality. It is because of these tensions and the resulting negotiations, and because they recur across various aspects of social and cultural life, that the pawnshop is a site where modernity and tradition constitute one another. This mutual constitution here is even more dramatic than in the secondhand marketplace, given the nature of the objects in focus, valuables that embody the core of the Tongan traditional order.

Pawning has a variety of other consequences. Becoming a pawnbroker in Tonga presupposes substantial material, social, and cultural capital, or at least access to this capital: large amounts of cash to loan out, storage and office facilities, entrepreneurial know-how and risk taking, expertise in assessing the exchange value of objects and converting it into monetary value, and so on. But it also presupposes a certain imperviousness to potentially shame-inducing allegations of seeking to make money from poorer people's customary obligations. This imperviousness is not unlike the disregard of shame extant among some secondhand marketplace traders. Not surprisingly, the first pawnshop entrepreneurs were not only wealthy but also on the fringe of society, in one fashion or another. The continuities and discontinuities embedded in the commodification of Tongan valuables are closely tied to the agency of a few, whose privileged position results from both their material and symbolic position in the system. Pawning is potentially very lucrative, and this potentiality was not lost on those who sought to invest their early-retirement packages in the business after 2006. But because it is lucrative at the expense of the poor and those who are by necessity traditionally oriented, the industry also exacerbates patterns of material inequality already operative in Tongan society.

Koloa Faka-Tonga, "Tongan Valuables"

I referred in passing in the previous chapters to *koloa faka-Tonga*, "Tongan valuables," which are the main focus of attention in pawnshops. *Koloa faka-Tonga*, or simply *koloa*, fall into two main categories: mats (*lālanga*) plaited from treated pandanus leaves (*fā*) and barkcloth or tapa cloth (*ngatu*), labori-ously manufactured by soaking, beating, and adjoining fragments of the inner bark of the paper mulberry tree or *hiapo* (Brussonetia papyrifera) and gener-ally decorated, through a process referred to as *koka'anga*, with set stylized designs painted or stenciled with natural brown and black dyes (look again at Figure 3.2). High-prestige mat and barkcloth textiles can attain enormous dimensions: Barkcloth pieces, for example, are often 3 m wide and up to 80 m in length and can be seen in all their magnificence being aired out on dry days across lawns. The term *koloa* also refers to goods or cargo of any type or origin; for example, it appears in the compound *fale koloa*, "store" (literally, "house of goods"). But it acquires a particular meaning, and one that connotes importance and continuity, when it refers specifically to mats and barkcloth. There are also marginal forms of *koloa* that people term *koloa si'i* (literally, "minor valuables"), which include machine-sewn quilts, barkcloth lined with paper or plastic, and nontextiles such as decorated baskets and bottles of fra-grant coconut oil. When I taught secondary school in Vava'u in the late 1970s, students would learn the names and types of these objects from mimeo-graphed textbooks that were still in use in the first decade of the millennium, testimonies to the traditional importance that the society attaches to them.[2]

In old-style village contexts, all adolescent commoner women would learn to make *koloa*. Today only some rural women actively engaged in its manu-facture. Tongans hold conflicting views on their production: They associate it with very hard manual work and low-prestige village life, but women who can and do produce valuables are also held in high regard as upholders of tra-dition. Textile manufacture is often a group occasion because the work is so tedious, and the objects thus carry the imprint of a village communalism that many urban or overseas Tongans, in principle at least, value nostalgically. The manufacture of barkcloth has remained an almost continuous process in the course of modern history, except for the interlude of two years during the late 1870s when the "Law on Tapa" was in force (Chapter Two). After the repeal of the law, barkcloth regained its original importance as a ritual object, al-though not as an item of clothing. Elsewhere in Polynesia (for example, Cook Islands, Tahiti, Marquesas, Hawai'i), prohibitions enforced by nineteenth-century missionaries and traders were much more successful in obliterating or reducing the importance of barkcloth production (Thomas 2003).

For decades, Tongan women have also manufactured fragments of deco-rated barkcloth and mats for the skeletal tourist trade, which seems to have reached its apex as a source of income for poorer Tongans during the 1970s, when cruise ships would call with greater frequency than today. The sheer size and lack of obvious practical use of *koloa* that Tongans exchange in prestation contexts render them of no interest to most visitors. So, like handicraft manufacturers in other parts of the world (for example, see Davis 1999; Rasmussen 2003), Tongan women adapt the objects in size, style, and function to what tourists expect, can carry away, and find useful: table mats, baskets, and fans decorated with turtles and dolphins, maps of Tonga, and stylized figures drinking kava, for example. Sold in temporary markets on cruise-ship days, tourist handicrafts are also on sale in some specialty shops around town and at the Langa Fonua women's handicrafts cooperative, which Queen Sālote III founded in 1953. When speaking English, Tongans use the term *handicraft* ambiguously to refer to both *koloa faka-Tonga* and souvenirs designed for sale to tourists. This conflation has the unfortunate consequence of devaluing *koloa faka-Tonga*, particularly when the term *handicraft* emerges in interactions with people unfamiliar with the local context, such as development aid representatives. Both handicraft and *koloa* production are viewed as rural manual labor, but, given a choice, women choose making *koloa* over handicrafts.[3]

On ritual occasions (*kātoanga*), low-ranking women fold large yardages of textile in a highly prescribed way under the supervision of high-ranking women, prior to presenting them formally in large bundles. Men present the product of agricultural efforts (*tokonaki*) alongside *koloa*, and in addition both women and men provide cash, store-bought food, and other objects, sometimes in large amounts. The less important *koloa si'i* can appear in these rituals as complements to canonical valuables. Cash is also inserted into an envelope called *sila pa'anga* (literally, "money envelope"), the form of which is important: It is usually white, hand lettered with the name of the recipient, and conspicuously placed on top of the folded bundles of *koloa*. Gift giving has both short- and long-term significance. In the short term, food ensures the success of the feast it accompanies and the distribution of leftovers, which is more and more frequently rendered an organic element of the feast by the practice of serving food in Styrofoam take-away trays. In the long term, durable wealth affirms the propitiousness of the family and the reproduction of the hierarchical order (Young Leslie 2004).

The royal family and other families of very high rank own centuries-old and densely plaited mats, which bear names and are brought out on very special occasions such as royal weddings (Kaeppler 1999). For nobles and commoners alike, these textiles encapsulate the essence of both *koloa faka-Tonga* and the rank-based social order. Because they do not circulate they are inalienable possessions of the lineages that hold them. Other mats may circulate but retain only the specific imprint of their givers during ceremonial presentation, whose names and gift lists are called out by the master of ceremony. The mats lose this imprint soon after joining the often-enormous piles of textiles, illustrating the fleeting nature of inalienability (Laidlaw 2000; Mosko 2000). However, in other instances, *koloa faka-Tonga* retain a metaphorical potential of inalienability because people tacitly associate them with the inalienable named mats that epitomize *koloa faka-Tonga*, another illustration of the upwardly focused mimesis operative throughout the society that I introduced in Chapter Two. Status climbing through rank mimesis is very much part of constructing selfhood for Tongan commoners. Few people, however, would admit to it and agree with this analysis, preferring to highlight instead the honorification and self-abasement in which they engage when the high-ranking are present, or *faka'apa'apa*, "respect."

Koloa faka-Tonga play a central role in the exchange-based division of labor between island-based Tongans and their overseas relatives. In ideal circumstances, the latter provide remittances in cash or kind, which the former repay in important objects that are unobtainable overseas, among which prominently figure *koloa*. Overseas Tongans still need the latter for rituals, perhaps in even larger quantities than in the islands to demonstrate their allegiance to *anga faka-Tonga*, "the Tongan way," sometimes even when they have thoroughly assimilated into the host societies. For diasporic Tongans, remittances to island-based relatives ensure their ongoing access to valuables and therefore their ability to demonstrate their competence in "doing culture" and allegiance to tradition. These concerns are mainly operative among Tongans who live in overseas locations among large numbers of their compatriots. In diasporic locations like Japan, where Tongans are few and dispersed and where they lead a profoundly urbanized existence, no exchange of traditional valuables takes place.

Cash and valuables are becoming more intertwined as *koloa* becomes further commodified. Because very old mats and barkcloth pieces are found in museum collections around the world (Addo 2004b; cf. Linnekin 1991a on Samoa), it is clear that selling them, to outsiders at least, is not a new practice. In both the islands and the diaspora, the demand for *koloa* is increasing rather than waning, for reasons ranging from the rising unpredictability of weddings (because young people today want to marry for love and do so far too fast) to the increasing anxiety of diasporic Tongans about displaying their allegiance to *anga faka-Tonga*. This anxiety inflates quantity rather than quality; hence the increased production and ritual presence of *koloa siʻi* like thick-gauge mats and paper- and plastic-lined tapa cloth. Until the 1990s, these valuables, which are much easier to manufacture, were viewed with contempt, but today their presentation in ordinary rituals barely generates gossip, as long as it does not involve large quantities of them. Furthermore, the qualifier *faka-Tonga*, "in the Tongan style," that Tongans use to modify the word *koloa* indexes a self-conscious reflexivity constitutive of this anxiety. It is congruent with the self-conscious discourse of distinctiveness that people often develop through comparisons of "the Tongan way" with what they present as characteristic of life in the industrial world.

The increasing demand in *anga faka-Tonga* poses problems for those who do not have direct kinship ties to the increasingly fewer women capable of manufacturing the textiles or willing to do so. Outside of ritual exchange, Tongans may obtain *koloa* from relatives or friends in exchange for another piece of *koloa* or a gift. *Koloa* can also be purchased at the market. In the upstairs ("handicraft") section of Talamahu Market, several entrepreneurs regularly sell *koloa*, including one (in 2001) who sold repossessed *koloa* from a pawnshop. In New Zealand and Hawaiʻi, Tongans sell *koloa*, generally of poorer quality, at fairs and markets. Back in Tonga, the continued importance of *koloa* is not lost on those involved in a growing industry that keeps *koloa* circulating: breaking into other people's houses. Widely blamed on "deportees," who are said to train idle Tongan youths in the art of thieving, house break-ins often focus on *koloa*, demonstrating that the perpetrators are hardly alienated from *anga faka-Tonga*, "the Tongan way," after all. People have on occasion sighted and recognized large bundles of stolen *koloa* being loaded into shipping containers, on their way to being sold in more lucrative markets in the diaspora, where the goods would also have lost some of their recognizability. Far from being marginalized, as Gailey (1987) argued it was during Tonga's early modernity, *koloa faka-Tonga* have gained enormous importance in the contemporary social landscape.

In other contexts, people sell *koloa* because they are constantly short of the cash they need for prestation as well as for everyday requirements: groceries, transportation, utility bills, family feasts, church collection contributions, school fees and uniforms, helping relatives in need, entertaining relatives visiting from overseas, making telephone calls to ask them for more money, trips overseas, and bonds for visas. In its advertisement in the 2008 national telephone directory, one pawn shop exhorts customers to obtain a loan for their "*fai'aho* (birthday), *putu* (funeral), *fakalaka ho fāmili* (development of your family), *tikiti folau* (airline ticket), *me'a fakafāmili* (family event)" (my translations). Because of the constant need for it and the limited employment opportunities, cash generally falls through people's fingers and is the subject of ever-increasing anxiety, particularly for those with few or less-than-dependable overseas relatives. Selling *koloa* may alleviate this anxiety, but it is stigmatized as an act of desperation. Not having ready access to valuables for emergencies brings shame on persons and families and puts into question their commitment to tradition because *koloa* continues to be an expression of Tongan identity, especially for women. A problematic yet expedient solution to the dilemma of meeting both cash and valuable needs is to pawn *koloa*.

Pawnshops

Nuku'alofa pawnshops provide short-term cash loans in various amounts, and request that customers guarantee the loan with *koloa faka-Tonga* (Figure 4.1). They accept as collateral for loans neither minor valuables nor high-quality *koloa* such as very fine and ancient mats. The latter are very difficult to resell, and few people would consider parting with such objects anyway. Pawnshop operators rarely accept other forms of collateral, such as cars, electronic equipment, and other consumer goods because they do not resell well and are difficult to store out of the reach of unruly children and destructive teenagers. More importantly, despite the popularity of consumer goods as prestige markers of modernity, they still pale in importance against the persistent value of *koloa faka-Tonga*.

Pawnshop operators generally set prices for different categories of textiles (Table 4.1). In 2000, loans generally amounted to between T$100 and T$1,000 but could go as high as T$5,000. Customers have one month to repay the loan, at a monthly interest rate of 10 to 15 percent. Should a customer default on a loan, the pawnshop owner advertises the *koloa* over national radio or takes it to the marketplace, selling it for two to three times

Figure 4.1.   One of the smaller pawnshops in 2000 (now out of business), with folded mats and barkcloth on shelves or wrapped in black plastic, run at the time by Nenase Afu, who would become my research assistant in 2008.

the amount of the loan, depending on the entrepreneur and on the time of the year. Demand is so great, particularly in high season, that the textiles are commonly gone within a couple of hours.

Pawning *koloa faka-Tonga* is potentially a very profitable business, a potential that was clearly not lost on civil service early retirees in 2006. Businesses in the 2000 sample reported annual profits of up to T$30,000, an extraordinary amount of money in Tonga. The most successful business had T$27,000 loaned out, while the most modest averaged T$500 to T$1,500 in loans at any given time. The inventory of textiles left as collateral ranged from T$1,500 up to T$60,000 per business, the largest inventories requiring entrepreneurs to store the valuables in relatives' houses in nearby villages. These figures are not surprising given the fact that people at the time would pay over T$1,000 for a well-made mat for a prestation that will impress (and this amount has increased dramatically since then), but they contrast sharply with most fami-

TABLE 4.1.
Collateral and resale values of *koloa*, 2001 and 2008.

Category of *koloa*	Mid-2001		Mid-2008	
	Collateral	Resale	Collateral	Resale
Ngatu 50-langanga (*launima*, with decorations)	300–750	800–1000	450–1000	1500–2000
Ngatu 10-langanga ("*fuatanga*," with decorations)	100–250	300–400	100–300	380–500
Ngatu 4- or *5-langanga* (with decorations)	20–40	80–100	20–40	60–100
Ngatu pepa (low-quality synthetic barkcloth), 10-*langanga*	80–100	300–450	60–80	250–300
Double-layered floor mat (*fala*), length:				
10 feet	100–190	250–350	100–200	250–400
12 feet	150–180	300–400	100–300	450–600
15 feet	170–280	350–500	100–450	550–800
20 feet	200–300	500–800	400–500	750–1000
Single-layered fine mat (*kie tonga*), width:				
4 feet	20–50	100–120	40–70	80–200
6 feet	30–80	120–150	no data	no data
8 feet	40–80	140–160	no data	no data
10 feet	80–150	160–200	80–100	250–400

Note: The prices are in Pa'anga, not adjusted for inflation. A *ngatu launima* may be used as a gift to a particularly significant person or at an important ceremony, but it may also be cut into four-*langanga* or five-*langanga* pieces, which are the standard sizes for gift exchange between commoners.

lies' modest incomes. They explain the extent of many people's anxiety over both money and valuables.

Pawning is seasonal for the same reasons that render secondhand marketplace trading seasonal. While Tongans need money for ceremonial occasions that can fall at any time, everyone is under pressure to obtain money at festival times. For example, business is at its most brisk before Christmas, before annual donations to the various churches in May and September, and in the weeks leading up to school fee due dates. To counterbalance this seasonality and in tune with the "multiple mode of livelihood" that characterizes middle-class entrepreneurialism in Tonga (Chapter Two), pawnshops in Nuku'alofa and Auckland are often part of business ventures that offer an inventory of services ranging from travel bookings, assistance in dealing with immigration problems and visa applications, and transnational shopping services. One pawnshop in Tonga also rents out a mobile refrigerated mortuary for customers' funeral needs. These various services cross-fertilize one another: A customer can bring a *koloa faka-Tonga* and obtain in return an airline ticket and a filled-out visa application. This "one-stop" process avoids customers having to patronize several businesses for these different transactions and allows them for example to "gamble" on the money they hope to make at their travel destination by working temporarily in a relative's business or by selling additional *koloa faka-Tonga* that they transport in their personal luggage, counting on the high demand for them at destination.

The operational scope of pawn businesses varies, some being exclusively local while others operate across borders and oceans. For example, one business operative in 2001, located in one of the cubicles of a shopping center on the edge of town, drew its clientele only from rural villages of Tonga. Started in mid-1999 with capital loaned to the owner by a New Zealander friend, it held only a couple of dozen *koloa* pieces at any given time. In contrast, the couple who owned the only Auckland *kautaha nō pa'anga* at that time operated an ambitious and astute transnational commerce with forfeited goods. Attuned to currency exchange rates, which in 2001 favored the U.S. and Australian currencies over the New Zealand dollar, the wife regularly visited relatives in Sydney and Salt Lake City, selling valuables that she brought along and turning a profit even after deducting her travel expenses. This kind of transnational trade, opportunistically intertwined with personal travel but also carefully planned, resembles the practices of agents in many other areas of the developing world (for example, see Freeman 2001 on Barbados).

The ability to engage in transnational operations of this kind is predicated on the entrepreneur's ability to travel or access trustworthy agents. So while this particular entrepreneur can take trips out of New Zealand, another entrepreneur is tied to Tonga because the business is a side operation to his employment as a high-ranking civil servant. He also knows no one overseas whom he can trust, who can judge *koloa* quality, and who knows how to handle business. An overseas agent would need to "have connections," and diasporic contacts who fit the bill "have no time." The mobility of others is curtailed by stringent visa requirements that they cannot meet. These various cases represent the range of different approaches among pawnshops and bear witness to the interconnected nature of tradition-enhancing concerns (such as visiting relatives), modern-style business planning, and the constraints that state and other authorities place on movements and ambitions. Pawnshops bring together local and diasporic agents, money and textiles, and modernity and tradition in an economy of obligation as well as entrepreneurialism that encapsulates the way in which modernity is domesticated in Tonga and elsewhere.

Entrepreneurs

Pawn businesses are all owned and run by Tongans, as the know-how and social connections that pawnbrokering presupposes are quintessentially Tongan, in contrast to other entrepreneurial ventures (including retail, construction, and hospitality), which involve a much more varied population. Yet all pawnbrokers whom we interviewed in 2000, who were in many ways the pioneers in the business, also maintained markedly extra-local connections and identifications, which categorized them as "local others": For example, one was married to a locally based businessman from another country, another was involved in a morally tainted *faka-Suva* "in the fashion of Suva" nonmarital relationship with a *Pālangi*, and most had spent considerable amounts of time overseas and maintained strong links to the diaspora. Religious affiliation also set them apart from the rest of the population: As among secondhand marketplace traders, a disproportionate number of pawnshop proprietors, six out of nine, were LDS adherents (at the time, Mormons constituted 14 percent of the total population). The LDS Church's embracement of modernity and capitalism, here again, plays a strong role in placing entrepreneurs in a liminal position vis-à-vis the status quo, as well as enabling their entrepreneurialism. The irony, which echoes examples discussed in Chapter Three, is that pawnshops deal with the very objects that are the focus of competitive gift giving from which Mormons distance themselves.

Pawnshop owners vary in terms of the "hard-nosed" fashion with which they conduct business. In 2000, one entrepreneur admitted to asking even his own wife to pay for valuables that she needed to fulfill their kinship prestation obligations. Others occasionally bent their own rules by offering grace periods, reducing interest rates, and loaning money to relatives. Another entrepreneur often shares his profit with the original owner of repossessed valuables, particularly at times of high profit, and his business was also one of the most actively patronized. The resulting loyalty and trust were precisely what he believed, when I interviewed him again in 2008, had given him the upper hand in the cutthroat competition in the post-2006 burgeoning of pawn businesses. As in other contexts where cash is chronically short (for example, see Williams 2004: 102), the success of pawnshops depends on the nurturance of long-term relationships through rule-bending as well as other manifestations of *'ofa*, "empathy, compassion, generosity," and willingness to *tokoni*, "help out," the less fortunate. Each business and each transaction embodies a different manifestation of the convergence of capitalist enterprise and Tongan values, allowing business owners to negotiate, on a transaction-by-transaction basis, the morality of their capitalistic ventures, and by implication their own otherness.

To run a pawnshop, entrepreneurs need to have knowledge of categories, values, and resale potentials of textiles, knowledge that is normally the domain of older tradition-oriented women. This requirement makes pawnshops one of the few areas of business that are decidedly immune to infiltration by Chinese immigrants. More recently, an additional skill has been essential to pawnshop management: having an eye for stolen *koloa* through a broad knowledge of which family has what mat or piece of barkcloth in its possession, for example, and being particularly suspicious of young or unknown people coming to pawn valuables. In 2008, interviewees in the business reported having been stung by raids on their stocks by the police who had received a tip that a particular pawnshop was (knowingly or not) storing stolen valuables.

Of the businesswomen who were operating pawning businesses in 2000, some acquired this knowledge through trial and error, while others relied on knowledgeable employees to estimate the acceptability and value of *koloa*. Male entrepreneurs place themselves in a more complex situation, in that they take an interest in handling objects that in all other respects are the purview of women. Male entrepreneurs either rely on women relatives to evaluate textiles or learn the skills from them, but this knowledge potentially threatens their masculinity and undermines women's control of this aspect of prestation. Significantly, men dominate the pawnshop business (in 2000, five out of eight, plus one couple).

Customers

There is no dearth of pawning customers, a symptom of the constant need for cash that most Tongans experience. When one of the pioneer entrepreneurs opened for business in 1999, he initially ran ads on national radio and in the newspaper but quickly realized that advertising was unnecessary: By the end of the first week, he already had forty customers, and now relies solely on word-of-mouth. Other entrepreneurs in 2000 only advertised at festival times. Yet by 2008 the competition had become fierce, and signs directing potential customers to pawn businesses had become a ubiquitous feature of the urban landscape, although it is doubtful that customers need them, as they know whose business they will patronize, and everyone knows who lives where.

Customers come from all walks of life and occasionally even include people of rank. In interviews and surveys she conducted among forty customers in Nuku'alofa and on 'Eua, Ping-Ann Addo learned that pawnshop customers are primarily women, although 20 percent of them were men who were pawning their wives' *koloa*. They ranged in age from their early twenties to their mid-eighties, demonstrating that people are concerned with both *koloa* and money at every life stage. Tongans from all religious denominations patronize pawnshops, including Mormons (15 percent of respondents), even though they are not under as much competitive pressure to give to their church as members of other denominations. For people across the social spectrum, *koloa faka-Tonga* are important sources of stored wealth and afford them the appearance of meeting the material demands of both traditional and modern life.

Customers approach pawnshops with diverse and conflicting emotions. Lātū, a sixty-seven-year-old retired teacher living on the outskirts of Nuku'alofa, member of the elite Church of England, and a distant relative and staunch supporter of the royal family, said that she had only once patronized a pawnshop, at the advice of co-workers. She recalls the experience with distaste, saying that all she could think of was repaying the loan: "Going to the pawnshop is like being imprisoned . . . I would rather be poor than go to a pawnshop again." Others, in contrast, patronize pawnshops routinely. Mana, a young man in his late twenties with a wife and small children, is a regular, as multiple family obligations, a demanding father, and poor management create a constant need for money in his life, which his job as a low-ranking employee of a service company cannot even begin to meet.

He pawns family *koloa faka-Tonga* and has also succeeded on a couple of occasions to pawn his car (another drain on his limited resources) to a willing pawnbroker. Sometimes, a loan from one pawnshop goes to pay off a loan from another pawnshop. He has borrowed money from friends and acquaintances (including me), which he has serious trouble paying back, sometimes requesting another loan before he has paid back the previous one. While one cannot imagine that the constant pressure associated with these activities brings much peace and comfort, pawning is part of his everyday existence, and his case is not atypical.

Pawning and Shame

Of the panoply of emotions in the Tongan cultural landscape, one emotion dominates pawnshop transactions: *mā*, which roughly translates as "shame," but which also partially overlaps with what English speakers would characterize as "embarrassment," "shyness," and "humiliation." There is a long genealogy of works in psychological and social anthropology on the operation of this and related emotions in the precapitalist world, particularly the Pacific Islands, which recognizes it as socially grounded, presupposing an audience witnessing the experiencer's loss of face, and experienced in response to one's own or one's kin's transgressions of the social order (for example, Fajans 1983; Heller 2003; Rosaldo 1983; Shweder 2003; Strathern 1975). More recently, inspired by Sahlins's (1992) contention that agents come to experience historical rupture only if they first experience a collective feeling of inadequacy for what they have in contrast to a referential (commonly Western) Other, a number of scholars (Robbins 2003a; Robbins and Wardlow 2005) have examined critically the role of a cognate emotion, humiliation, in bringing about radical cultural change. The relationship between shame and humiliation is not straightforward. "If shame is the consequence of not living up to what one ought to, then humiliation is the consequence of trying to live up to what we have no right to," states William Miller (1993: 145). Tongans do not seem to uphold this distinction—nor does Nussbaum (2004: 203)—and consider *mā* to be the operative emotion in both types of situations, although for them the second type is particularly problematic because it is symptomatic of not knowing one's place in the ranking system, not an unusual occurrence in this status-climbing society.

In Tonga, *mā*, "shame," underlies covertly many contexts, particularly where performance and exchange are foregrounded. One such context is ceremonial gift giving at ritualized events (*kātoanga*). In these contexts, the nature and quantity of what each family or village gives is announced publicly and, in the case of large-scale events such as church conferences and state events (such as royal weddings, coronations, and king's birthday celebrations), announced on national radio and nowadays recorded for television broadcasting. In the dominant ideology, gift giving is thought of being as fueled by *'ofa*, "empathy, compassion, generosity," which I discussed in Chapter Two. This ubiquitous emotion is what drives people, families, and businesses, caught by the enthusiasm of the moment, to announce unexpected gifts of money or goods or to increase dramatically the amounts or quantities that they had originally pledged to demonstrate their empathy for the recipient (as well as increase their own prestige). In considerably more covert fashion, *mā*, "shame," is also operative: the shame of not having enough to give, the shame of not being able to persuade one's kin to contribute, the shame of seeming stingy, or the shame of appearing to be turning one's back to *anga faka-Tonga*, "the Tongan way."[1]

When people patronize pawnshops, shame is preeminent in regulating microscopic aspects of the transaction. For example, some customers travel to the other side of the island to pawn their valuables to reduce the risk of being seen by relatives or neighbors, whereas others worry about being caught carrying *koloa* from their parked car to the pawnshop. While it is considered shameful for a woman to *kole* "beg for" textiles from her relatives (Addo 2004a), it is even more shameful to be seen alienating one's textiles when one is in need of cash. Shame derives from the fact that Tongans prescriptively expect the kinship system to provide for everyone's financial, emotional, and ceremonial needs, an expectation that is often frustrated by the complexities of modern life (as well as those of tradition). Patronizing a pawnshop implies that one is poor not only in material goods but also, and more importantly, in social relations and therefore ultimately poorly integrated into the traditional system. Pawning is viewed as the last recourse, but it is a last recourse that many depend on frequently, hence the particular anxiety that surrounds it. This anxiety is distributed equally across genders. Just as women find it shameful to *mole*, "waste, lose," their family valuables, men experience shame if seen as unable to meet their family's financial needs. Family reputation is the responsibility of both genders.

That shame is central is demonstrated by abundant ethnographic evidence. When they pawn their valuables, people often take a circuitous route to the pawnshop to minimize the possibility of becoming the topic of gossip among bystanders, on constant alert for signs of others losing face. One can also read shame in customers' silent approach, stooped shoulders, worried brows, and shifting gazes as they arrive at or leave the pawnshop and in their own accounts and other people's comments (cf. Toren 2005: 277). My working next door to a pawnshop in 1999–2001 afforded me many opportunities to witness these dynamics and to hear friends' commentaries about them. Shame is inscribed in an abundance of body habitus and decision making, and is the frequent topic of conversation. It is this overelaboration that demonstrates that shame is the operative emotion, and one that shows remarkable resilience over time.

Pawnshop owners are intimately aware of the importance of shame, and some admit to capitalizing on it. One entrepreneur described in 2000 the advantage of his shop being located away from the main road, affording customers the relative assurance that they will not be seen approaching or leaving it. Another pioneer entrepreneur had originally set up shop in one of Tongatapu's larger villages, but when he shifted his operation to the capital, where anonymity is easier to maintain than in the village, his business tripled. These examples suggest that emotion maps onto a politics of space and onto the organization of modernity and tradition across the landscape. Strategizing on the emotional weight of pawning is an example of larger processes through which Tongans subtly seek to use the possibility of others' shame to further their own interests (Figure 4.2). One infamous money-lending business catering to Tongans in Auckland, owned by a pair of Tongan brothers, provides perhaps the most blatant manifestation of the manipulation of shame. If the recipient of a loan defaults, the business publishes his or her photograph, name, age, reason for taking a loan, and church affiliation in a grim full-page gallery published weekly in the Tongan-language press, a practice that has received the critical attention of New Zealand parliamentarians and journalists (Snow, Druett, and Crawford 2006). Here, the sole collateral is the potential of shame.

Shame also concerns pawnshop owners, whose entrepreneurial activities are easily deemed antithetical to traditional values and practices, a widely attested pattern throughout the Pacific (van der Grijp 2002, 2003; Williksen-Bakker 2004). At best, like other entrepreneurs, they were viewed as turning away from a traditional order based on kinship ties and rank-based ob-

Figure 4.2. "*Kautaha Nō $$*": Sign directing customers to a pawnshop at the end of a secluded side road on the outskirts of Nukuʻalofa (2000).

ligations. At worst, they were vulnerable to criticism for banking on other people's desperation, which runs counter to the ideal of *foʻofoʻofaʻaki*, "mutual empathy." Early pawnshop owners managed this situation by generally refraining from lending money to relatives, preferring to maintain with them a relationship of ongoing reciprocity (as well as knowing that pressing relatives to repay loans is a lost cause). The framing of pawning as *tokoni*, "helping, rendering service," an image that comes up frequently in conversations with pawnshop operators, serves to further cushion the more jarring aspects of the practice, embedding it into a traditionalist discourse of mutual assistance. But, more importantly, their structural position as "local others" enabled them to remain relatively unaffected by the fear of shame, although of course this further contributed to their marginality. The proliferation of pawnshops after 2006 may have somewhat altered these dynamics, although it has also meant that the share of business (as well as the share of concomitant emotions) that each venture can claim is now considerably reduced.

In addition, for male entrepreneurs who constitute the majority of pawn-shop owners, shame potentially suffuses the gendered complexities of pawn-shop ownership. The pawnshop transaction involves a reversal of the gen-der order: Women customers worry about money, while male owners worry about possessing women's objects and expertise. Furthermore, men's en-gagement with women's valuables and knowledge normally associated with women potentially threatens their masculinity and the expectation that they should rather concern themselves with the agricultural activities that pro-duce men's ceremonial gifts or *tokonaki*. This gendered version of shame can be read, for example, in one of our male informants' initial insistence that the business belonged to his wife, which later clearly proved not to be the case. Other men highlighted the business functionality of their knowledge of valuables because entrepreneurial ambition is primarily the domain of men (notwithstanding Tonga's small but visible cadre of women entrepreneurs). For all pawnshop-owning men, the threat that too intense an involvement with women's material culture poses to their masculinity was somewhat di-luted by the fact that pawning represents only one of several previously es-tablished entrepreneurial ventures.

The pawnshop thus emerges as a central nexus in Tonga's economy of feelings, in which shame (*mā*) and empathy (*'ofa*), the two most elaborated emotions in Tongan culture, operate in different, sometimes contradictory, sometimes complementary ways. They enable customers to balance the shame of being monetarily poor with the shame of being perceived as poor in valuables and social relations, the empathy of giving with the shame of not giving, and being the recipient of empathy with being shamed by not being it. For entrepreneurs, anxiety around shame arises from their desire to do well in business while not appearing to violate the traditional order, and, for male entrepreneurs, being involved in women's valuables generates the potential of shame. The pawnshop therefore both exacerbates and al-leviates emotions: It amplifies the shame of poverty and relieves it; it high-lights the shame of business while anchoring business in rank-related presta-tion; it threatens gender roles while reinforcing gendered responsibilities for maintaining the reputation of families. Whether in Tonga or the diaspora, changing anxieties about the place of tradition and modernity in individuals' lives continue to be worked out at the pawnshop, although in partial fashion and with problematic outcomes. The situation exemplifies the open-ended nature of all projects of modernity and the simultaneous emergence of traditional in deeply modern contexts.

Pawning and Modernity

By providing a deeply modern mechanism in which Tongans can realize the value embodied in traditional valuables without necessarily alienating them forever, pawnshops enable individuals to negotiate their own positionality between kinship-oriented exchange-based *anga faka-Tonga* and the needs of the individual in a capitalist and diasporic modernity. Both traditional and modern dynamics are at play in pawning, for customers who pawn, for customers who buy, and for entrepreneurs. Tradition characterizes the emotional experience of exchange, with shame figuring prominently in all aspects of pawning, in the same way that it is one of the dominant, if covert, emotions in ritualized exchange. Whether entrepreneurs or consumers, sellers or givers, men or women, homeland- or diaspora-based, tenaciously traditional or adventurously modern, Tongans are subject to the abiding relevance of *mā* as an emotion. How they negotiate their own shame vis-à-vis the shame of others will continue to play a role in how they incorporate money into systems of traditional exchange and how traditional valuables continue to be markers of identity. Ruptures are found in the social relations between transactors and in the uneven distribution of shame (or perhaps of the fear of shame) among the participants. Both rupture and continuity characterize patterns of social inequality: The preexisting uneven distribution of wealth makes pawning possible, but pawning aggravates this uneven distribution, turning possibility into necessity.

Pawnshop owners' place in the moral order and the exchange system illustrates the multiple and contradictory opinions about what it means to be a cultural insider in modern Tongan society. Just as "the pawnbroker both precedes capitalism and is marginal to it, at least in its later manifestations" (Stallybrass 1998: 200), he or she is both of tradition and on the margin of tradition. Furthermore, the identity markers of pawnshop customers—the average Tongan—are also in flux. Tongan identities are not fixed, and when Tongans ask one another about people they gossip about, "What denomination does she [or he] belong to?" they are demonstrating how aware they are of the importance of church affiliation as a concentrated index of people's position in the system, in its past as well as its future. Church affiliation in Tonga tells you whether the person is likely to be burdened by obligation but also staunchly traditional, or at the forefront of modernity but flirting dangerously with the margin. It also tells you about the person's emotions, rank, aspirations, and body habitus (cf. Watson-Gegeo and Gegeo 1991).

While modernity is indeed diffuse, shifting, and ungrounded, it is also the object of considerable desire and the cause of a great deal of anxiety for our informants, requiring a nuanced approach to subjectivities of modernity, to which members of society bring different emotions, different intensities of emotions, as well as different material strategies vis-à-vis objects and money. And it is in the crevices between these different subjectivities that we should seek an understanding of modernity and its relationship to tradition.

Chapter Five

Modern Bodies on the Runway

Since 1980, the Tonga Tourist Association, an organization of private citizens concerned with the tourism industry, and the Tonga Visitors Bureau, a government agency, have earmarked two weeks of the year for a celebration called the "Heilala Festival." The festival, generally held in late June and early July, is named after the fragrant flower of the *heilala* bush (Garcinia callophylum), the national flower of Tonga, which occupies a particularly important place in songs and poems (Helu 2006; Kaeppler, Wood-Ellem, and Taumoefolau 2004). In its initial decade and a half, the Heilala Festival coincided with a public holiday on the occasion of King Tāufaʻāhau Tupou IV's birthday on July 4, and because the weather is driest and coolest at that time of the year, its timing was not changed after George V's accession to the throne. The birthday of the king's younger brother and crown prince, Tupoutoʻa Lavaka, opportunely falls on July 12, so the timing is still anointed with the proximity of a royal birthday.

Official brochures, press coverage, and publicity campaigns present the festival as a stimulus for tourism: "'The main objective of the festival is to attract visitors to Tonga', stated Semisi Taumoepeau, Tonga's Director of Tourism" (*Matangi Tonga* 1999: 3). Practically speaking, the bulk of the "tourists" are overseas Tongans who flock back to Tonga, principally to Nukuʻalofa, in increasing numbers every year for festivals, church conferences, high school reunions, family celebrations (*kātoanga*), and funerals, as well as to attend to their own entrepreneurial ventures. The few *Pālangi* tourists who venture to Tonga continue to be largely constituted of (to the chagrin of tourism officials and business owners) backpackers, whale watchers, divers, a few visitors to the offshore island resorts, and a few wealthy visitors who generally go straight to Vava'u to rent yachts from a time-share transnational corporation that operates a branch there. When they attend Heilala festivities, foreign tourists tend to find them a little bewildering, as little context is provided for them to understand what is going on. For example, in some years, official programs have been difficult to obtain, and schedules can change with little warning, which means that one needs to be part of local information networks to know where and when to show up. At most events, little accommodation is made for the benefit of audience members unfamiliar with the language and social context. This lack of accommodation to outsiders is not significantly different from general patterns extant in Tongan society: Foreigners are tolerated, but the agenda is not changed for their benefit or comfort even if they have dollars to spend, other than the occasional acknowledgment in sermons and speeches.

The rise of the Heilala Festival to the status of national event in the last couple of decades of the twentieth century coincided with the decline and eventual disappearance of the yearly agricultural show. The agricultural show carried a great deal of symbolic meaning, as I discuss in Chapter Two, although it was of interest exclusively to locally grounded participants. It is particularly significant that it was replaced with a festival designed, in the official version at least, for the ears and eyes of an extraneous audience. Its demise is of course a sign of the decline of agriculture, even in its most ritual form. More subtly, the festival that replaced it is a sign of the growing importance of bifocality, the consciousness of the copresence of multiple audiences, both local and extralocal.

The Heilala Festival is a complex event that involves several simultaneous agendas. It is primarily an occasion on which the state (which itself is made up of several distinct entities) displays itself to the people. The sovereign parades through the city, while lesser royals and sundry officials act as patrons and judges in various events. Perhaps as importantly and in tandem with state-affirming displays is a celebration of Tongan identity, in which overseas Tongans play a prominent role as both agents and spectators. In 2008, the festival was scheduled for the weeks prior to the king's coronation on August 1, and July and August were filled with extravagant celebrations of identity, statehood, and hierarchy. Invitations, sumptuary requirements, and tight policing carefully regulated who could perform and who could watch, as well as who could occupy what space. The generalization one can make about the festival foregrounds what it means to be Tongan in a modern context and affords both local and diasporic Tongans the opportunity to negotiate this meaning.

The festival features performances of many kinds, including a float parade through the streets of the capital, traditional dances, brass band concerts, military and police parades, and handicraft exhibitions. Church and school choirs compete with one another. Sports and other events include a children's fishing contest, a canoe championship, school sports competitions, a rugby tournament at Teufaiva Stadium, a boxing tournament at 'Atele Indoor Stadium, a sewing contest, and competitions in the manufacture of various traditional ornaments such as flower garlands. Elite and middle-class Tongans and local expatriates hold tennis and golf tournaments and a minitriathlon, and they vie for invitations to mix with royalty and VIPs at cocktail parties. The program weaves together, rather astutely, events that Tongans would self-consciously deem to represent *anga faka-Tonga*, "the Tongan way" (for example, traditional dancing, making ornaments, singing in church choirs), with events that symbolize a forward-looking modernity, embedding Tonga in a larger world of activities, representations, and competitions.

The pièce-de-résistance of the festival is a beauty contest or *fili misi* (literally, "choosing of miss"), the Miss Heilala pageant, which had been staged intermittently since 1958, organized by private interests before the tourism associations took over the responsibility in 1980 and turned it into a regularly scheduled showcase event. Originally held at the Dateline Hotel (still the only international-class hotel in Nuku'alofa, despite the fact that it has seen much better days), it moved in 1995 to then-newly built Queen Sālote Memorial Hall, the largest venue in the country, on one of Nuku'alofa's busiest intersections (Figure 5.1). The nexus of the traditional and the modern, the pageant showcases Tongan and part-Tongan unmarried young women from both the kingdom and the diaspora, who compete for the duration of a week for a title that will make them Tonga's national representative on the international pageant circuit. The pageant is the focus of everyone's attention during the weeks leading to it: The contestants are paraded in various venues, and their looks, attributes, and locations in the kinship landscape are the focus of conversations in hair salons, shops, and private homes, on website linking Tonga to its diaspora, and in intense media coverage.

Figure 5.1.   Queen Sālote Memorial Hall, the grandest venue in the country, inaugurated by King Tāufaʻāhau Tupou IV in March 1995 (April 2008).

While Miss Heilala is the most official, important, and orthodox pageant in the country, it is not the only one. First, it has a very serious competitor in the Miss Galaxy pageant organized by *leitī* or transgender males, which most consider to be considerably more entertaining than the contest for *misi moʻoni*, "real misses." Not to be outdone by their island-based compatriots, diasporic Tongans stage pageants for both "real misses" and *leitī* in San Francisco, Auckland, and Sydney. In Tonga, more or less impromptu beauty pageants are held throughout the year in increasing frequency. For several years around the millennium, Vavaʻu staged a Miss Cosmos transgender pageant, although this effort has now ceased. Since 2001 a local entrepreneur has been organizing a "Miss Face of Tonga" pageant for young women in their late teens, that is, a few years younger than Miss Heilala contestants, "with the aim to build-up [*sic*] the self-esteem and confidence of local girls" (*Matangi Tonga* website, November 7, 2007). In February 2008, another entrepreneur with business training from an elite university in the United

States organized a Miss Valentine pageant at the Dateline Hotel, which drew four contestants, the obligatory royal patron, and an audience of middle-class spectators. In July of that same year, the same person organized a wildly successful and much appreciated Top Model Search, which drew female and male teenagers from around Tongatapu and Vava'u, bringing twenty-seven finalists to Nuku'alofa's Queen Sālote Memorial hall for a competition that made the families of two winners T$500 richer. Here again, the discourse was one of youth empowerment, self-esteem, and self-reliance, themes that have all become the focus of anxious attention since the 16/11 events, although no one seems to question how modeling competition winners would implement this particular success for further empowerment, beyond paying off their families' overdue electricity bills.

While the middle classes of the industrial world have long contemptuously turned their collective back on beauty pageants, heeding second-wave feminist critiques of them as retrograde and puerilizing objectifications of women, in other parts of the world the genre is flourishing. Tonga is no exception. The contrast immediately suggests that beauty pageants are probably much more complex than dismissive criticisms depict them to be. The suggestion is further confirmed by the conflicts and controversies, the extreme interest and studied disdain, and the heightened emotions of which pageants routinely are the object across contexts.[1] To apprehend the social, cultural, and political meanings of pageants, thus, we must reach beyond simplistic readings of their literal form. In this chapter, I explore why pageants command so much attention in Tonga through a detailed exploration of the main two pageants, Miss Heilala and Miss Galaxy. My analysis is based on attendance of numerous pageants since the mid-1990s, active participation in the organization of several Miss Galaxy and Miss Cosmos pageants (as a judge and general hanger on), and the videotaping of both pageants in 1997 and 2000, plus, in 2001, a Miss Tonga New Zealand in Auckland, which my Tuvaluan namesake Niko Alefaio videotaped for me while I was busy judging.

The Miss Heilala Pageant

In traditional Tongan households, Tongan adults teach children to be seen and not heard, to be obedient (*talangofua*), and to wait for and follow instructions (*fakaongo*) from their elders (Morton 1996: 91). Traditional Tongans consider independent initiative and strong will to be signs of *talangata'a*, "disobedience," and *fie lahi*, "pretending to be older and more important than one really is," traits of which they disapprove particularly strongly in girls. Children bring the messages that this socialization conveys to school, where they avoid standing out from among their peers through independence, initiative, or curiosity, a fact that raises fascinating and yet unanswered questions when juxtaposed with the academic success of so many Tongan adolescents and young adults, particularly women. There are specific contexts in which children are expected to perform in front of adults. Such is the case, in most church denominations, of "children's Sunday" on the first Sunday of May (*faka-Mē*), on which children stand up in front of the entire congregation to recite well-rehearsed Biblical passages, prayers, and short sermons. These contexts, however, are carefully bracketed, and the performances that the children produce are carefully scripted.

This socialization does little to prepare young women to later present themselves with as much aplomb as they can muster before a large and distinguished audience at the Miss Heilala pageant, whose patron, seated at the head of the runway, is a member of the royal family. In the early days, the patron was the crown prince himself (Figure 5.2). Every year, a dozen or so contestants partake in the pageant, often under pressure from mothers and other female relatives. When competing, they are expected to display characteristics familiar from pageants in other part of the world: poise, charm, self-assurance, and articulateness, in addition to aesthetic qualities. By parading under the evaluative gaze of an audience that necessarily includes men, the young women are also potentially violating their role in maintaining the sister–brother avoidance relationship, which dictates that they remain modest and not draw attention to their bodies whenever there is the slightest possibility that a same-generation classificatory cross-sibling be present. This dilemma is resolved in a variety of ways: by brothers and male cousins eschewing the pageant in which their classificatory sister is competing; by families adopting progressive ideas; and by everyone acting in a way that desexualizes the pageant contestants. But it is precisely the contrast between these qualities and the qualities that traditional socialization nurtures that defines the Miss Heilala pageant as a rupture with traditionalism, village life, and localness. The contestants are required to be Tongans in and of the world, but still Tongans. This expectation is further reinforced by the fact that the Miss Heilala of the year goes on to represent the country, this

Message From the Patron

The Heilala Festival is an annual celebrations of special significance which plays an important role in ensuring that the essentials of culture are presented in harmony with the modern day world. The festivities, parades and feasts appropriately presented to mark the 77th Birthday of His Majesty King Taufa'ahau Tupou IV symbolise Tonga's great pride in its cultural heritage.

During this week for fun and enjoyment the Tongan gift for song, poetry and dance will find ready expression. You will witness the splendour and grace of traditional dancing, art and craft making of which the intricacies stretch back through the midst of antiquity. The Tongan people's great love for the outdoors will be exemplified by the myriad of events such as traditional boat races, fishing tournaments and sports.

On behalf of the people of Tonga it is my pleasure to extend a warm welcome to our overseas visitors and family members who have specially come to the Kingdom to join us in celebrating Heilala Week. I wish you all a memorable and enjoyable stay in Tonga.

HRH Crown Prince Tupouto'a
Patron

Figure 5.2. "Message from the Patron" in the introduction to the official program of the 1995 Heilala Festival, emphasizing the festival's role in "ensuring that the essentials of culture are presented in harmony with the modern day [sic] world."

time under the title "Miss Tonga," in the international Miss South Pacific pageant (launched in 1986), and hypothetically continues from there to Miss World and Miss Universe.[2]

The winner acquires substantial visibility and the attention of prominent citizens, as do her sponsors and relatives, and is immediately involved in various follow-up engagements that last a year if she lives in Tonga, until her reappearance on the runway at the next pageant. "The principal task of the winner of the Miss Heilala title," declares the 2006 pageant website (www .planet-tonga.com/events/heilala2006/index.shtml, retrieved in June 2010), "is to act as a roving ambassador for Tonga's tourism industry, joining delegations to overseas trade shows and promotions. She will also participate in the promotional activities of the Festival's major sponsors." The material rewards for winning, provided by the corporate sponsors of the pageant, are not unsubstantial. In 2008, the winner of the pageant received two sets of round-trip airline tickets to Australia and Vava'u, as well as a T$3,000 cash prize; the first runner-up tickets to Auckland and T$1,500; the second runner-up tickets to Fiji and T$750; and the third runner-up tickets to Vava'u and T$500. These prizes are obviously oriented to travel and tourism, but they are equally clearly circumscribed within the boundaries of the diasporic Tongan world, the assumption being that the primary goal of leisure travel is to visit relatives.

The jury judging the contestants in the various components of the pageant consists of pillars of Tongan society, high-ranking individuals, business owners, and other important people, including Western expatriates of visibility, although the latter are generally not entrusted to judge components that presuppose knowledge of Tongan dancing or outfits. According to the official website of the 2006 pageant, the contestants that year were judged in five events, which resemble closely, except for a few variations, the program that the pageant has followed over the years: an initial presentation and interview, a "traditional *tau'olunga*" event, a "sarong swimwear" event, a talent quest, and "island creation."[3] Five finalists were subjected to further interviews on stage. This program bears witness to the bifocal consciousness of locality and cosmopolitanism, represented perhaps in the program coordinators' intentions by the potential (but largely unrealized) presence of foreign tourists: the qualification of the *tau'olunga* as "traditional," the use of the term *sarong* (rarely used in Tonga, where the garment is referred to with the Samoan term *lāvalava* or simply *tupenu*, "cloth"), and the generic appellation "island creation," a concept that has seeped into the local repertoire of self-representations but that assumes a distant gaze (in the same way that the often heard expressions "floor show" and "island feast" do).

The actual implementation of the pageant program brings together a traditional and a modern world, as the 1995 "Message from the Patron" makes explicit. Modernity suffuses the pageant itself, the poise expected of the contestants, and their self-presentation. Contestants who speak English competently and demonstrate an educational background or educational aspirations win judges' and audiences' approval. The gait of their walk should reflect that of a model and not be the slow and tired foot-shuffling walk of a village woman. They are expected to answer the interview question confidently. They need to appear at ease in a ball gown and a swimsuit (albeit with the extra cover of the sarong), neither of which is part of the wardrobe of average young Tongan women.

At the same time, to be taken seriously, Miss Heilala contestants must be able to put on acceptable performances of Tonganness through "correct" bodily and linguistic habitus, competence in reified symbols of high culture, and the espousal of values and priorities that are consistent with dominant local discourses. While it is a deeply modern event, the pageant is also deeply embedded in what Tongans view as traditional and important. For example, the "island creation" costumes are outfits that encode both tradition and inventiveness. Contestants' families or sponsors are expected to create them exclusively from materials from the local environment, which include fragrant leaves, flowers, mats, and barkcloth. As the contestants model the outfits on the runway, a voice-over announces, in a poetic style called *heliaki*, "allusive," the nature of each material, locating it in a cultural landscape by specifying place names or personal names associated with each ingredient in the Tongan poetic canon.[4]

Even more importantly, the *tau'olunga* that contestants must perform, which many consider the make-or-break event of the pageant, represents the epitome of proper gender relations and hence the entire Tongan social order (despite its Samoan origin). As in Samoa, where the original *taualuga* is associated with the exalted village ceremonial virgin or *tāupōu*, the graceful and intricate dance is viewed in Tonga as the prerogative of unmarried high-ranking young women. The dancer enters the performance space clad in a fine mat covering her from the upper chest to the knees, pouring coconut oil between the palms of her hands, alternating from one to the other, her body glistening with oil. During the performance, spectators stick paper money onto her body dripping with oil, a symbol of virginity, to show appreciation for her performance and the moral righteousness it implicates. To the accompaniment of a song or combined sung and instrumental backing, the dancer performs intricate hand- and footwork of prescribed but not necessarily choreographed form, punctuated by discrete and ostensibly spontaneous quick head tilts that give style to the performance, while the torso remains static and the dancer smiles rapturously (Kaeppler 1987, 1993). The general effect is one of both joy and control. This effect is further emphasized when men and sometimes older women, inspired by the *māfana*, "warmth," of the performance, come up and dance around the *tau'olunga* performer in a style called *tulāfale*, the studied exuberance of which contrasts sharply with the controlled style of the solo dancer, showcasing her as the center of attention. The dance is fiendishly difficult to execute, and its semiotics fascinating. The female dancer's restricted movements and smile iconicize society's control of virginal femininity and her acquiescence of it, but the fact that she occupies the center of everyone's attention is also semiotic of high rank. Controlled female virginity itself indexes a rank order and the rank order in turn indexes the entire society, in a pattern of "fractal recursivity" (Irvine and Gal 2000). The dance therefore links the female body to the entire Tongan polity through a chain of semiotic associations and embeddings. "The *tau'olunga* is more than a dance; it is an expression of the essence of Tongan culture," asserts quite perceptively the program of the 1995 pageant.[5]

In the early years of the pageant, the *tau'olunga* was the shibboleth that separated local contestants from contestants from the diaspora. The latter's families often had access to greater wealth and more varied resources than most local contestants' families, thus ensuring nicer clothing, better coaching (at least for the Western-style tests), and greater individualistic confidence. These young women traveled to Tonga during their holidays with an entourage of relatives, often at great expense. Some even brought American or New Zealander girlfriends who formed a fair-skinned retinue that contributes enormous symbolic capital, judging by young Tongan men's gaping mouths as the women were paraded on floats through Nuku'alofa streets. Contestants with one Caucasian parent had the advantage of looking more attractive in Tonga, where light skin tones are as prized as they are in many other parts of the postcolonial world. Yet, in the olden days, overseas Tongan contestants rarely could perform the *tau'olunga*, relying instead on hula steps or similar "generic Polynesian" gambits. In an insightful analysis of the

Miss Heilala pageant she wrote in the early 1990s, the late Jehanne Teilhet-Fisk quotes the Princess Royal explaining, "There aren't enough teachers of Tongan dance for them to be able to understand the movements and like it. Hula and Tahitian is [*sic*] very popular, you can look in the telephone book and find a hula teacher in Foster City [California] who was born in Hawaii. So they dance the hula to show their pride in being Polynesian" (1996: 193).

In early pageants, Tongan judges and critics also found that some overseas-based contestants had inadequate proficiency in Tongan. This lack of proficiency represented a disadvantage in a context whose unarticulated subtext was (and still is, to a lesser extent) to demonstrate that locality, despite its association with relative poverty and disadvantage, ultimately triumphs over cosmopolitanism, transnationalism, and the industrial world. (*Pālangi* judges are carefully assigned to judge events that are not imbued with localness.) As a result, few overseas Tongans managed to win the Miss Heilala pageant until the turn of the millennium, and winners were invariably members of the local bourgeoisie. The wording of a magazine story about the 1999 pageant is particularly revealing of both the inevitability of the outcome of the contest and the marginality of nonlocal participants at that time: "The representatives of the Tongan communities from Hawai'i, New Zealand and Australia, enriched the Miss Heilala festival bringing overseas entrants. But again the title stayed in Tonga" (*Matangi Tonga* 1999: 2, punctuation as in the original).

Things, however, have changed, and some overseas Tongans are increasingly striving to be more Tongan than their island-based relatives. Perhaps as part of this identity-asserting project, they have numerically dominated the pageant in recent years. In 2008, out of thirteen contestants, twelve were from overseas, and the winner was Fiona Makisi, a twenty-one-year-old Tongan Australian studying at the University of Sydney. The overseas Tongan contestants come much better prepared than their predecessors of yesteryear with the visible markers of *anga faka-Tonga*, as witnessed by Fiona having won not only the entire pageant but also the individual *tau'olunga* event.

The pageant places on trial not only the young women contestants but also the standards of beauty, competence, decency, and worthiness according to which they are judged, standards that are the objects of divergent opinions. Beauty is one major focus of difference. I have already alluded in prior chapters to the politics of beauty in Tonga, which requires further elaboration here. The hegemonic ideals of female attractiveness demand a pale complexion, but the most attractive fairness of skin is one that is also slightly swarthy, in contrast to the Northern European pallor that Tongans do not find particularly attractive. This preference is one reason why the discourse of skin tone is not one of race but one of rank. The favored pigmentation indexes protection from the sun and hence dispensation from physical work outdoors and has done so throughout Polynesia since precontact days, earlier than any awareness of racial difference other than in comparison with darker-complexioned Fijian neighbors (cf. Miller 2006: 35–37; Schulz 2000). In Tonga, traditionally, the bodies of high-ranking women were massaged; anointed with chewed candlenut, coconut oil, and turmeric; and carefully shielded from the elements so that they kept a pale complexion (Gifford 1929: 129).[6]

In addition, the traditional aesthetics require that a beautiful woman have well-defined features, a full mouth, expressive eyebrows, a high forehead, and an oval face, features that are prevalent among members of high-ranking families (Teilhet-Fisk 1996: 195–196). As I will discuss at greater length in Chapter Seven, Tongans have bodies that on some measuring scales place them among the largest in the world. In some contexts, beauty is attached to these features in that large bodies can encode abundance, well-being, and fertility. Miss Heilala contestants who sport tall and full figures are not necessarily disadvantaged by these attributes.

As is the case of all hegemonic ideals, this prescriptive aesthetics is not without competing idealizations. Slim (but not thin) figures have also long been admired in Tonga. Years of health campaigning have communicated to most people the fact that fat too easily turns into obesity, with which come high-blood pressure, heart disease, and diabetes (the ravages of which are all too real), even if health campaigns do not provide people with the material means to change their diets. Plumpness may be a marker of both high rank and the abundance of food, but it is also the marker of the carbohydrate-rich and protein-poor diet with which the poor have to make do, while slimness bears witness to one's material ability to make diet choices. Many Tongans explain away these co-occurring body ideals as a competition between Tongan and Western body aesthetics (Teilhet-Fisk 1996: 196). Western commentaries on Pacific Island bodies are replete with comparable explanations, some attempting to rehabilitate and celebrate the fat body while paying lip service to the fact that "modernization" has introduced new ideals of thinness (for example, Pollock 1999). These explanations fail to contend with the fact that competing body size ideals have long coexisted in the Pacific Islands and the diasporas. Whether Tongans find a fat or thin body attractive (and whether they care at all) is contingent on the gender, age, rank, social class, and relative urbanity of both the observer and the observed, just as these parameters of difference (plus ethnicity) are deeply implicated in such judgments in industrial societies. Western commentators' statements about "cultural ideals" of fat and thinness ultimately remain embedded in underexamined orientalizing assumptions of cultural homogeneity and difference and more often than not in an understanding of "the West" suffused with Occidentalism. Predicated on an understanding of culture as seamless (Gremillion 2005: 16), these accounts also assume a simplistic cause-and-effect relationship between large-scale social conditions and body ideologies, implying for instance that someone who moves from the village into town or from Tonga to the West, or who comes into wealth, will mechanically adopt a new understanding of the body, which is of course not the case.

At the pageant, attractiveness, as well as standards of decency, poise, and confidence, is the subjective call of judges, who are of heterogeneous backgrounds, in terms of rank and nationality at least, and who bring to the task their own intuitive standards. The task of judging, frankly, is too frantic to leave much opportunity to ponder over criteria of beauty and suitability beyond the intuitive, and the complimentary liquor served to the judges in some cases lubricates their judgment to the point where the contestants begin to blend together into an impressionist scenery. As a result, the choice of winners has sometimes been surprising, as well as deeply disappointing for some contestants. Rumor has it that, in early years of the pageant, particular high-ranking people would influence the outcome in ways other than the simple application of criteria. The blind voting and auditing that is adhered to today make such rank pulling unlikely. The young women come from different backgrounds and represent a heterogeneous panoply of body types, from the plump to the slim, with features that correspond to traditional ideals to features that reflect mixed ascendance, years overseas, and the partaking in beauty consumption. Miss Heilala winners over the years have ranged widely, from classical Tongan beauties to young women whose physical appearance reflects cosmopolitan yet also locally relevant aesthetics.

Where the pageant remains firmly grounded in a local context is in the requirements of the *tau'olunga*, which are at once a matter of skill, practice, body type, and commitment to one of the most overelaborated semiotic forms of tradition. The twist is that this localness, which overseas Tongan contestants once found so difficult to achieve, is now well within their reach, as diasporic

Tongans have become deeply interested in demonstrating their Tonganness and have developed the means to do so in Auckland, Sydney, and the San Francisco Bay Area. It is this showcasing of localness, this reification of tradition that figures so prominently in the judging of the pageant that has so consistently disadvantaged, with a couple of exceptions, the Tongan winners as they step up to the next pageant level, the Miss South Pacific pageant. There, one's skills in dancing the *tau'olunga* with all its exacting details, one's proficiency in the Tongan language, and one's ability to come across as a virtuous, rank-conscious, and modest young Tongan woman are largely irrelevant.

The Miss Heilala pageant is thus a site deeply steeped in certain forms of modernity. Contestants are expected to present themselves as articulate and worldly subjects and to parade with confidence before the cream of Tongan society, setting aside the shame of exposing their bodies to the public gaze, thereby potentially compromising their *faka'apa'apa*, "respect," relationship to their cross-siblings. At the same time, it is a site that both represents tradition and produces it, by encapsulating in very specific performable products: the *tau'olunga*, the language, and a particular performance of the self.

The Miss Galaxy Pageant

Emcee: Next contestant is, Miss LADY MARIA BOUTIQUE! Sōnia- Ines-Trula Morgan.
((*heckler calls out, Sōnia waves regally, audience laughs*))
Twenty years old, she comes from Vava'u.
She weighs sixty-eight kilograms,
her hobbies are, dancing, netball, and fishing.
((*audience laughs*))
((*collusive intonation*)) God knows what she is fishing for.
((*audience laughs*))
Her occupation is, computer programmer.
((*audience applauds*))
Future plans is to be a good wife, with ten children.
((*audience applauds*))
((*collusive intonation*)) (She's going to do a lot of sitting at home).
((*audience laughs*))
((*concluding the introduction*)) Miss Lady Maria Boutique, Sōnia Ines Trula Morgan!

This monologue, with which the emcee of the Miss Galaxy pageant introduced one of the thirteen contestants in 1997, encapsulates much of the flavor of Tonga's "other pageant." That pageant showcases transgender males,
to whom Tongans refer as *fakaleitī* or *leitī*, members of a small but visible
minority in Tonga, whose numbers, by all accounts, are growing every year.
The word *leitī* is borrowed from the English word *lady*, but it is used only in
reference to transgender males, while *faka-* is a polysemic prefix ubiquitous
in Tongan, which in this context means "in the way of" (as it does in *"anga
faka-Tonga"*). For reasons that I will explain presently, transgendered men
prefer to call themselves *leitī* rather than *fakaleitī*. This is the term I use in
this book, unless I index the perspective of mainstream Tongans, most of
who continue to use the prefixed form. More rarely, nontransgender Tongans speak of them as *fakafefine* (literally, "in the way of a woman").

Started in the late 1970s as an underground event held in dingy discos
around town, during which contestants would have to fight off straight male
audience members' drunken pawing, the Miss Galaxy pageant has grown
over the years into an astonishingly popular and increasingly mainstream
three-day-long event. For several years, it was held at the Dateline Hotel, but
in 1997 the noble who presided over the hotel's management committee, an
Evangelical Christian, barred the pageant from the hotel, an illustration of
what Rosalind Morris aptly calls the "transnational circulation of prohibi-
tion" (1997: 56–61). It then moved to the Queen Sālote Memorial Hall, and,
at the 1997 pageant, the patron, Princess Lupepau'u Tuita, who was then a
twenty-year-old student in the University of Auckland's Anthropology Department, delivered an articulate and pointed speech subtly criticizing anti-
leitī sentiments among government officials. Ironically, the move to the new
venue gave the pageant much greater visibility and dignity, the opposite effect from what its detractors intended, as the hall seats many more people
than the hotel and its raised runway insulates contestants from unwanted
hands-on attention.

Even when not informed by Evangelical Christianity, male (and some female) public officials have mixed feelings about the pageant and *leitī* in general. They voice an embarrassment fueled by concerns about "what visitors
might think" and by layers of anxiety about masculinity, Christianity, and, if
one believes *leitī*, their own past activities when they were young men. This
ambivalence is reflected in the way in which official acknowledgment of the
pageant has lagged behind its popularity. For years, there was no mention of

it in the *Tonga Chronicle*, the government-run newspaper, and brief coverage began appearing in the back pages only in the mid-1990s. The Tonga Visitors Bureau did not list the pageant in its official festival program until the turn of the millennium. In the meantime, *Matangi Tonga*, a privately published magazine (later web-based), and *Taimi 'o Tonga*, a Tongan newspaper published in Auckland, had been publishing lavish photo spreads about the pageant every year, eventually giving other media little choice but to follow suit. Today, the pageant is listed in the Heilala Festival program, featured on government official websites, and broadcast on national television.

Over the years, some of the most prominent women in Tonga, such as the princess royal and her daughters (whose regular entourage includes *leitī*), anoint the pageant with their official patronage, bestowing upon it the endorsement of rank. *Leitī* regularly assert that royal patronage has been directly responsible for the improvement of their public respectability, reducing the bullying to which young *leitī* are subjected in schoolyards, for example. The pageant today receives financial sponsorship from Air New Zealand, and is co-organized by a cadre of influential elite Tongan women d'un certain âge and by the emcee Joey Mataele, the transgender scion of an entrepreneurial family in Tonga with distant blood ties to the Tongan royal family, whose introduction of contestant Sōnia opened this section. As in the Miss Heilala pageant, the jury of six or seven is composed of nontransgender dignitaries (for example, businesspeople, intellectuals, high-ranking army officers, the current Miss Heilala) and "distinguished" expatriates (such as banker's wives, diplomats, visiting professional athletes, the occasional anthropologist).

The contestants are younger *leitī*, generally poor, low ranking, and multiply marginalized (Figure 5.3). The prizes are similar to and sometimes more substantial than the Miss Heilala prizes, but they mean a great deal more to Miss Galaxy contestants, who are generally much poorer than Miss Heilala contestants. Unlike Miss Heilala, the reigning Miss Galaxy does not go on to represent the country in any supranational contest, to the relief of some. Sponsored by various businesses and organizations (including hotels, hairdressing salons, taxi services, rugby teams), contestants appear on stage in various costumes, ranging a gamut familiar from South Pacific pageants in general, which includes evening dress, "island wear" *puletaha*, and "their own creations." The outfits are the product of careful development by contestants, members of their family, and friends, and they end up covering the full range from stunningly beautiful to over-the-top camp. Most contestants are serious

Figure 5.3.   Contestants in the 1997 Miss Galaxy pageant, flanked to the right by emcee Joey Mataele, surrounding the beaming winner, Vaisima Langi (Natasha Pressland), whose beautiful gown was later ruined by a glass of red wine that another contestant "accidentally" spilled (August 1997).
(Source: Tod Kent.)

about the pageant and the possibility of winning, although a few enter the pageant knowing full well that their age, rugby-player thighs, or corpulence leave them with little chance of winning, and take the opportunity to clown, to the delight of the audience and the annoyance of other contestants.

Each appearance is ostensibly designed to allow contestants to present themselves as attractive and feminine persons, following familiar patterns of beauty pageants around the world. The core of the pageant consists of several judged events, including an individual talent display, a brief interview, and runway parades. Interspersed are entertainment routines, which may include a hula performance by the emcee, a Tongan R&B standard sung by a local talent, a dance routine performed by all contestants to a popular Tahitian or disco tune, and a short classical and torch-song concert by nontransgender performers.

In many ways, the Miss Galaxy pageant is the antithesis of the Miss Heilala pageant, and it is precisely the quality of carnivalesque inversion that it embodies that makes it so attractive to audiences. Unlike Miss Heilala pageants, which many have long declared to be plodding and interminable, Miss Galaxy pageants, when successful (which they are not always), have attracted large eager audiences. Some are dressed to the hilt; others, in the back, whoop and scream in various stages of inebriation. All segments of society are represented: from the high-ranking to ordinary villagers, from elderly grandmothers to babies falling asleep in the arms of their teenage brother, from urban sophisticates driving up in late-model SUVs to rough-looking village teenagers who don't quite know where they are going to end up at the end of the evening but harbor the hope that they might find a solution among pageant contestants. Completing the audience are expatriate residents, members of the various overseas volunteer organizations, and a few tourists, many of who come to see what they think is an event of outstanding exoticism. Although audience members come to the pageant with a wide variety of expectations (including being entertained by *leitī*'s antics and hoping to have a laugh at their expenses if a bra slips off or a wig falls off), most attend Miss Galaxy to see beauty, inventiveness, and glamour inscribed in the creativity of the outfits and the spectacular effects of dance routines and talent displays. Because for many Tongans the pageant epitomizes *leitī* identity, and because beauty making is the overt purpose of the pageants, the link between beauty and transgender is overelaborated, overflowing into day-to-day contexts, such as appointments at the beauty salon, as I will discuss in the next chapter.

Coming up with a precise definition of who a *leitī* is in Tongan society, and in the other Polynesian societies in which comparable identities are prevalent, is neither possible nor fruitful, for the same reasons that trying to define "man" or "woman" in any social context is not a useful project. Nevertheless, one can attempt to circumscribe the identity in two ways: by comparing it to the normative gender standards from which it departs and by identifying the stereotypes of which it is the subject. Tongan "hegemonic masculinity," to invoke an oft-used concept that we owe to R. W. Connell (1997) despite its shortcomings (for example, see Demetriou 2001), is sustained by highly constricting codes of hypermasculine identification and performance of virility, which are in turn related to rank. Constitutive of this identification are a controlled emotionality; a competitive orientation enshrined, for example, in intersibling status rivalry; a grounding of the self in the local rather than the transnational or in addition to selected tokens of the transnational; indifference for homebound and aesthetic pursuits and ambivalence toward intellectual ones; little overt concern about body image after early adulthood; friendship networks grounded in exclusively male circles; and, particularly among young unmarried men, relations with non-kindred women that are almost exclusively sexualized. In all these respects, *leitī* score a "failing grade," often from early childhood.

Focusing on stereotypes is another way of circumscribing the identity, and those abound, as they do wherever they concern a minority partially defined through sexuality. These stereotypes provide a working definition of the category, although they remain prone to distortions, underlain with moral judgments, and subject to manipulation and resistance. Focusing on them, however, is particularly pertinent to an analysis of the pageant, because the latter is a site in which the stereotypes are formed, played with, and contested. According to stereotypes, *leitī* enact an emotionally demonstrative and impulsive presentation of self; are particularly concerned about beauty, creativity, and domesticity; worry about body image well into adulthood; befriend women, who in turn often seek out their company; enthusiastically engage with and index the outside world and its cosmopolitan possibilities; define "straight" men as objects of erotic desire; and act as the "receiving" partner in oral and anal sexual intercourse. "Straight" men in turn often flirt with *leitī* openly without jeopardizing their masculinity, as is the case in many other societies with comparable gender-crossing categories (Gutmann 1997), and during intercourse take the "inserter" role, at least in theory (*leitī* themselves have other stories to tell), which maintains their masculine identity intact. These patterns are changing because of the growing awareness of the stigma associated with same-sex flirting in the mainstream societies in which the diaspora is embedded. Normatively, *leitī* do not express sexual desire toward one another. (For further discussion, see Besnier 1994, 1997, 2000, 2002, 2003, 2004.)

Transgender people are part and parcel of contemporary Polynesian societies and exist more ambiguously in other parts of the Pacific. They are known in Samoa as *fa'afafine* (Dolgoy 2000; Drozdow-St Christian 2002; Mageo 1996), the Cook Islands as *laelae* (Alexeyeff 2000, 2008a), in Tahiti and surrounding islands as *māhū* (Elliston 1999; Kuwahara 2005: 9–11), in Hawai'i under the same appellation (Matzner 2001), and among New Zealand Māori they self-refer with the neologism *takatāpui*. New Zealanders refer to Pacific Island transgender people generically with more or less garbled versions of the Samoan term, which ends up coming out of the mouths of *Pākehā* (Anglo) New Zealanders as *"fafifine"* or *"fafa."* The only unambiguous (but copious) reports of the presence of the transgender at early contact are for Tahiti (Besnier 1995: 288–295). In the early nineteenth century, Will Mariner, who was intimately acquainted with Tongan society and animated by an Enlightenment-era relativistic curiosity, made no mention of transgender people in Tonga in the recollections of his four years in Tonga.[7] Some mainstream Tongans today insist that the identity is the result of "Western influence," in tune with the cross-culturally common anxiety to attribute an external origin to what people see as undesirable aspect of society. In contrast, indigenous gays and lesbians in postcolonial New Zealand and Hawai'i are busy searching for evidence of the existence of the transgender in pre-contact days. It is, however, clear that transgender categories are historically grounded in the "structure of the conjuncture" (Sahlins 1981: 35), which is congruent with the "in-between" and performative nature of the identity (Balme 2007; Wallace 2003).[8]

Mainstream society's response to *leitī* wavers between the bemused, the annoyed, and the admiring, particularly of the industriousness and creativity of some *leitī*. There is a wonderfully matter-of-fact ethos to most face-to-face rapports between *leitī* and mainstream Tongans because *leitī* continue to be embedded in structures of kinship that, for them as for everyone else, is the foundation of social legitimacy. Women in particular find in *leitī* a source of friendship, pleasurable gossip, and flattery. At the same time, some Tongans express mock annoyance at the fraudulence of *leitī* self-presentation and identity, to which *leitī* retort that they are "ladies," and that men prefer their intimate company to that of real women. Mainstream Tongans, particularly men, respond to these claims with impatience. They consider them frivolous, particularly in the context of serious issues such as kinship-related rituals.

Boys are sometimes teased or bullied mercilessly when they show early signs of effeminacy, one telltale sign of which is a lack of enthusiasm in playing rugby. Parents of a *leitī* child respond to their child's gendering variously. Some welcome it, quietly thankful that they will have one unmarried child to take care of them in old age. Others worry about the inherently exploitative relationships that *leitī* form with "straight" men, as I will discuss presently. In the context of the sister–brother dyad, *leitī* are expected to behave as brothers to their female classificatory female siblings, at least in public. The most edgy people around *leitī* are their own "straight" brothers. Senior male siblings, as guardians of their female siblings' reputation and dignity, patrol social spaces to prevent any violation of the *faka'apa'apa*, "respect," owed to their sisters. Much more than parents, straight boys find it problematic when a young sibling shows sign of becoming a *leitī*, as they see the very persona of the latter as foregrounding sexuality, and they often exert serious physical violence in a futile attempt to "straighten up" the child. *Leitī* who have no older brother report a much more hassle-free childhood and early adulthood than those who grew up with older male siblings.[9]

As is the case in all societies other than postindustrial "post-Stonewall" societies, transgender identity is primarily a matter of gender, that is, constituted by boys acting in a feminine manner (although a particular form of femininity, which does not simply emulate local forms), from which logically derives sexual desire for masculine men, as well as masculine men's desire for a feminine-acting person, although the latter is much more secretive. Tongans generally assume that men who are slightly less than virile desire other men and that they exclusively desire "straight" men, even if they are married with children, as occasionally happens, and even when they are simply "sensitive New Age males" who grew up in the diaspora. However, they also assume that a male person who is predominantly attracted to other men desires "straight" men, and that they are or should be feminine acting. Thus both mainstream and *leitī* agree that Western-style nongendered gay identity is puzzling at best, fraudulent and deeply transgressive at worst. ("What's 'gay,' again?" one *leitī* would sometimes ask me, years into our friendship.) Like transgendered Tausug in the Southern Philippines (Johnson 1997: 207), some Tongan *leitī* continue to express unmitigated scorn for what they interpret as the foregrounding of sexuality in Western gay identity (for example, in lesbian and gay pride parades or in same-gender couples living together openly) and are scandalized at the thought of non-feminine-acting men having sex together ("God created man and woman," they point out sanctimoniously).

For years, my *leitī* friends and I silently agreed not to raise the issue of my own sexual identity (to my face at least), and as a gay man I maintained a prudent profile in this deeply homophobic society. Only after successive waves of crystal-clear evidence, including my partner accompanying me to Tonga, *leitī* encountering me at the 2002 Gay Games and various Mardi Gras festivals in Sydney, and several *leitī* coming to stay with me in Wellington and later with my partner and me in California, did the issue of my sexuality become less of a "secret." Tongan mothers of "good families" stopped insinuating that I would be a good match for their daughters, and no longer warned me, "Don't spend so much time with *fakaleitī*, they are going to try to sleep with you!" (while, unbeknownst to them, their own sons were having a fabulous time in the company of *leitī*).[10] Significantly, the comments of which I would eventually become the object focused on the lack of clear "fit" between my gender identity and sexuality. "Niko, he's man during the day and he dances the hula at night!" once teased one *leitī* friend within my hearing range (the hula being associated primarily with femininity in Tonga). "I don't understand why some *leitī* think that they have to behave in a manly way," my female assistant, an uncompromising *leitī* groupie, once declared to me, ostensibly in reference to a *leitī* whose demeanor was not as flamboyant as the rest.

Of course, all this is in constant flux. People, *leitī* or otherwise, now know what *gay* means. Several middle-class gay-identified Tongan men live in the islands, most remaining extremely discreet about their sexual orientation. Tongans who grow up in the diaspora "come out" as gay men without identifying as *leitī*, and some come to Tonga on visits (none stays very long). Their coming out has prompted some parents to react, "You can come home as a *fakaleitī* if you want, but not as a gay man!" Some young Tongans moving overseas, both *leitī* and straight, redefine themselves as gay, while Auckland and Sydney sex clubs are regularly visited by Polynesian "MSMs" ("men who have sex with men" but who self-identify as straight, a category not without its problems). Clearly, in the same way that the substance of any identity lacks determinacy, the boundaries between *leitī*, "straight," and gay identities are porous.

Leitī identity formation is crisscrossed by dynamics that reach far beyond the confines of narrow characterizations of gender and sexuality. An important theme is the notable way in which *leitī* orient their lives toward modernity, to an extent and in ways that many Tongans do not. While mainstream Tongans tacitly recognize, in their rapports with and attitudes toward *leitī*, that this orientation is part and parcel of who they are, they do not explicitly point to it as a characteristic marker of the identity, yet *leitī*'s modernity-oriented projects are as central to understanding their place in Tongan society as their gendering. A focus on language use offers a particularly striking entry point into the intricacies of the problem, particularly in the way English plays a prominent role in *leitī*'s linguistic repertoire. The name of the category itself says it all: The word "*leitī*" in and of itself indexes the English language, its contexts of use and its symbolic associations with modernity and cosmopolitanism, an indexicality that probably operates largely at a subconscious level. This indexicality is further reinforced by two factors: the original meaning and connotation of the English word "lady" (evoking sophistication, class, good breeding) and *leitī*'s own preference for the unsuffixed version of the term, which "denativizes" the term even further by stripping away the Polynesian morpheme *faka-*, which sounds too much like "fuck," an issue for people anxious about other people's perception of them as oversexualized. Furthermore, no matter how elementary or fluent their English proficiency may be, *leitī* pepper their conversations with one another and others with English. In doing so, they risk becoming the butt of gossip for being "hurry mouth no grammar." And here is where I return to the Miss Galaxy pageant.

The most striking contrast between the Miss Heilala and the Miss Galaxy pageants is the fact that contestants in the former are expected to perform a local identity that a significant number find difficult to perform, while contestants in the latter perform a nonlocal identity.[11] The different parties involved present this nonlocality in various ways, but it usually involves a mixture of modernity, cosmopolitanism, upward mobility, and Westernness that is not bound by the strictures of local moralities, power dynamics, and economic realities. However, for many Miss Galaxy contestants lacking the resources and consequent familiarity with the outside world, the task is a difficult one to enact, just as some Miss Heilala contestants find it taxing to dance the *tau'olunga* competently and speak credible Tongan.

Nonlocality is embedded in the very name of the pageant. Both funny and poignant, "Miss Galaxy" lays claim to an ambitiously cosmopolitan context and plays on hyperbole in the same fashion as some of the campier aspects of the pageant (such as the more extravagant costumes and performances) by creating humor while attempting to retain control of it. While it lasted, Vava'u's Miss Cosmos made an even grander claim. But nonlocality also saturates other aspects of the pageant. For example, in one of the events contestants are required to appear in "national" costumes as representatives of foreign "countries" (for example, Miss Rarotonga, Miss Switzerland, Miss South America), despite the fact that most contestants have no affinity whatsoever with those places. Participants refer to the nonlocal in numerous other ways: At the organizing stage for instance, they provide their ages, vital statistics, occupations, and personal aspirations—information that one of the organizers enters on bio-data sheets.[12] By emulating international pageant practices, participants in the pageant aim for glamour, of a kind that reaches beyond the confines of the local context.

In addition to bearing the names of the countries they represent, Miss Galaxy contestants go by female-sounding stage names of their own choosing, which they often use in everyday contexts. These names are generally coinages that bear linguistic similarity to the bearers' original Tongan names (for example, Susi from Sōsefo) and are either English names (such as Priscilla Pressland) or names chosen for their exotic sounds (such as Aisa De Lorenzo or Aodushi Kiroshoto). The stage names are never Tongan. The nonlocal flavor also pervades the stage decorations (in 1997 there were flower arrangements and rather unfortunate bouquets of phallic-shaped multicolored balloons), the background music (for the 1997 opening event, a medley of triumphalist classical themes including the William Tell Overture), and the singing and dancing numbers. When events are explicitly designed to add local color, such as a *tau'olunga* that some *leitī* perform expertly (better than many Miss Heilala contestants) or a popular Tongan tune sung by one of the organizers, they are bracketed entertainment routines designed to fill time while contestants are getting changed or squabbling backstage. When a contestant does decide to perform a Tongan dance for the talent event, it is generally a spoof.

Throughout the pageant, the dominant language is English, in contrast to Miss Heilala, where the Tongan language is the focus of elaboration, as well as anxiety for contestants from the diaspora. When Miss Galaxy contestants first present themselves, for instance, they do so in English. Following is contestant 'Aisa's brief introductory speech in 1997:

> 'Aisa: ((*walks up to the mike*)) Good evening ladies and gentlemen. My name
> is Aisa De Lorenzo, I'm eighteen years of age, and I represent,
> ((*pauses dramatically, raises arms triumphantly*)) BLUE PACIFIC
> TAXIS! ((*walks down runway*))
> [1997:Sony:2 1:07:36–1:08:20]

Each contestant will have memorized and rehearsed her lines prior to the pageant and will take utmost care to utter them correctly and loudly. This does not prevent occasional slip-ups, which the audience will immediately ridicule boisterously. The important point is that, for most contestants, speaking English before a large and distinguished audience of elite Tongans (many of whom are bilingual) and foreigners represents a serious challenge. Many *leitī*, particularly pageant contestants, speak only minimal English because poverty and marginality have hindered their access to opportunities to learn the language. A significant number have not traveled overseas, and those who have resided in industrial countries have not done so under privileged conditions.

By centralizing the English language and its associations, *leitī* position themselves on the side of prestige, worldliness, and nonlocality and in opposition to the use of Tongan and its localizing connotations. But their sociolinguistic practices, both in and out of the pageant, adds further complexity to the situation. Indeed, despite the obvious difficulties that *leitī* experience in speaking English during the pageant, many Tongans expect them to speak English more readily on a day-to-day basis than nontransgendered Tongan men for a number of reasons. First, Tongans generally see *fakaleitī* as self-assured and brash creatures that know no shame (*ta'emā*). While in actuality some *leitī* can be relatively self-effacing, the demeanor of others underscores this stereotype. One illustration of their alleged shamelessness is the participation of some *leitī* in a pageant that constitutes the prime reinforcement of popular *fakaleitī* stereotypes: Contestants' behavior in the pageant can be moderately outrageous and certainly exhibitionistic, as many imbibe large quantities of liquor prior to appearing on stage. Second, stereotypes of *leitī* depict them as oriented toward modernity, the West, transnationalism, and change. Once again, the extent to which this stereotype reflects reality varies among individuals, but the uncompromisingly nonlocal design of the pageant reinforces the stereotype. Viewed in this light, the prominence of English in the pageant is hardly surprising since English is the language of nonlocality. Finally, Tongans tend to view the use of English as having feminine undertones: As in many other societies in which a language of modernity competes with a code of traditionalism (for example, Gal 1979; Meyerhoff 2003), the former is associated with women's aspirations for upward mobility and emancipation from the strictures of tradition. When I questioned them about this topic, most Tongan men and women I knew explained that women speak better English overall than men due to the fact that girls study harder in school and that women are "by nature" talkative. These familiar-sounding assertions demonstrate that the gendering of language use is tacit and embodied in practice rather than explicit and grounded in overt consciousness.

As a result of this gendering, men who speak "too much" English do so at the risk of compromising their masculinity in the eyes of others. This concerns *fakaleitī*, who willingly go to great lengths to disassociate themselves from their masculine attributes. Interestingly, it also concerns Tongans born or brought up overseas: Their awkwardness in performing Tongan maleness (including speaking Tongan as a preferred language) frequently brands them as *fakaleitī*-like, regardless of whether they present any identifiable signs of effeminacy in their comportment. The use of English has many associations in addition to nonlocality: it potentially indexes deficient Tonganness, deficient masculinity, femininity, and transgendered identity, traits that overlap only partially but that are readily lumped together. Thus failure to perform Tonganness may easily become a sign of imperfect masculinity and vice versa, unless it is mollified by convincing mitigating factors, such as rank or wealth.

The elaboration of nonlocality in the pageant is not without irony. As discussed earlier, most contestants live in relative poverty, and sustaining the level of nonlocality expected of them is difficult for many contestants as a result. In particular, the difficulties contestants have in maintaining English as their working language during the pageant places them in an awkward position, and they switch to Tongan once they have delivered simple memorized lines. For example, in the interview event, contestants are given the choice of answering in English or Tongan, and most contestants choose the latter. In 1997, however, one contestant chose English, and the audience initially reacted with a loud murmur of temporary admiration for her courage. It took little time, however, for her to stumble, as she searched for an English word while waving her hand campily. The audience, apparently satisfied by the expected proof of the fraudulence of her claim to cosmopolitanism, began hooting and ridiculing, forcing her to abort her brave attempt:

> *Emcee:*   What would you say about being a hairstylist, or- being- a working- what- what does it mean, like, to be working at Joy's Hair Styles?
> ((*sotto voce, summarizes the question in Tongan*)) *Ko e hā e meʻa ʻoku ke fai ʻi he* hair salon?
>
> *Masha:*   ((*takes cordless mike*)) Well thank you very much.
> ((*audience laughs, then shouts with admiration and encouragement*))
> If you want your hair to be curled, ((*beckons with her hand*)) come over.
> ((*audience explodes in laughter and whooping, Masha laughs and then becomes serious and requests silence with her hand*))
> Uh, I like it very much, and uh- I enjoy working there, with uhmm-
> ((*pauses, word-searches, waves her hand, audience explodes in laughter, drowning the remainder of the answer*)) blowers,
> ((*unable to finish, mouths*)) (thank you).

((hands mike back and returns to her position))
[1997:Sony:4 0:02:45–0:03:55]

Contestants are thus in a difficult position: If they answer in English and make mistakes, the audience will laugh at them; if they answer in Tongan, the audience will see it as evidence that they are unable to carry off the artifice of nonlocality. The ridicule that greets the choice of Tongan is congruent with many other aspects of mainstream Tongans' attitudes toward *fakaleitī*, both at the pageant and in day-to-day interactions. Most mainstream Tongans I know consider *fakaleitī* identity essentially bogus: Here are men pretending to be women, and not just women but cosmopolitan sophisticates, but they cannot hold their end of a simple conversation in English. At the pageant, it is not uncommon for drunken men or women to try to rip contestants' outfits and expose them for what they "really" are, namely persons with male anatomies. Nothing generates greater hilarity than contestants losing their bras.

When I asked *leitī* and non-*leitī* why nonlocality was so central to the Miss Galaxy pageant, they responded variously: It increases the sophistication and glamour; it is for the sake of the tourists; it allows one the freedom to explore new outfit ideas unconstrained by the blandness of dominant dress codes. Without downplaying the validity of these motivations, I propose that a full explanation must appeal to a larger context (at the risk of provoking among Tongans the reaction that I am "overreading"). Many mainstream Tongans have told me that, in everyday contexts, the only men who have sex with *fakaleitī* are older male tourists and marginal members of Tongan society, such as old widowers. Yet it takes very little time in the company of *leitī* to realize that their sexual activity is limited to neither tourists nor marginal Tongans. Tourists with an interest in *fakaleitī* are far too few to cater to all sexually active Nuku'alofa *leitī*. The stereotypical association of *leitī* with potential *Pālangi* partners, however, is an enduring one, through which mainstream Tongans distance themselves from the morally repugnant possibility that their own male relatives may have sexual liaisons with *leitī*. Yet a walk through Nuku'alofa streets in the company of a *leitī* demonstrates clearly that many Tongan men see themselves as a *leitī*'s potential sexual partner. One of the most common interactional styles between "straight" men and *leitī* is sexual and gender-based banter, which frequently focuses on the alleged fraudulence of *leitī* identity but just as often broaches the possibility of sex. For many "straight" men, these dynamics end when the banter ends.

For a number of others, it leads to sexual encounters that do not jeopardize their heterosexual masculinity, although these trysts are generally shrouded in silence. For a small minority, it leads to romantic attachment and the possibility of an exclusive sexual liaison—at least for a while.

For many underprivileged *leitī*, however, sexual relations with "straight" Tongan men leave much to be desired. They are often onerous, as they have to be backed up with liquor, entertainment, and monetary gifts at the *leitī*'s expense, in part because alcohol and other gifts absolve the "straight" partner of the responsibility for desiring what is after all another male body. A sexually active *fakaleitī* may thus have to spend a lot of money "to take care of all his boyfriend's needs" (a recurrent phrase from *leitī* conversations, always uttered in English and with moralistic reprobation about other *leitī*'s actions). These dynamics define sexual relations between men and *fakaleitī* as distinct from pre- or extramarital relations between men and "real" women (in which the woman stereotypically provides sexual favors while the man provides economic resources), and thus emphasize the fact that *fakaleitī* are not real women. During one of my fieldwork visits, one *leitī* "disappeared" for three days with three young strapping lads who had just returned from a successful sport competition overseas. Wagging tongues in the know whispered that she had spent her meagre wages on liquor and a rental car (not cheap by any standard in Tonga), taking everyone and everything to the beach and calling in sick. Her irresponsibility, for disregarding her own family's needs and jeopardizing her job in a market where employment is scarce, did not go unremarked. Furthermore, everyone assumes that "straight" men will eventually marry a woman and that their sexual encounters with *leitī* (as well as loose women) are meaningless. The serious affective bonds that occasionally arise between "straight" men and *leitī* undermine this assumption, but this possibility constitutes a hidden discourse that no one (other than *leitī*) talks about. *Leitī* themselves often disparage each other's sexual and affective relations, describing them as *palakū* "ugly," as I will elaborate in the next chapter. Ironically, more privileged *leitī* are in a much better position to establish long-lasting liaisons that are not based on unreciprocated exchange patterns, perhaps because privilege enables them to be more assertive in their relations with less privileged "straight" men.

It is in this general context, in which the dignity and welfare of *fakaleitī* potentially fare poorly, that subscribing to a nonlocal modernity provides useful symbolic resources. It enables *leitī* to claim that they are exempt from local regimes of morality and exchange, including marriage, that marginalize and potentially degrade them. Presenting oneself as part of a larger context is a defiant attempt to limit the scope of locally grounded morality and interpersonal dynamics. Perhaps more importantly, this strategy supports the "occidentalist" idealizations that many *leitī*, particularly those who do not have much firsthand experience of industrial countries, harbor about the West.[13] According to these idealizations, a *leitī* in the West can marry a man, or at least enter into a marriagelike relationship, which many *leitī* (particularly underprivileged ones) see as a desirable solution to their exclusion from marriage in Tonga. Furthermore, establishing a romantic relationship with a *Pālangi* man provides an escape from onerous and dignity-compromising local expectations of unreciprocated generosity. Westerners are wealthy by definition, and a relationship with an older *Pālangi* man represents material security for *leitī*. Perhaps more importantly in recent years, it offers the possibility of an immigrant's visa to New Zealand or Australia, which since the 1990s have granted permanent residence to the nonnational same-sex domestic partners of nationals. This possibility is not to be underestimated in a climate in which border crossing, particularly by poorer Third World citizens, is increasingly criminalized; immigration authorities in industrial countries are closing national borders for reasons that range from nationalistic paranoia to the scapegoating of economic migrants as the sources of all ills.

However, the quality of the possibilities that relations with foreigners offer is mitigated. The stereotype of a *leitī*'s potential *Pālangi* partner is that of an older and unattractive man, albeit comfortably middle-class. Like other stereotypes, the image is not without grounding in experience, but it is not quite what *leitī* have in mind when they talk of their desires for hypermasculine, handsome, younger, and ultimately heterosexual Tongan men. Wagging tongues comment derogatorily that *leitī* who enter in relationships with a *ki'i motu'a Pālangi 'ulu tula*, "little old bald-headed Westerner," in the diaspora have compromised their own dignity, in addition to having turned their back on the Tongan Way in pursuit of material designs. Attractive *Pālangi* heterosexual men are for the most part absent from the range of possibilities. There is of course no dearth of young strapping *Pālangi* gay men in New Zealand, Australia, and the United States who desire brown-complexioned men, but their desires are generally oriented to younger masculine-acting Polynesian men and not *leitī*. Because they desire straight-acting men, Tongans categorize these men as *leitī*, no matter how butch the latter may consider themselves, and therefore *leitī* do not consider them potential sexual or romantic partners.[14]

The reality of most Miss Galaxy contestants' lives, however, is that the association with nonlocal modern life projects often remains confined to the symbolic. Most will not be able to migrate overseas, legally at least. Those who will are unlikely to find in the West the better circumstances that they think are available. Many Tongan *fakaleitī* who migrate to New Zealand, for example, become "Pacific Islander queens" or *fa'afāfine*, the Samoan equivalent of *fakaleitī* and a term that has been incorporated into New Zealand English to refer to all Polynesian transgender men, as I mentioned earlier. In New Zealand, they may join the ranks of transgender prostitutes lining certain streets of Auckland or Wellington, or at most they will eke out a living through multiple poorly paid part-time jobs, like most other Tongans. But the containment of *leitī*'s occidentalist constructions of Otherness within the realm of fantasy is supported by more than the material unattainability of these fantasies. Indeed, *leitī* (particularly those who have resided overseas) frequently express disappointment about many aspects of what the West has to offer. In New Zealand, for example, most *leitī* want nothing to do with Western drag queens, transgendered persons, or gays and lesbians, categories with which mainstream New Zealanders naïvely lump Pacific Islander *fa'afāfine*, often with the most liberal of intentions.

Similarly, while the pageant frequently includes one or two overseas-based transgendered persons from other Pacific Islands (for example, Samoa, Fiji, Cook Islands), local *leitī* (and many other Tongans) often find the nonlocality that these contestants embody to be at odds with their own vision of Otherness, even though the overseas contestants have an easier time performing Otherness than local contestants and sometimes end up winning the contest. For example, when one overseas Tongan contestant showed up to rehearsals in 1997 with a goatee (which she shaved off before the pageant), local *leitī* were scandalized, and when the same contestant chose lip-synching as her talent performance during the pageant, she received nearly unanimous zero scores from the judges. (Her choice also led to tense moments as technicians unfamiliar with lip-synching rushed on stage, thinking that she had switched off the mike by mistake.)

In 1999, 2000, and 2008, the overseas transgendered contestants who won the contest clearly had had access to hormones and perhaps a surgeon's scalpel to help them along with performing femininity. In 2008 in particular,

Japanese-Hawaiian Selena Nagaoka from Las Vegas, a hair and make-up art-ist who had come to Tonga to prepare female royal heads for the coronation, won the pageant even though she had never heard of Tonga until a week before her arrival. While these contestants' seriously worked-through femi-ninity impressed some of the judges, they generated scorn among local *leitī*, among whom they were the subject of furious gossip, not only because they represented the already privileged winning privilege but also because their understanding of being transgender is at odds with *leitī*'s. The referent of *leitī*'s performed nonlocality is therefore not the reality of what the West offers but, like occidentalism in general, a self-contained, self-referential re-ality, the terms of which are determined in local standards of aesthetics and social action (cf. Johnson 1997: 193–210).

Nevertheless, the relationship between nonlocality and modernity on the one hand and locality and tradition on the other is an uneasy one. Indeed, many Tongans who are locally grounded in structures of wealth, rank, or power have a secure stronghold in transnational endeavors. Today they are enthusiastic migrants and consumers of tokens of capitalism and cosmopoli-tanism, while remaining solidly grounded in local structures of traditional-ism from which they also derive benefits. When these individuals publicly embrace modernity and cosmopolitanism (by using English in daily conver-sation for example), no one accuses them of rejecting locality and tradition-alism. Even if they were criticized, they would have little to worry about. Wealth and power ensure their hegemony over the local context and enable them to dictate what counts as local in the first place. In contrast, when a poor or low-ranking Tongan embraces transnationalism and modernity too candidly, in the form of the use of English for example, that person is per-ceived as rejecting locality and tradition, a rejection that exposes him or her to ridicule. Miss Galaxy contestants' performed nonlocality fits into this cat-egory. Whatever the contestants' intentions, they risk being perceived as ar-rogant or as attempting to rise above their stations despite the tangible lack of material grounding to substantiate these claims of upward mobility.

Like all ideological linkages that disadvantage some and benefit oth-ers, however, these judgments are not immune to contestation on the part of the marginalized. This was powerfully illustrated by a minor incident in the 1997 pageant, when quick-witted contestant 'Āmini or Lady Amyland, sponsored that year by Joey's Unisex Hair Salon where she was working (see Chapter Six), turned the tables on the audience during the interview event, and perhaps on society at large, if only for a fleeting moment. Before she had a chance to answer the emcee's question, she was heckled by a drunken *leitī* in the audience who urged her to answer her interview question in English (*faka-Pālangi*). The heckling drew some laughter because many knew that Lady Amyland's English was poor and that she would make a fool of herself if she tried. But Lady Amyland had the last word:

Emcee:	Miss Joey's Unisex Hair Salon! What do you have to say to promote Joey's Unisex Hair Salon?
	(((*lowers voice, translating into Tongan*)) *Ko e hā e me'a 'oku ke fai ke* promote *ai 'a e-* ((*rolls eyes, searches for Tongan word*)) *fakalakalaka ai 'a* Joey's Unisex Hair Salon.
Heckler:	*Faka-Pālangi, 'Āmini!*
Audience:	((*laughter*))
'Āmini:	Sorry excuse me, I'm a Tongan ( ) ((*the rest of the answer drowned by deafening laughter, vigorous applause, catcalls*))

[1997:Sony:4 0:05:42–0:06:26]

Lady Amyland answered the heckler by reaffirming her Tongan identity and therefore her duty and privilege to answer the question in Tongan. The unexpected nature of the claim, which the audience found humorous to the extreme, stems from the fact that Lady Amyland makes it in a context in which everything is done to foreground nonlocal modernity. The humor had already begun with the heckler, who spoke in Tongan while urging the contestant to speak English, also referring to the contestant by his everyday male name ('Āmini) rather than her stage name (Lady Amyland). What Lady Amyland did here was part of a wider tacit ongoing project of at least some contestants to take greater charge of the pageant and its effect on the audience. This project consists of stripping the audience, and society at large, of its privilege to ridicule contestants and take control of the boundary between humor and seriousness. It is this project that some audience members bemoan when they complain about *fakaleitī* taking themselves "too seriously."

But the project goes further, and its meaning becomes clear when viewed in light of the previous analysis. Note that Lady Amyland asserted her claim to Tongan identity not in Tongan but in English. The covert message is that one can assert one's Tonganness while controlling the tools with which one does so and while using tools that are not part of the sanctioned repertoire.

In addition, the preface of her repartee ("Sorry excuse me") was an inside joke that mainstream audience members were unlikely to make sense of, a reference to another *leitī*'s awkward attempt, a few years earlier, to speak English to a prospective *Pālangi* date. The overall effect of the repartee contests the power of dominant forces to dictate what counts as markers of locality and what does not; asserts that claiming to be part of the "galaxy" does not necessarily mean denying one's local identity; reminds people that the Miss Galaxy pageant is part of a festival designed to celebrate Tongan identity; and proclaims that being a *leitī* does not mean giving up one's place in Tongan society. I do not wish to imply that Lady Amyland's act of resistance was the result of a carefully engineered strategy on her part. For one thing, she was seriously inebriated. If we have learned anything from Scott (1985, 1990), however, it is that everyday acts of resistance need not be the outcome of calculated designs.

So far I have focused on the subtle but consequential struggles that pitch *leitī* and non-*leitī* Tongans against one another both in and out of the pageant. But, as I have already indicated, not all *leitī* are on equal footing socially, materially, and symbolically. While pageant contestants who are principally involved in these struggles are located at the lower end of the socioeconomic and prestige ladders, more privileged *leitī* are also involved in the production of the show, some quite centrally so. And the same struggles that characterize relationships between *fakaleitī* and mainstream Tongans are also at play in the relationships between more and less privileged *leitī*.

Interactions between contestants and the *fakaleitī* emcee provide copious illustrations of this struggle. The main organizing force behind the pageant, the emcee, is a member of an economically successful family who was part of the first wave of entrepreneurs, and she works hard to make the pageant possible, relying on her powerful social connections and cosmopolitanism. At the same time, her position during the pageant and related situations is ambiguous and shifting. Joking sometimes with the contestants and sometimes at their expense (thereby undermining some contestants' efforts to claim control of humor), she engages in a complex play of allegiances and collusions, which mirrors and informs her general position vis-à-vis both other *leitī* and Tongan society at large.

The dynamics I describe here illustrate ways in which patterns of inequality, other than those directly associated with transgenderism, are as relevant to interpersonal dynamics within the ranks of *fakaleitī* as they are to

Tongan society as a whole. In particular, the many forms of power found in the structure of Tongan society at large also exist in structure hierarchies among *leití*. As Ortner (1995) aptly remarks, the marginalized have their own politics through which the very concept of marginalization is negotiated and contested.

Modern Bodies on the Runway

Beauty pageants highlight several constitutive aspects of modernity: They objectify gendered bodies by placing them under the evaluating gaze of audiences; they are designed as competitions based on allegedly meritocratic principles; they afford the winner the opportunity to become a confidently cosmopolitan citizen in charge of her future; they are organized on a homogenized pattern set by cognate international events; and they put forth a morality that mediates between local and presumably universal standards of acceptability. This quintessentially modern essence goes some way toward explaining the enormous popularity of beauty pageants across the developing world, which contrasts sharply with their waning status in the postindustrial world. Beyond these simple remarks, however, one finds that different pageants enact this modernity differently, bearing witness to the shifting nature of modernity. That beauty pageants differ across societies is now amply documented. What we are less aware of is that different beauty pageants can mean different things within the same society, as I have demonstrated in this chapter.

While they both seek inspiration from the same international events, the Miss Heilala pageant and the Miss Galaxy pageant showcase different forms of Tongan modernity, each associated with different constraints, different constituencies, and different projects. Miss Heilala elaborates a strong sense of locality, but of course a sense of locality that is deeply modern, equipped with the distancing that makes possible, for example, the outfits in the "island creation" category, inventive creations made of leaves, flowers, barkcloth, and mats, displayed with a poetic voice-over that identifies specific people and places in the country with which each ingredient is associated. The anxiety surrounding the *tau'olunga* performance as a clearly bounded and concretely defined form of traditionalism results from the modernity of the participants' increasingly common overseas residence. How can one, the pageant tacitly asks, be a modern Tongan at ease in a cosmopolitan world of possibilities and self-making while at the same time recuperating a sense of local identification?

In contrast, the Miss Galaxy pageant (which also includes its own "island creation" category) showcases an extravagantly nonlocal modernity, which articulates with the complicated politics of sexuality and respectability between the contestants (and those that they represent) and the rest of society, as well as among *leitī* themselves. The questions that the Miss Galaxy pageant asks are similar to the ones that the Miss Heilala pageant asks, but the answers diverge. While Miss Heilala contestants begin with the modern cosmopolitanism and must perform localness, Miss Galaxy pageants begin with localness, and a marginalized one at that, and must perform modern cosmopolitanism. Both projects nevertheless involve an awareness of multiple audiences, inspirations, and desires, some distant and some near. With this bifocality, contestants, organizers, audiences, judges, sponsors, and high-ranking patrons all contribute to the simultaneous construction of tradition and modernity, which emerge from these events in different configurations that relate to wider contexts in different ways. For the young contestants, partaking in the pageants is a delicate project, particularly as they perform before a consequential and critical public, but the Miss Galaxy contestants perhaps put even more on the line than the "real misses": While performing localness poorly has no effect on the transnational privilege that many Miss Heilala contestants already have, the *leitī* must ensure that their localness is not compromised because ultimately that is all that they have. This is perhaps why the prizes for which Miss Galaxy contestants compete are more attractive than the prizes that the Miss Heilala winner receives.

Chapter Six

Coloring and Straightening

Mara's Hair Attraction is located near the end of a row of commercial units that open onto the parking lot of a shopping center on the edge of Nuku'alofa's main business area, the first of its kind to be built in Tonga.[1] During the events of 16/11, the shopping center's peripheral location was its saving grace, as neither the looters nor the flames got to it. A medium-sized supermarket, which has seen better days, occupies the main commercial space of the one-structure center. It is often devoid of customers all day, its three or four employees trying to drown boredom in conversations that they do not interrupt for the sake of the occasional customer, adding to the desultory atmosphere. A sewing shop, a shipping agent, a Chinese-owned supermarket, a garage, a plastic flower rental shop, a pawn shop, an Internet center, a karaoke bar, an insurance agency, and a mobile-phone repair shop have occupied the other units, staying open as long as the managers were not too insistent about back rent. The shopping center as a whole has long begun to show the effect of age and poor planning. After a heavy downpour, the seriously potholed parking lot transforms into a veritable swimming pool, with water deep enough that cars find it impenetrable, and the water level often reaches such heights that the various shops are flooded, damaging inventories and requiring a tedious day of cleaning.

In 2008, the salon's employees were two *leitī*, one in her late twenties and the other, from Vava'u, in her early forties, who lived together with the family of the former. The salon is often full of friends who drop by, often on their way out of the country or on visits from overseas, chatting and teasing, uproarious laughter punctuating every utterance, risqué jokes alternating with rapid-fire whispered gossip. The hairdressers talk and laugh with customers, many of whom are regulars, and those who have just come to catch up on the news, the *leitī* often performing their signature mixture of femininity and over-the-top sexuality for the benefit of "real" women customers and visitors.

Despite the name that was originally bestowed onto it ("Joey's Unisex Beauty Salon"), the salon is a decidedly female and *leitī* world.[2] Non-*leitī* adult men sometimes come in for a quick haircut. Younger men occasionally drop in to have their hair colored blond, an increasingly popular statement of hipness among Nuku'alofa boys and men, or to flirt with the *leitī*, but they generally time their visits when the salon is quiet. When it is busy, the din of hairdryers barely manages to cover peals of laughter, whooping, and concurrent animated conversations, dominated by the dramatic intonation contours of *leitī* talk. News and gossip alternate with lewd talk and updates on upcoming beauty pageants. When they walk in, customers are greeted effusively with flattering comments about their appearance, and it is this effusiveness that some identify as one of the things that make them want to come back. Under the previous owner, a serious royal hanger-on, young female members of the royal family would occasionally have their arrival announced with a phone call, at which point the salon would be off-limits to other customers and hangers-on. These visits no longer happen, as princesses have found more upscale ways to have their hair done.[3]

Everything about the salon is designed to produce an inviting atmosphere, one steeped with sophistication, cleanliness, and cosmopolitanism, attuned to the attention to the self that indexes these values. Women customers arrive, usually in one of the better cars that crowd Nuku'alofa streets, because spending T$20 and up to get one's hair done presupposes a certain level of wealth, and park right in front of the salon, thus avoiding an uncomfortable walk under the unforgiving sun. The bold blue-and-white tiles are color coordinated with some of the walls and the frames of the oversized mirrors. Hair color charts and glamour posters adorn the walls, although some have seen better days, but this is true of many such decorations in Tongan lived environments, whether commercial or private. The chairs are as comfortable as one can find in the kingdom, and the generous piles of fashion and gossip magazines from New Zealand, Australia, and the United States make one almost forget that most are years out of date. The stereo, with the volume turned up, is generally tuned to Radio Tonga's eclectic music offerings, which these days in Tonga combine *hiva kakala* (literally, "songs of the fragrant flower"), Tongan R&B, Pacific Island pop and hip-hop, and an eclectic selection of Western popular tunes.

The business was founded many years ago by a prominent *leitī* from a wealthy business family. Time has somewhat obscured the salon's exact inaugural moment, but this uncertainty did not prevent the owner, in 2000, from throwing a lavish party to mark the business's twenty-first birthday. A few eyebrows were raised as people calculated in their heads that twenty-one years ago she would have been awfully young to start a business. Never mind, the party was enjoyed by all, as half of the crowd sat primly drinking sodas at tables set up in the parking lot, watching the other half (which included "real women," "straight" men, and *leitīs*) become progressively more inebriated on cheap rum and rowdier as the evening wore on. Not long afterwards, the owner sold the business to another *leitī*, for reasons that depend on whom one asks. She claims that she had more important endeavors to attend to, such as travelling overseas as a consultant (of a difficult-to-determine nature) and accompanying royalty on various missions. Others suggest that a formidable stack of unpaid bills had encouraged her to sell out.

The salon's single air-conditioner broke down a decade ago. Even if it were in working order, the salon workers would be unlikely to use it because of the prohibitive cost of electricity. Two ceiling fans provide relief from the heat, which can be oppressive in the shopping center's stuffy units. Coolness, however, is a key feature of the hair treatment, which usually begins with a long shampoo session in the specialized tubs fed by rainwater, the purpose of which is as much to prepare the hair as it is to *fakamokomoko* "cool off." If the water pump feeding water from the shopping center's tank is out of order, the salon employees will have gone in a taxi to fill buckets from the water tank of the nearby Wesleyan church. The stylists pay much care to the shampooing (as long as they are not interrupted by "booty calls" on their mobile phones), studiously massaging customers' heads, making the salon visit an "experience" characterized by a sought-after coolness and relaxing comfort (cf. Ossman 2002: 71–72). The other activity that is the object of much attention is styling with hairdryers, which make up for the heat that they generate by producing an aura of power, cleanliness, and artistry. Stylists often say that they enjoy working with hairdryers, and the hours that they spend blow-drying and styling clients' hair bear witness to this enjoyment. To complete the "experience" of visiting the salon, the original owner had partitioned off part of the salon into a massage area, where she had set up a massage table acquired on a trip overseas. The demand for body massages, however, was virtually nonexistent, as Tongans are reluctant to remove their clothes in front of others, an act that is both disrespectful and lacking in self-respect.[4]

I became intrigued by Nuku'alofa's beauty salons in the course of my earlier research on *leitī*. As in many other parts of the world (see, for example, Johnson 1997 on the Muslim Philippines and Reid 2007 on rural South Africa), transgender identities in Tonga are intimately connected to the creation of beauty, its institutionalization as an industry, and its professionalization. The search for beauty inscribes itself on the very body and in the very actions of the transgender, particularly in the context of and leading to beauty pageants. The relationship between hair styling and transgender identity, however, is not a simple one. It is not so much that *leitī* dominate numerically the beauty industry at any given moment, but that they take turns holding jobs over time. There is also an unarticulated sense, in Tonga as elsewhere (for example, Reid 2007: 117–118), that the transgender have to "work" harder and more self-consciously at creating gender than ordinary people, so that their being "experts" at working on one of the most gendered aspects of the body, the hair, makes perfect sense. Several salon patrons allude to these dynamics when they identify hair styling as inscribed in their "nature" (*nātula*):

> *Pea 'oku 'i ai pē fa'ahinga fakanātula ia 'o e fakaleitií, 'oku nau ngāue- nau fili ngāue kinautolu mei ha ngāue 'oku- 'oku ma'ama'a fe'unga mo e me'a pē 'oku nau lavá, pea mo e me'a 'oku fakasanisani ke nau fakamanimani pē ai he taimi kātoa pē.*
> [Nuku'alofa Interviews Salon 'A 05-02-08, 3]
> And it is an aspect of the natural constitution of *fakaleitī* that makes them work- makes them choose among the jobs that are light enough for them to do, as well as things that are sanitary so that they remain clean all the time.

This remark links *leitī*'s "nature" to cleanliness and light work, congruent with the delicate version of femininity that they assiduously cultivate. At the same time, a number of respondents reminded the interviewer that *leitī* are still men, and as such they have greater strength than women (*nau ivi lahi* "they have a lot of energy") and are more earnest in their work (*nau*

Figure 6.1. Lady Amyland ('Āmini) in front of Joey's Unisex Hair Salon in 2000, where she was employed at the time.

fai fakamāatoato 'enau ngāué). The latter remark echoes similar themes that recur in the discourse about the transgender across Polynesia and beyond (Besnier 1994: 296). In particular, it is *leitī*'s hands that are deemed strong, and the employees of this particular salon capitalize on this assumption by giving each customer a powerful and soothing head massage, which is not available in competing salons. Informants' explanations of *leitī*'s attraction to hairstyling bypass the possibility that becoming a hairstylist is one way of coping with poverty while claiming a sense of dignity associated with creativity, cleanliness, and beauty (Figure 6.1).

A Very Brief History of Tongan Hair

The head, and in particular the hair, is a semiotically laden body part in Tonga as is the case everywhere else in Polynesia. In pre-Christian times, the head of chiefs was *tapu* because it was the seat of their efficacious power (to which anthropologists commonly refer as the overdetermined notion of *mana*). Only designated people could cut chiefs' hair, and after the foundation of the kingdom this restriction was applied most saliently to the king. Since Christianization, the tabooing of the head, and in particular of the hair, has undergone democratization, as it is no longer only chiefly heads that cannot be casually touched, but also those of commoners. The taboo applies particularly to certain kinship relations: For example, a son is specifically proscribed from touching his father's head, in tune with the avoidance affect that suffuses father–son relations (Bott 1981: 15–16). More generally, touching someone's head is a serious insult that calls for retaliation, a fact not lost on angry young men eager to provoke one another.

It is in this context that the hair and its grooming historically embodied a particular significance that persists to this day. In precontact days, chiefly hair, whether female or male, was worn long while commoners' hair was generally, although not always, cropped (Cummins 1977: 87). Comments about hair length occupy a central place in many early travelers' journals (hair, like clothing or the lack of it, being one of the easiest things to notice without taking the trouble of trying to interact with the Other). The following remarks are from the journal of Dutch navigator Abel Janszoon Tasman, the first European visitor to Tongatapu, to which he "gave the name of Amsterdam because of the abundance of refreshments we got there": "At noon a small prow with three men in it put off from land and came near our ship; these men were naked, of a brown colour and slightly above the ordinary stature; two of them had long, thick hair on their heads, the third wore his close cut; they had only their privities covered with a curious small bit of cloth" (1644 [1965]: 26). The skimpy barkcloth garments and the fact that the men came out on a canoe suggest that they were of low rank, while the cropped hair on one of the men possibly was a sign of mourning. "Their women . . . wear their hair shorter than the men; the beards of the latter are as a rule the length of three or four finger's breadths, the hair on the upper lip being cut pretty short so that their mustachios are no longer than about two straw's breadths" (1644 [1965]: 28).

Missionization and attendant social change altered this semiotics as nineteenth-century men, regardless of rank, began wearing their hair short. Commoner women's hair was more resilient to change: Photographs show them, well into the mid-twentieth century, wearing their hair relatively short. Despite the short hairstyle that most people find appropriate on men, the association of male hair with power remains, although it is only foregrounded when explicit attention is drawn to it. This is the case, for example, when men grow their hair long, a sight that remains unusual in Tonga. It is associated with "born again" Tongans in the diaspora and "deportees" (*tīpota*) searching for the historical roots of Tongan masculinity, often with inspiration from symbols associated with Hawaiian and Māori activist indigeneity. Baldness is another trait that draws attention to the link between hair and power: While rare in Tonga, baldness does occur, and men lacking hair are often ashamed of the condition. Its sight often arouses comments, which vary in tone from derision to contempt to pity. In Tongan eyes, the frequency of baldness among Western men confirms the latter's general weakness: As I discussed in the previous chapter, *ko e kiʻi motuʻa Pālangi ʻulu tula,* "a bald *Pālangi* little old man," is a descriptor through which Tongans package together references to Western men's stereotypical ineffectiveness, lack of virility, and unattractiveness.

Long hair on women became commonplace in the course of the 1960s, although it was worn braided (*fī*) or bound (*faʻu*). As elsewhere in Polynesia (see Mageo 1994; Shore 1989; Valeri 1985), the binding of female hair in Tonga iconicized and continues to iconicize social control and in particular sexual restraint. In contrast, loosening the hair (*tuku ange*), which in the case of Tongan women often frees up a thick mane whose luxuriousness is accentuated with coconut oil, iconicizes sexuality, individualism, lack of so-cial control, and danger, categories that are tightly connected with one an-other. It is permitted in very restricted public situations, such as when young women perform the *tauʻolunga*, which I analyze in the previous chapter. It is no wonder that dangerous spirits, who are known to seduce young men before killing them, sport long hair (Gifford 1929: 293). It is also no wonder that traditional women loosen their hair only in private and that schools have strict rules requiring girls to wear their hair braided.

The semiotic importance of hair length is dramatically demonstrated in funerary rituals, in the context of which the warp and woof of Tongan society is exposed most explicitly. Allegiance to the traditional order demands that women mourn by wearing their hair loose. On the tenth day of a funeral, the eldest sister of the father of the deceased (*mehekitanga*), or alternatively the most senior relative in the position of *fahu* to the deceased, cuts the hair and sometimes shaves the eyebrows of mourners, male or female, who are of lower rank (*tuʻa*) than the deceased (that is, related to the deceased through his or her mother), as well as anyone else who wishes to demonstrate respect (*fakaʻapaʻapa*) for the mourning family. Those who undergo this process are said to *liongi*, and their hair is either cut short or even burnt (*tutu*), resulting in some tufts of hair being shorter than others. Like the oversized, coarse, and frayed *taʻovala* that *liongi* relatives wear at and following funerals, the particu-lar appearance resulting from hair cutting and burning is iconic of mourning. It operates as a sign that one is so bereft that one no longer cares about one's appearance. In pre-Christian days, *liongi* relatives would also mutilate them-selves in various ways on the occasion of the illness or death of a high-ranking person, particularly by chopping off the last phalanx of their pinky, or which-ever next was available, a practice referred to as *toʻo nima*. Western visitors to Tonga never failed to note the number of people lacking fingertips (for example, Tasman 1644 [1965] in the seventeenth century, La Pérouse 1799 in the eighteenth century, Brenchley 1873 in the nineteenth century).

At the 2006 funeral of King Tāufaʻāhau Tupou IV, who had no sister and therefore whose children and grandchildren had no *fahu*, the *liongi* relatives had their hair cut by Heeni Katipa, a Māori princess, who as a high-ranking outsider was theoretically one of the only people entitled to touch their hair. (In practice, low-ranking Tongans and foreigners regularly style princesses' hair.) An "impromptu" hair-cutting event had also taken place earlier in the week: Because overseas Tongans who were *liongi* had to return home, the king's eldest granddaughter, Lupepau'u Tuita, cut their hair before the tenth night, an event that is norm-breaking in two ways, timing and kinship. As these examples demonstrate, considerable semiotic meaning is attached as a marker of allegiance to a traditional order, meaning that modernity both transforms and perpetrates, a complexity in which Nuku'alofa hair salons are deeply involved.

Professionalizing Beauty

Documenting the historical trajectory of the professionalization of hair care in Tonga requires a fair amount of reading between the lines because hair salons, of all businesses, are not legible in historical records: Not only does hair care concern very small-scale ventures, but beauty shops are also run by and for the least visible citizens, namely women and *leitī*.

When I originally lived in Vava'u in the late 1970s, there was nothing in sight that resembled a hair salon. A few barbers were in operation, cutting men's hair (thick on top, sides and back buzz-cut) under trees or in private backyards, small businesses that continue to operate today. One man from Niuē (a New Zealand territory east of Tonga), Sione Tuna, was Nuku'alofa's barber for many years, operating from a shop on Tāufa'āhau Road. Another Nuku'alofa barber who operated in the early 1980s in a tiny shack across from Cowley's Bakery is still there today. In contrast to men's barbering, women's hair care was a private affair confined to washing and cutting, conducted in the privacy of homes, perhaps in the company of sisters or daughters. When asked about hair care back in the 1980s (a decade I chose for my interview protocol so that it still stood in people's memories while predating hair salons), most interviewees laughed at the thought of calling what women did at the time "doing one's hair" (*ngaahi 'ulu*), some adding that what went on in those days was not a matter of "style" (*sitaila*) but of basic hygiene.

It was in 2000 that I noticed that salons had proliferated. What is behind this proliferation is difficult to assess precisely. It is suggestive that the 1990s were also the time when the secondhand marketplace began growing, and that Nuku'alofa's business landscape expanded. The decade also saw an influx of money through the squash boom, while it lasted. By that time, some overseas Tongans or their children had managed to extricate themselves from the underclass migrant slot, earning much more than members of earlier migrant generations, which allowed them to send more money to relatives or to invest it themselves in businesses that relatives would run. One salon that opened in the late 1990s, for example, is run by the spouse of an athlete employed in professional rugby in Japan. Piggybacking on this new wealth were new ideas about appearance and consumption.

In mid-2008, my assistant and I enumerated forty-one salons in Nuku'alofa, and we probably missed some and did not cover salons in outlying villages of Tongatapu. Some appear, more or less consistently, in the Yellow Pages section of yearly editions of the telephone directory (Table 6.1), bearing witness to their longevity and better financing. However, telephone directory listings are only suggestive, as they include only businesses that have a dedicated fixed landline and are not too far behind in paying their telephone bills. They do not include salons that share a phone number with another business, that are reachable only on a mobile number (which is increasingly the case of phone users since the introduction of mobile technology in the early years of the millennium), and whose phone service has been cut off. Conspicuously absent from the phone list are salons operated on the side by Chinese immigrant entrepreneurs, who have begun to present stiff competition to Tongan-owned businesses, as in all other areas of retail and service in Tonga.

The figure of forty-one salons is equivalent to a little under one salon for every 500 inhabitants of Nuku'alofa. Even Nuku'alofa inhabitants who are attuned to the business report the feeling that they cannot keep track of new ventures. Opening a hair salon represents an attractive way of going into business. Unlike other kinds of business (such as food handling), it is not only viewed as clean but also designed to create beauty, concepts that go hand in hand. Doing people's hair can provide schedule flexibility, allowing its operators to give their attention to children and other family matters while running the business. Opening a hair salon does not require an onerous initial investment. The training can be acquired while washing and cutting relatives' hair or helping out at a salon (no styling training is in fact available in the country). At the same time, hair work enables agents to claim a degree of professional expertise. Hair salons thus represent a convenient, adaptable, clean, professional, and "appropriately feminine" business venture (cf. Gimlin 1996; Harvey 2005; Jacobs-Huey 2006).

When asked about the efflorescence of salons in recent years, interviewees invoke a variety of explanations. Some complain in exasperated tones:

TABLE 6.1.

Hair salons listed in available telephone directories, spelled as in the original.

Salon name	1976, 1979, 1981	1985–86	1989	1990–91	1992	1993	1995	1997	1998	1999	2000	2002	2004	2005	2006	2007	2008	2009
'Ana Hair Stylist										✓	✓	✓	✓	✓	✓	✓	✓	✓
Angelina Hair Fashion															✓		✓	
Baby Blue										✓	✓	✓	✓	✓	✓	✓	✓	✓
Hair Style											✓	✓	✓	✓	✓	✓	✓	✓
City Hair Studio		✓																
Dateline Hotel Beauty Salon					✓	✓	✓											
Florence Piliu Hair Dresser				✓	✓	✓	✓											
Hair Trend												✓	✓✓	✓	✓	✓	✓	
Halaevalu Hair Stylist																		
Joey's Unisex									✓	✓	✓	✓	✓	✓	✓	✓		✓
Beauty Salon (now Mara's Hair Attraction)									✓									
Joyces Hair Stylist						✓	✓	✓										
Leslies Hair Fashion		✓																
Longo's Hair Stylist					✓	✓	✓	✓	✓					✓	✓		✓	
Mafi Tu'akoi				✓	✓	✓	✓	✓	✓									
New Image Hair Company										✓✓								
'Ofa Hair Stylist			✓	✓	✓	✓	✓	✓	✓	✓			✓✓	✓✓✓	✓✓✓	✓✓	✓✓	✓✓
Pioneer Hair Fashion											✓							
Setaita Hair Dresser			✓	✓	✓	✓	✓	✓	✓	✓								
Siosi's Hair Stylist		✓											✓✓	✓✓	✓		✓	✓
Victoria Hair Stylist																		
Wailoa Hair Salon																		

Source: Phone directories issued by the Telegraphs and Telephones Department [1976–1981], Tonga Telecommunication Commission [1985–2000], and Tonga Telecommunications Corporation [2002–2009]).

"Tongans are all that way, one person comes up with a good idea, and then everyone tries to imitate what he or she has done!" Among the other themes that emerge is the explicit link between the proliferation of hair salons and the increasing importance that women attach to their appearance, of which the hair is one of the most important aspects. Urban women are no longer satisfied with letting a sibling or a neighbor cut their hair, nor do they feel comfortable with graying hair, yet they do not have the confidence to dye or straighten their own hair (and chemicals, in any case, are not readily available locally). Other informants, particularly younger ones, allude to the fact that paying attention to one's appearance is one aspect of the inexorable march toward development (*fakalakalaka*), of keeping up with the times, and of a desirable openness to new things. "We have to think, we have to explore the world *mo e ngaahi foʻi* latest *ko iá* [and the various *latest*]," affirms, with audible impatience, a young secondary-school teacher in a characteristic code-switched style that embodies her modern outlook on life.

The extent to which hair salons are successful as business ventures is debatable. In high season, prior to Christmas and during the Heilala Festival, salons exude activity, particularly on Fridays and Saturdays. Some appear to be consistently busy at other times as well, but in reality this image is often created by friends who drop by and get their hair washed and blow-dried for free. Particularly at times of the year when potential customers' pocketbooks have been emptied to pay for feasts, prestation to church conferences, or school uniforms, the salons can stay depressingly vacant all day. At such times, the hair stylists at Mara's Hair Attraction while the day away, leafing absentmindedly through magazines, watching intently who is coming into the adjacent businesses, commenting on who is who and who did what to whom, or sleeping under the tree on the other side of the parking lot, from which one can catch the sea breeze that elsewhere in the shopping center the design of the building blocks. The bills, including electrical bills for the ceiling fans and the stylists' salaries, continue to accumulate even if there are no paying customers. Yet the image that hair salons strive to exude is one of success, and many young salon employees are convinced that if they operated their own salon they would be much richer.

Operating a salon presupposes access to an overseas source of hair products, as the few products available in Nukuʻalofa shops are overpriced, and finding relevant products at the Tuʻimatamoana and Tofoa secondhand marketplaces is a matter of luck that cannot be counted on to run a business.

Consequently, like other business owners, salon owners design their trips to New Zealand, Australia, and the United States so as to combine private engagements (such as visiting relatives, attending weddings, partaking in funerals) with shopping for large supplies of shampoo, conditioner, coloring products, hair straightening products, gels, hair clips, scissors, brushes, combs, and towels, as well as more substantial purchases such as hairdryers and furniture. They bring these supplies back either as personal luggage, which has the advantage of being easier to slip by customs agents but the disadvantage of incurring excess-baggage charges, or packaged in a box and shipped as sea cargo back to Tonga; on arrival the business owner will have to pay consumption tax, customs duty, and a quarantine fee.

Consuming Hair Care

Nuku'alofa women bring to the salon desires that their predecessors did not know existed or did not think of as within their purview: for cosmetics, individualized styles, and the experience of professional care. These desires are congruent with the new centrality that consumption occupies in people's lives in urban Tonga and resemble those that draw people to the secondhand marketplace and that encourage them, if they can afford it, to travel overseas to shop or patronize shopping services. While the salon draws a wide cross-section of the urban female population, a sizeable number of customers are middle-aged working women. They have both the means and a reason to have their hair done, in contrast to their compatriots who, in the words of one of my informants, "stay home and boil the root crops and sweep the floor." In their own words, busy working women have no time to do their own hair, but they have the means to pay for the salon rates: in 2008, T$25 for shampooing, blow drying, and styling; T$50 for straightening. The salon affords them the opportunity to feel that they are saving time, even if in fact they end up spending more time getting their hair washed, cut, blow-dried, straightened, and dyed, as well as catching up on the latest gossip, than if they were to do it themselves at home. In their own eyes and in the eyes of bystanders, time spent at the salon nurtures the image of a successful career woman with a full professional agenda. Professionalized hair care is thus situated in a capitalist logic of both production and consumption. By paying for hair care, customers demonstrate an ability to participate in modern consumption, implying access to money (and other resources), whether from their own earnings, their husband's or children's income, or remittances from overseas. Here as elsewhere, the *idea* of consuming is perhaps more important than the *act* of consuming (Baudrillard 1988).

In particular, the white-collar workplace requires managers and employees to look "clean," well dressed, and well coiffed, as part of the regime of capitalist discipline that also demands such qualities as punctuality. For example, customers evaluate restaurants in terms of the cleanliness of employees' appearance and self-presentation, and these evaluations often come up in conversations among friends. Government departments, particularly ministries and comparable venues potentially frequented by the high-ranking, require that female employees and visitors wear the *kiekie* (tasseled belt) over a *pule-taha* (tailored two-piece matching ensemble), and that male employees and visitors wear a *tupenu* (tailored man's skirt) with a plaited *ta'ovala* wrapped around it. (Western-style trousers are not allowed, except for *Pālangi*.) As I discussed in Chapter Two, these outfits became "traditional clothing" during the modernity-making reign of Queen Sālote III, and they index a commitment to *anga faka-Tonga*, which also encompasses a host of other ideals. Tidy, controlled, and well-groomed hair, particularly for women employees, is part and parcel of this desirable presentation of self.

For employees of the dwindling civil service, as well as for private sector workers, NGO employees, and entrepreneurs, the appearance of the body becomes a project of its own, one that is embedded in self-definition. Hair straightening, for example, opens a host of styling possibilities to individuals whose naturally kinky hair (*'ulu mingimingi*) otherwise does not. One aspect of this project consists in keeping oneself youthful and thus to pay regular visits to the hair salon to get one's hair dyed to hide graying hair, a practice that began, according to informants in the know, in the early 1980s. As one interviewee, the owner of a small but successful restaurant, asserts (in accented English), "When you do your hair, you look renew again . . . Heh? And like when I dye my hair, I look- I feel to myself I look young. Even though I'm not young, but I- I- I just feel it." The quest for youthfulness is evident in the demand for hair coloring products, high on the shopping lists that salon owners take with them overseas and those that friends who own salons have asked me to bring to Tonga. It also requires the professional services of salon employees, as women do not feel confident enough to dye their own hair with do-it-yourself products and equipment and do not trust anyone in their own family to do it for them. The possibility of coming out of an amateur job looking like hell is more onerous than paying for the services of a professional.

As in the industrialized West (for example, see Wolf 1991), monitoring the most visible markers of aging such as white hair is embedded in a larger context of modernity, business success, and careerism in which modern middle-aged Tongan women seek to partake. This larger context contrasts sharply with a traditional ideology in which the body and its appearance are not mirrors of the individual but attributes of social relations, particularly kinship. In the latter context, which dominates rural lives and the lives of the less privileged, people pay little attention (or at least appear to do so) to the gradual decline in the aesthetic appeal of the body that accompanies aging. There the social body is not bounded by the individual's skin but instead encompasses kindred, particularly descendants (cf. Becker 1995; Reischer and Koo 2004: 306). Despite their own aesthetic and physical deterioration, aging persons continue to access beauty and youthfulness through their children and particularly grandchildren. Where this logic is in operation, being concerned about the visible signs of aging would demonstrate an inappropriate engagement with selfish pursuits, as does an interest in modern comforts, for example, and opens one to scorn and ridicule. Being coquettish is a prerogative of the young, not the old, although older traditional Tongan women do take care of their appearance before church and in similarly marked contexts. We find echoes of this morality in modern Western contexts, of course (for example, see Furman 1997: 3–4), but they are particularly close to the bone in Tonga.[5]

For patrons, regular visits to the salon index a break with the past, village life, lack of privilege, and the definition of the body as socially rather than personally owned. First, these visits are enabled by and demonstrate the capacity to consume, and thus one's embeddedness in a capitalist order that situates one firmly in a modern order. Second, the consumption of professionalized hair care enables one to be good-looking (*matamata lelei*) but also to appear youthful and thus to perform modern anxieties about aging and appearance. Third, salon visits both result from an individualization of bodily appearance and further embed it in the realm of the individual, confirming the body's progression from being owned by the collectivity to being owned by the self. In the words of one younger female informant, '*Kou tui lahi ko e fale 'ulu pē 'oku malava ke kakato ai 'eku fiema'ú*', "I strongly believe that it is only at the salon that my desires can be completely met." In the words

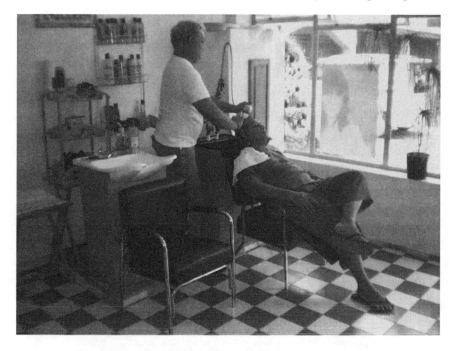

Figure 6.2. The desirable coolness of the hair wash (August 2009).

of another interviewee, the quality of the hairstylists' work feeds customers' desire (*fakatupu manako*). In these testimonies, the individual has desires (*fiema'u, manako*) that he or she can experience, talk about without fearing shame, and purchase. Having one's hair cut professionally does preclude certain practices, such as saving the hair cuttings to braid a valued belt (*kafa 'ulu*), but the kind of woman who seeks to wear such a tradition-encrusted garment is not the kind who patronizes hair salons.

Women come to the salon for a wide variety of explicit reasons. Some come on a regular basis, once a week or once every two weeks, a pattern that presupposes a comfortable and steady income. Professional women come to get their hair done ahead of important meetings and similar events. Others drop by on a whim, having done their shopping at the nearby supermarket or picked up clothing at the sewing shop next door. The inviting coolness of a hair wash was a recurring theme in interviews, which were conducted during a particularly uncomfortable summer heat wave (Figure 6.2).

Perhaps the most interesting motivation for visiting the hair salon is to have one's hair cut short during a funeral. Recall that, if relatives who are of inferior rank (*tuʻa*) to the deceased are anxious to demonstrate their allegiance to *anga faka-Tonga*, they must submit to having their hair roughly and unevenly cut (and sometimes burnt) by the father's sister of the deceased or someone who can act as *fahu*. This treatment yields a look that, together with the mourning *taʻovala*, is easily recognizable and inviting of respect. It does little, however, for the aesthetic appeal of the person (being designed in fact to obliterate it), and modern subjects concerned with beauty and with prolonging youthfulness are presented with a dilemma: Should they sacrifice looks and neatness for the sake of performing tradition, or should they give in to their individualized modern desires? This dilemma is inscribed in the following excerpt from a spontaneous conversation between a customer ('A) and a hairstylist (L) while the latter was doing her work:

'A   *Ko e mele pe ia ʻa e taimi ko ē ʻoku fai ai ko ē ʻetau putu faka-Tongá.*
        "When we have our Tongan funerals, it's a real drag."

L   Um.=
        "Hm"

'A   *=Hē? Pea tau ō ko ē ke kosi hotau ʻulú =*
        "Uh? And we come over so that we get our hair cut"

L   ((laughter))

'A   *= ʻikai ke siʻi ʻai ʻo kosi fakalelei kae fuʻu maʻu pē ʻo =*
        "they don't just cut it nicely, but instead go at it and-"

L   *Tuʻusi.*
        "Cut it."

'A   *= tuʻusi. Pea ʻosi pea te toki haʻu ʻo lele takai holo he ʻū fale kosi ʻulú ke =*
        "cut it. And then afterwards one has to run around to all the salons to-"

L   ((laughter))

'A   *= ke ngaahi =*
        "to get it done"

L   *= Ke fakaleleiʻi.*
        "To get it fixed properly."

'A   *= ke fakaleleiʻi angé, ko- ʻai hano kiʻi tuʻu lelei. 'Ai ai ko e taimi ko ē ʻoku kosi ai e fahú ia ʻoku kaila atu ha taha ia, "ʻai ke lahi, he ko e =*
        "to get it fixed properly again, so that it regain some shape. When the *fahu* is about to cut someone always has to shout, 'cut a lot of it, so that it"

L   *Kosi ke-*
        "Cut it so that-"

'A   = *vao, 'osi pea tutu! Kosi'i hake ki 'olunga!" Tahanī te te toe lava kita lea.*
        "look like a bush, then burn it! Cut it all the way to the top!" And one
        does not dare say anything."

Salon Conversation 'A 01-04-08

This excerpt displays a particular interesting pronoun switch: The customer begins the conversation referring to "our funerals" and "our hair" using the plural inclusive ("ours including you") possessive pronoun *'etau* and
hotau (one alienable, the other inalienable), as well as the corresponding subject pronoun *tau* in *Pea tau ō ko ē ke kosi hotau 'ulú*, "And we come over so that
we get our hair cut," stressing the inclusivity and plurality of the actions and
events. At the end of the commentary, however, she switches to the indefinite singular subject pronoun *te* (and its emphatic form *kita*) in *Tahanī te te
toe lava kita lea*, "And one does not dare say anything," indexing that the perspective (that the agent dares not express) has now switched to an intimately
personal one. This play of pronouns, from the generalized inclusive plural
to the intimate singular, is a particularly revealing microscopic index of the
dilemmas embedded in doing tradition at funerals.

The salon offers a solution to these funerary dilemmas by embedding the
iconic relationship between funerary haircuts and mourning into a larger
context. In this larger context, the mourning look now becomes a dishev-
eled look, one in need of attention and care, which the salon is there to pre-
empt. Mourners can pay a quick visit to the hairstylist ahead of the haircut
ritual to get their hair trimmed short in a stylish and orderly way, and significant numbers of customers patronize the salon before the tenth day of a
funeral. As in other realms of social life in Tonga, tradition and modernity
do not simply coexist, and one is certainly not being obliterated by the other,
but they are deeply entangled with one another, through simple acts such
as visiting the hair salon to get one's hair cut to required funerary length.
Of course, echoing the alienation that classically accompanies consumption,
such visits also remove the subject from the direct engagement with kinship
embodied in the father's sister's scissor-wielding. But it allows the person to
perform tradition in the eyes of others while satisfying personal desires for
beauty. Furthermore, as more and more funerals are no longer presided over

by a *fahu* because families are increasingly scattered across the world (remember the tradition bending that took place at the late king's funeral), the ritual often no longer has the kinship-related significance that it once had.[6]

Underlying this example and the many other motivations that bring customers to the salon is the theme of cleanliness. Historically, cleanliness occupied a prominent place in the teaching of Christian missionaries and other agents of "progress." These agents came from a world in which bourgeois sensibilities distanced themselves from the filth and stench of the peasantry and the poor, and in which hygiene was equated with morality, modernity, and order and heralded as the essence of "civilization" (see, for example, Frykman and Löfgren 1979 [1987]: 174–220). Classically, Tongans were quick to make these images their own, a process in which consumption, colonialism, and commodification are all embroiled (cf. Burke 1996; Comaroff and Comaroff 1992; Fife 2001; Masquelier 2005). What is intriguing is that Tongans in pre-Christian times were also deeply concerned about cleanliness, which indicates that this concern is not solely the product of nineteenth-century missionary zeal. Witness Enlightenment-era thinker Will Mariner's remarks about Tongans in the first decade of the nineteenth century:

> Another circumstance must be noticed, as connected with morality, and that is, personal cleanliness, in which no nation can excel (without ridiculous refinement), the people of these islands; and it is not unworthy of observation, that personal cleanliness often argues cleanliness of mind and idea. (Martin 1817: II: 178).

Contemporary Tongans bathe at least twice a day, change clothes frequently, and use as much fragrance as their pocketbooks can afford. They estimate that Westerners (as well as members of their own younger generation, particularly boys) are seriously lacking in hygiene, a stereotype that is confirmed by some of the more colorful (or malodorous) expatriate inhabitants of Nuku'alofa.

Whatever course the history of hygiene in Tonga actually took, cleanliness plays a central role in people's understanding of modernity. However, reminders of the lack of hygiene are everywhere, both in "traditional" forms, such as the excrement with which free-ranging pigs and fowl adorn the landscape, and in "modern" forms, such as the car carcasses that litter the island, the household rubbish that the new state-of-the-art transfer station has not yet managed to control, and the swampy and litter-strewn areas that constitute large portions of Nuku'alofa. Environmental cleanliness is a worry for many modern subjects in Tonga. "When I come back from overseas and drive to town from the airport," one informant asserted to me in a completely different context, "I feel ashamed by the mud and rubbish, *ko e palakū*" (*palakū*, "disgusting, repulsive"), continuing with a description of the contrasting beauty of the drive from the airport in Apia, Samoa, and Suva, Fiji. Like Freudian polymorphous desires, lack of hygiene never completely vanishes, looming dangerously and ubiquitously around the modern condition, so that for Tongans the maintenance of cleanliness represents a constant effort, a focus of attention that is often the topic of conversation, particularly when hygiene is found wanting.[7]

It is in this context that the salon emerges as a haven of desirable cleanliness closely linked to two other dominant aspects of salons, beauty and the transgender. The association of beauty with cleanliness is illustrated by salon customers' common references to physical beauty as *mata ma'a*, "clean-faced," the effect that they desire to achieve through their salon visits. (The opposite term, *palakū*, cited in the previous paragraph, translates as both "ugly" and "dirty.") Beauty and cleanliness are mutually constitutive features of the salon, one implying the other, and the clean habits of the stylists generate beauty. The connection between cleanliness and transgender identity resembles that between beauty and the transgender that I analyzed earlier in this chapter, but like the latter it is not straightforward. For many, *leitī* lead lives that are anything but "clean." The overt sexuality that many associate with them, for example, is often referred to as *palakū*. So is their stereotypical propensity to get roaring drunk and find themselves by the side of the road at dawn wearing very little clothing and not quite remembering how they got there (Besnier 1997, 2004). Nevertheless, the opposite stereotype, that of *leitī* as producers of beauty and cleanliness, operates just as readily, illustrating the complexities of stereotype formation and its relationship to practice.

As is the case of beauty businesses across the world (for example, Gimlin 1996: 514–518; Reid 2007: 104; Spitz 2004), urban Tonga hair salons are spaces to which women come to interact with one another, sometimes across otherwise significant social divides, nurturing bonds among themselves and between themselves and their *leitī* friends and attendants. "Even the relatively brief moments spent washing and cutting a customer's hair require a certain degree of intimacy" (Willett 2000: 197; cf. Weiss 2009: 159). Gossip and the concomitant "emotion work" occupy a central place in this sociality. But while the form of the sociality resembles its manifestations in other cultures, its meaning has a local flavor in Tonga. In rural Tonga, women generally do not socialize unless they are also working. The quintessential socializing context for village women is collective barkcloth making, or *koka'anga* (Teilhet-Fisk 1991: 44), arduous work during which women engage in conversation, joking, and general banter. Village men, in contrast, frequently get together for the sake of socializing, particularly in the form of informal kava drinking parties, to which many devote long hours of the day or night. The inequality inherent in this gendered use of time is not lost on village women, who have been known to complain bitterly about men's lack of productivity and their own never-ending list of tasks.

Salon patrons are of course not barkcloth-beating villagers but urban professionals. Office work does allow for more downtime than village life, although working women must still juggle business or professional engagements with caring for husbands and children and running households. In this context, a visit to the salon to be pampered and flattered may be one of the very few occasions that many have to claim time for themselves, an escape akin to romance reading among middle-class housewives in the American Midwest (Radway 1984), and to make them feel that, in contrast to village women, they are part of a world in which leisure occupies a prominent place in people's lives. It is no wonder that the term *fakalata*, "to make one feel comfortable, at ease," occurs so frequently in interviews and in casual conversations in the salon, as a descriptor or a spontaneous exclamation.[8]

Interviewees repeatedly alluded to *leitī*'s particularly fine-tuned ability to nurture sociability, to come across as affable and fun and to make one feel *lata* "comfortable." *'Okú nau- poto hono faka'ai'ai kita ke te-, ē?, ke te ongo'i 'okú te talavou neongo 'ene fōlahi mo e me'á, ka 'okú te pehē pē 'e kita ko kita 'okú te talavou tahá,* "[*leitī*] are good at encouraging you to, uh?, so that you feel pretty, despite being overweight and such, yet you end up feeling like you are the prettiest." This flattering treatment is part and parcel of the salon "experience": *Ko 'ete hū mai pē he matapaá, 'oku 'osi mali ange pē te'eki ke kamata, pea ko e fo'i* service *ia ko iá 'okú te 'osi* feel at home *pē kita ia,* "as soon as one shows up at the door, they are already smiling even before anything begins, and this is the kind of *service* that makes one *feel at home.*" In the eyes of many Tongans, "service" (*sēvesi*) is a particularly rare commodity in Tonga, where salespeople, government workers, and other service employees generally go about their work in rather dour fashion (although this is rapidly changing, as some business owners have caught on to the potential profitability of service with scripted affability). The enthusiasm that *leitī* demonstrate and the flattering way in which they treat salon customers, whether genuine or feigned, stand out particularly vividly.

The Salon and the Modern Self

The Nuku'alofa beauty salon does not simply exist to satisfy already established needs. On the contrary, the salon actively constructs patrons' needs, helping customers build a sense of who they are: women with a well-coiffed appearance appropriate to specific events, aging but still attractive subjects, busy businesswomen with no time to do their own hair, urbanites laying claim on leisure time denied to them in the traditionalist order, and so on. These images are addressed to both bystanders and the subject herself, just like other forms of what Simmel called "adornment," through which the individual seeks to distinguish him- or herself from others and at the same time be the object of attention (1950: 338). They firmly ground the person in a late capitalist modern order in which, in Tonga as elsewhere, consumption is the force that drives action and the body in particular represents a project that requires personal care and professional attention (Featherstone 1991).

The salon and its workers interweave together a number of themes, some of which are the subject of some anxiety among urban Tongans concerned with leading cosmopolitan lives, or at least with being recognized as doing so. Most straightforwardly, the salon experience associate beauty, cleanliness, pleasure, leisure, and sociability with one another, and it does so through consumption, which patrons have learned (or are learning) to associate with these other dynamics. Because tradition continues to loom large, the salon helps its customers distance themselves, at least partially, from a world of kinship, mutual dependence, endless work, and doubtful hygiene and align themselves with a world of individualized desire, leisure, and cleanliness that money can buy (cf. Giddens 1991; Miller 2006; Stambach 1999). But at the same time it enables customers to appear, at least, to pay allegiance to a traditional order in which personal desires are subordinated to the common good, as when they patronize the salon to get their hair cut to funerary length but not in funerary style. The beauty salon also nurtures intimacy and reinforces gendered solidarity among women and between women and the transgender. It encourages customers to craft, in their own eyes and the eyes of one another, a modern self, acceptable to both modern and traditional audiences, local and extralocal onlookers. Bifocality is, once again, at play.

An important aspect of the modern self is an understanding of the body that differs from that which operates in the traditional order. However, the extent to which the Weberian "ideal types" of the socially distributed body and the individualized body map simplistically onto dualities such as rural versus urban, traditional versus modern, underprivileged versus privileged, local versus cosmopolitan, or Tongan versus Western is an issue that should be treated with caution, as I discussed in the previous chapter.[9] The reality is more complex and much more interesting. Abiding by a particular body ideology can also be determinative of how one situates the self, particularly in a context such as Tonga since the turn of the millennium, where people (particularly young men) feel that they can gain access to an individuality expressible by sporting hairstyles that sometimes diverge radically from local conventionality (for example, cornrows, dreadlocks, shaved heads, rat's tails, hair dyed blond). Understandings of the body are context bound and shifting: Persons adopt different ideologies in different situations and are also subjected to different ideologies at once, as the well-documented double bind of consumption and control in Western modernity illustrates (Bordo 1993; Thompson 1994). For example, a rural, nonprivileged young person in Tonga can seek to transform his or her place in society by watching his or her weight, dying his or her hair blond, and adopting a fashion that stands out. While the urban sophisticates who patronize Nuku'alofa hair salons go to great lengths to distance themselves from traditional village-based morality, urban lifestyles are still only insulated from that morality by a wafer-thin partition, and one that is produced in the hair salon.

Chapter Seven

Shaping the Modern Body

Inaugurated by King Tāufaʻāhau IV in 1992, Teufaiva Fitness Centre is located slightly on the edge of town, near the police compound. Next to it is the country's main stadium with the same name, built on the occasion of the 1989 South Pacific Mini-Games on a site dedicated until then to the yearly agricultural show. With a capacity for 10,000 spectators in bleachers and on open-air grassy mounds, the stadium serves as the venue for rugby games, athletic competitions, large-scale dance performances, concerts, and other events of consequence. Members of the Tongan national rugby team, to whose training needs the gym was originally dedicated, came up with the name "Teufaiva," which can be translated as "ready [for] performance."

The gym is a high-ceiling cinder-block hangar with few frills. Officially, the daily admission fee in 2008 was T$3 a session (up from T$2 in the early years of the millennium), and there are also monthly and yearly memberships, but most users make alternative "arrangements" with the two employees to use the facilities. Lining the otherwise bare white walls are posters of Tongan and other champion bodybuilders, stretching exercises, and announcements. A sound system transmits the local FM station offerings or provides the music for aerobic classes. To one side are changing rooms and bathrooms, although most patrons do not use them, and the showers have long since stopped functioning. The spacious room is lined with fitness equipment and racks of free weights (Figure 7.1), most of which have seen

Figure 7.1.   The interior of Teufaiva Gym (August 2008).

better days, tired from the less-than-delicate handling by muscular young men. Some of the equipment has been replaced over the years, although machines do not stay new very long. Many of the pulleys and cables would need to be attended to if there were funds to do so. But everyone makes do in a good-natured way with what the gym has to offer.

Despite the formidable physique of some of its patrons, the gym is relatively unintimidating, and it attracts a broad range of users. Outsiders can easily partake in its casual sociality, as regular patrons quickly approach newcomers, Tongan or other, to find out who they are and what brings them to the gym. The most conspicuous regular patrons are the bodybuilders, who do not present the forbidding and menacing presence of their homologues in North American gyms. Casual users include a few young men who come to lift weights and socialize, as well as visiting overseas Tongans, expatriate residents (particularly members of overseas volunteer organizations), and members of minor rugby teams who use the facilities for cross-training. Elite rugby players of the 'Ikale Tahi ("Sea Eagles") national team now have their own, much more posh, fitness facility elsewhere in town. Generally speaking, patrons cultivate an easygoing egalitarianism and ethos of togetherness. The few nobles and high-ranking officials who use the facilities rub shoulders, with studied insouciance, with younger men and women of little social significance. Elsewhere they would be very ill at ease in each other's presence. The unspoken message is that they are all partaking in congruent modern projects of cultivating health and well-being.

In the early evening, young and not-so-young women, as well as a few Tongan and expatriate men, converge on the gym for a one-hour aerobics session, led by a Tongan or overseas instructor, sometimes a man, other times a woman. The weightlifting benches are placed against the wall and weight-lifters cannot use the equipment while the class is in session. In 2008, a volunteer of the Japan International Cooperation Agency (JICA) also conducted an aerobics class in the grassy seaside area of town in front of the Treasury building. In its heyday around the turn of the millennium, the aerobics classes attracted many, from teenagers to grandmothers in housecoats and slippers. The latter would come accompanied by a young grandchild, an example of the symbiotic relationship that grandmothers often have with their younger grandchildren, with the grandmother keeping an eye on the child while the child keeps her company, which also demonstrates to onlookers that she is attending to household chores rather than nurturing an inappropriately selfish concern for her personal health. Bodybuilders rendered idle by the temporary ban on working out sometimes join in, ensuring that their movements are laconic enough not to betray an enthusiasm that might call their masculinity into question. In earlier days, a crew from TV Tonga would sometimes film the aerobics class, providing entertainment to people sitting comfortably on their sofa with junk-food snacks within reach, proffering comments on the movements, expressions, and outfits of aerobics students. Since the decline of the fitness movement in Tonga, the classes have become smaller and fewer. Television crews no longer show up. These changes have lent greater visibility to the bodybuilding constituency of the gym.

In 1999–2001, I participated in many activities at Teufaiva, from aerobics and weight training to socializing, becoming one of the regulars and working out with companions. In 2008, I again used the facilities, although to a lesser degree given the greater time pressure I was under. During that year, my assistant Tyron Langi conducted a series of interviews with gym patrons, from which the analysis that follows benefits.

Bodies

To understand Teufaiva as a site of modernity, it is necessary to delve in some detail into a number of issues, including the historical constitution of Tongan bodies, the medicalization of size, and the place of sports and physical activities in the context of contemporary Tongans' lives. I will begin by further developing the discussion of bodies that I began in prior chapters, particular the meaning of size, which I broached in Chapter Two.

Since early contact with Tongans, outsiders have commented on the impressive size of Tongan bodies, alternating between admiration, condemnation, ridicule, and alarm, depending on the historical moment and the intentionality at play. It is the case that, in the traditional order, a corpulent body was classically a desirable marker of abundance, fertility, and status. This desirability operates within a logic in which the body is not a personal attribute and a signifier of individuality, as in Western middle-class modernity. Rather, the body is a communal attribute, whose health and abundance indexes telescopically collective wealth and health (particularly in the case of the high ranking), and whose boundaries with family, village, and society at large is porous (cf. Becker 1995 on Fiji; Brownell 1995 on China; Sobo 1993 on Jamaica).

Large bodies were and are associated in particular with chiefly status because the body of the high ranking is iconic of the polity. "The idea prevails that a chief is normally a large, portly person," states Edward Gifford, the first modern-day ethnographer of Tonga, "On one occasion my interpreter remarked, 'Can't you see he is a chief? See how big he is'" (1929: 124). The impressive stature of Queen Sālote III, who in 1924 was reported to stand at 6′3″ and weigh 300 lbs (Lambert 1941), indexed the wealth of the nation. It demonstrates the nation's ability to keep its sovereign supplied in vast quantities of food and metonymically inscribes the propitiousness of the nation. A similar logic underlay some readings of the body of the late king, Tāufaʻāhau Tupou IV (200 kg in the 1970s), but his body would eventually become the object of derisive exoticization by Western journalists and writers, as Tonga caught their attention with increasing frequency in the course of his reign.

As age turns size turns into corpulence, aesthetically pleasing and socially approved plumpness gives way to unsightly rolls of fat. In the traditional order, however, this matters little because beauty is collective, not personal. Village grandmothers derive a sense of aesthetics not from attempts to remain youthful through attention to clothing, make-up, or trips to the hair salon, but from the beauty of their grandchildren, because the body is an instrument that connects people together, and kinship (and in particular descent) is the obvious conduit of this connection. In this context, older people's attempts to remain youthful or beautiful not only go unnoticed but also, if too obvious, are the object of scorn.

The logic of body size is gendered. In the traditional order, women are encouraged to become large. They carry within their persona the rank, prestige, and potential upward mobility of the family, which means that the larger the body, the greater the reflection and claim of rank. Men are also prescriptively dynamic while women are static, as symbolized, for example, in the contrast between the controlled form of female *tauʻolunga* dancing and the exuberant male *tulāfale* dancing that supports and complements it. Ideally, low-ranking women work while sitting, even when their tasks involve physically strenuous work, as it does in the manufacture of *koloa faka-Tonga*. In contrast, low-ranking men's traditional work involves walking, standing, digging, and planting, all of which are high energy-expending activities, particularly in a tropical climate. But stasis increases the propensity to gain weight. As a result, in rural contexts, women have a greater propensity to obesity than men (Young Leslie 2004: 404).[1]

However, traditional conceptualizations of the body, attractiveness, and body size have long been operating alongside other dynamics. Gender, age, rank, social class, relative urbanity, and many subtle forms of identification are implicated in the valuation of the body and its size. The body of a fat young man, for example, has a radically different meaning from that of a fat elderly woman. Body size and its evaluation are also contingent on history and, in a simplistic sense, exposure to alternative modes of evaluation coming from elsewhere (cf. Becker 2004 on Fiji). None of these caveats is specific to Tonga because the valuation of the body, just like the valuation of the self that I analyzed in Chapter One, is transversed by all sorts of parameters of social difference in contemporary Western societies (for example, Davis 2003; Nichter 2000: 159–180).

The most consequential historical transformation that Tongan bodies have undergone results from their sudden medicalization in the 1990s, in the elaboration of the fact that, while corpulence may inspire respect, it comes with health problems such as diabetes, high blood pressure, respiratory ailments, and gout, as well as a shorter life and general discomfort, and that these issues matter. This medicalization is widely attributed to the example set by King Tāufaʻāhau Tupou IV, who in 1995 embarked on a diet and exercise regime, eventually loosing a third of his weight. (He could afford excellent healthcare at the Stanford Medical Center in California.) The king would come to Teufaiva Gym every Tuesday and Thursday morning for his workout, at which time the facilities were off limits to everyone else.

As is typical of a society in which ideas and practices flow down the social hierarchy, the nation followed the king's example, or at least the scenario is widely presented as having taken this configuration. For about a decade, fitness programs, weight-loss competitions, weight watchers group meetings, and aerobics classes proliferated (Englberger et al. 1999). Overseas volunteer agencies were centrally involved in the fitness and slimming programs, with JICA volunteers playing a leading role, the Japanese agency having specialized since the 1990s in providing paramedical expertise to Tonga. It was then that Teufaiva Gym was packed. The programs generated caught the attention of overseas journalists as eager as ever to fill slow news days with the oddities of the little island kingdom ruled by the fat king. While the trend has somewhat abated now that the late king is no longer there to lead the movement, NGOs, overseas volunteers, and government bodies continue the struggle to persuade people to change their ways (Figure 7.2). Many operate under the tacit assumption that if only Tongans would get over their "traditional culture," they would succeed in losing weight. This assumption, as well as the practices and institutions it fosters, is informed by a scientific rationality suffused with a middle-class modernity that pitches itself as the antithesis of tradition.[2]

Most people today are aware of the desirability to keep fit and eat healthy. But many find it difficult to translate this knowledge into practice (Evans et al. 2001), particularly in the context of skyrocketing food prices and taste buds that have long become used to fatty food. Whether it is acted on or not, this knowledge demonstrates that the body, its aesthetics, and norms of size and health are all subject to coexisting and potentially contradictory discourses. While the campaign continues, formidable hurdles get in the way of

Figure 7.2.   Billboard placed by an NGO at a well-traveled crossroad in Nuku'alofa urging viewers to "eat well" (*kai lelei*), adding, in English, "it's so easy" (March 2008).

reducing obesity and associated ailments. One hurdle is the disillusionment with agriculture following the failures of export monocropping for most except the wealthiest landowners, coupled with the depletion of nutrients in the wake of pesticide, fungicide, and fertilizer overtreatments. The eclipse of agriculture has had the effect of reducing the amount of locally grown food and the level of physical exertion inherent in daily activity, for men in particular. Women in villages continue to be relatively active throughout the day, particularly if they beat barkcloth and plait mats, but in town they are employed in large numbers in white-collar work and thus much more sedentary. Another issue is the increasing reliance on private vehicles for transportation instead of walking and taking the bus (or in earlier days the village truck). It is thus not "tradition" that is the problem, but the very same modernity that medicalized the body in the first place.

The biggest obstacle, however, may be the consequence of the state's neo-liberal policies concerning one central commodity: food. When they can afford it, Tongans' source of protein are mutton or lamb flaps, or *sipi*, byproducts of New Zealand and Australian meat production exported frozen to the few markets that will consume them, namely Tonga, Samoa, the Solomon Islands, and Papua New Guinea (Gewertz and Errington 2010).[3] In mid-2008, a kilo of *sipi* cost T$7.60. If money is short, there is always fatty chicken imported from the United States (T$4.80) or mutton fat (*ngako'i sipi*), which contains no meat but can flavor a meal of tubers and greens (T$1.99). The deregulation that comes with abiding by the requirements of WTO membership makes it very unlikely that the government will ever restrict the import of this low-quality meat, in contrast to Fiji, which banned it in 2000.

At the present time, most Tongans have no alternative source of protein. In addition, conditions of production and consumption have reconfigured the Tongan meal, which conforms to the configuration of the modern meal elsewhere (Mintz 1985: 201–202, 1996: 119–122). With the exception of people for whom the traditional after-church Sunday lunch is still a reality, people increasingly consume food as the occasion arises rather than in planned meals. What they consume is increasingly prepared outside the home, particularly by small-scale entrepreneurs engaged in multiple livelihood strategies, going door-to-door with containers of cooked food wrapped in foil or running small fast-food restaurants. At the time of writing, no fast-food transnational corporation franchise operated in Tonga yet, although, like other diasporic Pacific Islanders, Tongans are known to travel back from New Zealand carrying with them on the flight large quantities of fried chicken bought from a well-known transnational fast-food conglomerate. Rumor has it that a very high-ranking businessperson is negotiating with this corporation to open a local franchise.[4]

The weight-loss campaign is up against serious challenges that result in giving it a particular sociocultural profile: Because it focuses on the body as the property of the individual, it is modern; because it is most accessible to those with the means to find protein sources other than *sipi*, it is middle-class; because it involves exercising in public (and sometimes on camera for the entire nation to see), it is young; and because it centralizes a care of the self centered on the way in which the body is seen and assessed, it has feminine connotations, although not exclusively.

Sports

Gender is the category of social differentiation that leads to another pivotal factor in understanding Teufaiva as a modern site, namely sports. There is no doubt that the constitutive elements of physical activity for the purpose of leisure (such as playful competition, persons representing groups, the practice of "fair play") have long been part of Tongan society and culture, for both men and women. In early contact days, Tongan men engaged in a variety of combat sports such as wrestling and club fighting, while both women and men boxed in gender-segregated matches (Ferdon 1987: 184–191). Artists travelling on early European expeditions to the Pacific Islands, most famously John Webber (the official artist on James Cook's third voyage to the Pacific), immortalized Tongan sport scenes in the illustrations accompanying maritime journals.

At the dawn of the modern era, students who had gone to study at Newington College in Sydney, the first school in Australia to play rugby, introduced rugby union to Tonga around the turn of the twentieth century, the sport having already fissioned in Britain in 1895 into two codes, rugby union and rugby league (Dunning and Sheard 1976). While we have no records of its early development in Tonga, one can well imagine that rugby, locally referred to as *'akapulu* (literally, "ball-kicking"), quickly attained the popularity that it has today, as it embodies qualities that resonate particularly well with preexisting images of youthful manhood. Such is the case of the emphasis on work as a joint accomplishment and on the importance of age-based cohorts, characteristics that suffuse many other aspects of the social order. The association of the game with schools would also have given further legitimacy to the sport, as schools had already developed into institutions that, as they did elsewhere in the British Empire, centralized loyalty, hierarchy, and discipline, as well as a certain conceptualization of manliness that resonates with both the brutality of the sport and Christian morality (Hall 1994; MacAloon 2007;

Mangan 1998). Last but not least, King Tāufaʻāhau Tupou IV's own athletic accomplishments as a youth and his subsequent support of team sports, even before the beginning of the health campaign he heralded, sealed the fate of rugby in particular and sports in general as a national project.

Also relevant is the rather overused stereotype of the virile brawn of male Polynesian bodies. According to this representation, rugby provides a socially sanctioned modern recycling of the role of the warrior of precontact days, an image that dominates international journalistic coverage of games in which Tongans and other Polynesians are involved. It is a two-edged sword: While it generates worldwide admiration, it also confines in not so subtle ways Tongan and other Polynesian men to the "savage slot" (Hokowhitu 2004). Images of the modern warrior in the rugby field can easily slip into allegations of an unpredictable temper and a lack of discipline, embodying the contradictory representations of the colonial subject as alternatively hypervirile and slothful (Alter 2004). In the 1960s, "lack of discipline" offered a pretext for rugby clubs in New Zealand to exclude migrant Samoan teams, and today the theme often emerges in commentaries about Polynesian players (Teaiwa and Mallon 2005: 212–214). Tongan rugby teams, particularly the ʻIkale Tahi, do turn the warrior image to advantage, awing international spectators by the muscularity of their game. This quality compensates somewhat for their inability to win, which results at least in part from their inability to practice as a team, because most international-level players are employed by teams in industrial countries and come together only shortly before international tournaments.

The "boys" further underscore this muscularity with a pregame performance of a bellicose and hypermasculine *kailao* dance entitled Sipi Tau, which has inscribed Tonga's existence into the awareness of the even most provincial parts of the world. The performance of this dance is an answer to the New Zealand All Blacks' pregame performance of the Māori *haka* Ka Mate. The *haka* has made them world famous but has also stirred vigorous controversy domestically for being yet one more appropriation of a symbol of Māori indigeneity in the service of white-controlled corporate interests (see, for example, Jackson and Hokowhitu 2002). The usefulness of these strategic deployments of savagery in promoting Tongan interests, including women's interests and men's interests outside of the rugby field, is limited and limiting. In particular, while it never fails to impress overseas audiences, the *kailao* performance also feeds images of Tonga's exoticism (often depicted in the

West as slightly ridiculous) and its suspension in a no-man's-land between savagery and civilization. The celebration of reified "culture" can easily turn into a straightjacket.[5]

Beginning in 1924, the country's top rugby players played biyearly tests against Fiji. The two colonial entities gradually became full participants in the areas of the British colonial empire where the sport diffused (Australia, New Zealand, South Africa, and the Pacific Islands), fueled by a Christian morality that emphasized discipline, controlled male violence, and allegiance to a higher authority, including the colonial metropole. In addition to school teams, amateur rugby clubs are found in all villages, associated with kava-drinking clubs (*kalapu*) or youth groups. At the national level, by the 1990s Tonga had maintained a noticeable presence in the by-then heavily professionalized international rugby scene, taking part in World Cups and giving the country an international visibility that it could never achieve through other means. Another sport that has had a similar effect, although on a smaller scale, is boxing. It attracts young men's attention but to a lesser degree than rugby, in part because it requires difficult-to-obtain equipment and does not foster the sociability associated with team sports. Young women and *leitī* have not been completely left out of the sport scene: With vigor and enthusiasm, they play netball, a slightly watered-down version of basketball popular in the British colonial sphere of influence. Compared to the passion that men's rugby generates among everyone in the country, however, other sports appear incidental.

In recent years, the importance of rugby has been boosted by another factor: its export potential. The best and luckiest Tongan rugby players can find relatively well-remunerated employment in professional teams in New Zealand and Australia and, increasingly, Japan, Britain, and France, as well as the United States, where they convert rugby skills to playing American football. From Jonah Lomu (a New Zealand-born Tongan who became arguably the best-ever rugby player in the 1990s) down, Tongan athletes have gained international recognition. Athletes who are lucky enough to be signed up overseas fuel their younger siblings' fantasies back home, of making it big and claiming the prestige of sending large remittances to parents and relatives. These high-profile migrant workers are recruited either directly from Tonga by scouts who periodically visit or, in many more cases, in New Zealand and Australia, where they benefit from better facilities, trainers, and coaches, and more readily available talent scouts. They provide a healthy corrective to the image of Pacific Island migrants as poor unskilled workers dodging immigration authorities while slaving at the bottom of the employment ladder.

Nevertheless, overseas rugby teams clearly see in Tongan and other Pacific Island players a source of relatively cheap and pliant labor. In Japan, for example, they are not allowed to hire managing agents, leaving them at the mercy of team managers, who are employees of the corporations that own the teams. While relatively well paid, professional players continue to be blue-collar workers, whose minute actions on and off the job are micromanaged and whose continued employment is contingent on sustained performance and behavior deemed acceptable by employers. Sports careers, which are open to only a fraction of talented players in the first place, are notoriously short, and the "burnout" rate is extremely high. In Japan, early 2009 was marked by two nationally well-publicized events: One rugby player tested positive for marijuana use, and the other, while inebriated, was accused of stealing a small sum of money from a taxi driver. Both players were immediately shipped back to Tonga, and the events may have damaged corporate interest in continuing to hire Tongan rugby talent. In short, while sports careers fuel millenarian fantasies in a field of employment and migration where few options exist, they come with serious drawbacks and hurdles (Besnier and Kitahara 2009).

Through many of its characteristics, stereotyped or not, Tongan rugby is deeply reproductive of a preexisting social and gendered order: the organization of younger men in a cohort under the control of higher-ranking coaches and patrons; the high value associated with the civilizing and Christianity-affirming legacy of Tonga's place in the British Empire; the affirmation of the subject's belonging to a particular social group (not just the team, but also the village, the neighborhood, the kava-drinking club, the nation); an instrumental disposition to the body, whereby the athlete's entire body is invested in achieving a goal (Bourdieu 1978: 838); and the showcasing of the performance of virility (Saouter 2000), of the same kind that attracts young Tongan men to soldiering or police work. More subtly, rugby also articulates millenarian fantasies that are not part of Tongan society's official discourse but nevertheless preoccupy almost everyone in Tonga, fantasies that search for validations and opportunities beyond the confines of the national-state (cf. Foster 2006: 754). Rugby thus both derives legitimacy from its grounding in the traditional order and provides the context for modernity-infused fantasies of cosmopolitan stardom and wealth.

Bodybuilders and Weight Trainers

In these respects, rugby players contrast sharply with the bodybuilders and weight trainers who patronize Teufaiva Gym at all hours of the day. These young men can play rugby, of course, because all young men can, but their primary interest lies elsewhere. Their physical activities are more individualistic than group based, even though visits to the gym also involve sitting around conversing with friends before or after a workout, as well as the sociability of "spotting" for one another at the bench press. In addition, their activities do not fall under the control of a higher authority, unless the person goes into competitive bodybuilding by joining the Tonga Bodybuilding Association, chaired by one of the nobles. Operative in gym activities is an approach to the body as an end in itself, not as an instrument to achieve a goal. Furthermore, unlike rugby, gym training does not lead to economic opportunities nor does it fuel fantasies of international fame, except in the limited possibility of winning regional or international bodybuilding competitions. Bodybuilding is no qualification for migrant status in postindustrial countries, although some bodybuilders of Tongan extraction have established a commercial presence as personal fitness trainers in the United States.

Significant numbers of regulars patronize the gym, predominantly younger men who come to train with weights and machines, an activity that they refer to as *hikihiki* (literally, "to lift repeatedly") or *'uekauti*, "work out" (*fakamālohi sino* "to strengthen the body" refers ambiguously to cardiovascular and strengthening activities). In addition, increasingly large numbers of young men have weights and some basic equipment at home, particular school-age teenagers too young or impecunious to come to Teufaiva but among whom the weightlifting trend has been spreading since the mid-2000s. At one end are the dedicated amateur bodybuilders, referred to as *pāpela*, a term with positive connotations, evidently borrowed a long time ago from the English "barbell" (Melenaite Taumoefolau, personal communication). They aim to partake in local bodybuilding competitions primarily held during the Heilala Festival, as well as regional and international events (Figure 7.3). The posters that adorn the walls of Teufaiva glamorize the international achievements of bodybuilders from Tonga and other Pacific Islands, inspiring novices with dreams of similar fame. At the other end are casual users who aim for what they call a *sino lelei*, "good body," namely a muscular and large body, which emphasizes mass and shape over

Figure 7.3.   Teufaiva bodybuilders posing on a Heilala Festival float among Miss Heilala pageant contestants (August 2008).
(Source: Matangi Tonga.)

definition. All are fluent in the language of weight training: "supersetting," chest-triceps-shoulders versus back-biceps versus legs, the necessity of rest days, and so on. All know their basic diet theory (three food groups, and so on), inculcated into them by years of radio and television broadcasts, posters, billboards, workshops, and friendly advice. Bodybuilding supplements brought in from overseas circulate, as well as, more furtively, steroids. But many Tongan men attain a bodybuilder's physique with relatively little effort because of their mesomorphic constitution. "Tongans just have to look at the weights," explained a friend, "and their muscles just start swelling up."[6]

Images of oversized male musculatures have long loomed large in the Tongan imaginary. As is the case in other Pacific Island societies (see, for example, Tomlinson 2009: 9–10), Tongans widely believe that their male ancestors had enormous bodies, a belief that conjures complex representations of the past as well as the present. During my early fieldwork in a Vava'u village, young men would reenact vivid descriptions of the extraordinary feats of *pāpela* that they had seen in movies that they referred to as *mitinaiti* (from "midnight"), which the entrepreneurial owner of a 16-mm film projector screened outdoors onto a bedsheet in different villages at different times between evening and dawn. The fare was a mixture of Hong Kong kungfu and B-graded features, many of which featured well-built men, also available in urban theaters precariously housed in crumbling buildings (Figure 7.4). The action that was the main attraction would then be the subject of extensive retellings and embellishments both during the film screening and later in young men's huts (Gailey 1989; Hahn 1994), but with action comes muscle. *Ben-Hur* (1959) left an indelible mark on memories because of its religious content but also because it showed substantial amounts of muscle. Audiences particularly appreciated later productions such as *Spartacus* (1960), *Enter the Dragon* (1973), successive *Rambo* productions (1982–), the *Terminator* series (1984–), the *Predator* series (1987–), all the way to *300* (2006).[7]

Muscle also features in images from quite a different provenance, in the form of "identity merchandise," namely T-shirts, caps, decals, and other items juxtaposing images of men of formidable muscularity with slogans like "Tongan warrior," "Tongan pride," "Native Tongan," and "Pride of the Pacific" (Figure 7.5). These images have a genealogy that links them to the diaspora in Hawai'i and New Zealand, locations where assertions of muscular power operate within the context of the politics of indigeneity and land restitution. In Hawai'i, these assertions are commodified on clothing merchandise for local consumption, announcing the wearer as being "Proud to Be Hawaiian" (a term that has now also been appropriated as the trademark of a garment corporation). Accompanying the slogan is the image of a warrior with hyperdeveloped musculature wearing a gourd helmet, a signature index of combative allegiance to the Hawaiian sovereignty movement (Linnekin 1997, 2004). The images come with their own gendered and postcolonial politics, being based on colonial representations of savage physicality (Tengan 2008: 43). But when translated to the Tongan context, they fall in line with representations of the bodies of male Tongan ancestors as enormous in size and power.

At the Honolulu flea market, the site of much of the creativity and commodification involved in the circulation of these items, vendors offer multiple versions of the same product to different consumers in the multiethnic

Figure 7.4. " 'Samson and the Slave Queen' [a 1963 sword-and-sandal production] is showing at the local picture house."
(Source: Walsh 1972: 34.)

configuration of Hawai'i: "Tongan Pride" and "Samoan Pride" stickers are offered alongside "Hawaiian Pride" and "Chamorro Pride" ones, each with an appropriate design (usually a seal or flag) but all the same size and shape. The easy reproducibility of the designs gives them the quality of "floating signifiers" (Lévi-Strauss 1950: xlix), whose meaning is intelligible only in the

Figure 7.5. T-shirts proclaiming "Tongan Warrior" and "Native Tongan: Pride of the Pacific" on sale at Fua'amotu International Airport (August 2008).

context of a contrast but which can be replaced at will with new significance. The proud Hawaiian warrior with oversized muscles is easily transformed into a Tongan warrior, and Hawaiian pride into Tongan pride, even though they are embedded in very different political contexts that give them radically different meanings.

Backgrounded by the overelaboration of hyperdeveloped male musculatures, weight training and bodybuilding in Tonga have not been saddled with the suspect character and the lack of legitimacy with which these activities have struggled in the United States (Stokvis 2006). In Tonga, these activities are primarily the purview of younger men, who are normatively expected to display a certain amount of pride in their bodies. Rugby boys, for example, strut their stuff along the streets of Nuku'alofa on their way to and from practice, wearing tank tops and shorts that reveal a great deal more thigh than rules of decency would normally allow. But rules of decency are suspended in two ways: The outfits are justified by rugby practice, and the boys are always in groups. These images of youthful pride in the body do bring up an important difference in body consciousness between Tonga and the West. In the former, the male gaze can evaluate another male body, and potentially develop a homosocial affiliation, without the need to avert the eyes, contrary to the Western male gaze, which needs to avert its focus on other men to ensure that homosociality not be confused with homoeroticism (Sedgwick 1990). Thus men can candidly appraise each other's bodies or comment on the attributes of images they see in bodybuilding magazines without the fear that intentions be questioned. These dynamics go some way to explain the lack of guile involved in Tongan bodybuilding and weight training—until, of course, agents are exposed to an alternative body consciousness in the diaspora, although bodybuilders with some experience in Tonga can also easily recontextualize themselves in Western bodybuilding consciousness without having to cope with the twisted complexities of the modern-day Western male gaze focusing on other male bodies.

While weight training and bodybuilding fit into a long-standing context of masculinity, performance, and legitimacy, at the same time they also constitute ruptures from this context in several ways. One is the fact that the images that inspire the activities bear the indelible mark of modernity. Movies are of course consumed in reference to local dynamics, as many scholars of popular culture have painstakingly demonstrated, but they also come with symbols and fantasies of power of much wider scope than anything available. For example, Arnold Schwarzenegger (locally referred to as 'Ānolo) conquers the world, annihilating America's (and thus Tonga's) enemies, even appropriating the main minority language of the United States in his trademark "*Hasta la vista*, baby!" (Hill 1993).[8] Identity merchandise, while also interpreted in terms of a locally relevant context, still potentially implies that the wearer maintains a link to Hawai'i and New Zealand, whether through residence, travel, or remittances. It is also appropriate to mention the image that most Tongans have of Teufaiva as a space where "deportees" (*tīpota*), as well as other overseas Tongans who returned to the country under problematic circumstances not of their own choosing, congregate and mix with impressionable local youth. It is quite clear that some of the activities that are organized there at moments of sociability are not completely above the law. The gym is thus the site of a modern economy inspired by some overseas Tongans' desperate attempts to get rich quickly in the diaspora, pressured as they are to provide remittances and conform to expectations of overseas success while confronting the economic reality of the migrant condition in crumbling postindustrial economies.

Rupture characterizes not only inspirations and pasts but also the care of the self associated in particular with bodybuilding. This care is contingent on the ability to maintain a daily regime grounded in individualistic daily routines, rather than in the communal kinship-based arrangements in which what one eats when is dependent on the needs of others and the availability of food. One respondent, a member of the bodybuilding team, describes a diet regime that strikes a familiar chord from bodybuilders' regimes elsewhere, in which he weighs the food he consumes, chooses to eat vegetables and lean steak (which most people cannot afford), and eats small portions five times a day (again, not an option open to the majority). The modern grounding of these practices is a matter not just of images but also of whether one is in a position to afford and organize them.

Not all weight trainers and bodybuilders are drawn to Teufaiva by similar motivations. As in similar contexts the world over, Teufaiva patrons are attracted to working out for a variety of reasons. The majority of patrons I interacted with stated that they were introduced to weight training by friends and relatives, drawn into its sociability, which mitigates somewhat the individualism associated with gym training. They explicitly identified images of *pāpela* as having a long-standing effect that inspired them:

> *Ko 'eku tupu hake pē he kei si'i 'o sio ko ē he kau pāpela, pea ku- pea faka'ai'ai ai pē kiu uu ke u siv- fie sino lelei pea fakataha pē mo e mo'ui lelei pe*
>
> When I was still young as I was growing up I'd see the bodybuilders (*kau pāpela*), and it inspired me to wish for a strong body (*sino lelei*), and along with it a healthy life (*mo'ui lelei*).

For many, images from magazines and films served as inspirational motivation. Asked what his goals were, another respondent stated, with a chuckle, *Fiema'u 'e au ia ke liunga au 'a 'Ānolo ia 'ia au*, "What I want is to be Arnold's double," testifying to the ubiquity of images of Schwarzenegger, even if one takes into account the irony and other interpretive modes that characterize their local consumption.[9]

There are two noteworthy associations in these depictions, which also come up in other conversations: the link between casual weight training and bodybuilding and the link between strength and health. These various aims are not discrete. Gym users see weight training as embedded in the campaign for greater health in Tonga, even though they are also aware of the fact that it does not in itself contribute to the decline of noncommunicable diseases. All respondents invoked the term *moʻui lelei*, "health" (literally, "good life"), as a prime motivation for lifting weights. However, the individualized meaning of *moʻui lelei* here differs from its meaning in rural Tonga, where it is intrinsically associated with the maintenance of appropriate social relations (Young Leslie 2004: 402). For some, weight training leads to competitive bodybuilding, while for others, its motivation is the desire to improve sports performance. One respondent stated that he had started weight training after he had become tired of losing in the boxing ring. The gym is often populated by rugby amateurs and professional hopefuls cross-training, both strength and fitness (the latter being a common weakness among Tongan athletes). But for a significant number, beefing up the body is an end in itself, independent of any concurrent participation in team or other sports.

The comparison with middle-class projects of fitness and physicality in postindustrial contexts does not stop here. Some respondents articulate a familiar economy of time and money, reasoning that they come to the gym for their own personal benefit (*ʻoku ou ngāue ʻaonga mo hoku sino, maʻaku ia*, "I am working for something useful for my body, for myself"). These choices are contrasted with the waste of money and time that drinking alcohol or kava, smoking, or idling represent but also, more quietly, with the collectivist goals of rugby training. It is perhaps not surprising that respondents who voiced these arguments were predominantly members of Pentecostal or charismatic churches, where the modern self is shaped through a personal relationship to God rather than the sociability of kava drinking or other activities. Indeed, there is a clear and explicitly acknowledged overlap between gym patrons and adherents and preachers of these religious denominations. The overlap is reminiscent of the conflation of muscle and faith in the nineteenth-century doctrine of muscular Christianity, as I elaborate in the next chapter.

The link between Teufaiva and Christianity invokes in particular the image of the gym as a space occupied by deportees, some of who have had a head start in both bodybuilding and redemption through Jesus behind bars overseas, as well as members of other segments that mainstream society deems problematic. In addition to the efforts of particular leaders of charismatic churches to recruit while working out, the gym has also been the focus of Christian ministries that encourage bodybuilding and related activities as

part of a Christian lifestyle. It is perhaps not by chance that a group catering to deportees, "youth at risk," and former prisoners called itself "Ironman
Ministry." Founded by Sione Koloamatangi, who struggled to fit into Tongan
society after being deported from the United States at the completion of a
prison sentence, the group received financial support from the British High
Commission and had a royal patron, Princess Siuʻilikutapu. While it lasted,
Tongan courts placed offenders on probation in its care. "Ironman Ministry," states its website, whose American flavor is not confined to the spelling,
"uses biblical principles and 'tough love' to train and disciple at-risk individuals about respect, responsibility, commitment, honor, faithfulness, integrity
and love for God, country and self" (Ironman Ministry 2005). These juxta-
positions echo a discourse of empowerment that has gained wide circulation
in Tonga since the turn of the millennium, as they work hand-in-hand with
national policies of neoliberal disengagement of the state from society. An example of the way in which the ministry operationalized this discourse was to
offer Tongan language classes to deportees who grew up in the diaspora. Underlying this effort is the belief that language competence somehow provides
a solution to contemporary social problems and a tool for drifting individuals
to pull their lives together. The fact that the gym is one of the prime sites for
the implementation of this discourse should not come as a surprise, given the
extent to which it elaborates various aspects of modernity.[10]

Shaping the Modern Body

Teufaiva gym is a site where divergent projects come together—yet all fall
under one large umbrella of the care of the self. The gym is a site of transformation: of the body, lifestyle, and diet. These transformations both presuppose and enact other kinds of transformations: from collective to individual
activity; from the instrumental body to the body as an end; from eating what
one is served to eating what one chooses; from mainstream Christianity
to accepting Jesus as one's savior and celebrating Him through the care of
the self; from a social order in which genders and ranks are carefully segregated, to one in which everyone gathers in the same space, focusing on
similar goals of self-improvement, articulating a sense of "we are all in this
together." Backgrounding these transformations is a panoply of different
cosmopolitan images: health campaigns promoted by NGOs and mediated

by JICA volunteers, cinematic images of hypermuscular men, and echoes of muscular Christianity with a long genealogy elsewhere.

One should take care, however, not to associate cosmopolitan images exclusively with gym training in its various guises. Other images with equally, and perhaps even more compelling, cosmopolitan possibilities fuel rugby playing, particularly millenarian images of athletic contracts and fame overseas. In the same way that young men consume images of bodybuilders through a local gaze, rugby, despite being viewed as a quintessentially local practice, is informed by its imperial origin and global possibilities. Here as elsewhere, the local and the global, the present and the future, and tradition and modernity are all involved in configuring people's lives, priorities, and imaginings.

There are of course many other ways in which people in Tonga cultivate both a modern body and self, including athletics, weightlifting, and boxing. These sports occupy an important place in the national project of modernity: super-heavyweight boxer Paea Wolfgramm, born in a Vava'u family of German-Tongan descent and living in Auckland, won Tonga's only silver medal ever at the 1996 Atlanta Olympic Games, while the country was represented at the 2008 Beijing Olympics by a shot put thrower ('Ana Pō'uhila), a runner ('Aisea Tohi), and a weightlifter (Maamaloa Lolohea). Golf, tennis, cricket, judo, and triathlon retain the attention of small groups of amateurs, generally middle class and with strong overseas links. For many years, the late Japanese-born Nuku'alofa hotelier Naoko Afeaki arranged for young Tongan men to undergo sumo training in Japan, in the hope that one of them might achieve the star status of Samoans Musashimaru Kōyō (Fiamalu Penitani) and Konishiki Yasokichi (Saleva'a Fuauli Atisano'e) or at least do well in the sport (which to date has not happened). All of these other avenues both presume and articulate possibilities that may differ or resemble in interesting ways the projects that I have analyzed in this chapter.

Chapter Eight

Reconfiguring the Modern Christian

It is Sunday morning in Nuku'alofa. Congregants of Tonga's numerous Christian denominations make their way to their respective churches, some on foot, others by car. Soon the clanging of bells (which have largely replaced the slit gongs that were formerly used) from the many imposing church buildings compete with one another to announce the start of the services, punctuated by the melodies of hymns emanating from the churches of the mainstream denominations, sung by proverbially powerful choir voices in highly professional and orderly harmony. But the sounds that emanate from the Light from Heaven Church (a pseudonym), in a suburban area of the town, are quite distinct. There, electric guitars, keyboards, and strong individual voices amplified by sound systems intone, in English, a lengthy hymn. The congregants clap, dance, and hop to the rhythm, young ones oozing gendered vigor, the boys punching the air with their fists, the young women gracefully swaying. All smile beatifically, and when the pastor takes the microphone at the end of the opening hymn, he invokes joy and happiness, while audience members endorse his remarks with enthusiastic responses.

Religious Affiliation, the Mainstream, and the Fringe

Situating this opening vignette requires a somewhat extended excursus into the historical trajectory through which Christianity became tightly enmeshed with Tonga's contemporary sociopolitical order. The first missionaries who attempted to Christianize the inhabitants of Tonga in 1797 were envoys of the London Missionary Society, which had established a base in Tahiti.[1] At that time, Tonga was in political turmoil, as chiefs were constantly at war with one another and frequently ensured each other's untimely demise. LMS missionaries' efforts were thwarted by this situation and a number of other factors, including conflict with European and North American beachcombers, Tongans' designs on their cargo, and the desertion of one from their ranks, George Vason, who "went native." In 1799, the embattled missionaries abandoned the venture. Missionizing efforts subsequently remained hesitant until 1826, when Wesleyan missionaries established a mission. After a rocky beginning, they saw their labor come to fruition in Nuku'alofa, which was then under the chieftainship of Aleamotu'a. This chief distinguished himself from other chiefs by supporting the missionaries and eventually allowing himself to be baptized, under the name of Siosaia Aleamotu'a, shortly before his death in 1830. The Wesleyans established schools and churches, baptized converts, and translated the Scriptures into Tongan. Their breakthrough came in 1831 with the conversion of Aleamotu'a's grandnephew, Tāufa'āhau, then a minor chief of Ha'apai. Tāufa'āhau would soon unite Ha'apai and Vava'u and conquer Tongatapu, establishing himself in 1875 as King George Tupou I, ruling over a society which by then was deeply steeped in Christian convictions and practices (Lātūkefu 1974).

The intervening years, however, were not devoid of turbulence. In 1836, Marist fathers had arrived and, also after several false starts, began to convert souls to Catholicism in Central and Eastern Tongatapu. Missionaries of both denominations became embroiled in chiefly rivalries that escalated into war in the 1850s. The conflicts were primarily matters of chiefly politics, but they pitted Catholic against Wesleyan converts, while colonial powers looked on with some interest (Laracy 1977). After the dust had settled, Tonga emerged as a multidenominational Christian nation. The denominational diversity was later further accentuated by fissions over theological and administrative dissentions, such as whether or not to maintain autonomy from outside church authorities. Today, the de facto state church is the Free Wesleyan Church of Tonga, to which belong the royal family and most nobles, except for a few who attend the Church of Tonga, another Methodist denomination. Fissions and mergers in the course of Methodism's history also gave rise to the Free Church of Tonga and the Free Constitutional Church.

Other arrivals dating to the beginning of the twentieth century include Seventh-Day Adventists and the Anglican Church, the latter being attended mostly by part-Tongan families descended from nineteenth-century European traders. Faiths of more recent vintage include the Salvation Army, Jehovah's Witnesses, Assemblies of God, and a host of small Pentecostal and charismatic churches, some connected to overseas organizations, others independent (Table 8.1).[2] Some of these denominations are today considered "mainstream," alongside the various Methodist denominations and the Catholic Church, while others are considered socially and theologically marginal. On the outer fringe are the Baha'i Faith, which has had a small but stable Tongan following since its introduction in 1954, and Islam, Hinduism, and Buddhism, all associated with South and East Asian immigrants and expatriate workers. But the most remarkable of the nonmainstream churches is by far the Church of Jesus Christ of Latter-day Saints (LDS) or Mormonism, which straddles the boundary between the mainstream and the fringe, as I will discuss presently.

Tonga's religious landscape has two important characteristics: the central place accorded to Christianity and denominational diversity. Christianity is enshrined in the Constitution of 1875. Breaking the Sabbath (for example, by swimming in public view or playing non-Christian music) is punishable by law, and the police immediately shuts down any business that stays open beyond midnight on Saturday (except, since the late 1990s, some restaurants). After the Saturday midnight curfew, however, some Chinese shops owners take risks and make brisk business selling liquor illegally through the back door. Denominational diversity has long provided social and theological legitimacy to shifts in kinship alliance, negotiations of power affiliation, and opportunity-seeking designs, in a society whose rigid stratification otherwise affords limited opportunities for upward mobility. The present king astutely acknowledges the importance of denominational diversity by attending a different mainstream service each Sunday.

Church affiliation operates as a major signifier of familial and personal identity. It is constitutive of people's social and political positions, material

TABLE 8.1.

Distribution of religious denominations by census year,
in percentages of the total population.

Denomination	1931	1939	1956	1966	1976	1986	1996	2006
Free Wesleyan	58%	53.9%	49.6%	49.9%	47.4%	43.4%	41.3%	37.3%
Church of JC & LDS	0	0.0	2.9	7.1	9.3	12.1	13.8	16.8
Roman Catholic	12	13.6	14.7	16.0	16.1	16.0	15.9	15.6
Free Church of Tonga	16	17.1	17.5	14.3	13.7	11.2	11.7	11.4
Church of Tonga	10	10.5	9.9	9.0	8.9	7.4	7.3	7.2
Tokaikolo Christian Church	—	—	—	—	—	3.3	3.0	2.5
Assemblies of God	—	—	—	—	0.4	0.6	1.1	2.3
Seventh-Day Adventists	—	0.8	1.5	1.8	2.1	2.3	2.5	2.2
Anglican Church	—	0.8	0.9	1.0	1.0	0.6	0.7	>.01
All others	4	0.1	0.3	0.8	0.9	1.5	2.5	3.6
Not stated	—	0.3	0.5	0.1	0.3	1.6	0.0	>.01
Total	100	100.0	100.0	100.0	100.0	100.0	100.0	100.0

Source: Decktor Korn 1978: 398; Tonga Department of Statistics 2008b.

conditions, life projects, presentations of self, and even body hexis. Church affiliation is most obviously inscribed in certain telltale forms of clothing, such as elderly Methodist men's heavy jackets and ties on Sunday, and the uniforms and nametags of young Tongan Mormons on their mission, but one can also "read" it from a person's gait, posture, everyday clothing, and manner of speaking (cf. Watson-Gegeo and Gegeo 1991). Membership in some denominations determines political alignment. Methodists are conservative supporters of the status quo, while the Catholic Church is an active supporter of proreform efforts. During the protests and strikes leading to 16/11, Catholic priests encouraged parishioners to take part in the demonstrations, to the irritation of government supporters. What one would identify as "social services" (including help to the needy, conflict resolution, youth guidance) are by and large the responsibility of churches. Church-related activities, from attending services to choir practice to meetings of all kinds, crowd most people's weekly schedules. Because these activities differ from denomination to denomination, religious affiliation brings cocongregants together by organizing their lives in a similar way and helps them distinguish themselves from members of other churches.

Mainstream churches are the recipient of substantial wealth from their congregants in the form of cash, food, *koloa faka-Tonga*, and *tokonaki*. Church adherents present this wealth to church hierarchies during competitive gift-giving rituals, such as the Wesleyan *misinale* (from English "missionary") held in September; during annual church conferences; on the occasion of weddings, funerals, or baptisms; or when a family benefits from a sudden windfall, in the form of remittances for example. Churches use this wealth to build more church buildings, maintain existing ones, and keep the pastor and his family living in the style to which they are accustomed. In *anga faka-Tonga*, "bearing the burden" (*fua kavenga*) is a virtue, and one gives to the church to display one's *'ofa*, "empathy, compassion, generosity," and to compete for prestige, even if it brings the family to the brink of bankruptcy. Giving to the church is part of a wider system of reciprocity: Some of the wealth is redistributed (for example, through assistance to the poor), and, more importantly, church personnel ensure their parishioners' divine providence and protection. The flow of resources is thus not completely unidirectional.

However, like all systems of inequality framed as exchange, particularly when they involve nontangible resources such as divine protection, the potential for negative reciprocity is great, and the system offers little to prevent it. Outside observers (for example, Wynhausen 2008) as well as Tongans who are critical of the status quo are known to express indignation at the inequalities that these practices engender and at the burden (*kavenga*) that they represent for families. Protest is rarely confrontational but takes the form of a "discursive negation" (Scott 1990: 104) of the terms of the exchange. Its most effective form is seeking divine protection from churches that practice fixed tithing rather than competitive gift giving. However, because mainstream Christianity and its institutions are deeply embedded in the structures of state and rank and tied to the cohesion and continuity of society, this discursive negation always comes with a price. In particular, agnosticism, atheism, church nonattendance, and adherence to non-Christian faiths continue to be unusual and stigmatized, representing a "bailing out" from mainstream life. Yet this ideology has undergone some changes, particularly among the middle classes, as evidenced by the emergence in the 1990s of the tongue-in-cheek category *lotu hangatonu*, literally, "straight church" (that is, straight to God) to denote people who have strayed from church membership in one fashion or the other.

The Church of Jesus Chris of Latter-day Saints

One of the churches that practices fixed tithing is the Church of Jesus Christ of Latter-day Saints, which underwent remarkable growth in the last decades of the twentieth century, as is evident from Table 8.1. Of course, census figures on religious affiliation are unreliable because they are based on reports by heads of households and because they fail to reflect degrees of religious commitment and take into account the constant movement of people in and out of Tonga. In the case of Tongan Mormons, the last point means that the figures are underestimates, given Mormons' particular propensity to migrate. The 2006 figure of 16.8 percent of the country's population is reputed to be the highest percentage of Mormons in any nation in the world, and there are rumors that the mother-church in Salt Lake City is eyeing Tonga as potentially the first Mormon nation.

Mormon missionaries reached other parts of Polynesia, such as the Tuamotus, as early as 1844, only fourteen years after Joseph Smith founded the church in the United States. Motivating these early efforts was the belief that light-complexioned non-Americans such as Polynesians were descendants of the lost tribes of Israel. The church appeared in Tonga in 1891, but the mission closed after six years because of the lack of converts and reopened in 1907. From 1922 to 1924, the young Queen Sālote III banned Mormon missionaries completely from entering the country, fearing their "democratic" ideas and associations with antiestablishment elements (Britsch 1986: 431–445; 1998). An official restriction on the number who could reside in Tonga at any given time remained in effect for a long time, and the church gained few converts until the 1950s.

That decade marked the beginning of the church's meteoric expansion. Local explanations of Tongans' enthusiasm for Mormonism foreground the theological and ideological convergence of certain aspects of Mormonism with Tongan social and cultural practices, such as a strong interest in genealogy. But these explanations leave history unaccounted for, and in particular the contrast between the original lack of enthusiasm for Mormonism and the later success of the church. The LDS's sudden growth in the second half of the nineteenth century coincides with the dramatic changes that Tonga experienced at the time, which arguably began with the U.S. occupation of 1942–1945 and Tongans' exposure to a world of wealth and new ideas emanating from America (Weeks 1987). Tongans also began to regard education as a means to an upward mobility that they did not previously know to be possible. Coincidentally, in 1952, the LDS Church opened Liahona High School, a sprawling institution built with U.S. funds and organized on American educational principles. Its state-of-the-art facilities contrast sharply with the understaffed, poorly equipped, and dilapidated state of other schools in the country. Not surprisingly, many non-Mormon families are attracted to its expansive, orderly, and well-appointed campus and from there to Mormonism. In addition, the possibility of obtaining an overseas education became one of the "selling points" of Mormonism, as nonelite Tongans began considering a university education as within the range of life's possibilities. The church's Lā'ie, Hawai'i, campus of Brigham Young University (BYU) became the meeting ground for the Church's expansionist policies and Tongans' desire for higher education and economic opportunities beyond it. The campus is adjacent to the Polynesian Cultural Center, a theme park also owned by the Church that features as a key destination for the numerous tourists visiting Hawai'i. The Center employs large numbers of Polynesian Mormons, including many BYU students who pay for their education by performing their (often genericized) "Polynesianness" with different degrees of concern for authenticity and varying doses of irony (Balme 2007).

The Mormon Church offers two important material advantages to Tongans. First, the church is the largest employer and contractor in the country outside of government, and one where salaries are considerably higher than elsewhere. Of course, church members are given first priority, and some business-owning LDS congregants have become very wealthy from church contracts, particularly in the building industry. Second, the church is a serious conduit for desirable emigration to the United States, in part through the medium of overseas education, in part through other means. Everything about the church and its congregants, from language choice to body hexis, conveys an orientation to American modernity, with a Tongan twist. This modernity speaks (American) English, or is at least resolutely bilingual ("Please speak English," exhorts a sign in the Liahona bus shelter). In the schoolchildren's parade at the king's coronation on August 1, 2008, Liahona High School had not only the largest contingent but the most noticeable, with its shiny brass instruments and American-style cheerleaders awkwardly parading in pompons and miniskirts, clearly embarrassed by the skimpiness of their outfits.[3]

Mormon churches have not only an obligatory basketball court built on their premises but also the only paved church parking lots in the country, and on Sundays the sheer density of parked cars is particularly noticeable, displaying congregants' affluence for all to see. Enclosed in chicken wire fences and all built on a common plan, Mormon Church compounds exude cleanliness, orderliness, and wealth. Tongan Mormons occupy the front lines of the march toward capitalistic middle-class modernity, the apex of which they locate in Salt Lake City (Gordon 1988). For Mormons, marrying a white Mormon American offers the additional possibility of not only acceding to middle-class status but also of distancing oneself of the very real possibility that, in the United States, Polynesian features confine one to the nonwhite slot. Not surprisingly, marriages among Tongan Mormons, particularly women, are common. "Mormons thus have a lot to show the Johnny-come-latelies of the world about how to reach white respectability quickly, by providing a specific path toward success in the American environment" (Ong 2003: 212).

Among other features that make the LDS Church attractive to new converts is the church's highly organized social welfare system. More subtly but also more consequentially, Mormonism is the religion of capitalism par excellence, the first Christian denomination to "resolve" the moral contradiction between capitalist accumulation and faith (Cannell 2005; Davies 2000; Mitchell 2001), a contradiction that figures uneasily in Weber's (1904 [1976]) classic hypothesis. These general traits also apply to the Tongan version of Mormonism. For example, tithing to the Church (*vahe hongofulu*), fixed at 10 percent, has liberated its members, economically and morally, from the sometimes enormously burdensome obligations that non-Mormons define as part and parcel of Tongan identity. It has attracted to the Church adherents of other denominations dissatisfied with the latter's expectations.

While the LDS Church has done away with many traditionalist practices, converts run the risk of distancing themselves from *anga faka-Tonga*, an issue of continued anxiety for Tongan Mormons. For example, the Church promotes worldwide a social organization and theological dogma predicated on the nuclear family. Mormon doctrine maintains that people of the same nuclear family will reunite in Paradise after death (a belief that leaves the souls of unmarried or divorced people stranded). This doctrinal "nuclearization" of the family diverges from the open-ended structure of the family generally operative in Tonga. In particular, it poses problems for what many Tongans consider foundational to social structure, the sister–brother relationship. In mainstream practice, this relationship comes in different versions, all suffused with some allegiance to *faka'apa'apa*, "respect." Very traditionalistic families implement it through the complete physical avoidance between cross-gender siblings. In progressive families, cross-siblings do not joke in each other's presence and are careful not to display or be exposed together to intimate matters or behaviors (for example, while watching television). Sisters are ranked higher than brothers, and brothers have a life-long obligation to ensure the material welfare of sisters, an expectation commonly offered as the justification for the exclusion of women from land ownership. Mormon families engage in diverse negotiations of the sister–brother avoidance, some by ignoring it, others by applying it selectively. Mormon sisters and brothers wear matching clothes and dance together at church socials, braving the ridicule and scorn of non-Mormon witnesses (Gordon 1990: 211–213), and when I described to non-Mormon friends in 2000 having witnessed a Mormon sister–brother pair working out together at Teufaiva Gym, they expressed revulsion, comparing the practice to the behavior of animals. In other contexts, the Church takes positions that others do not necessarily brand as contradictory to *anga faka-Tonga* but that are at odds with mainstream practices. An example is its vocal condemnation of *leitī*, a condemnation that tows the line of the Mother Church's virulent antigay activism in North America and contrasts with mainstream Tongans' bemused attitude toward *leitī*, as well as mainstream churches' silence on the topic (see Chapter Five).

These vignettes illustrate the kind of delicate footwork that Tongan LDS church members engage in between contradictory belief systems and competing ideologies. The decisions they make can place them on the margin of mainstream society, into which they are nevertheless drawn back through their sheer numbers and economic importance. It is perhaps because of this delicate positioning that the Church does not align itself with the prodemocracy movement. Individual church members, however, were taken to court by the state for having allegedly utilized their ascendance on deportees from the United States to play a pivotal role in the events of 16/11.

Pentecostal and Charismatic Christianity

The second important change in Tonga's late-twentieth-century religious landscape, to which the rest of this chapter is devoted, is the increasing prominence of Pentecostal and charismatic churches at the expense of orthodox denominations. Religious revivalism is certainly not a new phenomenon. As early as 1834, encouraged by British missionaries Peter Turner and David Cargill, a revivalist movement swept through Tonga, halting day-to-day activities as people filled their days with prayer meetings, public confessions, testimonials, and dramatic performances (Lātūkefu 1977: 128–129). But while the late twentieth century's turn to religious charisma has historical antecedents, it differs from earlier forms in that it is clearly here to stay, to the annoyance of many leaders and congregants of mainstream churches.

The pioneering events of modern-day revivalism in Tonga were the introduction of the Assemblies of God in 1966 and the founding of the Tokaikolo Christian Church, or *Maama Foʻou* ("New Light"), in 1978. The Assemblies of God are the most established of contemporary charismatic churches in Tonga and have the largest number of adherents. Affiliated with the international Assemblies of God church, founded in the United States in 1914 as a federation to fund missionary activities and scattered throughout the world as a result of these efforts, the Assemblies were originally introduced to the kingdom by missionaries based in Fiji (Ernst 1996: 29). They are particularly well represented in the diaspora, with congregations even embedded in the cradle of Mormonism, Utah. The teachings have a strong revivalist basis, calling for congregants' spiritual transformation through rebirth. The church maintains a lively program to recruit new converts, in line with the widespread belief that spiritual rebirth orients the person to the nonbeliever, who must be brought into the fold and saved (Harding 2001: 39).

The Tokaikolo Christian Church was founded by a Wesleyan pastor named Senituli Koloi, who after his death in 1980 was succeeded by Liufau Saulala. Koloi is reputed to have had healing powers, and both he and his successor loom large in the church's teachings. The church owns a school, Lavengamālie College, in a highly visible location at the entrance of Nukuʻalofa, and several primary schools and kindergartens. Its website (www .tokaikolochristianchurch.com, accessed September 2008) states that the church has 6,000 adherents, 50 percent living in Tonga and the remainder in the diaspora. It is politically and socially engaged, seeking social change through spiritual transformation, and key church members have had to defend themselves against accusations of being implicated in the 16/11 events. Preceding the riot and looting on that day, a march was held to protest the closure of a television station then owned by the church, which had become in the preceding year the principal outlet for the Pro-Democracy Movement.

Besides the two better-established charismatic churches, numerous small Pentecostal and charismatic churches dot the urban landscape, some independent, others connected in some fashion to churches overseas. All are based on doctrinal principles that echo those of Pentecostal and charismatic churches worldwide, particularly the centrality of the individual's direct relationship with God, marked by an act of rebirth, and the mediating role of the Holy Spirit. The proliferation of these churches bears witness to Pentecostalism's remarkable capacity for fission, perhaps the secrets of its popularity in Tonga and elsewhere. What attracts converts to these new denominations is a complex question, and it is to the task of finding a (partial) answer that I devote this chapter. Defection from mainstream churches, whose somber pews are gradually emptying as congregants opt to sing, dance, and praise the Lord in the newer churches, is provoking a great deal of anxiety among the authorities of the former.

The shift to charismatic Christianity operates at the juncture of several related dynamics. One is a general phenomenon that Joel Robbins provocatively calls "the paradox of global Pentecostalism," the fact that it is "a religion that localizes easily yet claims to brook no compromise with traditional life and that at the same time seems to have at its heart a set of globalized practices that often look very local in their makeup" (2003b: 224; also Robbins 2004). In addition, the turn to charisma in Tonga is embedded in the radical worldwide expansion of Pentecostalism, with increasingly well-attended Pacific Island Pentecostalist churches in New Zealand acting as a conduit (Macpherson and Macpherson 2001; Taule'ale'ausumai 2001). Another set of dynamics is the congruence among the spiritual, educational, and material bases of faith. The relationship between the first two is the easiest to apprehend: Tongans easily transpose their passion for education to the religious realm, and new churches provide more possibilities than mainstream churches to "learn more" about God, the Bible, and faith, for example through the workshops that many offer. The relationship between spirituality and materiality is a little more complex because its exploration runs the risk of falling into the trap of understanding denominational shifts in utilitarian terms. Yet one cannot ignore the congruence, given the prominence of prosperity in the teachings, which echo similar patterns elsewhere (Meyer 2004, 2007; Piot 2010; Robbins 2004). Tradition and modernity, the local and the extralocal, meaninglessness and meaningfulness, material slavery and economic agency: The foregoing analysis focuses on the way in which the contemporary Christian revival in Tonga provides the tools for the modern Christian to negotiate multiple tensions and refashion him- or herself as a new person in the process.

Two Charismatic Congregations

My fieldwork focused on two smaller charismatic churches, a Pentecostal church to which I refer pseudonymously as "Light from Heaven Church," and a revivalist church to which I refer as "Action Church." During fieldwork, I also interacted with leaders of the Christian television station, who conduct their own services in the station's premises. Light from Heaven Church has a single congregation in Nuku'alofa. The church is loosely associated with a long-standing New Zealand revivalist movement and is headed by a pastor assisted by several other preachers, all men. One of the preachers, a large, gentle, and eloquent man, makes frequent appearances on television to preach the message. Action Church is connected to a megachurch based in an Auckland amphitheater, with branches in Northern Europe. In Tonga it is headed by a dynamic diaspora-born Tongan who is a former member of the Auckland church and who came to Tonga a few years ago to preach, answering a calling from God. Following in the steps of the head church in Auckland, which operates a comprehensive Christian educational institution, this church is heavily invested in offering a variety of courses in Bible study, theology, ministry skills, and leadership. All these themes evoke with the "empowerment" ideology extant in post-16/11 Tongan society and present to potential followers an educational orientation to which many react enthusiastically.

Preachers at both churches radiate an air of cosmopolitan ease and forward-looking dynamism. They travel to New Zealand with some frequency to attend to church business and private matters. Many Tongans state that Pentecostalism and charismatic Christianity, when they originally appeared in the country, attracted the poor, the marginal, and the disgruntled, and in many people's opinions they continue to do so. One of the two churches brings from its sister churches overseas a focus on reaching out to young people. Pentecostal and charismatic churches are often said to hold particular appeal to deportees, and casual inquiries confirmed that some young men in the congregation had returned from the diaspora under less-than-agentive conditions.[4] The Ironman Ministry that I described in the last chapter is an example. The founding pastor of another charismatic congregation is widely known to have been a drug dealer (*tīlā*) in the United States. He makes no effort to conceal this information because recognizing one's sinful ways before one finds Jesus is solidly embedded in born again practices. The congregations of both churches I attended, however, cut a wide swath through the demographics of Tongan society. One church included close family members of a prominent politician (currently a member of the Pro-Democracy Movement), while a mixture of middle-class people, a few Tongans married to Westerners, and a Korean family attended the other.

An emphasis on popularity and growth is both indexed in and generative of worldwide charismatic ideology. In many parts of the world, this emphasis is embodied in the evangelical expansionist drive that is fundamental to the movement, the dramatic amplification of speech and music through high-tech sound systems, the sheer vastness of megachurches, and the ability to reach vast and dispersed television audiences. In Tonga, the churches' active orientation to recruitment is illustrated in the warm welcome extended in the services to any potential adherent. It is the case, however, that expansiveness is constitutive of Pentecostalism's self-representation. It is heavily imbued with a particular self-fulfilling ideology, which one should approach analytically (Coleman 2000). While the efflorescence of charismatic churches in Tonga since the 1990s is undisputable, many of the new churches are fragile, and some have not lasted long, for lack of adherents and funding. For the leaders of the two churches I focused on, the recruitment and retentions of congregants are matters of explicit concern, fueled by an interest in both saving souls and expanding the church's resource base. One of the churches, for example, continues to hold services in rented premises in Nuku'alofa several years after its beginning. The pastor brings up this issue quite frequently as he expresses the hope that the church gain access to the funds to have its own home, which members could organize as they wish.

Light from Heaven Church and Action Church present both similarities and differences in their structure and practices, but above all they contrast sharply with the mainstream denominations from which their adherents have turned away. It is in this contrast that I seek to understand how congregants and leaders view themselves as breaking from the traditionalism of mainstream churches and, more quietly, from the traditionalism of society as a whole. These simultaneous ruptures and continuities are at the root of the growth and efflorescence of charismatic denominations in Tonga.

Effervescence, Informality, and Modernity

As soon as the service begins at the Light from Heaven Church, the seasoned congregant from mainstream denominations is struck by the particular quality of the atmosphere. In contrast to the stolid predictability and solemnity of Methodist and Catholic services, the Light from Heaven service overflows with effervescence. This effervescence emerges with the opening act, a lengthy English hymn in praise of the Lord, sung at very high volume on an upbeat R&B tune, to the accompaniment of two electric guitars, two keyboards, and a full set of percussions, all played by young men on stage. There is no altar, and the lectern is rarely used, as the pastors prefer to pace back and forth onstage, engaging directly with the congregation. A young woman clutching a microphone leads the congregation in a soulful hymn, periodically shutting her eyes tight, supported by a group of ten adolescents and children standing in choir formation in one corner. The spirited performance ends with a few minutes of glossolalia (speaking in tongues) by the lead singer and a few congregants. The details of the glossolalia are difficult to make out over the soft drone of the keyboard, but it clearly weds together emotion, body, and communication (cf. Csordas 1990: 26). Every person on stage exudes the youthful radiance and clear-eyed attractiveness that so often characterizes young Tongans. Local cynics often claim that the new denominations bank on the prominence of music in their services and the opportunity to play modern and expensive acoustic instruments to attract youth, in a society in which music occupies such an important place.

Standing before their plastic chairs, congregants sing, dance, clap, hop on both feet, raise their hands in testimonial fashion, and punch the air with their fists. Some older, heavier, or more hesitant congregants content themselves with swaying their bodies to the music. The body hexis that dominates hymn singing (as well as other parts of the service) contrasts sharply not only with mainstream services but also with most other public contexts, where the fear of ridicule and shame (*mā*) ensures a dignified and controlled comportment, particularly for adults. Histrionic hexis (including joking, clowning, gesticulating) draws attention to the body and conjures the possibility of sexual undertones. Underlying the fear of shame is the possibility that one's classificatory cross-sibling witness behavior that foregrounds bodily or sexual matters, or that someone witness it in the presence of his or her classificatory cross-sibling. Nonnormative body control potentially violates the cross-sibling avoidance at the foundation of the Tongan social order (*faka'apa'apa*).

The only sites where Tongans allow themselves greater kinetic abandon than normal are dance clubs and bars (for young people), drunken parties (for men), and traditional dance performances (particularly for older women). At clubs and bars, cross-siblings manage *faka'apa'apa* by not patronizing these locations at the same time or, if they are more progressive, by sticking to different areas of the venue. Drunken parties are off limits to reputation-conscious women, unless a fight erupts, in which case a sister can intervene to shame a classificatory brother into desisting. Traditional dance performances are the context in which participants and spectators can demonstrate their *māfana* (literally, "warmth"), a state of rapture conducive to an exuberance of gesture and word (Johnson-Hill 2008; Kaeppler 1987; Moyle 1987: 40–41). In gift-giving rituals, being moved by *māfana* can prompt people to give even more than they had originally intended. Dancers in traditional performances experience *māfana* when their bodies and voices identify completely with the singing, poetry, and choreography, reaching what Csikszentmihalyi (1990) would call "flow." Spectators at these events, particularly older women, also perform *māfana* by standing up on the sidelines and clowning, gesticulating wildly, lifting their skirts, and spoofing the choreography. They must carefully calculate their position vis à vis classificatory cross-siblings if the performance of *māfana* involves clowning, which generally has sexual overtones. Audiences and performers of moving speeches, sermons, and prayers are also said to experience *māfana*, although their body hexis remains generally controlled.

Where charismatic church services differ from services of mainstream denominations is in the quality and frequency of *māfana*. In mainstream services, only particularly moving sermons or prayers bring on *māfana*, while in charismatic services it is the expected effect of every service, every hymn, and every sermon. Church members who have accepted the Lord into their hearts no longer need the contextual bracketing of drunkenness or dancing that other people require to suspend the fear of shame when behaving exuberantly. Because the church is sacred and because congregants see themselves as free from the strictures of traditionalism, the expression of *māfana* with the body is divorced from its potential sexual or bodily undertones. God has also set them free from the constraints of *faka'apa'apa* between cross-siblings. For them, the context of the service sacralizes vigorous body hexis. Onlookers from mainstream denominations, in contrast, disapprove of this hexis as profaning the service.

The exuberance of feelings that the Lord brings about among charismatic Christians is ingrained in several other dynamics. One is the predominance and active participation of young congregants, who have little trouble contributing to the atmosphere of energy and enthusiasm. Mainstream services, in contrast, are steeped in gerontocracy and patriarchy. Another manifestation of effervescence are practices such as the applause that punctuates the entire service, sometimes prompted by the pastor; at Action Church, the pastor periodically asks the congregations to "give God a big round of applause" (in English, as I will explain presently). Occasionally, effervescence prompts a congregant to break out in sobs and wailing.

Exuberance is also foregrounded explicitly in the services: At both churches, the service opens with the pastors jumping to their feet and asking the congregation whether they "feel happy." "Are you happy this morning? Let me hear you, are you happy this morning?" a young lead singer asked the congregants at the beginning of the service, speaking through a microphone, and continued: "Let me see you smile so I can see that you are happy!" and, probably referring to my rather stiff composure, "Don't just stand there, show your happiness in the Lord!" These references to happiness, which pepper the entire service, refer to people's relationship with God and the presence of the Holy Spirit among worshipers, but contrast sharply with the relative absence of any talk about "happiness" in ordinary Tongan interactions (cf. Piot 2010: 68–71). In the eyes of noncharismatic churchgoers, however, this exuberance lacks authenticity, and tradition-oriented members of other denominations find it particularly riling. Noncharismatic Christians value *māfana* in religious and other contexts precisely because it is a special occurrence triggered by an appreciation of the unusual quality of feelings and performances. For charismatic congregants, it is a routine sensation that is an integral part of expressing and experiencing their faith. It climaxes in glossolalia, in one of the two churches at least (cf. Fer 2005 on Tahitian Pentecostalists).

Besides their effervescent quality, services at Light from Heaven Church and Action Church are notable for their casualness. Informality is particularly evident in congregants' clothing. In contrast to people who attend mainstream services, for which they put on their best fineries, charismatic Christians go to church in faded jeans, "three-quarter pants," T-shirts, rugby jerseys, and other items of clothing associated with youthful informal style. One sees none of the heavy *tupenu* and *ta'ovala* that older Methodist men wear to church, often supplemented by heavy jackets and sober neckties. Few women wear the *puletaha* and *kiekie*, which, as I discuss in Chapter Two, are prime indexes of formality, respect, and a commitment to *anga faka-Tonga* and therefore outfits that are particularly appropriate to mainstream church services. Priorities at the Pentecostal and charismatic churches lie elsewhere: in inner faith rather than outer appearance, in communing with God rather than meeting the expectations of others, and in freedom from the yoke of traditional expectations (cf. Brison 2007: 55–56; Fer 2005: 160).

Informality also permeates the conduct of the service, in words and action. During one service at Action Church, the pastor corrected himself several times, saying, "Ah, we forgot to do X!" He also regularly peppered his sermons with hip New Zealand English colloquialisms such as "cool," "awesome," "are you with me?" and "simple as!" (a superlative expression), which are intelligible to younger audience members who have spent time overseas but probably not to others. One of my respondents, who is not a member of the church, pointed to this lack of attention to order and formality as what he particularly disliked about the service. One preacher at Light from Heaven Church organized his entire sermon on the colloquialism, "Fasten your seatbelts!" (in a country where the prime purpose of seatbelts in vehicles is decorative). The studied casualness with which pastors walk into the church in the course of the opening hymn, the conversational tone of the sermon and other announcements, and the pastor's calling congregants to the front to demonstrate key points of his sermon all reinforce the unceremonious atmosphere. The individual needs no formality to communicate with God. But to those looking in from the outside, the joyful dancing, the Christian pop and R&B, and the electric band accompaniment all index a lack of gravitas and attention to form more appropriate to youthful parties than to Christian services.

Informality is a matter of liberation and personal freedom through the Lord, a powerful idea that permeates many aspects of the services and of the congregants' lives. I have already mentioned that congregants see their distancing from shame, from traditional concerns, and from the constraints on kinship relations such as sister–brother avoidance as "being free." "Freedom" is a common theme in the hymns sung at both churches, one of which is entitled "Break Free." Further afield, the notion of freedom informs born again people's actions and decisions in mundane contexts of life. In 2000, when I queried traders at the secondhand marketplace (*fea*) about the shame that the traditional ideology attaches to selling (Chapter Three), one of my interviewees, 'Ēseta, explained to me that her acceptance of the Lord had liberated her from the strictures of traditionalistic thinking:

> *Trader:*   In the past I was.
> *NB:*   Hm,
> *Trader:*   *'Ē?*
>   "You see?"
> *NB:*   Hm.
> *Trader:*   *'Eku- ko e- ko e::: me'a lahi, me'a 'oku to'o ai 'a e- 'a e- 'a e maá 'a*
>   *ia 'iate au ko e toki-* break *pē ia 'i he- 'i he f- aaa- 'i he ala 'a Sīsū 'o*
>   *fakatāu'atāina'i.*
>   "It's- the most important thing, thing that took away the- the shame
>   from within me was just- what broke me away from- from- the-
>   huh-[I went] the way through which Jesus sets us free."
> *NB:*   Ha, ha.
> *Trader:*   Because I'm a born-again Christian.
> *NB:*   Hm, hm, hm, hm!
> *Trader:*   *Ko e me'a lahi 'eni ne f- ne- MOLE 'aupito 'a e maá.*
>   "That's the most important thing that f- that made shame *DISAP-*
>   *PEAR* once and for all."
> [Tu'imatamoana, disk 4, 5:25:43–26:13]

'Ēseta explicitly links her success as a *fea* trader with having accepted Jesus into her heart, which liberated her (*fakatāu'atāina'i*) from being concerned about others' reactions. Here religious affiliation has two implications: It provides an enabling condition for entrepreneurial ventures and it disengages her from tradition-grounded structures of feelings (cf. Meyer 1999).

Perhaps the most distinctive characteristic of the services at both churches is the unequivocal and multifaceted orientation to a particular understanding of modernity, which has several notable characteristics: It speaks English; it is steeped in technology; and it is unabashedly embedded in a consumption-focused capitalist logic. I will tackle each of these themes in turn.

In Tonga, modernity speaks a cosmopolitan language to express cosmopolitan messages, although here (in contrast to other sites) there is little evidence of any interest in meshing traditionalist, Tongan-speaking concerns with the modern form and the modern message. The most audible and somewhat surprising form that this cosmopolitanism takes is language choice: The services are in English, and colloquial English at that (cf. Brison 2007: 52–54 on Evangelical services in Fiji). Hymns, sermons, testimonials, prayers, and announcements are almost all in English (save for some particularly intense healing prayers). Yet the pastors vary quite a bit among themselves in the degree of their linguistic competence and almost all congregants are Tongan, and some deeply so in the sense of having only a precarious command of English. In this respect, the churches contrast sharply with orthodox Christian practices, where the use of Tongan is de rigueur. In particular, mainstream services utilize the high codes of the language (Philips 1991, 2000, 2007), which consist of one special vocabulary to refer to the king or God or to speak in their presence and another to refer to or speak in the presence of chiefs and people that one wishes to honor (vocabulary replacement only concerns a few dozen terms, which are nevertheless of high frequency). During Methodist and Catholic services, honorific vocabulary replacement is obligatory. Because church talk makes frequent reference to God and the king, and frequently acknowledges the possible presence of nobles and other persons deserving of such language in the congregation, honorifics are a conspicuous feature of mainstream services, highlighting the difference with Pentecostal and charismatic services in a particularly striking way.

The surprising twist in the Pentecostal church (and to a lesser extent in the other) is that a young woman, elegantly dressed in a conservative Tongan outfit, translates the entire proceedings sentence-by-sentence into Tongan. The situation is thus one in which a native speaker of Tongan speaks in nonnative English to an audience of almost exclusively native speakers of Tongan through the mediation of a translator. Despite the expertise that the translator brought to the task, her mediating role in the entire two-hour service was clearly taxing and occasionally posed complex problems that she had to solve on the spot (for examples: How does one translate "CEO" into Tongan? Does it make any sense to specify that the brand of a car that appears in a parable is a Jaguar?).[5]

A similar semiotic mediation concerns another notable aspect of the services, technology. As is the case of Pentecostal and charismatic churches elsewhere around the world (Meyer 2006), the experience of faith and technological mediatization are inextricably intertwined with one another. I have already commented on the audibility of electronic instruments and voices amplified by obligatory and expertly handled microphones. Mediatization also addresses other senses, including the visual. In the better-off church, a couple of young congregants sitting in the back of the room operated a laptop and digital projector beaming onto a screen a digital presentation of the text of the hymns, while the other church, being less well-off, had to make do with a transparency projector. (To date, no mainstream denomination has made use of these tools.) At both churches, some congregants take notes in notebooks and agendas, evidence of the "educational" dimension that attracts them to the new denominations. Mediatization also brings the message into people's homes in the form of television, on both state-owned channels, where Pentecostal and charismatic churches compete with mainstream denominations for time and visibility, and on the one private evangelical channel, which has had a complicated history, during which it alternated between a religious and a secular channel and was ordered off the air during a governmental media repression that preceded 16/11.

As Birgit Meyer aptly argues, "Rather than offering new *content*, Pentecostalism offers converts above all a new, more adequate *form* through which to express their ideas" (1999: 215, emphasis in the original), and the conscientization of form through mediatization and translation foregrounds importance, newness, and modernity. But modernity suffuses not only the form and medium of the message but also its content. A striking assumption that preachers make in their sermons at both churches is that congregants are white-collar workers. In one sermon, the pastor talked of the disenchanted alienation of office work, the feeling that one is tired of one's job, that one is going nowhere in one's career, and that one is not recognized, concluding that, "instead of complaining, you should count your blessings." The feelings that he describes may be part of a desirable world (*pace* the dystopic depiction) of white-collar salaried employment, in which one has the choice of experiencing alienation. But they are clearly at odds with the precarity of the economic existence of most congregants, who are much more likely to depend on multiple livelihood strategies, remittances from overseas relatives, and other forms of bootstrapping than on office work. Yet white-collar employment, complete with disenchantment, is characteristic of the modernity that Pentecostal and charismatic Christians take as a default context.

This modernity resolutely turns its back on the traditionalism of kinship, ritual, rank, and religious orthodoxy, in tune with the rupture that Christianity represents for members of other societies (Robbins 2007). At one service, this orientation was made explicit in the instructions, beamed from the laptop, on how to fill out the wallet-size "prayer cards" that are distributed every Sunday at Action church: "Freedom from spiritual, personal, and traditional bondage."[6] One service I attended fell on the first Sunday of May, which in other denominations is a celebration centered on children referred to as *faka-Mē*. On this occasion, children in mainstream denominations wear new white clothes and the family's finest *ta'ovala* and perform prayers and Scriptural readings before the congregation, before retiring with their families for a hearty midday feast.[7] That Sunday, the preacher at Action Church, which of course does not partake in the ritual, referred to the fact that the rest of the country was looking forward to *kai pola*, "eat from the feast table," but what was much more meaningful was to *kai pola* at the feast of faith. The contrast he made between the meaningfulness of faith and meaninglessness of traditional beliefs and practices is echoed time and again in the Pentecostal and charismatic churches. For example, a young man about to be rebaptized mentioned in a testimonial, while snickering sarcastically, that he had been rebaptized before, at a Mormon church, and that it had cost him "ten bucks." In contrast, the Christian modernity embodied in Pentecostal and charismatic faith is meaningful (cf. Gershon 2006 on New Zealand Samoan charismatic Christians).

Modernity is inscribed onto the bodies of the participants. I already commented on the casualness of the outfits that people wear to church. Youthful casual clothing indexes an orientation to a modern presentation of self and a turn away from the traditionalism of the *tupenu* and *ta'ovala*, *puletaha* and *kiekie*. In addition, among male congregants and pastors, one sees a preponderance of gym-buffed bodies, leading one Tongan friend to casually refer to one of the churches as the *siasi 'o e kau pāpela*, "church of the bodybuilders." There is of course the strong possibility that, for some, the link between bodybuilding and faith is mediated by time spent in overseas prison gyms. Whether this is the case or not, male charismatic Christians work on their bodies at both church and Teufaiva Gym, turning it into an index of a modern, well-built masculinity that echoes the revival of nineteenth-century muscular Christianity characteristic of some new religious movements. The muscular body is the product of a Foucauldian care of the self, a calculated and highly rational work to dominate nature (Coleman 2000: 143–50, 2007). It is resolute in its faith and in converting others, no longer satisfied with passive obedience to traditional authority. I queried one of the pastors about his own gym visits, to which he had referred without prompting in his sermons. After overcoming a very quick moment of embarrassment (perhaps reacting to the possibility that bodybuilding may be seen as a sign of self-indulgence), he explained that he had begun going to gym because the only people he was interacting with were fellow born again Christians, and he had wanted to meet "non-Christians" (by which he meant members of noncharismatic churches). Indeed, Teufaiva Gym has become one of his main recruiting sites. In bodybuilding, a relatively unusual activity in Tonga among middle-aged men, several images converge: perfecting one's God-given temple, nurturing a modern muscular Christian self, and meeting future Christians.[8]

An important aspect of the modernity of the message at the two churches is its embeddedness in a capitalist order that foregrounds giving-as-investment. A parable recounted as part of one of the sermons I heard at one of the churches illustrates this point. The parable is based on the well-known "six degrees of separation" hypothesis, although the pastor here inadvertently changed it to five. However, rather than presenting the hypothesis (which incidentally bypasses kinship altogether) as any random pair of persons being separated by six degrees, the preacher explained it as "five degrees separate you from famous and rich people like CEOs and politicians." He then went on to tell the parable of a millionaire lady stranded in her expensive car with a flat tire in a dangerous part of New York, afraid to leave the car, until she is rescued by a black man who changes her tire and refuses to take money from her, telling her to give it to someone who truly needs it. She then goes to have coffee at a "simple restaurant," where the waitress is very pregnant, and when pressed the latter tells the lady that she cannot afford to stop working. The lady leaves her a large tip, and it turns out that the waitress is married to the man who had helped the lady, while he was on his way to look for work. The moral with which the preacher concluded the parable is that it demonstrates the kind of providence that God enables. "If you give generously," he concluded, "you receive generously."

The parable, which is clearly inspired by American religious literature, may strike a familiar chord from other locales: It is prosperity faith, characteristic of some Pentecostal and charismatic movements (although not all). Surrendering to God ensures bountifulness. As Meyer (2007) remarks, because Pentecostal and charismatic churches are embedded in the logic of the market, we must begin our analysis with the problem of how religion and economy are enmeshed with one another. As elsewhere, this logic of the market is deeply capitalistic, but it is also distinctively *late* capitalistic, as evidenced in its foregrounding of consumption. Thus, when I first made an appointment with a preacher of one of the churches, he suggested that he pick me up from home in his SUV so that we could hold our interview over breakfast at one of Nuku'alofa's premier New Zealand-style cafés, where the offerings are not inexpensive, and of which less well-off and more tradition-oriented Tongans stay clear. When I insisted on paying for our food and drinks, he expressed his disappointment, given the fact that he had invited me, a stance that few traditional Tongans would take. "Doing breakfast" is part-and-parcel of church leaders' lifeways.

Another illustration of this orientation to late capitalism is illustrated by a testimonial at one of the services I attended given by a Tongan man living in New Zealand, flanked by seven of his eight children (an infant had remained with its mother in New Zealand), dressed in matching aloha shirts and *puletaha*. Walking to the front of the church, he told the congregation that until recently he had been making just enough money to cover the family's expenses in Auckland, but that he had been dreaming of buying property in Tonga. Suddenly, the Lord gave him NZ$70,000, which to his amazement turned into an even larger sum of money (T$100,000) once he had exchanged it into Tongan currency. He had come to Tonga for a family gathering, but it was in coming to church, rather than attending the family event, that he found *fiefia*, "happiness." His narrative reinforces the conviction that it is not in the traditionalism of kinship but in faith that one finds joy. His windfall (the earthly source of which he never specified) would enable him to buy one of the public servant houses that, in its downsizing efforts, government had placed on the market. After his testimonial, the children, all embarrassed in their cuteness, performed a carefully rehearsed "Polynesian floor show" routine to a Hawaiian Christian hula tune, the choreography of which strung together hula movements, generic dance steps, *tau'olunga*, and *ma'ulu'ulu* (group dance performed sitting down). By performing a hybridized and genericized Polynesian dance to Hawaiian-style music, the children were providing another example of the church's modern outlook. While they were performing, the proud father, having whipped out a late-model micro-camcorder, videotaped the performance from the aisle, true to the mediatizing impulse of Pentecostalism. "God gives when you give," concluded the pastor. As elsewhere, God promises "a miraculous return on a limited spiritual investment" (Comaroff and Comaroff 2000: 325), enabling one, in this case, to cash in on the state's neoliberal divestments.

The interesting twist is that all denominations, orthodox and heterodox, emphasize the intertwining of faith and exchange in Tonga. Competitive gift giving in mainstream churches rests on the belief that gifts to the church demonstrate a commitment to God, in that *'ofa*, "empathy, compassion, generosity," fuels the gift in the same way that it does in rituals of kinship. As in kinship-based exchange, gifts to the church assume delayed reciprocity, although the return gift is spiritual: While one can possibly expect material assistance from the church in times of need, gifts to the pastor and the church are more importantly paid back in the form of divine protection. The difference between this traditional logic and the logic of Pentecostal and charismatic Christianity is that, for the latter, divine providence manifests itself, like a capitalist investment, in material terms. In this respect the new denominations resemble the LDS Church, for whom spirituality and materiality are deeply intertwined, although the millenarianism that underlie exchange for Pentecostal and charismatic Christian Tongans is not shared by Mormon Tongans. The latter are more likely to emphasize, like their American counterparts, a faith in hard work and capitalist accumulation as the key to prosperity.

Unlike mainstream churches (but like the LDS Church), Pentecostal and charismatic churches expect their congregants to provide a 10 percent tithe in a sealed envelope, which at one church children are delegated to drop in an enormous yellow wheelbarrow at the end of the service. Here the gift is no longer something one provides in a large system of generalized reciprocity, but something from which one expects results on a personal basis. Giving is no longer a formal public performance, announced in loud voice for all to hear, and prone to being doubled or tripled if the giver feels *māfana*.

Rather, it is a private act, hidden from the scrutiny of others, even entrusted to children.

Returning the Country to God

"I want to return this country to God," the pastor of Action Church affirmed at the beginning of our interview, a statement that may cause consternation in those who already see Tonga as a deeply religious country. The statement is based on a familiar revivalist critique of established denominations having lost track of the importance of faith in their pursuit of materialism, hierarchy, bureaucracy, and ritual. But it may also have a specifically local connotation, namely the fact that the events of 16/11 indicate to many that the kingdom is in danger of loosing track of its Christian foundation. Pentecostal and charismatic Tongans like him are on a mission of faith, seeking meaning by finding God and living through Him. But as many other aspects of services illustrate, while it remains critical of the materialism of mainstream churches, the Pentecostal and charismatic mission also operates in a particular material context from which it cannot be analytically divorced. In fact, as Meyer (2007) insists, for Pentecostal and charismatic Christians, the material and the spiritual have the same ontology.

Unlike their Methodist and Catholic relatives, Pentecostal and charismatic Tongans look resolutely to a future filled with the abundance that God promises, even as everyday realities are increasingly filled with material anxieties, as the cost of living rises, as jobs are becoming even scarcer because of government downsizing, and as remittances decline because of global economic crises and overseas relatives' waning interest in their obligations. This abundance is intertwined with a late capitalist logic that foregrounds a consumption that eclipses production and a trust in the intertwining of faith and neoliberalism (Comaroff and Comaroff 2000: 295–298). It distances itself from the abundance one expects from the kind of divine protection mediated by traditionalist churches and structures of rank, in that it is understood by congregants as a personal contract with God rather than a social one. Its idiom, inscribed in bodies, clothing, language practices, parables, and faith itself, is deeply embedded in a modernity that rubs shoulders with the modernity of the secondhand marketplace, the gym, the neoliberal state, and the diaspora but nevertheless has its own distinctive configuration. In particular, unlike many of these other sites, the charismatic church pays little attention to the problem of reconciling tradition and modernity, a reconciliation that many see as the root of political problems. For church members, answers lie in the future.

It is in this respect that, among the sites that I have ethnographized in this book, the Pentecostal and charismatic church emerges as the most concerned with turning its back on tradition. Unlike other sites, where tradition is constructed alongside modernity and the porous boundary between them placed under scrutiny, participants here articulate explicitly a resolute break with the past, the ritualized, and the taken-for-granted, in short with what they see as the traditional order. Yet while their practices do place new emotions, language practices, and conducts in center stage, they also nurture experiences and practices that are eminently recognizable as continuous with mainstream society: the emphasis on "studying," for example, and the faith that religious experience is an act of exchange. I would also add that the constant emphasis on newness, the comparison between one's actions and what the rest of society does, is itself a generative act, the creation of a traditional order from which one distances oneself but that nevertheless remains essential to defining the newness of who one is.

Conclusion: Sites of Modernity

In the last two decades, anthropologists have counterbalanced the total-izing characterization of modernity emanating from some social theoretical quarters by arguing that modernity is not a monolithic entity that glo-balization disseminates around the world in a one-way flow. This book is squarely grounded in this critique, in its demonstration that people actively engage with both the new possibilities and the new constraints of global-ization and configure modernity in accord with the local. In the introduc-tory chapter, however, I took issue with the concept of "multiple" or "local" modernities as a theory of the modern condition, arguing instead that the recognition of modernity's multiple forms must be followed by an analysis of how different modernities operate and articulate with one another and by a search for generalizations about how people engage with modernity in local contexts. These endeavors must be attentive to the dynamics of local social life and its place in a larger context. Societies such as Tonga, which see themselves as occupying the margins of globalization at the same time as they resolutely engage with it, present particularly rich contexts in which to examine this process because they are neither thick in the stream of glo-balization nor completely bypassed by it. The ethnography I have presented in this book portrays the dense flows that link the local to the global, par-ticularly those that are tied to diasporic dispersal, and demonstrate that it is not just the global that localizes but also the local that globalizes. Modernity and its twin, tradition, emerge out of the resulting multidirectional entanglements.

Objects and bodies have played particularly important roles in my discussion, precisely because they figure prominently in people's engagements with modernity in Tonga and, I suggest, in many other societies "on the edge." The objects on which I have focused in particular are clothing and textiles, which become commoditized through pawning and through their circulation between the islands and the diaspora. Objects may originate as gifts and become commodities or vice versa, and these transformations contribute to the constitution of the modernity in question. Also important to everyday engagement with modernity are the commodification and modification of the body's movement, size, gender, and aesthetic value. The ways in which agents define modernity through objects and bodies showcases the way in which modernity is engrained at once in the intimate details of the quotidian and in large-scale dynamics of globalization and social transformation. Objects and bodies in turn provide the groundwork for negotiations of the self, as people strive to present themselves as both locally grounded agents and forward-looking moderns, while navigating the shoals of being perceived as too "bush," or at the other extreme too pretentiously cosmopolitan, too anxious to distance themselves from the local moralities and traditional obligations (*fie Pālangi*, "seeking to act like a Westerner"). Achieving this delicate balance is an unfinished project, one that constantly requires close monitoring of the feedback of others, unless of course one is living a life of privilege or one has completely opted out of local moralities and constraints.

A focus on the tensions between rupture and continuity, between the local and the global, has enabled this ethnography to mediate between grand narratives of modernity *and* particularism run amok. This approach enables a reconciliation of two seemingly contradictory analytic trends in recent social theory, particularly in anthropology: a call for greater intimacy with the object of ethnography and a call for deterritorialization and the search for explanations in large-scale dynamics. The analytic bifocality of the analysis, which mirrors the experience of the people whose lives are described here, demonstrates that an integrated approach is not only possible but also desirable.

Rethinking 16/11

For most Tongans, the looting and arson of Nuku'alofa on November 16, 2006, an account of which opened the introductory chapter, were deeply disturbing events. Unlike members of societies for whom social unrest is a fact of life (including an increasing number of Pacific Island countries), Tongans see their society as being held together by a very robust organic solidarity founded on a hierarchical order in which everyone is expected to know his or her place. That this order and its underlying covenant should have been so dramatically and unexpectedly overturned is, for many, difficult to fathom. Some simply refuse to talk about it: When I raised the topic during interviews with people I did not know well, they simply fell silent, seemingly unable and unwilling to articulate any comment. Others expressed utter incomprehension: "What are we supposed to do?" is a common rhetorical reaction. Still other commentators blamed the events on specific agents of change: overseas-born Tongans, ne'er-do-well youth, adherents of newly imported religions, politicians who conflate the Pro-Democracy Movement with their own ruthless ambitions, or the infamous deportees. With these agents come new ideas, which equally frequently are made to bear the burden of responsibility: individualism, lack of self-control, lack of "self-esteem," unrealistic expectations, "laziness" (*fakapikopiko*), and "disrespect" (*ta'efaka'apa'apa*). Whatever the reaction, there is a strong sense that, for many Tongans, 16/11 has had the irreversible effect of generating a cynicism and disillusionment that did not exist before.

What I have tried to demonstrate in this book is that 16/11 may be more complex than a sudden fall into anomie. The tensions that erupted on that day are operative, in subtle and manageable ways, in the structuring of daily life in Tonga at the beginning of the twenty-first century. This structuring is produced through ongoing negotiations over the meanings of tradition and modernity, negotiations that are never quite resolved and that concern some of the most commonplace aspects of daily life, such as bodies, hairdos, and clothing, as well as not-so-banal ones, such as worshipping, the circulation of traditional valuables, and the source of one's livelihood. For example, the authority of the local confronts the seduction of cosmopolitan modern as a customer and trader at the secondhand marketplace negotiate the local appropriateness of a blouse that reveals a little too much skin, while subtly seeking to demonstrate to one another both their local grounding and their engagement with a broader context. In these situations, agents operate bifo-cally with the simultaneous awareness of these various contexts, knowing that their actions and sense of self can become the object of evaluation according to unexpected criteria. While these dynamics are easy to overlook analytically and easy to dismiss as utterly inconsequential (as many Tongans do), I argue that they inform more visible and consequential dynamics, such as the call for democracy, the return to traditionalism, the drive toward the neoliberalization of the economy, and debates over citizenship.

What I have highlighted in this book is the fact that the traditional and the modern are not preexisting entities that come into contact with one another in banal or consequential encounters but that they are both produced by these encounters, they both arise out of trite and not-so-trite objects and practices. This perspective runs against the grain of local discourses in Tonga and in comparable places, which maintains that a preexisting moder-nity clashes with a preexisting tradition. Rather, I have demonstrated in the ethnographic chapters that modernity is a production (recalling aspects of Latour 1991 [1993]), that tradition is also a production (recalling aspects of Hobsbawm and Ranger 1983), and that their production arises out of their meeting, out of agents' negotiations over boundaries and structures of differ-ence. Uncertainty permeates these negotiations, in part because boundaries are always shifting, not only over time but also from site to site: Modernity and tradition, and the boundary between them, operate differently at the secondhand marketplace, the pawn shop, the beauty pageants, the hair salon, the charismatic church, and the gym.

It is in the context of these uncertainties that we may seek a better under-standing of the events of 16/11 than the straightforward representation of these events as arising out of a clash between the traditional and the modern, or out of the breakdown of traditional authority under the threat of mo-dernity. As is well established, the riot and arson took place in the context of deep political tensions, escalating conflict among parliamentarians and other prominent agents, and mounting frustrations over the course and pace of political reforms. Yet Ian Campbell is right in arguing that "the riot was not simply an indignant blow struck for democracy and justice" (2008: 108), because in fact it occurred *after* the government had finally begun address-ing calls for reform. Furthermore, it is amply clear that most of those impli-cated in the riots were motivated more by personal greed and revenge than by more noble causes. In addition to seeking the source of the events in the specific political moves of specific agents driven by specific motives (if these can ever be discovered), I suggest that we also understand them as having arisen in a particular social and cultural context that does not constitute a cause but provides an enabling structure, a framework in terms of which the riot no longer appears as an extraordinary event completely at odds with the structuring of life up to the moment of their occurrence or as the product of forces emanating from elsewhere. The uncertainties about what course of action is locally acceptable, the multiplicity of local definitions of modernity, and the complexities of bifocal vision are the characteristics that make the events of 16/11 much more legible than more common explanations that locate them at the point of collision between a tradition that is set in stone and a disruptive modernity. These uncertainties operate in the course of ordinary life, demonstrating that the riots, while appearing deeply disruptive (and being experienced as such by commentators since then), in fact exhibit a great deal more structural continuity than meets the eye.

This structural continuity, however, is not analytically intelligible from the perspective of Durkheim-inspired social theoretical positions. Most simply, 16/11 involved people from many walks of life, including at one extreme very sophisticated agents backed by capital (legitimate or not), church positions, and political status. At the other end of the spectrum were the young naïve agents who interpreted the events as a carnival, though which they could obtain the fridge that their family had always wanted or simply have fun setting fire to building and cars, mugging for the tourist's camera without giving a thought to the fact that the footage could later be used against them, and entering a burning building whose self-locking doors they had no familiarity with. This is modernity in Tonga, as well as elsewhere: a complex array of positions, some tied to cosmopolitanism, others tied to locality, to power, to sheer greed, or to the wish to meet one's family's basic needs while despairing over how to do so.

Retheorizing the Modern

Societies like Tonga are often depicted as being on the edge of globality, occupying a marginal position in world economies, and being suspended in a time warp, depictions that are sustained by Western journalists, travel brochures, and development reports. Tonga in particular is featured in newspapers and magazines with a frequency that is disproportionate to the size and importance of the country. Most of this coverage is in the New Zealand and Australian presses, but journalists in other locations find in the country useful material to fill column on slow news days. Invariably, whatever the topic of the coverage, what journalists underscore is the quaint remoteness and anachronism of the island country, the seeming absurdity of royalty and rank, and the oppressive power they attribute to the churches. Ironically, despite the fact that Tongans are often irritated by Western representations of their country, they reinforce, rather than contradict, certain aspects of these representations. For example, conservative Tongans' arguments against political reform often go roughly like this: "Tonga is a small country, away from everything, steeped in tradition, so don't bring ideas of democracy from larger countries here." Similarly, when ordinary Tongans produce what I called in Chapter Two the "discourse of *fiemālie*," romantically depicting life in Tonga as free of stress, they emphasize that their society is, in their eyes, removed from a wider world of individualism, greed, and anxiety, while in reality these dynamics are as operative in Tongan society as they are in any other context. These representations and their somewhat forced relationship to everyday realities provide a window into why modernity in societies of the developing world is such a difficult condition to apprehend analytically.

The discourse of marginality can mean different things in different contexts, as well as different things at once. For those who see the source of Tonga's problems in "influences" from elsewhere whose vectors are "deportees" and other problematic agents, it means "don't bother us." For others, it embodies a longing for a past when things were apparently simpler: Men felt pride in growing food in gardens, families' main concern was ensuring they had just enough money to cover children's school fees, and church and rank structured society. Even if a past that resembles these images ever existed, it has long been supplanted by other ways of organizing life, new designs, and ambitions and desires of a much great scale. It is suggestive that, historically, the U.S. occupation of Tonga during World War II suddenly implicated Tongans' life projects in a larger context, from which they have not looked back ever since. More consequentially perhaps, a poignant feeling of disaffection now obscures these projects, for having been bypassed by development and stranded in an economic standstill, which increasingly difficult migration to New Zealand, Australia, and the United States does not necessarily alleviate.

As they elaborate, motivated by diverse reasons, an ideology of being on the edge, Tongans also engage fully with modernity, which for them is not just an abstract construct. If anything, modernity is at the forefront of all social action in their society, perhaps more so than in societies that have convinced themselves that they are the proprietors of modernity. Tongans construct different kinds of modernities in different sites of social life, public contexts in which they attend to the necessities of everyday life (or to things that they have come to define as necessities), attempting to earn a living, attending to cash emergencies, taking care of the body, developing new standards of beauty and shape, and seeking hope and answers in a personal relationship with God. At the same time, sites overlap in their semiotic configurations: Some men become bodybuilders because they are inspired by images of muscular Christianity associated precisely with born-again movements. I have demonstrated in this book that what takes place in these sites is not just what they are primarily designed for but also a complex array of performances and negotiations over the meaning of modernity.

A number of additional projects take place in each of these sites. One is the construction of tradition, as agents are anxious to appear to be, in addition to being modern and cosmopolitan, upstanding traditional subjects by elaborating through their words and actions a loyalty to traditionalism, with various degrees of success. Such is the case, for example, of the Miss Heilala pageant, whose organizers make it their duty to elaborate explicit criteria for tradition, as well as the hair salon and the pawnshop, deeply modern sites where agents engage in intensely modern action designed to fulfill traditional obligations. These are clear illustrations of the fact that we should not think of preexisting forms of modernity and tradition as "clashing." Rather, modernity and tradition are constantly emergent, being actively produced in these sites. They acquire their quality through iteration, the repetitive assertion of what they are, but like all dynamics that are constructed through iteration, "what they are" is always potentially open to disruption (Butler 1997). This is why one finds in Tonga (and undoubtedly elsewhere) such a strong sense of what it means to be traditional (for example, producing and exchanging textile valuables, attending funerals, giving generously to the church), while at the same time this traditionalism is susceptible to change in big and small ways. Change can take unpredictable contours. The increasing frequency with which people don "traditional" outfits on a day-to-day basis (Chapter Two), an example of change toward greater traditionalism, contrasts with the increased reliance on event management businesses for the organization of funerals (Besnier 2009b: 249), an example of change toward greater commoditization and autonomy from kinship in one of the most kinship-affirming contexts of the cultural order.

Another project is the indexical projection of people's actions onto a larger world. For example, bodybuilding at the gym references an international competition circuit, while worshipping at the Pentecostalist church embeds agents in a larger context of modern born-again Christian subjectivity. This indexical projection onto a larger world is perhaps what distinguishes dynamics of modernity in societies "on the edge" from comparable dynamics in the industrial world, where it is easy to forget the existence of a larger world "out there," despite the fact that this larger world produces all goods consumed in industrial societies and provides a substantial proportion of the low-level labor. An analytic bifocality, attentive to both local and global dynamics, is particularly relevant to comprehending how lives are lived in societies like Tonga, because it is not just an appropriate analytic strategy but also a reflection of the way agents lead their lives. Social action, particularly when it has performative qualities (as most of the examples I have analyzed do), always takes place with an awareness, somewhere in the background, of at least two types of audiences: one local and immediate, embodied in the people one interacts with; the other global and distant, but no less important. The latter is the larger world, and in particular the diaspora in the case of diasporic societies like Tonga, which local agents know are always potentially judging and evaluating their actions. In some cases the evaluative relevance of the distant audience has very materially specific consequences. At the national level, that audience controls foreign aid funds, which are always contingent on the donor being satisfied that some of its conditions be met to its satisfaction, be it "good governance" or the condition that funds bounce back to the donor's own consultants. On a more specific level, the distant audience may include overseas sports scouts for rugby teams, fueling young men's hopes of salaries of a scale they had never dreamt of. It also includes salaried relatives overseas, on whose remittances entire island-based families rely, and whose opinion (as well as material destiny) can easily translate into increased or decreased remittances. Maintaining one's gaze on the global as well as the local is of crucial importance on the edge of the global, whether in Tonga or in other locations of the Global South.

Gender comes into play in this bifocality, but in ways that defy simplistic generalizations that maintain that one gender group is more oriented to modernity than another, that one gender is more bifocal than another. It is the case that, in Tonga, men appear to be more localized in their practices and outlooks than women. Men, for one thing, continue to be the exclusive owners the primordial symbol of localness, the land, even if the land is no longer used to produce wealth. Women are the ones who are portrayed as speaking English more readily than men, which explains why men who opt out of masculinity, namely *leitī*, are so thoroughly oriented to the English language and its social and cultural connotations. Men's stereotypical activities (such as politics, kava drinking, and rugby) have a more local grounding than women's stereotypical activities, if one equates the latter with fashion, appearance, and upward mobility.

These differences, however, are more ideological than tangible. In the first place, women in villages have little choice but to be grounded in the local, as they spend their day strenuously beating barkcloth, plaiting mats, minding the children, and preparing meals. Furthermore, even men's seemingly local preoccupations, like rugby, are embedded in a larger context: not only in the imperial origins of the game but also in its international career potentials (even if for the majority it remains only a largely illusory hope) and its role as symbolic representation of the nation-state to the larger world. The *kailao*, "war dance," that Tonga's national rugby team performs before international matches, to which I refer in Chapter Seven, is a particularly interesting example of the complicated entanglements of the local, the global, and gender: The performance, inspired by the New Zealand All Blacks' performance of the *haka*, is presented as a "traditional" manifestation of Tongan masculinity, but it only takes place in international sports venues (and never in Tonga), from which it is consumed as a metonym of the Tongan nation by television spectators around the globe. Clearly, the gendering of modernity and its byproduct, tradition, defy simple generalizations.

Where generalizations do emerge, but do so in a surprising manner, is in the emotional quality that consistently recurs across sites of modernity in Tonga. While everyone in the country would agree that modernity as a general concept is desirable (and I have provided numerous examples of this desirability), hanging over all sites of modernity that I have analyzed is a cloud of stigma, embarrassment, and shame. What is at play here is a strongly elaborated emotion in Tonga as in all other societies of the Pacific Islands, as I explained in Chapter Three. This affect is prominent for everyone involved in the pawning of traditional valuables, as I demonstrate in Chapter Three. Shame is also uneasily close to the surface for sellers of goods at the second-hand marketplace and in the commodification of beauty that Miss Heilala contestants are expected to take part in, as they parade around in "sarongs" before large audiences, temporarily bracketing both sister–brother avoidance and the risk of showing too much bare skin. *Leiti*'s subversions of gender categories and norms of decorum and respect constantly risk bringing shame onto families. The individualized and monetized body-care regimes of modernity of the hair salon and the gym require becoming immune to possible criticism that one is shamelessly foregrounding the individual self at the expense of children, families, and society. The proliferation of nonmainstream, non-rank-oriented, individualized forms of Christianity are congruent with a modern orientation to faith and a world cash economy all at once. Once a Tongan joins one of these new congregations, she or he is no longer vulnerable to shaming gossip, as one of my informants explains in Chapter Eight, and can dance, clap, sing, and speak in tongues with abandon.

To understand how this affect and its bracketing operate, one must remember that modernity is not only symbolic but also deeply material. The appropriation of modernity by the high ranking and the wealthy (or lucky) has a long genealogy in Tonga, in a pattern familiar from many other areas of the world. It is historically embedded, for example, in the fact that education, particularly at the tertiary level, was originally the privilege of the well born. The genealogy continues today in the fact that wealth and rank more often than not overlap, as the high ranking have been able to transform traditional forms of wealth (such as land) into capitalist wealth, as some did during the squash boom. The fact that modernity is "owned" by default is further illustrated by the fact that some citizens have been able to accumulate considerable wealth, which enables them to travel, maintain residences in several locations, and display conspicuous forms of consumption, while the rest of the population is heading in the other direction.

The appropriation of modernity, however, does not take place without being counterbalanced by other dynamics, and one of these is the mimesis inherent in the relationship between the high ranking and commoners. In the course of my discussion, I provided several examples of this mimesis at work: the conspicuous consumption of cars, which I discussed in Chapter Two; the royal patronage of *leitī* projects (Chapter Five), which has contributed, according to *leitī*, to the improvement of their lot; and the mimetic response of commoners to the late king's personal project to lose weight and improve his health (Chapter Seven). In Besnier (2009b), I argue that this mimesis also colors in modern times the relationship between social classes in Tonga, demonstrating that class and rank are homologically structured, and operate in parallel to one another, rather than one replacing the other. I also suggest that the rivalry that characterized the life of the high ranking in premodern times now colors the relationships between ordinary people and their superiors, as well as among ordinary people themselves. These qualities give to social relations a competitive spirit that I have documented throughout this book, a spirit that deeply embeds the society in a capitalist order, while at the same time retaining the traditionalism of a rank-based system. But it also means that, when they claim a share of the ownership of modernity, the low-ranking are stepping beyond their position in the traditional order; they are risking becoming the target of criticism for not knowing their place. Hence the specter of shame.

More generally, I have argued for an approach to the modern condition that is analytically sensitive to the emotions that surround it, as the global, or at least the large-scale, is domesticated, understood, and argued over in the local context in terms of locally elaborated emotions, not just some vague universal notion such as "the imagination." It is through attention to the entanglement of emotion and modernity that we can arrive at a much more precise (as well as much more interesting) understanding of how the global engages with the local.

In the introduction, I argued that much can be gained from close analytic attention to the way in which modernity is embedded in language and interaction. However, it is not just in linguistic form (for example, words that translate "modernity," if they exist) that we should look for this embedding, but also, and probably much more importantly, in the way in which agents "do" modernity through the indexical qualities of interaction, in their day-to-day and not so quotidian conversations, gossip, speeches, announcements, commentaries, online discussions, social networking websites, and so on. In the ethnographic chapters I provided several illustrations of how this micro-analytic approach can proceed and how the insights it yields can enrich more traditional forms of ethnographic observation. Examples include second-hand marketplace traders and customers negotiating the local appropriateness of New Zealand fashion, the recurrence of particular metaphors in the discourse of *fiemālie*, emcees' running commentary on beauty pageant contestants, contestants' handling of interview questions, hair salon small talk, and the uses of translation and mediatization in charismatic church services. In my analysis of these examples, I have demonstrated that agents construct modernity and their position vis-à-vis modernity through not only what they say but also how they say what they say: whether they opt for Tongan or English, switching from one to the other or superposing the two languages in sometimes unexpected ways, the phonology they use, whether they appear concerned about fluency and grammaticality, the imagery they invoke, the jokes they crack (both widely understandable and not), their pronoun choices, and so on. In other words, people in societies like Tonga rarely talk *about* modernity, but they "talk modernity" all the time. I am not arguing, of course, that modernity is located only in verbal interaction: Movements, the shaping of the body, people's relationships to objects, the decision that agents take are equally pregnant with meaning. But easy-to-overlook, largely unconscious aspects of interactional production can be mined for fascinating insights into local meanings and their complexities, in a way that very few scholars of modernity have attempted to date, and the methods I have utilized at strategic moments provide a methodological model for future endeavors.

I have demonstrated in this work that modernity is a heterogeneous condition, whose shape in different societies can take on unpredictable configurations. Yet this book departs from other works that have made similar points by showing that what gives modernity its specific configuration is not simply the engagement of entire societies with a global context, whose main project can be understood as the spread of modernity. What I have demonstrated is that modernity is produced through both this engagement and people's engagements with one another across sites of social life. Locating the production of modernity in both local–global and local–local engagements helps us understand how this production takes place in mundane sites that agents themselves either naturalize or pay little attention to. It also foregrounds the fact that agents of modernity are not always those whom we expect.

Reference Matter

Notes

Chapter 1

1. The Tongan currency, or Pa'anga (abbreviated TOP in international finance and T$ locally), was equivalent to US$0.66 in January 2000 and US$0.49 in July 2006. In early 2008, a basket of cassava, which can feed a medium-sized family for a week, cost T$10 at the market, a tailor-made school uniform T$15–25, and a liter of automobile fuel T$2.70.

2. Approximately 800 people were arrested in the days following the looting, resulting in 500 being charged, who are gradually being brought to justice as this book is going to press. Five members of parliament associated with the Pro-Democracy Movement were charged with sedition for statements made on or around 16/11, but the charges were eventually dropped. The Tongan government called in New Zealand and Australian armed and police forces for reinforcement, their continued presence well after 2006 illustrating Tonga's deep embedding in regional forms of modernity. Since 16/11, Tonga has boosted its police and armed forces recruitment, which it has no trouble doing given the high level of youth unemployment and the glamour that young Tongan men and women find in being uniformed and armed (as well as employed). The large-scale reconstruction of Nuku'alofa began in 2009, funded and controlled by the People's Republic of China. The 2006 events are carefully chronicled in Campbell (2006, 2008) and Moala (2007, 2009). I have relied for my synopsis on published accounts, informal narratives by eyewitnesses drawn from various segments of Tongan society, and anonymous video footage.

3. Among the more durable works that have explored early global interconnections in different ways figure J. Abu-Lughod (1989), Gilroy (1993), Mintz (1985), Wallerstein (1974–1988). I borrow the phrase "exotic no more" from the title of Jeremy MacClancy's (2002) edited volume, and "people without history" from that of Eric Wolf's (1982) celebrated volume.

4. These two Tongan terms are compounds, of a reduced form of the possessive pronoun *hono* "its" and *pō* "night" or *'aho* "day," followed by the clitic demonstrative *ni* "this" in the case of the first term.

5. Although the scholarship in this vein is far too vast to catalogue, we can match the various terminological proposals with illustrative works: "multiple modernity" with Eisenstadt (2002), "other modernity" with Rofel (1999), "vernacular modernity" with Piot (1999), "local modernity" with Robbins and Wardlow (2005), "parallel modernity" with Larkin (1997), "indigenized modernity" with Sahlins (1992), and "alternative modernities" (or rather its criticism) with Gaonkar (1999).

6. I refer to C. S. Peirce's tripartite semiotic distinction between symbols, icons, and indexes (Silverstein 1976; Singer 1984; Mertz 2007). One of the most important realizations of contemporary linguistic anthropology is that social and cultural meaning is often communicated through indexes, which are the most slippery of the three categories.

7. "Deportee" (*tīpota*) refers to Tongans from the diaspora, often brought up overseas but without the rights of citizenship, whom immigration authorities in industrial countries have "sent back" to Tonga after they have broken the law. Radio New Zealand International (2008) reports an official figure of 443 Tongans deported to the kingdom between 2002 and 2007, half of them from New Zealand and 116 from the United States (the rest, presumably, from Australia). I will later provide more details on this category, which emerged after the turn of the millennium. For an analysis of the comparable scapegoating of disaffected young men in Tahiti, see Elliston (2004).

8. One does not have to look hard for evidence of the fact that Tongan elites and the rest of the population seem to live in two different worlds. One Tongan intellectual told me that command of the Tongan language by members of the royal family leaves much to be desired, in a context where language continues to be a pivotal marker of local commitment (although the person may have used an assessment of linguistic competence as a judgment of habitus in general). Young Leslie (2007: 391–92) quotes another traditionalist stating that the Tongan Traditions Committee must actually teach city- or overseas-dwelling nobles with faraway rural estates how to fulfill their chiefly functions during their rare visits to their constituencies. Perhaps the most egregious markers of the gulf is a series of remarks that King George V made while crown prince, such as dismissing average Tongans in a television interview for spending their time "basket weaving or whatever it is that they do," an unfortunate line that was forever repeated in the New Zealand press (for example, Phare 2006).

9. Mauss has been thoroughly rethought in the last three decades in works such as Appadurai (1986); Carrier (1995); Godelier (1996); Graeber (2001); Gregory (1982); Parry and Bloch (1989); Sykes (2005); and Yan (1996).

10. For example, Bordo (1993); Butler (1990); Lacqueur (1990); and E. Martin (1997).

11. Anthropologists and others have analyzed the political meanings of such attributes as clothing and adornments (for example, Brenner 1996; Hansen 2000), bodybuilding (Alter 1992), cosmetic surgery (Brownell 2005; Edmonds 2007; Gilman 1999), fitness training (Spielvogel 2003), beauty regimes (L. Miller 2006), and other forms of body modification and enhancement (Hogle 2005; Reischer and Koo 2004). Conklin (1997) documents the politics of body adornments in indigenous Brazil, and tattooing in contemporary Polynesian and beyond are analyzed in Kuwahara (2005), Mallon (2005), and Schildkrout (2004).

Chapter 2

1. British imperial administration drew a distinction between "protectorates" and "protected states." In the former, the colonial power controlled both external and internal matters because it deemed the entity not to have had an organized government. Protected states had an organized internal government prior to colonization that the Colonial Office deemed viable, and the metropole was supposedly in control only of external affairs. Tongan people frequently characterize their country as "the last Polynesian kingdom," a coconstruction of local and international discourses. For example, the phrase appears on the U.S. Department of State webpage about Tonga (www.state.gov/r/pa/ei/bgn/16092.htm, retrieved in June 2010), and it is an oft-used selling point for tourism.

2. The first "ethnographic" account of Tongan society was based on a narrative by Will Mariner who, aged sixteen in 1806, was marooned on Vavaʻu when Tongan warriors seized the British privateer *Port-of-Prince* of which he was the clerk, massacred the crew, but spared his life when chief Fīnau Fangupō ʻUlukālala II took a shine to him. Mariner spent four years under Fīnau's protection. On his return home, he dictated to a London doctor an extraordinary account of Tongan society and the events in which he had taken part, which was very widely read, reprinted numerous times, and translated in several languages (Martin 1817). Details about Tongan society gleaned by missionaries, travelers, and beachcombers appear here and there in the writings of nineteenth-century evolutionary anthropologists. Radcliffe-Brown is the first modern anthropologist to have resided in Tonga, where he was director of education during Word War I. He wrote one brief typescript on Tonga (1940a) and passing references to Tongan society appear in his classic writings (for example, 1924, 1940b, 1950). The first two ethnographic monographs on Tonga in modern times are Gifford (1929) and Beaglehole and Beaglehole (1941). Works published since are too numerous to list exhaustively.

3. Population figures are calculated from the preliminary report of the 2006 population census (Tonga Department of Statistics 2008b). The Nukuʻalofa figures aggregate the populations of Kolomotuʻa (literally, "Old Town"), west of the Royal Palace, and Kolofoʻou (literally, "New Town"), east of the Royal Palace. The (undated) net migration rate and the median age (dated 1996), provided in the following pages, were obtained from Tonga Department of Statistics (2008c).

4. It is of course possible that Vavaʻu's population stability may be due to people moving there to find work in the tourist industry, including a significant number of foreigners, replacing Vavaʻu islanders who leave the island.

5. Diverse manifestations of mimesis are the focus of a large body of anthropological writings and ethnographic films, among which figure most prominently Basso (1979), Calavia Sáez (2004), Ferguson (2002), Herzfeld (2001), Lipset (2004), Rouch (1955), Stoller (1995), and Taussig (1993). Some scholars such as Boddy (1979) and Henley (2006) have cautioned against the too facile assumption that the colonizer is always the inspiration for mimetic appropriation.

6. Kalir (2005) argues for a theoretical shift away from the oft-cited notion of "culture of migration" (for example, Massey et al. 1993) to a concept of "migratory disposition," inspired by Bourdieu's (1972 [1977]) theorization of "disposition," that accounts for both migrants' agency and the structural constraints to which they are subjected.

7. These data are from, respectively, Statistics New Zealand (2001), Australian Bureau of Statistics (2001), and U.S. Census Bureau (2001). Details provided alongside the Australian figure indicate that it is highly unreliable (Helen Lee, personal communication).

8. Underlying the move were economic designs, as the state aimed not only to collect the substantial processing fee that applicants must pay but also to encourage overseas Tongans to inject money into the national economy. The new law became effective in the context of massive neoliberal deregulation and privatization.

9. The figures on household income are from Tonga Department of Statistics (2008d: 192), the figures for the national receipts from overseas for March–June 2007 from Tonga Department of Statistics (2008a), and the historical figures on remittances are from the website Tonga Now, which the government shut down in January 2008.

10. The role and form of remittances to Tonga and other Pacific states raise issues that feature as a central preoccupation in a vast corpus of writing (for example, Brown 1997; 1998; Brown and Connell 1993, 2006; Brown and Foster 1995; Faeamani 1995; James 1991; Lee 2007; Satō 1997; Sudō 1997; Vete 1995). Among these issues figure the impact of remittances on national budgets, whether remittances decline over time, and the extent to which remittances are "useful" (a concept often defined in very narrow terms).

11. The term *Pālangi* or *Papālangi* has a contextually shifting referent, like all terms referring to groups: Across different situations it can refer to Westerners, white people, foreigners, or speakers of English. It is not particularly flattering, particularly when it is applied to long-term residents, overseas Tongans whose demeanor bears obvious marks of a diasporic upbringing, or otherwise thoroughly integrated descendants of nineteenth-century European settlers. When referring to Westerners when tact is called for, Tongans occasionally use the euphemism *muli* "outsider" (also "overseas"), which in precontact days referred to Pacific Islanders other than Tongans. *Fie Pālangi* "pretending or wanting to be a Westerner," is a particularly damaging qualifier that Tongans level at those who somehow misjudge the boundary between those attributes and "being modern." The belief that the term *Pālangi* originally meant "heaven-bursting" or "wood from heaven" (as well as a host of other fanciful etymologies) has a long genealogy among Western observers, anxious to believe that ancient Polynesians thought that early Western travelers were heavenly creatures (Obeyesekere 1997). It is much more likely that the term is borrowed from the Malay word *barang* "cloth, commodity, cargo," carried to Western Polynesia by Malay-speaking sailors on seventeenth century Dutch ships (Tcherkézoff 1999; Tent and Geraghty 2001).

12. In Tonga and elsewhere in the Pacific (and many other parts of the world), a light skin tone is valued as both beautiful and a marker of high rank (Besnier 2002; Teilhet-Fisk 1996). However, what is valued is not the color of the average Northern European skin (which often ends up burnt and ugly under the tropical sun), but a cream-colored complexion, which indicates that race as a category is not the central issue in these aesthetic judgments. I will comment further on the matter in Chapter Five.

13. At the time of writing, the other long-standing colorful Nuku'alofa *Pālangi* is another Dutchman, who rides a bicycle with tiny wheels around town wearing large nose- and earrings and various combinations of Tongan women's clothing. He is well-known for wild and uncontrolled *tulafale* dancing (an exuberant male style that is difficult to execute properly, as I will explain in Chapter Five) and for keeping for himself the money that people stick on his body during his performances, which is generally meant to contribute to fund raising. Another legendary *Pālangi* was Preben Kauffmann, nicknamed Tavi, a Dane who settled in Tonga until his death, was a vegetarian and naturist (in a country where public nudity is abhorrent), but was saved from abjection by his friendship with King Tāufa'āhau Tupou IV and long-term residence on a small island off Niuatoputapu (Møller 2006).

14. The scheme is one of several consecutive blunders committed by the late king in his desperate attempts to trigger economic growth while seeking little or poor advice. In 1999, he would entrust the proceeds from the sale of passports (approximately US$30 million) to American businessman Jesse Bogdanoff, and the money vanished without a trace.

15. At the time of the general strike of 2005, anxious Chinese residents exported substantial sums of money, and the Tongan government counteracted by imposing a cap of T$10,000 a year per person on funds that one can export without a documentable reason, which is still in effect. This cap does not apply to the payment of invoices.

16. The GDP figure is from Tonga Department of Statistics (2005), and figures for 2001 are from Tonga Department of Statistics (2008d: 319–320).

17. Early-millennium reports on the squash industry all sing a less-than-encouraging tune: "The squash result in 2003 was very disappointing due to unforeseen market conditions" (Tonga Development Bank 2003: 5); "The 2005 squash industry was a disaster" (Tonga Development Bank 2005: 8); "the 2006 squash season was unsuccessful due to low yields, high costs of production and marketing and also a very low C&F price for the Japanese market" (Tonga Development Bank 2006: 7). Yet, continues the last quote, "in 2006 we continued to assist the development of the squash industry because of it's [*sic*] positive potential for the economy."

18. The sovereign, the nobles, and the government own the land and grant use-rights to commoners. Owners cannot take land away from commoners, and the latter cannot sell it. Since 1976, however, land can be leased or exchanged (James 1995; Maude and Sevele 1987; van der Grijp 1993). Land dealings require the approval of both the Ministry of Lands and the traditional owners, and if the latter is a noble these transactions are often predicated on the prestation of gifts (such as agricultural products, traditional valuables, cash). Women can lease but not own land, except in the case of widows, who can hold their deceased husband's land as long as they remain celibate. The exclusion of women from land ownership has been the subject of intense debate. Opponents of reform argue that it is counterbalanced by the lifelong cultural obligation of classificatory brothers to support their sisters, which many consider to be fundamental to the Tongan social order (Biersack 1996; Bott 1981; Gailey 1987; Herda 2007; Ortner 1981; Rogers 1977), and that allowing women to own land would undermine both the sister–brother covenant and *anga faka-Tonga*, "the Tongan way."

19. For example, a search I conducted (April 2008) on the term "MIRAB" in AnthroSource, which combs the content of thirty-two key North American journals in the discipline, returned only one mention of MIRAB in an article and two in reviews.

20. In one of his several less well-thought-through statements that was widely repeated in the foreign press, the Crown Prince blamed his future subjects for "see[ing] nothing wrong with allowing their pigs to run all over their townships leaving pig droppings everywhere. No one has yet made the connection between this and the failure of the tourism industry to attract the required number of tourists. . . . We have a very long way to go and many changes to make in Tonga's national life before we can even approach comparing ourselves to Singapore. Just

try getting Tongans to work in a factory from 9 to 5 every day without suddenly having to attend a funeral for a week" (Fonua 2000: 17). Of course, the first part of the statement obviates the possibility that tourists find free-roaming pigs to be part of Tonga's charm, as illustrated in the fact that one of the few postcards available to visitors depicts pigs foraging on a beach. More seriously, to the second part of the statement can be juxtaposed Hau'ofa's apt remark that "the poor adhere to some of their traditions because they have been consistently been denied any real benefits from their labour. . . . [T]he very sections of island communities that preach against adherence to what they think to be outmoded traditions, are the very groups that simultaneously try to force the dead weight of traditions on the poor" (1987: 12).

21. Fees that transnational corporations charge for money transfers to the Pacific Islands are some of the highest in the world (Gibson, McKenzie, and Rohorua 2006), and Tongans find it advantageous to both operate and patronize small-scale ventures that handle such transactions.

22. Sunday morning church services are the other notable context that gives rise to high concentrations of vehicles awkwardly parked along roads because church grounds were not designed for the possibility that space would be needed for them. The ironic consequence of the burning down of downtown Nuku'alofa on 16/11 is that now there is room for shoppers to park their oversized vehicles.

23. Tongans have long used localized versions of Biblical names or names in English and other languages (such as "Mele" for "Mary" or " 'Atolo" for "Adolph"), which are part of the large number of words borrowed from English into Tongan and adapted to Tongan phonology. In recent decades, however, they have transformed personal names back to their English version, as well as given their children English names. This pattern contrasts with trends among Native Hawaiians and Maori, who inscribe politically engaged indigeneity by changing their names to Hawaiian and Māori ones and giving their children names in the respective indigenous languages that evoke mythological and other themes associated with indigeneity.

24. There is a vast body of anthropological literature on tradition making in the Pacific Islands, variously referred to as (*aga*) *fa'a-Samoa* in Samoa, *na i-tovo vaka-Viti* in Fiji, *tuu mo aganuu* in Tuvalu, *la coutûme* in New Caledonia, or the best-known term *kastom* throughout areas of Melanesia where English-based creoles are the lingua franca. Much of this work flowed from the publication of Hobsbawm and Ranger's (1983) landmark but problematic volume, *The Invention of Tradition*, which was in fact preceded by a less well known and in many ways more subtle special journal issue on the subject, Keesing and Tonkinson (1982). The ease with which "invention" bleeds into "inauthenticity" and lack of legitimacy (Jolly 1992) has provoked acrimonious debates, involving agents of the politics of indigeneity in particular in Hawai'i (Keesing 1989, 1991; Linnekin 1991a, 1992: Trask

1991) and Aotearoa New Zealand (Goldsmith 1992; Hanson 1997; Thomas 1997). Richland (2008: 150–153) provides an excellent evaluation of the debate.

25. The foregoing remarks must be mitigated by the rather odd dress codes that were in place during King George V's coronation celebration in August 2008, which required morning coats and gowns, outfits that had to be imported at great expense. The sumptuary connotations of this dress code were in line with the decidedly non-populist tenor of the events, which was not lost on many Tongans. Because some invitations to the events did not go out until two days before the ceremonies because of disorganization at the Palace Office, many guests, unable to lay their hands on the required garments, skipped the proceedings entirely. Ushers at the coronation service went into the street and corralled bystanders to fill the empty pews.

Chapter 3

1. The constitution, Part I, Clause 6, modified by Act 3 of 1971, states: "The Sabbath Day shall be kept holy in Tonga and no person shall practise his trade or profession or conduct any commercial undertaking on the Sabbath Day except according to law; and any agreement made or witnessed on that day shall be null and void and of no legal effect." The word for "Saturday," *tokonaki*, literally means "preparation," and it also refers to the product of men's agricultural labor in prestation, as mentioned in the previous chapter.

2. The Tongan government agreed to the terms of World Trade Organization (WTO) membership on December 15, 2005 and acceded to membership on July 27, 2007, promising to lower customs duties to the WTO-mandated uniform rate of 15 percent, although it had not implemented it at the time of my 2008 fieldwork. The shift in emphasis from import duties to the consumption tax (CT) is part of this agreement, although during my last fieldwork both high import duties and the CT were in effect, the latter being levied on all consumer goods transacted through commercial channels, including food.

3. See for example Gregson and Crewe (2003), Herrmann (1997), Maisel (1974), and Miller (1988).

4. Since the funeral of even distant relatives dictates that one be in mourning for up to 100 days, many Tongans, particularly conservative elderly women, wear black on most days of the year. On the death of a very high-ranking person, such as a member of the royal family, the entire country goes into mourning, and black clothing is de rigueur. Such events create a high demand for black clothing at the *fea*, in commerce and tailor shops, and in exchange networks.

5. Other respondents to the 2008 survey indicated that they had purchased the merchandise themselves or that they were managing the stand for someone who had done the purchasing themselves, which suggests that in the intervening years

slightly more people were able to travel for entrepreneurial purposes or delegate selling to others.

6. The connection between objects and cash remittances has already caught the attention of development-studies scholars (Brown and Connell 1993) and an economist (van de Walle 1998), who attempted to quantify these gifts-for-sale and identified them as "hidden" forms of remittances, that is, remittances that bypass bank transfers or other means that can be institutionally monitored. While I welcome the insights provided by these prior projects, I find much to be desired in their methods and in the categories they bring to the context (for example, fetishization of cash, investment versus church obligations, goods paid for versus goods sent as gifts). They also take for granted a dual model contrasting informal with formal economic sectors, about which economic anthropologists have long been cautious (for example, Dannhaeuser 1989: 228–231). I also venture that these remittances in kind are hardly "hidden" to the people themselves, and characterizing them as such creates an alignment of one's analytic stance with a bureaucratic and institutional apparatus, which may not be the most fruitful approach.

7. In recent years, Customs has attempted to crack down on import-duty evasion. However, enforcing duty payment would undoubtedly force them to look into the practices of people in high places, which concerns about rank simply would not make possible. Small amounts of cash can readily be seen to discreetly change hands between arriving passengers at Fua'amotu Airport and petty customs officers.

8. In contrast, at the Talamahu Market, some sellers who occupy "regular" stalls (that is, for more than a couple of weeks) employ a relative, a friend, or an unrelated third party to tend their stalls. In a couple of cases, the employee has never actually met the owner of the merchandise, who lives overseas and prefers employing a stranger with a trustworthy reputation to entrusting the merchandise to an unremunerated relative, as the latter is likely to feel entitled to helping him- or herself to the goods or to the income generated.

9. The self-reported amounts correspond to what I have been able to ascertain informally outside the *fea*. Calculating net profits is not possible because sellers do not keep detailed accounts (although the more entrepreneurial do keep records of sales). It is suggestive that most small-scale sellers receive the merchandise they sell as gifts, and therefore the profit margin is, strict speaking, 100 percent, although this does not take into account the fact that gifts, like everywhere else, have to be reciprocated.

10. Many Tongan married couples, as well as parents and children, are geographically separated for extended periods of time, often years. Although separation always contains the possibility of abandonment, particularly when the husband is the party in residence overseas, it is considered a sign of mutual *fe'ofo'ofa'aki* "mutual care, reciprocal empathy," in that the spouses are viewed as sacrificing altruistically their self-centered desire to be "taken care of" by one another to meet each other's material needs (Gailey 1992).

11. Compare, among others, Alexander (1998: 211–214); Alexeyeff (2008b: 145); Bunster and Chaney (1985: 106–109); Seligmann (2001: 12–14). There are other cases in which trading can contribute more burden than flexibility to women, such as where the success of trading is contingent on a consistent present at the marketplace (for example, Clark 1994).

12. "When you marry a Tongan, you marry the whole family," people with other options often declare in Tonga. Viliami does have a live-in girlfriend, or *faka-Suva* (literally, "in the fashion of Suva," in reference to the capital of Fiji, which is for this part of the Pacific the main centre of modernity and hence a den of depravity) but, because the relationship is not sanctioned by kinship, church, and state, it frees him of obligations to her family, except when it suits him.

13. The classic cases of hypercorrection are the high proportion of standard features of English in the speech of lower-middle-class New Yorkers in the 1960s (Labov 1966) and middle-class Standard English–speaking African Americans' use of African American Vernacular English features in contexts where native speakers of the dialect would not use them (Baugh 1992). Baugh terms the latter case "hypocorrection" because the features that are the object of exaggeration have low prestige in mainstream society, even if they are indexes of race solidarity between hypocorrectors and native users. The example here is in fact a little ambiguous because the trader in fact emulates the pronunciation of lower-class New Zealanders but does so to index her familiarity with a non-Islander dialect of New Zealand English. But the intersection of social class and transnationalism is never straightforward.

Chapter 4

1. In Britain and probably other parts of Europe, pawnshops have been prominent features of the urban landscape since the eighteenth century (Hudson 1982). Pawnshops have a long history in urban New Zealand, the earliest and still most common destination for Tongan migrants, as they already appear in the 1897 phone directory listing for Wellington (Malcolm McKinnon, personal communication). Diasporic Tongans, who display all the resourcefulness of the urban poor, would have quickly become familiar with the concept and brought the idea back to the islands, ingeniously adapting it to the local economy.

2. There is a vast literature on the material culture of Tongan valuables and the ritual practices that showcase them, including Addo (2004a, 2004b), Filihia (2001), Gailey (1987), Helu (1999: 309–318), Herda (1999), Kaeppler (1978, 1995, 1999), Koch (1955), Kooijman (1972), and Teilhet-Fisk (1991).

3. Connelly-Kirch (1982) and van der Grijp (1993b) analyze the handicraft tourist trade, and von Gizycki (1997) provides the ethnographic background of Langa Fonua. The souvenir-producing industry alters the gender of objects be-

cause entrepreneurialism is generally the domain of men. Women often produce handicrafts that men sell to tourists, in contrast to *koloa* prestation, where women are in control. I provide an example of gender-based power realignment in the case of Viliami in Chapter Three, who exports souvenirs made of barkcloth and mat and signs them with his own name.

4. In a critique of the earlier publication on which this chapter is based, Dr. 'Ana Taufe'ulungaki, a widely respected Tongan intellectual, faulted me for fore-grounding *mā* as the dominant emotion in exchange, rather than *'ofa*, which she attributed to my perspective as an outsider and which in her view is at odds with a Tongan perspective. I take this criticism seriously and fault the original publication for not foregrounding what is after all of major importance to Tongan agents. At the same time, I continue to maintain that we cannot overlook the importance of shame as a regulator of exchange, even it is not part of the overt discourse about exchange. It figures abundantly in gossip about exchange, for example.

Chapter 5

1. Pageants and similar events (including fashion shows, debutante balls, and quinceañeras) have been the subject of controversies over a variety of issues, in-cluding the kind of beauty standards that should apply, which often uncomfortably foreground issues of ethnicity, indigeneity, and race (Banet-Weiser 1999; Borland 1996; McAllister 1996; Rahier 1998; Schulz 2000; Yano 2006); the nature of be-longing, authenticity, and national identity (Brownell 2001; Cohen 1996; Dewey 2008; McGranahan 1996; M. Rogers 1998; Schackt 2005; Schröder 2004; Wilk 1996); and whether they should take place at all (Assayag 1999; Lukose 2005)

2. So far, only two Miss Heilala laureates have won the Miss South Pacific title, and neither has made it further.

3. The program of the 1995 pageant lists a luncheon interview, a talent quest, a *tau'olunga* contest, a South Pacific evening, and a Heilala ball, during which the contestants parade in ball gowns. Events in which contestants would appear in swimsuit were then considered inappropriate in a society in which bare skin (particularly thighs) was considered beyond the bounds of propriety (Teilhet-Fisk 1996: 197–198). These standards have relaxed somewhat over the years, and the current pageants do require contestants to parade in beachwear. Some try to at-tenuate the risqué nature of their outfits by giving them a local flavor and design-ing them out of barkcloth, despite the fact (not lost on spectators in the know) that it would immediately disintegrate on contact with water.

4. "So what are the judges looking for?" the 1995 program asks rhetorically. "Certainly the glamour and sophistication of the Miss Heilala Ball is an important element. Nevertheless, of equal importance are events designed to access contestants'

knowledge of both Tongan and English language, of Tongan culture, and their general knowledge. Their communication skills are judged during a private luncheon interview. The Talent Quest provides opportunity for the young ladies [to] show off their entertainment skills during an evening of music and fun."

5. Teilhet-Fisk reports that when the Tonga Visitors Bureau assumed control of the pageant it decided to prevent audience members from supporting *tau'olunga* performers with *tulāfale* dancing because it considered it "distracting" and "lack[ing] a sense of professionalism" (1996: 193). What should be added is that men not infrequently perform *tulāfale* while drunk, and the Dateline Hotel, when it hosted the pageant, used to push alcohol sales quite insistently.

6. Of course, the valuation of pale complexion can easily morph into a racial judgment. The slip is almost made inevitable by the common etymologies of the words *'uli'uli*, "black, dark complexioned"; *'uli*, "dirty"; and *po'uli*, "darkness, uncivilized." One can easily elicit from Tongans explanations of their Melanesian neighbors' relative lack of development in terms of their darker skin tones. The common use of the term *nika*, borrowed from English, to refer to dark-skinned people, even though Tongans are well aware of the extremely pejorative connotations of the original English term, does not help. In the diaspora, in contrast, younger radicalized Tongans easily "become black," identifying with Māori or African American cultural symbols and racial politics.

7. He does make the following ambiguous statement: "As to certain preposterous habits, which so disgrace the moral character of nations west of them, and which have been said to infect the natives of some of the South Seas islands, we must do the Tonga people the justice to say, that they have not the most remote idea of any thing of the kind" (Martin 1817: II: 178). This sentence may be interpreted as a comparison of Tonga with Tahiti, where the presence of *māhū* had been lavishly described in early navigators' travel literature, in which Mariner was well versed, although Tahiti is to the east of Tonga, not to the west. The other possible reading of "preposterous habits" is a reference to cannibalism, but this interpretation is ruled out by the detailed description of Tongan cannibal feasts elsewhere in the book.

8. The exotic appeal of the category and its ambiguous place at the intersection of sexual and indigenous politics in New Zealand, Hawai'i, and diasporic Polynesia have given rise to a sizeable industry of particularly bad scholarship (cf. Towle and Morgan 2002).

9. One tired myth that keeps reoccurring in Western representations of Polynesian transgender identities is the assertion parents "turn" one of their boys into a girl when they do not have enough girls, in response to the need for a gendered balance in the distribution of domestic labor. I believe that the myth can be traced back to Margaret Mead's *Growing Up in Samoa*. While some mothers do playfully encourage effeminate behavior in their sons, they are few and far between, and extremely few parents would wish their child to grow up with the social disadvantage

of being a *leitī*. The detailed data I have gathered on *leitī*'s siblings and birth order suggest that, if any factor has a statistical effect, it is the prevalence of sisters, not brothers.

10. Mainstream Tongans represent *leitī* as sexually aggressive, while in fact it is straight men who constantly initiate sexually suggestive banter with them. Of course, most *leitī* hardly are shrinking violets.

11. The term *nonlocality* is abstract and stylistically awkward, but the alternatives (the Other, the foreign, difference, the exotic, the global, the Western, transnational identity, whiteness, and so on) are too specific (and in some cases misleading) to capture a category that remains crucially vague in the social practices concerned and that is defined in terms of what it is not. In fact, both vagueness and antithesis are essential features of pageant contestants' strategic deployments of nonlocality. Johnson (1997) grapples with a similar situation in an analysis of the Tausug transgendered construction of "America" in Jolo (Southern Philippines), which does not refer to a particular place but to a shifting, negatively defined entity evoking a variety of historical and symbolic associations.

12. Some of the information provided is fake or unrealistic, while other details are designed to be humorous. For example, contestants in 1997 claimed high-status feminine occupations such as "nurse" or "public relations" [*sic*], as well as future plans to become a "computer operator," a "flying attendant" [*sic*], or a "good wife." Johnson (1997) and Reid (2007) describe the same practice of emulating international beauty contests in Tausug transgendered pageants and in urban South Africa.

13. Following Lindstrom (1995: 35), I use the term *occidentalism* as the equivalent of what Carrier (1992: 198) terms "ethno-occidentalism," to refer to non-Western visions of the West that are characterized by the same reifications and constructions of difference and similarity as orientalism. Of course, orientalism and occidentalism operate within the context of distinct power dynamics.

14. Tongan attitudes toward women who marry older *Pālangi* men ostensibly for financial security are similar to those described for *leitī*. However, women in this situation are not generally criticized for having turned their back on the Tongan Way. Indeed, exogamy with Westerners is not only unstigmatized but also conforms, alongside the assumption that Westerners are wealthy, to a desirable hypergamy for low-ranking women that dates back to precontact days. The possibility that some *leitī* and some "straight" Tongan men may in fact desire older white men is not broached. Some young masculine-acting Polynesian men who quietly "turn gay" in the diaspora gravitate toward relationships with older white men, a pattern reminiscent of the attraction of younger Asian "potato queens" to older white "rice queens" in much of Asia (Jones 2000). The complicated structuration of sexual desire, material desire, and parameters of social identity such as age, ethnicity, and race deserves considerably more analytic attention than I can devote to it.

Chapter 6

1. In this chapter, I forego the use of pseudonyms for people and businesses at the request of those mentioned.

2. This gendering is a common characteristic of professionalized beauty care elsewhere in the world (see, for example, Furman 1997; Jacobs-Huey 2006; Labaki 2007; Miller 2006; Ossman 2002; Reid 2007; Willett 2000). Its specter looms large even when beauty work is done by men for men (see Ahmed 2006; Barber 2008; Weiss 2009).

3. At the coronation on August 1, 2008, female members of the royal family had their hair and make-up done by stylists flown in from overseas: part-Tongan Felicia from Auckland, Hawaiian Coco Chandelier from Honolulu, and Japanese-Hawaiian Selena from Las Vegas. The last went on to win Miss Galaxy 2008 the following week, as I describe in the previous chapter.

4. Massage (*fotofota*) is part of the repertoire of Tongan ethnomedical practices, but it differs radically from the Western-style body massage that the original salon owner had in mind. Some Chinese salons, in contrast, are offering massage services that attract expat and Tongan men and that, rumor has it, consist in a little more than an ordinary massage.

5. These dynamics are ubiquitous across Pacific Island societies and probably elsewhere and are congruent with some theoretizations of the Melanesian self as "partible" (see Chapter One). The immorality of vanity in the aged was demonstrated to me particularly dramatically while I was conducting fieldwork on Nukulaelae Atoll, Tuvalu, in 1990, when I showed people around me a photograph that a friend, a Midwesterner in her eighties, had sent me in the mail, depicting herself and a couple of age-mates at a restaurant, dressed up and made up in what would pass as a tasteful manner in the Midwest. The make up, coiffed hair, fineries, public setting, and the fact that old women would even allow themselves to be photographed provoked utter consternation among my Nukulaelae relations, who are deeply embedded in a politics of body aesthetics similar to that of rural or underprivileged Tonga.

6. With increasing frequency, funerals nowadays "belong to," to use the Tonga phrase (that is, are organized and presided by), the children of the deceased, particularly first-born daughters, rather than *fahu* senior relatives. Tupou IV's eldest granddaughter taking the responsibility of hair cutting at his funeral is congruent with this trend.

7. Recall Prince Tupouto'a's remarks, cited in Chapter Two, juxtaposing roaming pigs with the dearth of tourists, as well as Tongans' deficient work ethics. The contrast he drew between the dirt and lack of discipline on the one hand and, on the other hand, a modernized, technologically oriented nation favored as a tourism destination encapsulates themes that Tongan elites and aspiring elites often express.

8. Women's casual office gossip often consists of minutely detailed commentaries on clothing and hairstyles and thus builds on the conversations and practices that take place in salons, acting as one channel through which the desire to and the knowledge of doing hair get transmitted (Mary Good, personal communication).

9. For example, one should not overlook the shallow history, even in urban Western contexts, of dyeing one's hair to look younger. In his classic *Presentation of Self in Everyday Life*, Erving Goffman asserts, "Very recently the concealment of gray hair by dyeing has come to be considered acceptable, although there still are sectors of the populace which consider this to be impermissible" (1959: 61). He does not clarify what "segments of the populace" he alludes to.

Chapter 7

1. The gendering of the static–dynamic contrast maps onto rank because women within the family are of higher rank than men. In other parts of Polynesia and elsewhere in the world, the daughters of chiefs were "fattened" so that they developed large bodies (cf. Popenoe 2004 on Mali).

2. Comparable contrasts operate in industrial societies, this time in terms of social class. Pierre Bourdieu's comparison of middle-class sports activities like walking, jogging, and aerobics trainings, with working-class team sports (about which more anon) is instructive: The former,

> unlike ball games, do not offer any competitive satisfaction, are highly rational and rationalized activities. This is firstly because they presuppose a resolute faith in reason and in the deferred and often intangible benefits which reason promises (such as protection against ageing, an abstract and negative advantage which only exists by reference to a thoroughly theoretical referent). (1978:839)

3. Fish in Tongan waters is becoming rare; it is beyond the means of most, and young people have lost the taste for it. Local chicken is scarce and tough. Pork is reserved for feasts, and so are the products of the sea, such as fish, lobster, octopus, large shellfish, and crab. The smaller seashells (*fingota*) that constituted village diets during my early years in Tonga are now harvested and consumed only on the smaller outlying islands, and elsewhere people generally experience shame (*mā*) to be seen gathering them.

4. Dietary expectations have also changed over time. Until relatively recently, people did not expect to consume protein on a daily basis, and the day-to-day diet consisted mostly of staple carbohydrates (cassava, taro, breadfruit) and greens. Today, people expect to consume protein regularly, and bread manufactured with imported white flour tops the preference list of carbohydrates (Evans et al. 2001).

5. These contradictions are not confined to the rugby field. Tongans themselves have ambivalent feelings about them, sometimes feeding back to Westerners the exotic images that the latter want to see (a great leg-pulling strategy), and at other times defensively emphasizing their modernity. An excellent example of the former can be found in a popular article that the late Langi Kavaliku, who would become a long-serving minister of education, published in the late 1960s, recounting his arrival at Harvard University having never worn shoes or eaten with a fork (reading this article as a child left an indelible mark on me). The discourse of exoticism is not exclusively directed at outsiders, as I demonstrate in my discussion of the "discourse of *fiemālie*" in Chapter Two.

6. Pro Heavyweight Tēvita 'Aholelei, based in the United States and a veteran of the first Gulf invasion, whose posing DVDs sell on the Internet, has won international competitions. Young Teufaiva patrons also look up to bodybuilder Simi Tufunga, heavyweight bodybuilder with a high-profile personal trainer business in the San Francisco Bay Area.

7. At least one Nuku'alofa family named their baby Ben-Hur: Ben-Hur Kivalu, born in 1972, has become one of Tonga's leading international rugby players, last employed in Japan by the Kintetsu Liners (owned by a railway company).

8. In the last few decades, the Tongan state has been a staunch supporter of U.S. foreign policies, particularly when these involved invading non-Christian countries, and most Tongan citizens have enthusiastically approved. Tonga was one of the last members of the "allied coalition" in Iraq, where it maintained several dozen troops, at the expense of the United States.

9. Similarly, Rambo, symbol of resistance to hegemony with tools powerful enough to make a difference (muscles, machine guns, language, jingoism, a certain sex appeal), left in its time a particularly memorable impression among young people in Tonga (Gailey 1989) and around the Pacific (Jourdan 1995; Wood 2006).

10. By an independent twist of irony, private interests have set up a venture in Utah to send, for a hefty sum of money, American teenagers with a drug problem to Tonga for extended periods of time. The logic is that the youngsters will learn discipline from the Tongan context. In 2008, they were regularly seen working out at Teufaiva, trying to kill boredom and homesickness.

Chapter 8

1. Nonconformist and Anglican evangelicals founded the Missionary Society in 1795 for the purpose of promoting the evangelization of the colonies. It later became known as the London Missionary Society and gained enormous ascendance in South Africa (Comaroff and Comaroff 1991, 1997), in addition to Tahiti. From Tahiti, the society missionized Samoa and minor island groups like Tuvalu.

2. A detailed survey by Vakaoti (2006) enumerates the following: Gospel Chapels, Church of Christ, New Apostolic Church, Tonga Bible Baptist Church, United Pentecostal International, Tonga Fellowship for Revival, Christadelphians Worldwide, New Life Church, Church of the Rock, and Churches of Christ. By the time of my 2008 fieldwork, several of these had waned, and others had emerged. Tonga had a private Christian television channel for a decade, although it underwent complicated transformations resulting from personal disagreements and was finally closed down in a 2005 government crackdown on private media. For an earlier analysis of a charismatic church in Tonga, see Olson (2001).

3. When I turned to a friend and commented that Liahona was *tuʻumālie*, "wealthy," a bystander retorted, in American-accented English and with a tone of slight annoyance, "No, they work hard!" The retort embodies a classic American faith in the power of meritocracy, which in the case of Liahona High School is particularly disingenuous given the large input of funds from the United States that keeps the school functioning.

4. Not to be outdone, the Free Wesleyan Church also runs its own program for deportees.

5. Prior to the first service I attended at one of the churches, I had interviewed the preacher who conducted the service, and we had spoken Tongan. Aware of my competence in the language, he asked me during the service to introduce myself to the congregation and specified that I do so in Tongan. Congregants punctuated my little performance (which the in-house interpreter translated into English) with appreciative applause and vocalizations. Given that this introduction had already taken place, it is clear that the choice of English in the service was not for my benefit.

6. This particular service took place on the Sunday after the king's coronation. In his sermon, the preacher nevertheless paid tribute to the king, stating that God had anointed him to be in the position of ruler and describing the atmosphere of enthusiasm and deep unity that characterized the coronation celebrations.

7. Several video clips of children reciting texts at a *faka-Mē* are available on YouTube. Among mainstream Christian families whose means are modest or whose remittances have not come through on time, providing material evidence of parents' love for their children in a way that will also not bring shame on the family can be a source of deep anxiety in the days leading up to *faka-Mē*.

8. There is of course a strong gender dimension to this aspect of the charismatic movement in Tonga, in that the gym is a site dominated by men that exudes hypermasculinity. Masculinity emerges in some of the sermons at the church with the stronger connections to New Zealand, in the form of remarks about men's need to "regain control," reminiscent of the ideology of recent Christian men's movements like the Promise Keepers, which incidentally were very popular in New Zealand at its peak.

References

Abercrombie, Nicholas, Stephen Hill, and Bryan S. Turner. 1986. *Sovereign Individuals of Capitalism*. London: Allen & Unwin.

Abu-Lughod, Janet. 1989. *Before European Hegemony: The World System, A.D. 1250–1350*. New York: Oxford University Press.

Abu-Lughod, Lila. 1991. Writing against Culture. In Richard G. Fox, ed., *Recapturing Anthropology: Working in the Present*, 137–162. Santa Fe, NM: School of American Research Press.

Addo, Ping-Ann. 2003. God's Kingdom in Auckland: Tongan Christian Dress and the Expression of Duty. In Cloë Colchester, ed., *Clothing the Pacific*, 141–163. Oxford, UK: Berg.

———. 2004a. Kinship, Cloth, and Community in Auckland, New Zealand: Commoner Tongan Women Navigate Transnational Identity Using Traditionally-Styled Textile Wealth. PhD dissertation, Department of Anthropology, Yale University.

———. 2004b. *Pieces of Cloth, Pieces of Culture: Tapa from Tonga and the Pacific Islands*. Oakland and San Francisco: Center for Art and Public Life, California College of the Arts and California Academy of Sciences.

Ahmed, F.M. Faizan. 2006. Making Beautiful: Male Workers in Beauty Parlors. *Men and Masculinities* 9: 168–185.

Alexander, Jennifer. 1998. Women Traders in Javanese Marketplaces: Ethnicity, Gender, and the Entrepreneurial Spirit. In Robert W. Hefner, ed., *Market Cultures: Society and Morality in the New Asian Capitalisms*, 203–223. Boulder, CO: Westview.

Alexeyeff, Kalissa. 2000. Dragging Drag: The Performance of Gender and Sexuality in the Cook Islands. *Australian Journal of Anthropology* 12: 253–260.

———. 2008a. Globalizing Drag in the Cook Islands: Friction, Repulsion, and Abjection. *The Contemporary Pacific* 20: 143–161.

———. 2008b. Neoliberalism, Mobility and Cook Islands Men in Transit. *Australian Journal of Anthropology* 19: 136–149.

Alter, Joseph S. 1992. *The Wrestler's Body: Identity and Ideology in North India*. Berkeley: University of California Press.

———. 2004. Indian Clubs and Colonialism: Hindu Masculinity and Muscular Christianity. *Comparative Studies in Society and History* 46: 497–534.

Appadurai, Arjun. 1986. Introduction: Commodities and the Politics of Value. In Arjun Appadurai, ed., *The Social Life of Things: Commodities in Cultural Perspective*, 3–63. Cambridge, UK: Cambridge University Press.

———. 1996. *Modernity at Large: Cultural Dimensions of Globalization*. Minneapolis: University of Minnesota Press.

Assayag, Jackie. 1999. La "glocalisation" du beau: Miss Monde en Inde, 1996. *Terrain* 32: 67–82.

'Atiola, 'Aioema. 2007. Tongan Wesleyan Missionaries Abroad 1835–1985. In Elizabeth Wood-Ellem, ed., *Tonga and the Tongans: Heritage and Identity*, 87–102. Alphington, Victoria: Tonga Research Association.

Australian Bureau of Statistics. 2001. *Census of Population and Housing: Selected Social and Housing Characteristics, Australia*. Canberra: Australian Bureau of Statistics.

Bain, K. R. 1954. *The Official Record of the Royal Visit to Tonga, 19th–20th December, 1953*. London: Pitkin, published by the Government of Tonga by command of H.M. Queen Salote Tupou, G.C.V.O, G.B.E.

Balme, Christopher. 2007. *Pacific Performances: Theatricality and Cross-Cultural Encounter in the South Seas*. London: Palgrave Macmillan.

Banet-Weiser, Sarah. 1999. *The Most Beautiful Girl in the World: Beauty Pageants and National Identity*. Berkeley: University of California Press.

Barber, Kristen. 2008. The Well-Coiffed Man: Class, Race, and Heterosexual Masculinity in the Hair Salon. *Gender & Society* 22: 455–476.

Bashkow, Ira. 2006. *The Meaning of Whitemen: Race and Modernity in the Orokaiva Cultural World*. Chicago: University of Chicago Press.

Basso, Keith H. 1979. *Portraits of "the Whiteman": Linguistic Play and Cultural Symbols among the Western Apache*. Cambridge, UK: Cambridge University Press.

Bataille, Marie-Claire. 1976. Le salon de l'agriculture à Tonga et sa relation avec le passé. *Journal de la Société des Océanistes* 32 (50): 67–86.

Baudrillard, Jean. 1988. *Selected Writings*. Mark Poster, ed. Jacques Mourrain, trans. Cambridge, UK: Polity Press.

Bauer, Laurie. 1994. English in New Zealand. In Robert Burchfield, ed., *The Cambridge History of the English Language*, Vol. 5, 382–429. Cambridge, UK: Cambridge University Press.

Baugh, John. 1992. Hypocorrection: Mistakes in Production of Vernacular African American English as a Second Dialect. *Language & Communication* 12: 317–326.

Bauman, Richard. 2001. The Ethnography of Genre in a Mexican Market: Form, Function, Variation. In Penelope Eckert and John R. Rickford, eds., *Style and Sociolinguistic Variation*, 57–77. Cambridge, UK: Cambridge University Press.

Beadle, Rosalind. 2008. Letter from Tonga: Trying to Make an Island Connection. *Guardian Weekly* 179 (1): 29.

Beaglehole, Ernest, and Pearl Beaglehole. 1941. *Pangai: A Village in Tonga.* Wellington: The Polynesian Society.

Beaglehole, J. C., ed. 1961. *The Journals of Captain James Cook: The Voyage of the Resolution and Adventure, 1772–1775.* Cambridge, UK: Cambridge University Press.

Becker, Anne E. 1995. *Body, Self, and Society: The View from Fiji.* Philadelphia: University of Pennsylvania Press.

———. 2004. Television, Disordered Eating, and Young Women in Fiji: Negotiating Body Image and Identity during Rapid Social Change. *Culture, Medicine and Psychiatry* 28: 533–559.

Bertram, Geoff. 1999. The MIRAB Model Twelve Years On. *The Contemporary Pacific* 11: 105–138.

———. 2006. Introduction: The MIRAB Model in the Twenty-First Century. *Asia Pacific Viewpoint* 47: 1–14.

Bertram, Geoff, and Ray F. Watters. 1985. The MIRAB Economy in Pacific Microstates. *Pacific Viewpoint* 26: 497–519.

Besnier, Niko. 1994. Polynesian Gender Liminality through Time and Space. In Gilbert Herdt, ed., *Third Sex, Third Gender: Beyond Sexual Dimorphism in Culture and History,* 285–328. New York: Zone.

———. 1995. *Literacy, Emotion, and Authority: Reading and Writing on a Polynesian Atoll.* Cambridge, UK: Cambridge University Press.

———. 1997. Sluts and Superwomen: The Politics of Gender Liminality in Urban Tonga. *Ethnos* 62: 5–31.

———. 2000. Transvestism (Transgenderism). In Brij V. Lal and Kate Fortune, eds., *The Pacific Islands: An Encyclopedia,* 416–417. Honolulu: University of Hawai'i Press.

———. 2002. Transgenderism, Locality, and the Miss Galaxy Beauty Pageant in Tonga. *American Ethnologist* 29: 534–566.

———. 2003. Crossing Genders, Mixing Languages: The Linguistic Construction of Transgenderism in Tonga. In Janet Holmes and Miriam Meyerhoff, eds., *Handbook of Language and Gender,* 279–301. Oxford, UK: Blackwell.

———. 2004. The Social Production of Abjection: Desire and Silencing among Transgender Tongans. *Social Anthropology* 12: 301–323.

———. 2009a. *Gossip and the Everyday Production of Politics.* Honolulu: University of Hawai'i Press.

———. 2009b. Modernity, Cosmopolitanism, and the Emergence of Middle Classes in Tonga. *The Contemporary Pacific* 21: 215–262.

Besnier, Niko, and Takuya Kitahara. 2009. Zainichi Tongajin Ragubī Senshu: Gurōbaru na Idō to Supōtsu [Tongan Rugby Players in Japan: Global Movements and Sports]. *Kikan Minzokugaku* 130: 46–54.

Biersack, Aletta. 1996. Rivals and Wives: Affinal Politics and the Tongan Ramage. In James Fox and Clifford Sather, eds., *Origins, Ancestry, and Alliance: Explorations in Austronesian Ethnography*, 237–279. Canberra: Australian National University.

Boddy, Janice. 1979. *Wombs and Alien Spirits: Women, Men, and the Zâr Cult in Northern Sudan*. Madison: University of Wisconsin Press.

Bordo, Susan. 1993. *Unbearable Weight: Feminism, Western Culture, and the Body*. Berkeley: University of California Press.

Borland, Katherine. 1996. The India Bonita of Monimbó: The Politics of Ethnic Identity in the New Nicaragua. In Colleen B. Cohen, Richard Wilk, and Beverly Stoeltje, eds., *Beauty Queens on the Global Stage: Gender, Contests, and Power*, 75–88. New York: Routledge.

Bott, Elizabeth. 1981. Power and Rank in the Kingdom of Tonga. *Journal of the Polynesian Society* 90: 7–81.

Bourdieu, Pierre. 1970. The Berber House or the World Reversed. *Social Science Information* 9: 151–170.

———. 1972 [1977]. *Outline of a Theory of Practice*. Richard Nice, trans. Cambridge, UK: Cambridge University Press.

———. 1978. Sport and Social Class. *Social Science Information* 17: 819–840.

———. 1979. *La distinction: Critique sociale du jugement*. Paris: Éditions de Minuit.

———. 2004. The Peasant and His Body. *Ethnography* 5: 579–599.

Brenchley, Julius L. 1873. *Jottings during the Cruise of HMS* Curaçoa *among the South Seas Islands in 1865*. London: Longmans, Green.

Brenner, Suzanne. 1996. Reconstructing Self and Society: Javanese Muslim Women and "the Veil." *American Ethnologist* 23: 673–697.

Brightman, Robert. 1995. Forget Culture: Replacement, Transcendence, Relexification. *Cultural Anthropology* 10: 509–546.

Brison, Karen J. 2007. *Our Wealth Is Loving Each Other: Self and Society in Fiji*. Lanham, MD: Lexington Books.

Britsch, R. Lanier. 1986. *Unto the Islands of the Sea: A History of the Latter-day Saints in the Pacific*. Salt Lake City: Deseret.

———. 1998. Mormon Intruders in Tonga: The Passport Act of 1922. In Davis Bitton, ed., *Mormons, Scripture, and the Ancient World*, 121–148. Provo, UT: Foundation for Ancient Research and Mormon Studies.

Brown, Richard P. C. 1997. Estimating Remittance Functions for Pacific Island Migrants. *World Development* 25: 613–626.

———. 1998. Do Migrants' Remittances Decline over Time? Evidence from Tongans and Western Samoans in Australia. *The Contemporary Pacific* 10: 107–151.

Brown, Richard P. C., and John Connell. 1993. The Global Flea Market: Migration, Remittances, and the Informal Economy in Tonga. *Development and Change* 24: 611–647.

———. 2006. Occupation-Specific Analysis of Migration and Remittance Behaviour: Pacific Island Nurses in Australia and New Zealand. *Asia Pacific Viewpoint* 47: 135–150.

Brown, Richard P. C., and John Foster. 1995. Some Common Fallacies about Migrants' Remittances in the South Pacific: Lessons from Tongan and Western Samoan Research. *Pacific Viewpoint* 36: 29–45.

Brownell, Susan. 1995. *Training the Body for China: Sports in the Moral Order of the People's Republic.* Chicago: University of Chicago Press.

———. 2001. Making Dream Bodies in Beijing: Athletes, Fashion Models, and Urban Mystique in China. In Nancy N. Chen, Constance D. Clark, Suzanne Z. Gottschang, and Lyn Jeffery, eds., *China Urban: Ethnographies of Contemporary Culture,* 123–142. Durham, NC: Duke University Press.

———. 2005. China Reconstructs: Cosmetic Surgery and Nationalism in the Reform Era. In Joseph S. Alter, ed., *Asian Medicine and Globalization,* 132–150. Philadelphia: University of Pennsylvania Press.

Brubaker, Rogers. 2005. The "Diaspora" Diaspora. *Ethnic and Racial Studies* 28: 1–19.

Bunster, Ximena, and Elsa M. Chaney. 1985. *Sellers and Servants: Working Women in Lima, Peru.* Granby, MA: Bergin & Garvey.

Burke, Timothy. 1996. *Lifebuoy Men, Lux Women: Commodification, Consumption, and Cleanliness in Modern Zimbabwe.* Durham, NC: Duke University Press.

Butler, Judith. 1990. *Gender Trouble: Feminism and the Subversion of Identity.* London: Routledge.

———. 1997. *Excitable Speech: A Politics of the Performative.* New York: Routledge.

Calavia Sáez, Oscar. 2004. In Search of Ritual: Tradition, Outer World, and Bad Manner in the Amazon. *Journal of the Royal Anthropological Institute* [n.s.] 10: 157–173.

Campbell, I. C. 2001. *Island Kingdom: Ancient and Modern,* 2nd ed. Christchurch: Canterbury University Press.

———. 2006. Progress and Populism in Tongan Politics. *Journal of Pacific History* 41: 49–60.

———. 2008. Across the Threshold: Regime Change and Uncertainty in Tonga 2005–2007. *Journal of Pacific History* 43: 95–109.

Cannell, Fenella. 2005. The Christianity of Anthropology. *Journal of the Royal Anthropological Institute* [n.s.] 11: 335–356.

Carrier, James G. 1992. Occidentalism: The World Turned Upside-Down. *American Ethnologist* 19: 195–212.

———. 1995. Maussian Occidentalism: Gift and Commodity Systems. In James G. Carrier, ed., *Occidentalism: Images of the West,* 85–108. Oxford, UK: Clarendon Press.

Chakrabarty, Dipesh. 2000. *Provincializing Europe: Postcolonial Thought and Historical Difference.* Princeton, NJ: Princeton University Press.

Chalfin, Brenda. 2008. Cars, the Customs Service, and Sumptuary Rule in Neoliberal Ghana. *Comparative Studies in Society and History* 50: 424–453.

Chodorow, Nancy. 1978. *The Reproduction of Mothering: Psychoanalysis and the Sociology of Gender.* Berkeley: University of California Press.

Churchward, C. Maxwell. 1953. *Tonga Grammar.* Oxford, UK: Oxford University Press.

———. 1959. *Tongan Dictionary (Tongan–English and English–Tongan).* Oxford, UK: Oxford University Press.

Clark, Gracia. 1994. *Onions Are My Husband: Survival and Accumulation by West African Market Women.* Chicago: University of Chicago Press.

Clifford, James. 1994. Diasporas. *Cultural Anthropology* 9: 302–338.

Cohen, Colleen B. 1996. Contestants in a Contested Domain: Staging Identities in the British Virgin Islands. In Colleen B. Cohen, Richard Wilk, and Beverly Stoeltje, eds., *Beauty Queens on the Global Stage: Gender, Contests, and Power,* 125–145. New York: Routledge.

Cohen, Shana. 2004. *Searching for a Different Future: The Rise of a Global Middle Class in Morocco.* Durham, NC: Duke University Press.

Coleman, Simon. 2000. *The Globalisation of Charismatic Christianity: Spreading the Gospel of Prosperity.* Cambridge, UK: Cambridge University Press.

———. 2007. Of Metaphors and Muscles: Protestant "Play" in the Disciplining of the Self. In Simon Coleman and Tamara Kohn, eds., *Discipline of Leisure: Embodying Cultures of "Recreation,"* 39–53. Oxford, UK: Berghahn.

Comaroff, Jean, and John Comaroff. 1991. *Of Revelation and Revolution: Christianity, Colonialism, and Consciousness in South Africa.* Vol. 1. Chicago: University of Chicago Press.

———. 1992. Home-Made Hegemony: Domesticity, Modernity, and Colonialism in South Africa. In Karen T. Hansen, ed., *African Encounters with Domesticity,* 37–74. New Brunswick, NJ: Rutgers University Press.

———. 1997. *Of Revelation and Revolution: The Dialectics of Modernity on a South African Frontier.* Vol. 2. Chicago: University of Chicago Press.

———. 2000. Millennial Capitalism: First Thoughts on a Second Coming. *Public Culture* 12: 291–343.

Conklin, Beth A. 1997. Body Paint, Feathers, and VCRs: Aesthetics and Authenticity in Amazonian Activism. *American Ethnologist* 24: 711–737.

Connell, John. 2007. Islands, Idylls and the Detours of Development. *Singapore Journal of Tropical Geography* 28: 116–135.

Connell, John, and John P. Lea. 2001. *Urbanisation in the Island Pacific: Towards Sustainable Development.* London: Routledge.

Connell, R.W. 1987. *Gender and Power: Society, the Person, and Sexual Politics.* Sydney: Allen and Unwin.

Connelly-Kirch, Deborah. 1982. Economic and Social Correlates of Handicraft Selling in Tonga. *Annals of Tourism Research* 9: 383–402.

Crehan, Kate. 2002. *Gramsci, Culture and Anthropology*. London: Pluto Press.

Crocombe, Ron. 2007. *Asia in the Pacific Islands: Replacing the West*. Suva: Institute of Pacific Studies, University of the South Pacific.

Crocombe, Ron, and Marjorie Crocombe, eds. 1994. *Polynesian Missions in Melanesia: From Samoa, Cook Islands and Tonga, to Papua New Guinea and New Caledonia*. Suva: Institute of Pacific Studies, University of the South Pacific.

Csordas, Thomas. 1990. Embodiment as a Paradigm in Anthropology. *Ethos* 18: 5–47.

Csikszentmihalyi, Mihaly. 1990. *Flow: The Psychology of Optimal Experience*. New York: Harper Perennial.

Cummins, H.G. 1977. Tongan Society at the Time of European Contact. In Noel Rutherford, ed., *Friendly Islands: A History of Tonga*, 63–89. Oxford, UK: Oxford University Press.

Dannhaeuser, Norbert. 1989. Marketing in Developing Urban Areas. In Stuart Plattner, ed., *Economic Anthropology*, 222–252. Stanford, CA: Stanford University Press.

Davies, Douglas J. 2000. *The Mormon Culture of Salvation: Force, Grace and Glory*. Aldershot, UK: Ashgate.

Davis, Elizabeth. 1999. Metamorphosis in the Culture Market of Niger. *American Anthropologist* 101: 485–501.

Davis, Dona. 2003. Changing Body Aesthetics: Diet and Exercise Fads in a Newfoundland Outport Community. In Anne Bolin and Jane Granskog, eds., *Athletic Intruders: Ethnographic Research on Women, Culture, and Exercise*, 201–226. Albany: SUNY Press.

de Certeau, Michel. 1980 [1984]. *The Practice of Everyday Life*. Steven Rendall, trans. Berkeley: University of California Press.

de la Pradelle, Michèle. 1995. Market Exchange and the Social Construction of a Public Space. *French Cultural Studies* 6: 359–371.

Decktor Korn, Shulamit R. 1978. After the Missionaries Came: Denominational Diversity in the Tonga Islands. In James A. Boutilier, Daniel T. Hughes, and Sharon W. Tiffany, eds., *Missions, Church, and Sect in Oceania*, 395–422. Ann Arbor: University of Michigan Press.

Demetriou, Demetrakis Z. 2001. Connell's Concept of Hegemonic Masculinity: A Critique. *Theory and Society* 30: 337–361.

Dewey, Susan. 2008. *Making Miss India Miss World: Constructing Gender, Power, and the National in Postliberalization India*. Syracuse, NY: Syracuse University Press.

di Leonardo, Micaela. 1991. Habits of the Cumbered Heart: Ethnic Community and Women's Culture as American Invented Traditions. In Jay O'Brien and William Roseberry, eds., *Golden Ages, Dark Ages: Imagining the Past in Anthropology and History*, 234–252. Berkeley: University of California Press.

Dolgoy, Reevan. 2000. The Search for Recognition and Social Movement Emergence: Towards an Understanding of the Transformation of the *Fa'afafine* of Samoa. PhD dissertation, Department of Sociology, University of Alberta.

Drozdow-St Christian, Douglass. 2002. *Elusive Fragments: Making Power, Propriety, and Health in Samoa*. Durham, NC: Carolina Academic Press.

Douglas, Mary, and Baron Isherwood. 1979. *The World of Goods: Towards an Anthropology of Consumption*. London: Routledge.

Dunning, Eric, and Kenneth Sheard. 1976. The Bifurcation of Rugby Union and Rugby League: A Case Study of Organizational Conflict and Change. *International Review of Sport Sociology* 11: 31–72.

Durham, Deborah. 1999. The Predicament of Dress: Polyvalency and the Ironies of Cultural Identity. *American Ethnologist* 26: 389–411.

Edmonds, Alexander. 2007. "The Poor Have the Right to Be Beautiful": Cosmetic Surgery in Neoliberal Brazil. *Journal of the Royal Anthropological Institute* [n.s.] 13: 363–381.

Ehrenreich, Barbara. 1989. *Fear of Falling: The Inner Life of the Middle Class*. New York: Pantheon.

Eisenstadt, Shmuel N., ed. 2002. *Multiple Modernities*. New Brunswick, NJ: Transaction.

Elliston, Deborah. 1999. Negotiating Transnational Sexual Economies: Female Māhū and Same-Sex Sexuality in "Tahiti and Her Islands." In Evelyn Blackwood and Saskia E. Wieringa, eds., *Female Desires: Same-Sex Relations and Transgender Practices Across Cultures*, 232–252. New York: Columbia University Press.

———. 2004. A Passion for the Nation: Masculinity, Modernity, and Nationalist Struggle. *American Ethnologist* 31: 606–630.

Englberger, Lois, Vizo Halavatau, Yoshiko Yasuda, and Yisa Yamazaki. 1999. The Tonga Healthy Weight Loss Program 1995–97. *Asia Pacific Journal of Clinical Nutrition* 8: 142–148.

Englund, Harri, and James Leach. 2000. Ethnography and the Meta-Narratives of Modernity. *Current Anthropology* 41: 225–248.

Ernst, Manfred. 1996. *The Role of Social Change in the Rise and Development of New Religious Groups in the Pacific Islands*. Hamburg: LIT Verlag.

'Esau, Raelyn Lolohea. 2007. Tongan Immigrants in Japan. *Asian and Pacific Migration Journal* 15: 289–300.

Evans, Mike. 1999. Is Tonga's MIRAB Economy Sustainable? A View from the Village and a View without It. *Pacific Studies* 22: 137–166.

Evans, Mike, Robert C. Sinclair, Caroline Fusimālohi, and Viliami Liava'a. 2001. Globalization, Diet, and Health: An Example from Tonga. *Bulletin of the World Health Organization* 79: 856–862.

Fabian, Johannes. 1983. *Time and the Other: How Anthropology Makes Its Object*. New York: Columbia University Press.

Faeamani, Sione 'U. 1995. The Impact of Remittances on Rural Development in Tongan Villages. *Asian and Pacific Migration Journal* 4: 139–155.

Fajans, Jane. 1983. Shame, Social Action, and the Person among the Baining. *Ethos* 11: 166–180.

Featherstone, Mike. 1991. The Body in Consumer Culture. In Mike Featherstone, Mike Hepworth, and Bryan S. Turner, eds., *The Body: Social Process and Cultural Theory*, 170–196. London: Sage.

Fer, Yannick. 2005. Genèse des émotions au sein des Assemblées de Dieu polynésiennes. *Archives de sciences sociales des religions* 131–132: 143–163.

Ferdon, Edwin. 1987. *Tonga as the Explorers Saw It, 1616–1810*. Tucson: University of Arizona Press.

Ferguson, James G. 1999. *Expectations of Modernity: Myths and Meanings of Urban Life on the Zambian Copperbelt*. Berkeley: University of California Press.

———. 2002. Of Mimicry and Membership: Africans and the "New World Society." *Cultural Anthropology* 17: 559–569.

Fife, Wayne. 2001. Creating the Moral Body: Missionaries and the Technology of Power in Early Papua New Guinea. *Ethnology* 40: 251–269.

Filihia, Meredith. 2001. Men Are from Maama, Women Are from Pulotu: Female Status in Tongan Society. *Journal of the Polynesian Society* 110: 377–390.

Firth, Stewart G. 1973. German Firms in the Western Pacific Islands, 1857–1914. *Journal of Pacific History* 8: 10–28.

Fleming, Euan M. 1996. *Research Options for High-Value Agricultural Exports in South Pacific Island Nations*. The Hague: International Service for National Agricultural Research.

Fonua, Pesi. 2000. Tupouto'a Offers High-Speed, Wireless Telephone, Internet and Television. *Matangi Tonga* 14 (4): 14–18, 20.

Foster, Robert J. 2006. From Trobriand Cricket to Rugby Nation: The Mission of Sport in Papua New Guinea. *International Journal of the History of Sport* 23: 739–758.

———. 2008. *Coca-Globalization: Following Soft Drinks from New York to New Guinea*. New York: Palgrave Macmillan.

Foucault, Michel. 1975 [1979]. *Discipline and Punish: The Birth of the Prison*. Alan Sheridan, trans. New York: Vintage.

———. 1997. Technologies of the Self. In Paul Rabinow, ed., *The Essential Works of Michel Foucault*, Vol. 1 (*Ethics: Subjectivity, and Truth*), 223–251. New York: New Press.

Francis, Steve. 2003. Tongan Movement in Action: An Ethnography of Movement in Oceania. PhD thesis, Department of Anthropology, University of Melbourne.

Franklin, Marianne. 2005. *Postcolonial Politics, the Internet and Everyday Life: Pacific Traversals Online*. London: Routledge.

Freeman, Carla. 2001. Is Local : Global as Feminine : Masculine? Rethinking the Gender of Globalization. *Signs* 26: 1007–1037.

Frykman, Jonas, and Orvar Löfgren. 1979 [1987]. *Culture Builders: A Historical Anthropology of Middle-Class Life*. Alan Crozier, trans. New Brunswick, NJ: Rutgers University Press.

Furman, Frida K. 1997. *Facing the Mirror: Older Women and Beauty Shop Culture.* London: Routledge.

Fusitu'a, 'Eseta, and Noel Rutherford. 1977. George Tupou II and the British Protectorate. In Noel Rutherford, ed., *Friendly Islands: A History of Tonga*, 173–189. Oxford, UK: Oxford University Press.

Gailey, Christine W. 1987. *From Kinship to Kingship: Gender Hierarchy and State Formation in the Tongan Islands.* Austin: University of Texas Press.

———. 1989. "Rambo" in Tonga: Video Films and Cultural Resistance in the Tongan Islands. *Culture* 9 (1): 21–32.

———. 1992. A Good Man Is Hard to Find: Overseas Migrations and the Decentered Family in the Tongan Islands. *Critique of Anthropology* 12: 47–74.

Gal, Susan. 1979. *Language Shift: Social Determinants of Linguistic Change in Bilingual Austria.* New York: Academic Press.

———. 1995. Language and the "Arts of Resistance." *Cultural Anthropology* 10: 407–424.

Gaonkar, Dilip P. 1999. On Alternative Modernities. *Public Culture* 11: 1–18.

Geertz, Clifford. 1976. "From the Native's Point of View": On the Nature of Anthropological Understanding. In Keith H. Basso and Henry A. Selby, eds., *Meaning in Anthropology*, 221–237. Albuquerque: University of New Mexico Press.

———. 1998. Deep Hanging Out. *The New York Review of Books* 45 (16): 69–72.

Gershon, Ilana. 2006. Converting Meanings and the Meanings of Conversion in Samoan Moral Economies. In Matthew Engelke and Matt Tomlinson, eds., *The Limits of Meaning: Case Studies in the Anthropology of Christianity*, 147–163. New York: Berghahn.

Geschiere, Peter. 1997. *The Modernity of Witchcraft: Politics and the Occult in Postcolonial Africa.* Charlottesville: University Press of Virginia.

———. 2009. *The Perils of Belonging: Autochthony, Citizenship, and Exclusion in Africa and Europe.* Chicago: University of Chicago Press.

Gewertz, Deborah, and Frederick Errington. 1999. *Emerging Class in Papua New Guinea: The Telling of Difference.* Cambridge, UK: Cambridge University Press.

———. 2010. *Cheap Meat: Flap Food Nations in the Pacific Islands.* Berkeley: University of California Press.

Gibson, John, David J. McKenzie, and Halahingano Rohorua. 2006. How Cost-Elastic Are Remittances? Estimates from Tongan Migrants in New Zealand. *Pacific Economic Bulletin* 21 (1): 112–128.

Giddens, Anthony. 1990. *The Consequences of Modernity.* Stanford, CA: Stanford University Press.

———. 1991. *Modernity and Self-Identity: Self and Society in the Late Modern Age.* Stanford, CA: Stanford University Press.

———. 1992. *The Transformation of Intimacy: Sexuality, Love and Eroticism in Modern Societies.* Stanford, CA: Stanford University Press.

Gifford, Edward W. 1929. *Tongan Society.* Honolulu: Bernice P. Bishop Museum.

Gilman, Sander L. 1999. *Making the Body Beautiful: A Cultural History of Aesthetic Surgery*. Princeton, NJ: Princeton University Press.

Gilroy, Paul. 1993. *The Black Atlantic: Modernity and Double Consciousness*. Cambridge, MA: Harvard University Press.

Gimlin, Debra. 1996. Pamela's Place: Power and Negotiation in the Hair Salon. *Gender & Society* 10: 505–526.

Godelier, Maurice. 1996. *L'énigme du don*. Paris: Fayard.

Goffman, Erving. 1959. *The Presentation of Self in Everyday Life*. New York: Doubleday.

Goldsmith, Michael. 1992. The Tradition of Invention. In Michael Goldsmith and Keith Barber, eds., *Other Sites: Social Anthropology and the Politics of Interpretation*, 29–41. Palmerston North, New Zealand: Department of Social Anthropology, Massey University.

———. 2005. Culture in Safety and in Danger. *Anthropological Forum* 15: 257–265.

Gordon, Tamar. 1988. Inventing Mormon Identity in Tonga. PhD dissertation, Department of Anthropology, University of California at Berkeley.

———. 1990. Inventing the Mormon Tongan Family. In John Barker, ed., *Christianity in Oceania: Ethnographic Perspectives*, 197–219. Lanham, MD: University Press of America.

Goss, Jon, and Bruce Lindquist. 2000. Placing Movers: An Overview of the Asian-Pacific Migration System. *The Contemporary Pacific* 12: 385–414.

Graeber, David. 2001. *Toward an Anthropological Theory of Value: The False Coin of Our Own Dreams*. New York: Palgrave Macmillan.

Gregory, Anthony C. 1982. *Gifts and Commodities*. London: Academic Press.

Gregory, Derek. 1989. Presences and Absences: Time–Space Relations and Structuration Theory. In David Held and John B. Thompson, eds., *Social Theory of Modern Societies: Anthony Giddens and His Critics*, 185–214. Cambridge, UK: Cambridge University Press.

Gregson, Nicky, and Louise Crewe. 2003. *Second-Hand Cultures*. Oxford, UK: Berg.

Gremillion, Helen. 2005. The Cultural Politics of Body Size. *Annual Review of Anthropology* 34: 13–32.

Gunson, Niel. 1977. The Coming of Foreigners. In Noel Rutherford, ed., *Friendly Islands: A History of Tonga*, 90–113. Oxford, UK: Oxford University Press.

Gupta, Akhil, and James Ferguson. 1992. Beyond "Culture": Space, Identity, and the Politics of Difference. *Cultural Anthropology* 7: 6–23.

Gutmann, Matthew C. 1997. Trafficking in Men: The Anthropology of Masculinity. *Annual Review of Anthropology* 26: 385–409.

Hahn, Elizabeth. 1994. The Tongan Tradition of Going to the Movies. *Visual Anthropology Review* 10: 103–111.

Hall, Donald E., ed. 1994. *Muscular Christianity: Embodying the Victorian Age*. Cambridge, UK: Cambridge University Press.

Hannerz, Ulf. 1996. *Transnational Connections: Culture, People, Places.* London: Routledge.

Hansen, Karen T. 2000. *Salaula: The World of Secondhand Clothing and Zambia.* Chicago: University of Chicago Press.

Hanson, F. Allan. 1997. Empirical Anthropology, Postmodernism, and the Invention of Tradition. In Marie Mauzé, ed., *Present Is Past: Some Uses of Tradition in Native Societies,* 195–214. Lanham, MD: University Press of America.

Harding, Susan F. 2001. *The Book of Jerry Falwell: Fundamentalist Language and Politics.* Princeton, NJ: Princeton University Press.

Harvey, Adia M. 2005. Becoming Entrepreneurs: Intersections of Race, Class, and Gender at the Black Beauty Salon. *Gender & Society* 19: 789–808.

Hauʻofa, Epeli. 1987. The New South Pacific Society: Integration and Independence. In Antony Hooper et al., eds., *Class and Culture in the South Pacific,* 1–12. Auckland: Centre for Pacific Studies, University of Auckland, and Suva: Institute for Pacific Studies, University of the South Pacific.

———. 1994. Our Sea of Islands. *The Contemporary Pacific* 6: 148–161.

Heller, Agnes. 2003. Five Approaches to the Phenomenon of Shame. *Social Research* 70: 1015–1030.

Helu, ʻI. Futa. 1999. *Critical Essays: Cultural Perspectives from the South Seas: Aspects of Tongan Material Culture.* Canberra: Journal of Pacific History Special Issue.

———. 2006. *Ko e Heilala Tangitangi ʻo Sālote Pilolevu: Koe Vete moe Analaiso ʻo e Ngaahi Hiva, Maau, Taʻanga, Langi, Hiva Kakala, etc.* Nukuʻalofa: ʻAtenisi Press.

Henley, Paul. 2006. Spirit Possession, Power, and the Absent Presence of Islam: Re-viewing *Les maîtres fous. Journal of the Royal Anthropological Institute* [n.s.] 12: 731–761.

Herda, Phyllis. 1999. The Changing Texture of Textiles in Tonga. *Journal of the Polynesian Society* 108: 149–167.

———. 2007. The Political Aspects of Marriage in Traditional Tonga. In Elizabeth Wood-Ellem, ed., *Tonga and the Tongans: Heritage and Identity,* 179–193. Alphington, Victoria: Tonga Research Association.

Herrmann, Gretchen M. 1997. Gift or Commodity: What Changes Hands in the U.S. Garage Sale? *American Ethnologist* 24: 910–930.

Herzfeld, Michael. 2001. Irony and Power: Toward a Politics of Mockery in Greece. In James W. Fernandez and Mary Taylor Huber, eds., *Irony in Action: Anthropology, Practice, and the Moral Imagination,* 63–83. Chicago: University of Chicago Press.

Heyman, Josiah McC., and Howard Campbell. 2009. The Anthropology of Global Flows: A Critical Reading of Appadurai's 'Disjuncture and Difference in the Global Cultural Economy.' *Anthropological Theory* 9: 131–148.

Hill, Jane. 1993. *Hasta la Vista* Baby: Anglo Spanish in the American Southwest. *Critique of Anthropology* 13: 145–176.

Hirst, Paul, and Grahame Thompson. 1999. *Globalization in Question: The International Economy and the Possibilities of Governance*. Cambridge, UK: Polity Press.

Hobsbawm, Eric, and Terence Ranger, eds. 1983. *The Invention of Tradition*. Cambridge, UK: Cambridge University Press.

Hogle, Linda F. 2005. Enhancement Technologies and the Body. *Annual Review of Anthropology* 34: 695–716.

Horan, Jane C. 2002. Indigenous Wealth and Development: Micro-Credit Schemes in Tonga. *Asia Pacific Viewpoint* 43: 205–211.

Hokowhitu, Brendan. 2004. Tackling Māori Masculinity: A Colonial Genealogy of Savagery and Sport. *The Contemporary Pacific* 16: 259–284.

Hudson, Kenneth. 1982. *Pawnbroking: An Aspect of British Social History*. London: The Bodley Head.

Ironman Ministry. 2005. Vision: Go into the World of Tonga and Make Disciples. Retrieved in November 2008 from: www.planet-tonga.com/ironmanministry/Goals.shtml.

Irvine, Judith T., and Susan Gal. 2000. Language Ideology and Linguistic Differentiation. In Paul V. Kroskrity, ed., *Regimes of Language: Ideologies, Politics, and Identities*, 35–83. Santa Fe, NM: School of American Research Press; Oxford, UK: James Currey.

Jackson, Steven J., and Brendan Hokowhitu. 2002. Sport, Tribes, and Technology: The New Zealand All Blacks Haka and the Politics of Identity. *Journal of Sport and Social Issues* 26: 125–139.

Jacobs-Huey, Lanita. 2006. *From the Kitchen to the Parlor: Language and Becoming in African American Women's Hair Care*. New York: Oxford University Press.

James, Kerry E. 1991. Migration and Remittances: A Tongan Village Perspective. *Pacific Viewpoint* 32: 1–23.

———. 1995. Right and Privilege in Tongan Land Tenure. In R. Gerard Ward and Elizabeth Kingdon, eds., *Land, Custom and Practice in the South Pacific*, 157–119. Cambridge, UK: Cambridge University Press.

Johnson, Mark. 1997. *Beauty and Power: Transgendering and Cultural Transformation in the Southern Philippines*. Oxford, UK: Berg.

Johnson-Hill, Kelly. 2008. Inner Exhilaration and Speaking Truth through Metaphor: An Exploration of the Theological Significance of *Māfana* and *Heliaki* in Tongan Dance. *Studies in World Christianity* 14: 19–34.

Jolly, Margaret. 1992. Specter of Inauthenticity. *The Contemporary Pacific* 4: 49–72.

———. 2001. Damming the Rivers of Milk? Fertility, Sexuality, and Modernity in Melanesia and Amazonia. In Thomas Gregor and Donald Tuzin, eds., *Gender in Amazonia and Melanesia: An Exploration of the Comparative Method*, 175–204. Berkeley: University of California Press.

Jones, Rodney H. 2000. "Potato Seeking Rice": Language, Culture, and Identity in Gay Personal Ads in Hong Kong. *International Journal of the Sociology of Language* 143: 33–61.

Jourdan, Christine. 1995. Masta Liu. In Vered Amit-Talai and Helena Wulff, eds., *Youth Cultures: A Cross-Cultural Perspective*, 202–222. London: Routledge.

Kaeppler, Adrienne L. 1978. Exchange Patterns in Goods and Spouses: Fiji, Tonga, and Samoa. *Mankind* 11: 246–252.

———. 1987. Spontaneous Choreography: Improvisation in Polynesian Dance. *Yearbook for Traditional Music* 19: 13–22.

———. 1993. *Poetry in Motion: Studies of Tongan Dance*. Nuku'alofa: Vava'u Press.

———. 1995. Poetics and Politics of Tongan Barkcloth. In Dick A. M. Smidt, Pieter ter Keurs, and Albert Trouwborst, eds., *Pacific Material Culture: Essays in Honour of Dr. Simon Kooijman*, 101–121. Leiden: National Museum of Ethnology.

———. 1999. *Kie Hingoa*: Mats of Power, Rank, Prestige and History. *Journal of the Polynesian Society* 108: 168–232.

Kaeppler, Adrienne L., Elizabeth Wood-Ellem, and Melenaite Taumoefolau. 2004. *Songs and Poems of Queen Sālote*. Nuku'alofa: Vava'u Press.

Kalir, Barak. 2005. The Development of a Migratory Disposition: Explaining a "New Emigration." *International Migration* 43: 167–196.

Kapchan, Deborah. 1996. *Gender on the Market: Moroccan Women and the Revoicing of Tradition*. Philadelphia: University of Pennsylvania Press.

Kavaliku, Langi. 1977. '*Ofa*! The Treasure of Tonga. *Pacific Perspective* 6 (2): 47–67.

Kawamura, Chizuko. 2003. Tonga wo Nihon-sei jidōsha no hakaba ni shinai tameni: garōbaru tekunosukēpu no shiten kara [Tonga Is not a Grave for Japanese Reconditioned Vehicles: From the Point of View of Global Technoscapes]. *Social-Human Environmentology* (Daitō Bunka University) 4: 75–96.

Keane, Webb. 2003. Self-Interpretation, Agency, and the Objects of Anthropology: Reflection on a Genealogy. *Comparative Studies in Society and History* 45: 222–248.

Keesing, Roger M. 1989. Creating the Past: Custom and Identity in the Contemporary Pacific. *The Contemporary Pacific* 1: 19–42.

———. 1991. Reply to Trask. *The Contemporary Pacific* 3: 168–171.

Keesing, Roger M., and Robert Tonkinson, eds. 1982. Reinventing Traditional Culture: The Politics of Kastom in Island Melanesia. *Mankind* 13 (4), special issue.

Kintz, Ellen R. 1998. The Yucatec Maya Frontier and Maya Women: Tenacity of Tradition and Tragedy of Transformation. *Sex Roles* 39: 589–601.

Knauft, Bruce. 2002. Critically Modern: An Introduction. In Bruce Knauft, ed., *Critically Modern: Alternatives, Alterities, Anthropologies*, 1–54. Bloomington: Indiana University Press.

Koch, Gerd. 1955. *Südsee-gestern und heute: Der Kulturwandel bei den Tonganern und der Versuch einer Deutung dieser Entwicklung*. Braunschweig: A. Limbach.

Konstantinov, Yulian. 1996. Patterns of Reinterpretation: Trader Tourism in the Balkans (Bulgaria) as a Picaresque Metaphorical Enactment of Post-Totalitarianism. *American Ethnologist* 23: 762–782.

Kooijman, Simon. 1972. *Tapa in Polynesia*. Honolulu: Bernice P. Bishop Museum.

Kristeva, Julia. 1980. *Pouvoirs de l'horreur: Essai sur l'abjection*. Paris: Seuil.

Kulick, Don. 1992. *Language Shift and Cultural Reproduction: Socialization, Self and Syncretism in a Papua New Guinea Village*. Cambridge, UK: Cambridge University Press.

Kuwahara, Makiko. 2005. *Tattoo: An Anthropology*. Oxford, UK: Berg.

La Pérouse, Jean François de Galaup de. 1799. *A Voyage Round the World Performed in the Years 1785, 1786, 1787 and 1788 by the Boussole and Astrolabe, Published by Order of the National Assembly under the Superintendence of L.A. Milet-Mureau*. London: Printed by A. Hamilton, for G. G. and J. Robinson.

Labaki, Nadine, dir. 2007. *Sukkar Banat* [Caramel]. Feature film, 96 min. Distributed by Les Films des Tournelles Roissy Films.

Labov, William. 1966. Hypercorrection by the Lower Middle Class as a Factor in Linguistic Change. In William Bright, ed., *Sociolinguistics: Proceedings of the UCLA Sociolinguistics Conference, 1964*, 84–113. The Hague: Mouton.

Lacqueur, Thomas. 1990. *Making Sex: Body and Gender from the Greeks to Freud*. Cambridge, MA: Harvard University Press.

Laidlaw, James. 2000. A Free Gift Makes No Friends. *Journal of the Royal Anthropological Institute* [n.s.] 6: 617–634.

Lakoff, Andrew. 2006. *Pharmaceutical Reason: Knowledge and Value in Global Psychiatry*. Cambridge, UK: Cambridge University Press.

Lambert, S. M. 1941. *A Yankee Doctor in Paradise*. Boston: Little, Brown.

Laracy, Hugh. 1977. The Catholic Mission. In Noel Rutherford, ed., *Friendly Islands: A History of Tonga*, 136–153. Oxford, UK: Oxford University Press.

Larkin, Brian. 1997. Indian Films and Nigerian Lovers: Media and the Creation of Parallel Modernities. *Africa* 67: 406–440.

Latour, Bruno. 1991 [1993]. *We Have Never Been Modern*. Catherine Porter, trans. Cambridge, MA: Harvard University Press.

Lātūkefu, Sione. 1974. *Church and State in Tonga: The Wesleyan Methodist Missionaries and Political Development, 1822–1875*. Canberra: Australian National University Press.

———. 1977. Wesleyan Mission. In Noel Rutherford, ed., *Friendly Islands: A History of Tonga*, 114–135. Oxford, UK: Oxford University Press.

———. 1978. The Impact of South Sea Islands Missionaries on Melanesia. In James A. Boutilier, Daniel T. Hughes, and Sharon W. Tiffany, eds., *Missions, Church, and Sect in Oceania*, 91–108. Ann Arbor: University of Michigan Press.

Lee, Helen. 2003. *Tongans Overseas: Between Two Shores*. Honolulu: University of Hawai'i Press.

———. 2007. Transforming Transnationalism: Second Generation Tongans Overseas. *Asian and Pacific Migration Journal* 16 (2): 157–178.

Lefebvre, Henri. 1988. Toward a Leftist Cultural Politics: Remarks Occasioned by the Centenary of Marx's Death. In Cary Nelson and Lawrence Grossberg, eds., *Marxism and the Interpretation of Culture*, 75–88. Urbana: University of Illinois Press.

———. 1974 [1991]. *The Production of Space*. Donald Nicholson-Smith, trans. Oxford, UK: Basil Blackwell.

Lepowsky, Maria. 1993. *Fruit of the Motherland: Gender in an Egalitarian Society*. New York: Columbia University Press.

Lévi-Strauss, Claude. 1950. Introduction à l'œuvre de M. Mauss. In *Marcel Mauss: Sociologie et anthropologie*, ix–lii. Paris: Presses universitaires de France.

Lewis, James. 1982. Natural Disaster Mitigation: Environmental Approaches in Tonga and Algeria. *The Environmentalist* 2: 233–246.

Liava'a, Viliami T. F. 2007. Transnational Tongans: The Profile and Re-Integration of Returning Migrants. MSc thesis, Department of Geography, University of Waikato.

Liechty, Mark. 2003. *Suitably Modern: Making Middle-Class Culture in a New Consumer Society*. Princeton, NJ: Princeton University Press.

———. 2005. Carnal Economies: The Commodification of Food and Sex in Kathmandu. *Cultural Anthropology* 20: 1–38.

Lindenfeld, Jacqueline. 1990. *Speech and Sociability at French Urban Marketplaces*. Amsterdam: John Benjamins.

Lindstrom, Lamont. 1995. Cargoism and Occidentalism. In James G. Carrier, ed., *Occidentalism: Images of the West*, 33–60. Oxford, UK: Clarendon Press.

Linnekin, Jocelyn S. 1991a. Fine Mats and Money: Contending Exchange Paradigms in Colonial Samoa. *Anthropological Quarterly* 64: 1–13.

———. 1991b. Text Bites and the R-Word: The Politics of Representing Scholarship. *The Contemporary Pacific* 3: 172–177.

———. 1992. On the Theory and Politics of Cultural Construction in the Pacific. *Oceania* 62: 249–263.

———. 1997. Consuming Cultures: Commoditization of Cultural Identity in the Island Pacific. In Michel Picard and Robert E. Wood, eds., *Tourism, Ethnicity, and the State in Asian and Pacific Societies*, 215–250. Honolulu: University of Hawai'i Press.

———. 2004. Tradition Sells: Identity Merchandise in the Island Pacific. In Victoria S. Lockwood, ed., *Globalization and Culture Change in the Pacific Islands*, 324–338. Upper Saddle River, NJ: Pearson Education.

Lipset, David. 2004. "The Trial": A Parody of the Law Amid the Mockery of Men in Post-Colonial Papua New Guinea. *Journal of the Royal Anthropological Institute* [n.s.] 10: 63–89.

Lukose, Ritty. 2005 Consuming Globalization: Youth and Gender in Kerala, India. *Journal of Social History* 38: 915–935.

MacAloon, John J., ed. 2007. *Muscular Christianity in Colonial and Post-Colonial Worlds*. London: Routledge.

MacClancy, Jeremy, ed. 2002. *Exotic No More: Anthropology on the Front Lines*. Chicago: University of Chicago Press.

Macpherson, Cluny, and Liava'a Macpherson. 2001. Evangelical Religion among Pacific Island Migrants: New Faiths or Brief Diversions? *Journal of Ritual Studies* 15 (2): 27–37.

Mageo, Jeannette M. 1994. Hairdos and Don'ts: Hair Symbolism and Sexual History in Samoa. *Man* [n.s.] 29: 407–432.

———. 1996. Samoa, on the Wilde Side: Male Transvestism, Oscar Wilde, and Liminality in Making Gender. *Ethos* 24: 588–627.

Mahmood, Saba. 2005. *Politics of Piety: The Islamic Revival and the Feminist Subject*. Princeton, NJ: Princeton University Press.

Maisel, Robert. 1974. The Flea Market as an Action Scene. *Urban Life* 2: 488–505.

Mallon, Sean. 2005. Samoan *Tatau* as Global Practice. In Nicholas Thomas, Anna Cole, and Bronwen Douglas, eds., *Tattoo: Bodies, Art, and Exchange in the Pacific and the West*, 145–169. Durham, NC: Duke University Press.

Mangan, J. A. 1998. *The Games Ethic and Imperialism: Aspects of the Diffusion of an Ideal*. London: Frank Cass.

Marcus, George E. 1978. *The Nobility and the Chiefly Tradition in the Modern Kingdom of Tonga*. Wellington: The Polynesian Society.

———. 1980. Role Distance in Conversations between Tongan Nobles and Their "People." *Journal of the Polynesian Society* 89: 435–453.

———.1989. Chieftainship. In Alan Howard and Robert Borofsky, eds., *Development in Polynesian Ethnology*, 175–211. Honolulu: University of Hawai'i Press.

———. 2000. Book Review of Elizabeth Wood-Ellem, Queen Sālote of Tonga: The Story of an Era 1900–1965. *The Contemporary Pacific* 12: 526–528.

Martin, Emily. 1997. *The Woman in the Body: A Cultural Analysis of Reproduction*. Boston: Beacon Press.

Martin, John. 1817. *An Account of the Natives of the Tonga Islands, in the South Pacific Ocean, with an Original Grammar and Vocabulary of Their Language, Compiled and Arranged from the Extensive Communications of Mr. William Mariner, Several Years Resident in Those Islands*. London: Printed for the author.

Masquelier, Adeline, ed. 2005. *Dirt, Undress, and Difference: Critical Perspectives on the Body's Surface*. Bloomington: Indiana University Press.

Massey, Douglas, Joaquin Arango, Graeme Hugo, Ali Kouaouci, Adela Pellegrino, and Edward Taylor. 1993. Theories of International Migration: A Review and Appraisal. *Population and Development Review* 19: 431–466.

Matangi Tonga. 1999. Photo News: Heilala Festival 1999. *Matangi Tonga* 14 (3): 2–3.

Matzner, Andrew. 2001. 'O Au No Kēia: *Voices from Hawaii's Mahu and Transgender Communities*. [s.l.]: Xlibris.

Maude, Alaric M., and Feleti Sevele. 1987. Tonga: Equality Overtaking Privilege. In Ron Crocombe, ed., *Land Tenure in the South Pacific*, 3rd edition, 114–142. Suva: Institute of Pacific Studies, University of the South Pacific.

Maude, Harry E. 1981. *Slavers in Paradise: The Peruvian Labour Trade in Polynesia, 1862–64*. Canberra: Australian National University Press.

Mauss, Marcel. 1925 [1983]. Essai sur le don: Forme et raison de l'échange dans les sociétés archaïques. In *Marcel Mauss: Sociologie et anthropologie*, 145–279. Paris: Presses universitaires de France.

———. 1934 [1983]. Les techniques du corps. In *Marcel Mauss: Sociologie et anthropologie*, 363–386. Paris: Presses universitaires de France.

McAllister, Carlota. 1996. Authenticity and Guatemala's Maya Queen. In Colleen B. Cohen, Richard Wilk, and Beverly Stoeltje, eds., *Beauty Queens on the Global Stage: Gender, Contests, and Power*, 105–124. New York: Routledge.

McGranahan, Carole. 1996. Miss Tibet, or Tibet Misrepresented? The Trope of Woman-as-Nation in the Struggle for Tibet. In Colleen B. Cohen, Richard Wilk, and Beverly Stoeltje, eds., *Beauty Queens on the Global Stage: Gender, Contests, and Power*, 161–184. New York: Routledge.

Mertz, Elizabeth. 2007. Semiotic Anthropology. *Annual Review of Anthropology* 36: 337–353.

Meyer, Birgit. 1999. *Translating the Devil: Religion and Modernity Among the Ewe of Ghana*. Edinburgh: Edinburgh University Press.

———. 2004. Christianity in Africa: From African Independent to Pentecostal-Charismatic Churches. *Annual Review of Anthropology* 33: 447–474.

———. 2006. Impossible Representations: Pentecostalism, Vision, and Video Technology in Ghana. In Birgit Meyer and Annelies Moors, eds., *Religion, Media, and the Public Sphere*, 290–312. Bloomington: Indiana University Press.

———. 2007. Pentecostalism and Neo-Liberal Capitalism: Faith, Prosperity, and Vision in African Pentecostal-Charismatic Churches. *Journal of the Study of Religion* 20 (2): 5–28.

Meyer, Birgit, and Peter Geschiere. 1999. Introduction. In Birgit Meyer and Peter Geschiere, eds., *Globalization and Identity: Dialectics of Flow and Closure*, 1–15. Oxford, UK: Blackwell.

Meyerhoff, Miriam. 2003. Claiming a Place: Gender, Knowledge, and Authority as Emergent Properties. In Janet Holmes and Miriam Meyerhoff, eds., *Handbook of Language and Gender*, 302–326. Oxford, UK: Blackwell.

Miller, Dan, ed. 1995. *Acknowledging Consumption: A Review of New Studies*. London: Routledge.

Miller, H. Max. 1988. Patterns of Exchange in the Rural Sector: Flea Markets along the Highway. *Journal of American Culture* 11 (3): 55–59.

Miller, Laura. 2006. *Beauty Up: Exploring Contemporary Japanese Body Aesthetics*. Berkeley: University of California Press.

Miller, William I. 1993. *Humiliation, and Other Essays on Honor, Social Discomfort, and Violence*. Ithaca, NY: Cornell University Press.

Minister for Immigration and Citizenship (Australia). 1996. Drop in Number of People in Australia Unlawfully, MPS 31/96. Retrieved in October 2007 from: www.minister.immi.gov.au/media/media-releases/1996/r96031.htm.

Mintz, Sidney W. 1985. *Sweetness and Power: The Place of Sugar in Modern History*. New York: Viking Penguin.

———. 1996. *Tasting Food, Tasting Freedom: Excursions into Eating, Culture, and the Past*. Boston: Beacon Press.

Mitchell, Hildi J. 2001. Good, Evil, and Godhood: Mormon Morality in the Material World. In Paul Clough and Jon P. Mitchell, eds., *Powers of Good and Evil: Social Transformation and Popular Belief*, 161–184. New York: Berghahn.

Mitchell, Timothy. 2000. Introduction. In Timothy Mitchell, ed., *Questions of Modernity*, xi–xxvii. Minneapolis: University of Minnesota Press.

Moala, Kalafi. 2007. Media–A Tool for National Development. In Elizabeth Wood-Ellem, ed., *Tonga and the Tongans: Heritage and Identity*, 235–248. Alphington, Victoria: Tonga Research Association.

———. 2009. *In Search of the Friendly Islands*. Kealakekua, HI: Pasifika Foundation Press.

Møller, Leif. 2006. *Tavi fra Tonga*. Copenhagen: Ekstra Bladets Forlag.

Morris, Rosalind C. 1997. Educating Desire: Thailand, Transnationalism, and Transgression. *Social Text* 15 (52–53): 53–79.

Morton, Helen. 1998. Creating Their Own Culture: Diasporic Tongans. *The Contemporary Pacific* 10: 1–30.

———. 1996. *Becoming Tongan: An Ethnography of Childhood*. Honolulu: University of Hawai'i Press.

Mosko, Mark S. 2000. Inalienable Ethnography: Keeping-while-Giving and the Trobriand Case. *Journal of the Royal Anthropological Institute* [n.s.] 6: 377–396.

Moyle, Richard. 1987. *Tongan Music*. Auckland: Auckland University Press.

Munro, Doug. 1990. Transnational Corporations of Kin and the MIRAB System: The Case of Tuvalu. *Pacific Viewpoint* 31: 63–66.

Needs, Andrew P. 1988. *New Zealand Aid and the Development of Class in Tonga*. Palmerston North, New Zealand: Department of Sociology, Massey University.

Nichter, Mimi. 2000. *Fat Talk: What Girls and Their Parents Say about Dieting*. Cambridge, MA: Harvard University Press.

Nussbaum, Martha. 2004. *Hiding from Humanity: Disgust, Shame, and the Law*. Princeton, NJ: Princeton University Press.

Obeyesekere, Gananath. 1997. *The Apotheosis of Captain Cook: European Mythmaking in the Pacific*. Princeton, NJ: Princeton University Press.

Olson, Ernest. 2001. Signs of Conversion, Spirit of Commitment: The Pentecostal Church in the Kingdom of Tonga. *Journal of Ritual Studies* 15 (2): 13–26.

Olwig, Karen F. 1996. *Global Culture, Island Identity: Continuity and Change in the Afro-Caribbean Community of Nevis*. London: Routledge.

Ong, Aihwa. 1999. *Flexible Citizenship: The Cultural Logics of Transnationality*. Durham, NC: Duke University Press.

———. 2003. *Buddha Is Hiding: Refugees, Citizenship, the New America*. Berkeley: University of California Press.

Ortner, Sherry B. 1981. Gender and Sexuality in Hierarchical Societies: The Case of Polynesia and Some Comparative Implications. In Sherry B. Ortner and Harriet Whitehead, eds., *Sexual Meanings: The Cultural Construction of Gender and Sexuality*, 359–409. Cambridge, UK: Cambridge University Press.

———. 1984. Theory in Anthropology since the Sixties. *Comparative Studies in Society and History* 26: 126–166.

———. 1995. Resistance and the Problem of Ethnographic Refusal. *Comparative Studies in Society and History* 37: 173–193.

Osella, Caroline, and Filippo Osella. 2006. Once upon a Time in the West? Stories of Migration and Modernity from Kerala, South India. *Journal of the Royal Anthropological Institute* [n.s.] 12: 569–588.

Ossman, Susan. 2002. *Three Faces of Beauty: Casablanca, Paris, Cairo*. Durham, NC: Duke University Press.

Owusu, Francis. 2008. Conceptualizing Livelihood Strategies in African Cities: Planning and Development Implications of Multiple Livelihood Strategies. *Journal of Planning Education and Research* 26: 450–465.

Palmié, Stephan. 2006. Creolization and Its Discontents. *Annual Review of Anthropology* 35: 433–456.

Parry, Jonathan, and Maurice Bloch. 1989. Introduction: Money and the Morality of Exchange. In Jonathan Parry and Maurice Bloch, eds., *Money and the Morality of Exchange*, 1–32. Cambridge, UK: Cambridge University Press.

Peters, John Durham. 1997. Seeing Bifocally: Media, Place, Culture. In Akhil Gupta and James Ferguson, eds., *Culture, Power, Place: Explorations in Critical Ethnography*, 75–92. Durham, NC: Duke University Press.

Phare, Jane. 2006. The Madness of King George of Tonga. *New Zealand Herald* online. Retrieved in January 2010 from: www.nzherald.co.nz/world/news/article .cfm?c_id=2&objectid=10401690&pnum=2.

Philips, Susan U. 1991. Tongan Speech Levels: Practice and Talk about Practice in the Cultural Construction of Social Hierarchy. In Robert Blust, ed., *Currents in Pacific Linguistics: Papers on Austronesian Languages in Honour of George Grace*, 369–382. Canberra: Pacific Linguistics C–117.

———. 2000. Constructing a Tongan Nation-State through Language Ideology in the Courtroom. In Paul V. Kroskrity, ed., *Regimes of Language: Ideologies, Polities, and Identities*, 229–257. Santa Fe, NM: School of American Research Press; Oxford, UK: James Currey.

———. 2004. The Organization of Ideological Diversity in Discourse: Modern and Neotraditional Visions of the Tongan State. *American Ethnologist* 31: 231–250.

———. 2007. Changing Scholarly Representations of the Tongan Honorific Lexicon. In Miki Makihara and Bambi Schieffelin, eds., *Consequences of Contact: Language Ideologies and Sociocultural Transformations in Pacific Societies*, 189–215. New York: Oxford University Press.

Piot, Charles. 1999. *Remotely Global: Village Modernity in West Africa*. Chicago: University of Chicago Press.

———. 2001. Of Hybridity, Modernity, and Their Malcontents. *Interventions* 3: 85–91.

———. 2010. *Nostalgia for the Future: West Africa after the Cold War*. Chicago: University of Chicago Press.

Plattner, Stuart. 1989. Economic Behavior in Markets. In Stuart Plattner, ed., *Economic Anthropology*, 208–221. Stanford, CA: Stanford University Press.

Poirine, Bernard. 1998. Should We Hate or Love MIRAB? *The Contemporary Pacific* 10: 65–106.

Pollock, Nancy J. 1999. Fat Is Beautiful: The Body as Art Form in the Pacific. In Barry Craig, Bernie Kernot, and Christopher Anderson, eds., *Art and Performance in Oceania*, 58–63. Bathurst, NSW: Crawford House.

Popenoe, Rebecca. 2004. *Feeding Desire: Fatness, Beauty, and Sexuality among a Saharan People*. London: Routledge.

Prakash, Gyan. 1999. *Another Reason: Science and the Imagination of Modern India*. Princeton, NJ: Princeton University Press.

Radcliffe-Brown, A. R. 1924. The Mother's Brother in South Africa. *South African Journal of Science* 21: 542–555.

———. 1940a. *Notes for the Use of Visitors 3: A Note on Rank and Kingship in Tonga*. Aberdeen: Anthropological Museum, Aberdeen University.

———. 1940b. On Joking Relationships. *Africa* 13: 195–210.

———. 1950. Systems of Kinship and Marriage. In A. R. Radcliffe-Brown and Daryll Forde, eds., *African Systems of Kinship and Marriage*, 3–85. Oxford, UK: Oxford University Press.

Radio New Zealand International. 2008. Tonga Workshop Looks at Deportees' Problems. Retrieved in August 2008 from: www.rnzi.com/pages/news .php?op=read&id=40930.

Radway, Janice A. 1984. *Reading the Romance: Women, Patriarchy, and Popular Literature*. Chapel Hill: University of North Carolina Press.

Rahier, Jean Muteba. 1998. Blackness, the Racial/Spatial Order, Migrations, and Miss Ecuador 1995–96. *American Anthropologist* 100: 421–430.

Rasmussen, Susan J. 2003. When the Field Space Comes to the Home Space: New Constructions of Ethnographic Knowledge in a New African Diaspora. *Anthropological Quarterly* 76: 7–32.

Reid, Graeme. 2007. How to Be a "Real" Gay: Emerging Gay Spaces in Small-Town South Africa. PhD dissertation, Amsterdam School for Social Science Research, University of Amsterdam.

Reischer, Erica, and Kathryn S. Koo. 2004. The Body Beautiful: Symbolism and Agency in the Social World. *Annual Review of Anthropology* 33: 297–317.

Riccio, Bruno. 2001. From "Ethnic Group" to "Transnational Community"? Senegalese Migrants' Ambivalent Experiences and Multiple Trajectories. *Journal of Ethnic and Migration Studies* 27: 583–599.

Ribeiro, Gustavo Lins. 2009. Non-Hegemonic Globalizations: Alter-Native Transnational Processes and Agents. *Anthropological Theory* 9: 297–329.

Richard, Chris. 2008. Mom-and-Pop Imports: Murrieta Yard Sales Help Mexico's Underground Economy. *The Press-Enterprise* (San Bernardino, CA) April 28, B1, B4.

Richland, Justin B. 2008. *Arguing with Tradition: The Language of Law in Hopi Tribal Court*. Chicago: University of Chicago Press.

Robbins, Joel. 2003a. Given to Anger, Given to Shame: The Psychology of the Gift among the Urapmin of Papua New Guinea. *Paideuma* 49: 249–261.

———. 2003b. On the Paradoxes of Global Pentecostalism and the Perils of Continuity Thinking. *Religion* 33: 221–231.

———. 2004. The Globalization of Pentecostal and Charismatic Christianity. *Annual Review of Anthropology* 33: 117–143.

———. 2007. Continuity Thinking and the Problem of Christian Culture: Belief, Time, and the Anthropology of Christianity. *Current Anthropology* 48: 5–38.

Robbins, Joel, and Holly Wardlow, eds. 2005. *The Making of Global and Local Modernities in Melanesia*. Aldershot, UK: Ashgate.

Rofel, Lisa. 1999. *Other Modernities: Gendered Yearnings in China after Socialism*. Berkeley: University of California Press.

———. 2002. Modernity's Masculine Fantasies. In Bruce Knauft, ed., *Critically Modern: Alternatives, Alterities, Anthropologies*, 175–193. Bloomington: Indiana University Press.

Rogers, Garth. 1977. The Father's Sister Is Black. *Journal of the Polynesian Society* 86: 157–182.

Rogers, Mark. 1998. Spectacular Bodies: Folklorization and the Politics of Identity in Ecuadorian Beauty Pageants. *Journal of Latin American Anthropology* 3 (2): 54–85.

Rosaldo, Michelle Z. 1974. Woman, Culture, and Society: A Theoretical Overview. In Michelle Z. Rosaldo and Louise Lamphere, eds., *Woman, Culture and Society*, 17–42. Stanford, CA: Stanford University Press.

———. 1983. The Shame of Headhunters and the Autonomy of the Self. *Ethos* 11: 135–151.

Rosenblatt, Daniel. 1997. The Antisocial Skin: Structure, Resistance, and "Modern Primitive" Adornment in the United States. *Cultural Anthropology* 12: 287–334.

Rouch, Jean. 1955. *Les maîtres foux*. 30 min film, originally produced and distributed by Les films de la Pléiade.

Rouse, Roger. 1991. Mexican Migration and the Social Space of Postmodernism. *Diaspora* 1: 8–23.

Rutherford, Noel. 1971. *Shirley Baker and the King of Tonga.* Melbourne: Oxford University Press.

———. 1981. *Tonga Ma'a Tonga Kautaha*: A Proto-Co-Operative in Tonga. *Journal of Pacific History* 16: 20–41.

Sahlins, Marshall. 1981. *Historical Metaphors and Mythical Realities: Structure in the Early History of the Sandwich Islands Kingdom.* Ann Arbor: University of Michigan Press.

———. 1988. Cosmologies of Capitalism: The Trans-Pacific Sector of "The World System." *Proceedings of the British Academy* 74: 1–51.

———. 1992. The Economics of Develop-man in the Pacific. *Res* 21: 13–25.

———. 1999. Two or Three Things That I Know about Culture. *Journal of the Royal Anthropological Institute* [n.s.] 5: 399–422.

Said, Edward. 1984. The Mind of Winter: Reflections on Life in Exile. *Harper's Magazine* 269: 49–55.

Saouter, Anne. 2000. *"Être rugby": Jeux du masculin et du féminin.* Paris: Éditions de la Maison des Sciences de l'Homme.

Satō, Motohiko. 1997. Structure and Dynamics of MIRAB Societies in the South Pacific: An Economic Study. In Ken'ichi Sudō and Shuji Yoshida, eds., *Contemporary Migration in Oceania: Diaspora and Network*, 165–177. Osaka: The Japan Center for Area Studies, National Museum of Ethnology.

Schackt, Jon. 2005. Mayahood through Beauty: Indian Beauty Pageants in Guatemala. *Bulletin of Latin American Research* 24: 269–287.

Schein, Louisa. 1999. Performing Modernity. *Cultural Anthropology* 14: 361–395.

Scheld, Suzanne. 2007. Youth Cosmopolitanism: Clothing, the City and Globalization in Dakar, Senegal. *City & Society* 19: 232–253.

Schildkrout, Enid. 2004. Inscribing the Body. *Annual Review of Anthropology* 33: 319–344.

Schröder, Ingo W. 2004. Parades and Beauty Pageants: Encountering Authentic White Mountain Apache Culture in Unexpected Places. *Etnofoor* 17 (1–2): 116–132.

Schulz, Dorothea. 2000. Mesmerizing Missis, Nationalist Musings: Beauty Pageants and the Public Controversy over "Malian" Womanhood. *Paideuma* 46: 111–135.

Scott, James C. 1985. *Weapons of the Weak: Everyday Forms of Peasant Resistance.* New Haven, CT: Yale University Press.

———. 1990. *Domination and the Arts of Resistance: Hidden Transcripts.* New Haven, CT: Yale University Press.

Sedgwick, Eve Kosofsky. 1990. *Epistemology of the Closet.* Berkeley: University of California Press.

Seligmann, Linda J. 2001. Introduction: Mediating Identities and Marketing Wares. In Linda J. Seligmann, ed., *Women Traders in Cross-Cultural Perspective: Mediating Identities, Marketing Wares*, 1–24. Stanford, CA: Stanford University Press.

Shore, Brad. 1989. Mana and Tapu. In Alan Howard and Robert Borofsky, eds., *Developments in Polynesian Ethnology*, 137–173. Honolulu: University of Hawai'i Press.

Shweder, Richard. 2003. Toward a Deep Cultural Psychology of Shame. *Social Research* 70: 1109–1130.

Silverstein, Michael. 1976. Shifters, Linguistic Categories, and Cultural Description. In Keith H. Basso and Henry A. Selby, eds., *Meaning in Anthropology*, 11–55. Albuquerque: University of New Mexico Press.

Simmel, George. 1950. *The Sociology of Georg Simmel*. Kurt H. Wolff, ed. and trans. New York: Free Press.

Singer, Milton. 1984. *Man's Glassy Essence: Explorations in Semiotic Anthropology*. Bloomington: Indiana University Press.

Small, Cathy A. 1997. *Voyages: From Tongan Village to American Suburbs*. Ithaca, NY: Cornell University Press.

Snow, Amanda, Kate Druett, and Vicky Crawford. 2006. The High Cost of Easy Cash: Are Poorer Auckland Communities Being Exploited by Loan Sharks? *Te Waha Nui* (June): 20.

Sobo, Elisa J. 1993. *One Blood: The Jamaican Body*. Albany: SUNY Press.

Spielvogel, Laura A. 2003. *Working Out on Japan*. Durham, NC: Duke University Press.

Spitulnik, Debra. 2002. Accessing "Local" Modernities: Reflection on the Place of Linguistic Evidence in Ethnography. In Bruce Knauft, ed., *Critically Modern: Alternatives, Alterities, Anthropologies*, 194–219. Bloomington: Indiana University Press.

Spitz, Andrea, dir. 2004. *Hot Wax*. (Real Stories From a Free South Africa Series.) Documentary film, 49 minutes. Distributed by California Newsreels.

Stallybrass, Peter. 1998. Marx's Coat. In Patricia Spyer, ed., *Border Fetishisms: Material Objects in Unstable Spaces*, 183–207. London: Routledge.

Stambach, Amy. 1999. Curl Up and Dye: Civil Society and the Fashion-Minded Citizen. In John L. Comaroff and Jean Comaroff, eds., *Civil Society and the Political Imagination in Africa: Critical Perspectives*, 251–266. Chicago: University of Chicago Press.

Statistics New Zealand. 2001. Pacific Profiles 2001: Tongan People in New Zealand. Retrieved in May 2003 from: www.stats.govt.nz/domino/external/web/nzstories.nsf/htmldocs/.

Stokvis, Ruud. 2006. The Emancipation of Bodybuilding. *Sport in Society* 9: 463–479.

Stoller, Paul. 1995. *Embodying Colonial Memories: Spirit Possession, Power, and the Hauka in West Africa*. London: Routledge.

———. 2002. *Money Has No Smell: The Africanization of New York City*. Chicago: University of Chicago Press.

Storey, Donovan, and Warwick E. Murray. 2001. Dilemmas of Development in Oceania: The Political Economy of the Tongan Agro-Export Sector. *The Geographical Journal* 167: 291–304.

Strathern, Andrew. 1975. Why Is Shame on the Skin? *Ethnology* 14: 347–356.

Strathern, Marilyn. 1988. *The Gender of Gift: Problems with Women and Problems with Society in Melanesia*. Berkeley: University of California Press.

Sudō, Ken'ichi. 1997. Expanding International Migration by the Tongan People: Strategies and Socio-Cultural Effects on the Homeland. In Ken'ichi Sudō and Shuji Yoshida, eds., *Contemporary Migration in Oceania: Diaspora and Network*, 101–111. Osaka: The Japan Center for Area Studies, National Museum of Ethnology.

Sykes, Karen. 2005. *Arguing with Anthropology: An Introduction to Critical Theories of the Gift*. London: Routledge.

———, ed. 2007. Interrogating Individuals: The Critique of Possessive Individualism in the Western Pacific. Special issue, *Anthropological Forum* 17 (3).

Tasman, Abel Janszoon. 1644 [1965]. *Abel Jansz. Tasman's Journal of His Discovery of Van Diemens Land & New Zealand in 1642, with Documents Relating to His Exploration of Australia in 1644*. J. E. Heeres and C. H. Cootes, eds. and trans. Facsimile edition. Los Angeles: N.A. Kovach. (Gutenberg Project of Australia; available at http://gutenberg.net.au/ebooks06/0600571h.html)

Tale'ale'ausumai, Feiloaiga. 2001. New Religions, New Identities: The Changing Contours of Religious Commitment. In Cluny Macpherson, Paul Spoonley, and Melani Anae, eds., *Tangata o te Moana Nui: The Evolving Identities of Pacific Peoples in Aotearoa/New Zealand*, 181–195. Palmerston North, New Zealand: Dunmore Press.

Taussig, Michael. 1993. *Mimesis and Alterity: A Particular History of the Senses*. London: Routledge.

Taylor, Charles. 1989. *Source of the Self: The Making of Modern Identity*. Cambridge, MA: Harvard University Press.

———. 1991. *The Malaise of Modernity*. Toronto: Anansi.

Tcherkézoff, Serge. 1999. Who Said the 17th–18th Centuries Papalagi/Europeans Were Sky-Bursters? A Eurocentric Projection onto Polynesia. *Journal of the Polynesian Society* 108: 417–425.

———. 2003. On Cloth, Gifts and Nudity: Regarding some European Misunderstandings during Early Encounters in Polynesia. In Cloë Colchester, ed., *Clothing the Pacific*, 51–75. Oxford, UK: Berg.

Teague, Matthew. 2007. While the King Sleeps: Democracy Stirs in Tonga, the Pacific's Last True Monarchy. *National Geographic Magazine* 212 (5): 58–75.

Teaiwa, Teresia, and Sean Mallon. 2005. Ambivalent Kinships? Pacific People in New Zealand. In James Liu, Tim McCreanor, Tracey McIntosh, and Teresia Teaiwa, eds., *New Zealand Identities: Departures and Destinations*, 207–229. Wellington: Victoria University Press.

Teilhet-Fisk, Jehanne H. 1991. To Beat or Not to Beat, That Is the Question: A Study on Acculturation and Change in an Art-Making Process and its Relation to Gender Structures. *Pacific Studies* 14 (3): 41–68.

———. 1996. The Miss Heilala Beauty Pageant: Where Beauty Is More Than Skin Deep. In Colleen B. Cohen, Richard Wilk, and Beverly Stoeltje, eds., *Beauty Queens on the Global Stage: Gender, Contests, and Power,* 185–202. London: Routledge.

Tengan, Ty P. Kāwika. 2008. Re-membering Panalā'au: Masculinities, Nation, and Empire in Hawai'i and the Pacific. *The Contemporary Pacific* 20: 27–53.

Tent, Jan, and Paul Geraghty. 2001. Broken Sky or Shattered Myth? The Origin of *Papālagi. Journal of the Polynesian Society* 110: 171–214.

Thomas, Nicholas. 1997. *In Oceania: Visions, Artefacts, Histories.* Durham, NC: Duke University Press.

———. 2003. The Case of the Misplaced Ponchos: Speculations Concerning the History of Cloth in Polynesia. In Cloë Colchester, ed., *Clothing the Pacific,* 79–96. Oxford, UK: Berg.

Thompson, Becky W. 1994. *A Hunger So Wide and So Deep: American Women Speak Out on Eating Problems.* Minneapolis: University of Minnesota Press.

Thomson, Basil. 1894. *The Diversions of a Prime Minister.* Edinburgh: William Blackwood & Sons.

Tomlinson, Matt. 2009. *In God's Image: The Metaculture of Fijian Christianity.* Berkeley: University of California Press.

Tonga Department of Statistics. 2005. National Accounts Statistics, Year 2005: Provisional Estimates of Gross Domestic Product for the Kingdom of Tonga, 1993–94 to 2003–04. Nuku'alofa: Statistics Department, Kingdom of Tonga.

———. 2008a. Balance of Payments, Quarterly Bulletin, June 2007. Nuku'alofa: Statistics Department, Kingdom of Tonga.

———. 2008b. *Preliminary Result, Tonga Population Census 2006.* Nuku'alofa: Statistics Department, Kingdom of Tonga.

———. 2008c. Social Indicators. Retrieved in February 2008 from: www.spc.int/prism/country/to/stats/.

———. 2008d. Statistical Abstracts. Nuku'alofa: Statistics Department, Kingdom of Tonga.

Tonga Development Bank. 2003. Annual Report for 2003. [Nuku'alofa]: Tonga Development Bank.

———. 2005. Annual Report 2005. [Nuku'alofa]: Tonga Development Bank.

———. 2006. Annual Report 2006. Nuku'alofa: Tonga Development Bank.

Toren, Christina. 2005. Laughter and Truth in Fiji: What We May Learn from a Joke. *Oceania* 75: 268–283.

Towle, Evan B., and Lynn M. Morgan. 2002. Romancing the Transgender Native: Rethinking the Use of the "Third Gender" Concept. *GLQ* 8: 469–497.

Trask, Haunani-Kay. 1991. Natives and Anthropologists: The Colonial Struggle. *The Contemporary Pacific* 3: 159–167.

Trouillot, Michel-Rolph. 1991. Anthropology and the Savage Slot. In Richard G. Fox, ed., *Recapturing Anthropology: Working in the Present*, 17–44. Santa Fe, NM: School of American Research Press.

———. 2001. The Anthropology of the State in the Age of Globalization. *Current Anthropology* 42: 125–138.

U.S. Census Bureau. 2001. The Native Hawaiian and Other Pacific Islander Population: Census 2000 Brief. Retrieved in May 2003 from: www.census.gov/prod/2001pubs/c2kbr01-14.pdf.

Vakaoti, Patrick. 2006. Tonga. In Manfred Ernst, ed., *Globalization and the Re-Shaping of Christianity in the Pacific Islands*, 611–638. Suva: Pacific Theological College.

Valeri, Valerio. 1985. *Kingship and Sacrifice: Ritual and Society in Ancient Hawaii.* Chicago: University of Chicago Press.

van de Walle, Ferdie. 1998. Remittances in Tonga. Unpublished report to the National Bank of Tonga, Nuku'alofa.

van der Grijp, Paul. 1993a. *Islanders of the South: Production, Kinship and Ideology in the Polynesian Kingdom of Tonga.* Leiden: KITLV Press.

———. 1993b. Women's Handicrafts and Men's Arts: The Production of Material Culture in the Polynesian Kingdom of Tonga. *Journal de la Société des Océanistes* 97: 159–169.

———. 2002. Selling Is Poverty, Buying a Shame: Representations of Work, Effective Leadership and Market Failures on Wallis. *Oceania* 73: 17–34.

———. 2003. Between Gifts and Commodities: Commercial Enterprise and the Trader's Dilemma on Wallis ('Uvea). *The Contemporary Pacific* 15: 277–307.

Van Fossen, Anthony. 1999. Globalization, Stateless Capitalism, and the International Political Economy of Tonga's Satellite Venture. *Pacific Studies* 22 (2): 1–26.

———. 2007. Citizenship for Sale: Passports of Convenience from Pacific Island Tax Havens. *Commonwealth and Comparative Politics* 45: 138–163.

Vava'u Press. 1999. Discover Tonga 2000: Nuku'alofa & Tongatapu Maps and Guide. Fold-out brochure. [Nuku'alofa]: Vava'u Press.

Veblen, Thorstein. 1899 [1994]. *The Theory of the Leisure Class.* New York: Dover.

Vete, Mele. 1995. The Determinants of Remittances among Tongans in Auckland. *Asian and Pacific Migration Journal* 4: 89–116.

von Gizycki, Renate. 1997. Tapa in Tonga, Gestern und Heute: Aufzeichnungen zur Begegnung mit den Frauen von Langa Fonua 'ae Fefine Tonga. *Baessler-Archiv* 45: 63–84.

Wallace, Lee. 2003. *Sexual Encounters: Pacific Texts, Modern Sexualities.* Ithaca, NY: Cornell University Press.

Wallerstein, Immanuel. 1974–88. *The Modern World-System.* 3 vols. New York: Academic Press.

Walley, Christine J. 2003. Our Ancestors Used to Bury Their "Development" in the Ground: Modernity and the Meanings of Development within a Tanzanian Marine Park. *Anthropological Quarterly* 76: 33–54.

Walsh, A. C. 1972. *Nuku'alofa: A Study of Urban Life in the Pacific Islands*. Wellington: Reed Education.

Wardlow, Holly. 2006. *Wayward Women: Sexuality and Agency in a New Guinea Society*. Berkeley: University of California Press.

Watson-Gegeo, Karen A., and David W. Gegeo. 1991. The Impact of Church Affiliation on Language Use in Kwara'ae (Solomon Islands). *Language in Society* 20: 533–555.

Weber, Max. 1904 [1976]. *The Protestant Ethic and the Spirit of Capitalism*. Talcott Parsons, trans. New York: Charles Scribner's Sons.

Weeks, Charles J. Jr. 1987. The United States Occupation of Tonga, 1942–1945: The Social and Economic Impact. *The Pacific Historical Review* 56: 399–426.

Weiss, Brad. 2009. *Street Dreams and Hip Hop Barbershops: Global Fantasy in Urban Tanzania*. Bloomington: Indiana University Press.

Wilk, Richard. 1995. Consumer Goods as Dialogue about Development: Colonial Time and Television Time in Belize. In Jonathan Friedman, ed., *Consumption and Identity*, 97–118. Chur, Switzerland: Harwood Academic.

———. 1996. Connections and Contradictions: From the Crooked Tree Cashew Queen to Miss World Belize. In Colleen B. Cohen, Richard Wilk, and Beverly Stoeltje, eds., *Beauty Queens on the Global Stage: Gender, Contests, and Power*, 217–232. New York: Routledge.

Willett, Julie A. 2000. *Permanent Waves: The Making of the American Beauty Shop*. New York: New York University Press.

Williams, Brett. 2004. *Debt for Sale: A Social History of the Credit Trap*. Philadelphia: University of Pennsylvania Press.

Williksen-Bakker, Solrun. 2004. Can a "Silent" Person Be a "Business" Person? The Concept *Māduā* in Fijian Culture. *Australian Journal of Anthropology* 15: 198–212.

Wolf, Eric R. 1982. *Europe and the People without History*. Berkeley: University of California Press.

Wolf, Naomi. 1991. *The Beauty Myth*. New York: William Morrow.

Wood, Michael. 2006. Kamula Accounts of Rambo and the State of Papua New Guinea. *Oceania* 76: 61–82.

Wood-Ellem, Elizabeth. 1999. *Queen Sālote of Tonga: The Story of an Era 1900–1965*. Auckland: Auckland University Press.

Woolard, Kathryn A., and Bambi Schieffelin. 1994. Language Ideology. *Annual Review of Anthropology* 23: 55–82.

Wynhausen, Elisabeth. 2008. Give It Everything You've Got. *The Australian*, 20 September 20. Retrieved in September 2008 from: www.theaustralian.news.com.au/story/0,25197,24371630-28737,00.html.

Yack, Bernard. 1997. *The Fetishism of Modernities: Epochal Self-Consciousness in Contemporary Social and Political Thought.* Notre Dame, IN: University of Notre Dame Press.

Yan, Yunxiang. 1996. *The Flow of Gifts: Reciprocity and Social Networks in a Chinese Village.* Stanford, CA: Stanford University Press.

———. 1997. McDonald's in Beijing: The Localization of Americana. In James L. Watson, ed., *Golden Arches East: McDonald's in East Asia*, 39–76. Stanford, CA: Stanford University Press.

Yano, Christine R. 2006. *Crowning the Nice Girl: Gender, Ethnicity, and Culture in Hawai'i's Cherry Blossom Festival.* Honolulu: University of Hawai'i Press.

Young Leslie, Heather. 2004. Pushing Children Up: Maternal Obligation, Modernity, and Medicine in the Tongan Ethnoscape. In Victoria Lockwood, ed., *Globalization and Culture Change in the Pacific Islands*, 390–413. Upper Saddle River, NJ: Prentice Hall.

———. 2007. A Fishy Romance: Chiefly Power and the Geopolitics of Desire. *The Contemporary Pacific* 19: 365–408.

Index

Addo, Ping-Ann, 71, 96, 104–105, 109, 117, 119, 254n2
Afeaki, Naoko, 204
agriculture, 33, 55–60, 91, 126, 189
alienability and inalienability, 109, 110, 119, 123, 177
American football, 193
anga faka-Tonga, "the Tongan way." *See* tradition
anxiety, xiii–xiv, 2, 5, 12, 17, 55, 65, 70–71, 110–124, 129–140, 144, 148, 181, 212, 215, 236, 261n7
Appadurai, Arjun, 8, 13, 18, 93, 246n9
Assemblies of God, 214
Australia, 36–71 passim; dollar, 114; rugby, 39, 191, 193

barkcloth (tapa cloth). *See koloa faka Tonga* "Tongan valuables"
beauty. *See* beauty pageants, bodybuilding; hair; *palakū* "ugly"
beauty pageants, 15, 18, 22, 25, 60, 125–159, 237
bifocality, 12–17, 67, 74, 94, 99–100, 126, 132–133, 159, 182, 232, 234, 235, 238–239
body, xvi, 15, 20, 23–26, 99, 120, 124, 125–159, 160–182, 183–204, 208, 211, 218–220, 232, 237, 242
bodybuilding, 18, 27, 183–204 passim, 225–226, 237, 238, 247n11, 260n6
"born-again" Tongans. *See* overseas Tongans
Bourdieu, Pierre, 17, 23, 24, 26, 64, 194, 248n6, 259n2

boxing, 127, 193, 202, 204
Brigham Young University (BYU), 211

capitalism, xvi, xx, xxi, 7, 21, 24, 38, 77, 101, 105, 116, 123, 155, 172–174, 177; and Mormonism, 91, 115, 212, 228
cars, 65–69, 161, 190, 212, 251n22
Catholicism, 60, 206–208
China, People's Republic of, 42, 245n2. *See also* migration
Christianity, 29, 32, 92, 139, 193–194, 205–230; conversion to, 47, 50, 60, 165–166, 178; muscular, 202, 204, 226. *See also* Assemblies of God; Catholicism; Mormonism; Pentecostal and charismatic churches; Tokaikolo Christian Church; Wesleyan Church
Church of Jesus Christ of Latter-day Saints. *See* Mormonism
citizenship, 16–17, 37, 42, 51–52, 246n7; sale of passports, 3, 51–52, 249n14. *See also* deportees; migration; overstayers
class. *See* social class
cleanliness and dirt, 73, 76, 101, 161–173, 178–179, 250–251n20, 256n6, 258n7. See also *palakū* "ugly"
clothing, 71–73, 173, 197, 208, 220–221, 225, 247n11; barkcloth, 107, 166; gossip about, 259n8; mourning, 167, 176, 252n4; secondhand, 75–103
code-switching, 11, 95–98, 242
colonialism, 31, 47–48, 50, 96, 99, 178, 192–193, 247n1
comfort. See *fiemālie*
compassion. See *'ofa*

Japan's Dual Civil Society: Members Without Advocates
By Robert Pekkanen
2006

Protest and Possibilities:
Civil Society and Coalitions for Political Change in Malaysia
By Meredith Leigh Weiss
2005

Opposing Suharto: Compromise, Resistance, and Regime Change in Indonesia
By Edward Aspinall
2005

Blowback: Linguistic Nationalism, Institutional Decay,
and Ethnic Conflict in Sri Lanka
By Neil DeVotta
2004

Beyond Bilateralism: U.S.-Japan Relations in the New Asia Pacific
Edited by Ellis S. Krauss and T. J. Pempel
2004

Population Change and Economic Development in East Asia:
Challenges Met, Opportunities Seized
Edited by Andrew Mason
2001

Capital, Coercion, and Crime: Bossism in the Philippines
By John T. Sidel
1999

Making Majorities: Constituting the Nation in Japan, Korea,
China, Malaysia, Fiji, Turkey, and the United States
Edited by Dru C. Gladney
1998

Chiefs Today: Traditional Pacific Leadership and the Postcolonial State
Edited by Geoffrey M. White and Lamont Lindstrom
1997

Political Legitimacy in Southeast Asia: The Quest for Moral Authority
Edited by Muthiah Alagappa
1995